D1565897

SHE DAMN NEAR RAN THE STUDIO

HOLLYWOOD LEGENDS SERIES

CARL ROLLYSON, GENERAL EDITOR

SHE DAMN NEAR RAN THE STUDIO

The Extraordinary Lives of Ida R. Koverman

JACQUELINE R. BRAITMAN

UNIVERSITY PRESS OF MISSISSIPPI
JACKSON

The University Press of Mississippi is the scholarly publishing agency of
the Mississippi Institutions of Higher Learning: Alcorn State University,
Delta State University, Jackson State University, Mississippi State University,
Mississippi University for Women, Mississippi Valley State University,
University of Mississippi, and University of Southern Mississippi.

www.upress.state.ms.us

Designed by Peter D. Halverson

The University Press of Mississippi is a member
of the Association of University Presses.

First printing 2020

∞

Library of Congress Cataloging-in-Publication Data

Names: Braitman, Jacqueline R., 1953– author.
Title: She damn near ran the studio : the extraordinary lives of Ida R.
Koverman / Jacqueline R. Braitman.
Other titles: Hollywood legends series.
Description: Jackson : University Press of Mississippi, 2020. | Series:
Hollywood legends series | Includes bibliographical references and
index.
Identifiers: LCCN 2020017820 (print) | LCCN 2020017821 (ebook) | ISBN
9781496806192 (hardback) | ISBN 9781496830371 (epub) | ISBN
9781496830364 (epub) | ISBN 9781496830388 (pdf) | ISBN 9781496830395
(pdf)
Subjects: LCSH: Koverman, Ida R., 1876–1954—Biography. |
Metro-Goldwyn-Mayer—History. | Motion pictures—United States—History.
Classification: LCC PN1998.3.K684 B73 2020 (print) | LCC PN1998.3.K684
(ebook) | DDC 791.43092 [B]—dc23
LC record available at https://lccn.loc.gov/2020017820
LC ebook record available at https://lccn.loc.gov/2020017821

British Library Cataloging-in-Publication Data available

For Sara, Susan, Mom, and Tim

CONTENTS

"SHE DAMN NEAR RAN THE STUDIO!"

TURN ON ANY CLASSIC MOVIE CHANNEL AND YOU WILL SEE SCORES of films that have brought the hand of Ida R. Koverman into millions of homes for generations. An internet search results in hundreds of listings, and targeting historical newspapers brings even more, including one 1935 article claiming, "When it comes to women executives, Ida Koverman seems to stand alone."[1] Ida R. Koverman was a talent scout, mentor, executive secretary, and confidant to the vice president of Metro-Goldwyn-Mayer, movie mogul Louis B. Mayer. Viewed as the power behind Mayer's throne, at times, she was considered the most powerful woman in Hollywood during the 1930s and 1940s, the golden era of the Metro-Goldwyn-Mayer studio. Nevertheless, only smatterings of biographical sketches have been written about her, and much of it is unfounded, unexamined, and untrue—that is, until now. Because specialized fields of inquiry perceive the past through narrow lenses, a full portrait of Ida Koverman's compartmentalized lives have remained just beyond the field of vision looking at diverse aspects of Hollywood history. The sequential nature of her reincarnations is only visible through a prism that reflects the broader spectrum of California women in partisan politics and its symbiosis with the rising motion-picture industry, and MGM in particular.

Ida Koverman is a fixture in the history of MGM and some of Hollywood's most colorful characters. She has appeared as a minor character in theatrical and television productions about actresses Judy Garland, Greta Garbo, and gossip columnists Hedda Hopper and Louella Parsons. One of Koverman's colleagues, however, suggested that, while the legacies of Hopper and Parsons persist, "Ida Koverman's name was not known to the public as much as these were but I would say she had more influence."[2]

Nevertheless, this is the first full account of the mysterious puzzle of Ida Koverman's extraordinary life, a long one lived in distinct incarnations, each segment of it invisible to the others. There were few raw materials on which to build a comprehensive narrative, but it grew from disparate pieces that eventually led to revelations of what are clearly sequential demarcations of her personal existence, each with layers of larger historical themes embedded within. This seminal account thus begins as a story within a story, and when viewed as part of the whole, it makes explicable why biographers have failed to look beyond the surface or to challenge what appears to have been a conscious effort to shroud her past in a mythical portrait.

A national financial scandal surfaced in 1909 that soon forced her to give up her life in Cincinnati, Ohio. She escaped and reinvented herself in New York during a decade that would inspire the origin story that has survived to this day. After the first world war, her next incarnation came in Southern California, where she capitalized on the major transformations of the region—changing demographics, partisan politics, and popular cultural. She established herself as a hardcore political operative, a kingmaker, and as such was the matchmaker for the growing motion-picture industry and the state Republican Party. This led to her partnership with a growing network of professional women, the city's elites, and Louis B. Mayer, who facilitated her most visible and last incarnation in her elevated perch at MGM. Soon she became the studio's premiere star maker, bringing talent to or nurturing the careers of the biggest stars, and she became "one of the invisible power centers in both MGM and the city of Los Angeles."[3]

This work offers new perspectives about well-known figures in Hollywood and politics, but when viewed in proximity to Ida Koverman, their context takes on new historical meanings. This includes a network of men and women whose alliance with Ida Koverman shaped public policy, political power, and popular culture. Recent interest in women, in and out of power, in Hollywood and beyond, makes Ida Koverman a timely subject, and she fits neatly into distinct scholarly analyses that look at the rise of the Hollywood-Washington connection and the rise of twentieth-century conservative political movements.[4] Regarding the first, this work places Ida Koverman at the center and not in the shadow of Louis B. Mayer in facilitating the marriage of politics and pictures, and it pushes the roots of modern conservatism back to the immediate post–World War I years when Ida R. Koverman planted herself in the Golden State. The early chapters were first drafted during the 2016 presidential primary season when, just as in 1920, the Republican Party candidates reflected similar ideological factions that threatened the very soul of the party. What's more, the outcome of the general election epitomized the fruition of a century of the evolution of celebrity politics, enabled by the media technology and tactics first employed by Ida Koverman's tenure in partisan politics and motion pictures.

There are only a handful of files in even fewer archives to form the basis of a full portrait of Ida Koverman. There are no collections of Ida Koverman's papers, diaries, or published memoirs. Any knowledge about her life and legacy rests on consistent references to a catalogue of scholarly and popular works about Hollywood and the talent and executives of Metro-Goldwyn-Mayer studio. Bosley Crowther noted in his 1960 *Hollywood Rajah* that Koverman was responsible for Louis B. Mayer's entry into Los Angeles Republican Party politics. Subsequent accounts describe Koverman as Mayer's "formidable secretary" and a "capable but rather humorless widow," who was "extremely efficient and politically well-connected."[5] She was neither humorless nor was she a widow.

Neal Gabler's 1988 classic *An Empire of Their Own* more colorfully spins Koverman's persona, acknowledging that Mayer's "real entrée [into political life] was a middle-aged bulldog of a woman named Ida Koverman." To close friends and associates, she was known as "Kay," but some at MGM called her "Mt. Ida," since she was the last and toughest obstacle before anyone got in to see Mayer. Necessity dictated the industry become increasingly politicized, so as Scott Eyman argued, Mayer recognized that Ida Koverman was a vital link to bridging his world with that of "bankers, politicians, and other members of the Eastern establishment." Charles Higham's *Merchant of Dreams* (1993) describes her as "perhaps considered the most important person in the studio next to Mayer and [Irving] Thalberg."[6]

Ronald Brownstein's 1990 *The Power and the Glitter* acknowledged Koverman's place at the outset of his book about the integration of Hollywood and politics. While elevating attention to Koverman, Steven Ross's 2011 *Hollywood Left and Right* asserts that she was only able to exercise her considerable talents because of Mayer's superior vision and leadership. Author J. E. Smyth recently concurred in her 2018 *Nobody's Girl Friday*, suggesting that "whatever Ida Koverman may have achieved at MGM, she still operated in the large shadow cast by L. B. Mayer's egocentric bulk."[7]

Ida Koverman rarely operated in the shadows, even if history has pushed her there. As "the political boss of Los Angeles County," she was the premiere matchmaker in the courtship between Hollywood and national partisan politics.[8] After Ida Koverman's story finally took shape, I realized I fulfilled my initial goal of finding out who Ida Koverman really was. But, I also affirmed that she had, and still does, live up to her legacy, and unlike her origin story, it was not a mythical construct perpetuated without scrutiny. This portrait of Ida Koverman emerged after a long journey dictated by where the sources took me. And, so, it is important to acknowledge that, while there are parallel stories and alternative contexts within which her life can be framed, this is a biography about one woman, a white woman, who lived in a primarily white world. But, to the extent it is discernible, she did not accept race as an impermeable divide, and, in fact, she spent much of her indefatigable energy promoting talent wherever she found it, and her mission was to elevate and to enhance citywide access to the musical arts and culture. In this, her broader legacy not only reaches across generations and geographies, but reaches into the lives of local, diverse, and multiple communities.

Outside of the studio, she nurtured the city's cultural transformation and popular tastes, fostering the performing arts and a new way of publicly financing them. Ida R. Koverman was not just a naturalized citizen of the realm. In fact, she was perhaps the lioness of Hollywood, who, according to MGM executive Robert Vogel, at times "damn near ran the studio," as she reigned over its kingdom.[9]

ACKNOWLEDGMENTS

CONSTRUCTING THE DISPARATE INCARNATIONS OF IDA R. KOVERMAN'S long life has required obsessive detective work, and the resolve that, because of my insight into women in early twentieth-century California politics, I was uniquely prepared to write her consummate portrait, which has been previously overlooked and even unimagined. My confidence in Ida Koverman as a subject, and in my ability to bring her untold story to fruition, however, has relied on the unconditional patience, support, and counsel of two individuals. Anthony "Tony" Slide graciously offered his time and assistance from the first articulated conception of Koverman all the way to her full breath of life in a completed manuscript. If Tony was the birthing coach, Susan Klein Margulies was the midwife, without whom Ida Koverman would have remained a legacy without a life story. Tony Slide's optimism garnered early interest from Leila Salisbury, then at the University Press of Mississippi, followed by Director Craig W. Gill's patience and Valerie Jones's continuity in shepherding the manuscript along, and allowed this work to gestate through repeated labors of research and writing until a coherent narrative emerged. I am thankful for Emily Snyder Bandy's confidence and enthusiasm for the ultimate version and for Robert J. Norrell's concerted attention to detail to smooth out its rough edges.

Part of the challenge was the diversity of audiences to whom Ida Koverman could speak. My first inkling of her came while completing research on California progressive Katherine Philips Edson. Jo Freeman, feminist political scientist, sent me a document that only later took on significance while researching my book on California Supreme Court justice Stanley Mosk, when I found a collection of letters written by and to Koverman. It became clear that Ida Koverman and Katherine Edson were iconic symbols of the ideological divide in post-WWI feminism, and within the Republican Party, as well their uncanny connection to Metro-Goldwyn-Mayer and its vice president, Louis B. Mayer. This ultimately led to my inspired exploration into the unknown, mysterious, and extraordinary lives of Ida R. Koverman as she reincarnated herself during seven decades of monumental shifts in American society and world history.

Finding relatives through websites and emails led to important leads, but few solid sources. Email communications with distant family members took on more significance as the disparate pieces of the Ida R. Brockway Koverman puzzle began to make sense. This included descendants Pam Koverman, great-granddaughter to cameraman Irby Koverman; Howard "Bud" Koverman, whose father was a cousin to Ida's husband Oscar; and Eileen Coppola, granddaughter of Ida's uncle, Henry R. Brockway. The biggest break came through Vikki McAllister, Koverman's great-grand niece, who introduced me to her aunt, Mary Louise Hawkins Troffer, the granddaughter of Ida Koverman's sister Phoebe May Brockway. Vikki's effervescence and Mary's willingness to share memories and a handful of documents were clues to my eventually revealing what was to them still their mysterious relation. A telephone interview with the acclaimed singer Marni Nixon elevated my mood and motivation. It reinforced what she had written about Koverman in her memoir, but I was jubilant after I realized I had been talking to the voice that brought me and my family such joy, to say nothing of decades of other movie-musical lovers.

Grants awarded during incipient research came from the Historical Society of Southern California and Haynes Foundation research fellowships at the Huntington Library. Assistance from archivists and librarians were crucial there and at the Library of Congress, the Bancroft Library at the University of California, Berkeley, and the Department of Special Collections at the Los Angeles campus. Ned Comstock, who is a living legacy in his own right at the Cinema-Television Library University of Southern California, provided a few key documents, as did archivists at the Hoover Presidential Library, and Genevieve Maxwell and others at the Margaret Herrick Library at the Academy of Motion Picture Arts and Sciences.

During the incubation stage, conversations, insights, or assistance came from individuals including Josh Getlin, Max Holland, Steven Ross, Taylor Coffman, Cari Beauchamp, Darrell Rooney, Alicia Mayer, Marc Wanamaker, Lynne Crandall, Martin Turnbull, Bret Arena, Amanda Russell, and Susan Wladaver-Morgan, who provided helpful commentary during a conference of the Western Association of Women Historians. Throughout the gestation process, friends and family mitigated the solitary nature of the writing process, while they reinforced my resolve, and shared my epiphanies and the milestones of seeing Koverman's emergent life take form. They are Elyse Flier, Tim Schwarz, Collette Dutray, Ann Trank, the late Wendy Gordon, Bobby Gilmore, my mother Mili Lang and her life-givers Cha Cha and Jethro, my brother Stephen M. H. Braitman, Emily Rader, especially for generously sharing her expertise, and above all, my loving daughter, Sara L. M. Golden.

LIFE ONE— TROUBLE MAKER

Scandal and Survival

CHAPTER 1

Secret Meeting, Part I

Wanted Woman

ONE DAY AFTER THE LABOR DAY LAUNCH OF THE 1932 PRESIDENTIAL campaign season, a small group of people clandestinely assembled in the executive suite of Louis B. Mayer, vice president of Metro-Goldwyn-Mayer in Culver City, California. These colleagues, who had gathered for countless brainstorming sessions or public events, were now pondering a potential crisis affecting their personal fortunes and those of an army of workers depending on what was becoming the premiere motion-picture studio of the twentieth century. They had no idea at the time that they were going to be central players in a still-unsolved mystery, a standout in Hollywood's scandal-rich history. This exigency of the moment came in the final months of their effort to re-elect President Herbert Hoover, however unlikely that was after he had failed to inspire hope during the early years of the Great Depression. Now they were gathered to discuss Jean Harlow, the "blond bombshell," a rising star at MGM, who had recently married the studio's popular producer Paul Bern who, the day before, was found dead, lying naked in the bedroom closet of the newlyweds' Benedict Canyon home.

Questions have lingered for decades about what really happened to the German born, forty-two-year-old affable Bern, known among MGM's stars as "the Father Confessor." At the time of his death, no one knew whether he had public enemies or private demons, and his broader fame would soon come, not through his marriage to the exotic actress, but through his untimely and suspicious death. Most observers thought he was an intriguing, intelligent figure, but one whose slight frame and sexually ambiguous demeanor made him an unlikely suitor, let alone husband, to the sultry Jean Harlow. It was an odd match to be sure, but beyond the facade of Hollywood glamour, Harlow was drawn to him in part because she felt he appreciated her mind as well as her beauty. But now he was dead.

A dozen or more chronicles cover the gamut of hyperbole speculating whether Paul Bern committed suicide or was murdered; and if the latter, then by whom, how, and why; and then whether and how MGM's top brass conspired in their response to Bern's premature demise. Ida R. Koverman always had a unique view of how MGM executives handled unsavory incidents involving studio personnel, but this seemed an altogether different magnitude of either misbehavior, malfeasance, or misfortune. Koverman's friendship with Jean Harlow and her proximity in the immediate aftermath of Bern's death offer insight into the world of fantasy she helped to create and to flourish, and now had to protect. And the meeting in Mayer's office, as if a photograph captured that moment in time, encapsulates how multiple layers of meaning are invisible before our very eyes.

That Ida Koverman attended the meeting illustrates her central place inside the corridors of MGM power; but it also provides a new, deeper historical context within which to interpret the gathering tasked with handling the momentary crisis. Previous accounts of Paul Bern's death and the subsequent scandal have failed to place the events within the broader sweep of national politics. Ida Koverman and the others in Mayer's office had spent years together pursuing a political mission that inadvertently forged a successful marriage between partisan politics and the movie industry. Paul Bern's ill-timed death could threaten their grand vision, and this longer view has remained obscured until now gleaned through the path of Ida Koverman's life and how she came to the inner circle secreted inside the executive suite. This snapshot of Koverman's life offers a way of perceiving how the threads of personal lives are woven into the larger fabric of history.

The meeting in Mayer's office recalled the derailing of her own life two decades earlier, which eventually led her to MGM in the fall of 1929. Ida Koverman instinctively knew that Jean Harlow would be feeling as though her life were out of control. And for a while it would be. Koverman knew first-hand how it felt to be at the center of a national scandal, hounded by the press, and to be suspected of a criminal act. When her own life was sidetracked by a national scandal, she had no idea when the

notoriety would end or where it would lead. While at MGM, Ida Koverman remained just beyond the glare that illuminated everyone around
her, dead or alive, and until now, this opaque posture kept the details of
her own past in the shadow of her growing living legacy.

Decades earlier, in November 1909, Miss Ida R. Brockway was a wanted
woman. Henry T. Hunt, the Hamilton County, Ohio, prosecutor, wanted
her regarding the explosive news of the crime of embezzlement against the
railroad conglomerate commonly known as the "Big Four." First elected
in 1908, Henry Hunt's youthful exuberance and lofty family connections
made him a star among progressive Democrats, and as a reformer, he was
on a mission to weed out the entrenched corruption flourishing under
the Republican mayor of Cincinnati, George "Boss" Cox. Soon after, in
1912, Hunt won the election as Cincinnati's "boy" mayor. In 1909, though,
Henry Hunt issued an arrest warrant for Miss Ida R. Brockway regarding what he soon learned was a decade-long crime-spree that included
blackmail, extortion, adultery, violent assault, deadly gunfire, and sexual
debauchery. He was convinced Ida Brockway was somehow involved with,
or knew more about than it had first appeared, the sordid details of what
was ultimately an inscrutable conspiracy filled with colorful characters
that nearly brought down a railroad empire. For now, though, no one
had a clue where she was.

One person who might have known was Thomas J. Cogan, an attorney
and long-time friend of Ida Brockway's family, with whom the press believed she had consulted before she disappeared. Thomas Cogan insisted
that if she had indeed approached him, he would have advised her to stay
put.[1] He had known her father, John R. Brockway, so he authoritatively
assured the press that Ida R. Brockway was a "good girl," who came from
a respectable family.

He was right. John Brockway's wife, Laura Harrison Brown, was a
great-granddaughter of President William Henry Harrison. Unfortunately,
this historic lineage did not pass on an uplifted social or economic status,
so the Brockways lived modestly at 97 Laurel Avenue, a few miles north
of the Ohio River in the rural suburb between the towns of Hartwell and
Valleydale. City directories indexed John R. Brockway as an "artist" or as
a "photographer," and he was both, making his living as a professional
portrait photographer, blending the technical skill of the craftsman with
the eye and sensibility of the artist.

He rented a succession of storefront studios in the booming central business district, where other members of the Brockway clan also lived and
worked, specializing in more traditional trades crucial to building modern

cities and suburbs. Charles was a nail maker who lived with his brother Henry, who was either a paperhanger, a printer, or both. John Brockway's last photo studio across the Ohio River in Newport, Kentucky, on Freeman Street, is where he stayed until, at the age of fifty-nine, he died in 1899.[2]

John R. Brockway also had a passion for baseball, but he didn't just love it, he played it, and baseball was a big deal in Cincinnati, which had hosted the country's first professional team, the Cincinnati Reds. Brockway was a founding member, director of the Live Oak Baseball Club, played left field, and was an umpire of suitable temperament and good enough judgment to earn a reputation for respectful calls during two National League games, in 1877 and 1879.[3]

On May 10, 1866, John and Laura Brockway gave birth to their first child, Phoebe May Brockway. Their second daughter, Martha, was born in July 1869, but she died after eight months. The family eventually moved to Dayton, Ohio, where Ida Ranous Brockway was born on May 15, 1876. To close friends and family Ida was "Kay," and early on, it was clear she was a bright child, earning promotion to second grade in the fall of 1881, at a wee five years old.[4]

The Brockways lived within the flourishing, urban, ethnic "Over-the-Rhine" cultural district, still a thriving creative-arts center and renowned as the largest zone with national historic designation. Comparable to Europe's distinctive quarters, the Over-the-Rhine neighborhood nurtured public spaces filled with lush gardens, community orchestras, and ties to old-world identities. Along with the ever-popular, boisterous beer halls, tourists flocked to its world-class operas and symphonies. Ida Brockway's passion for opera and classical music inspired her flirtation with a career in the arts, which left her with mastery of the piano and later, her most prized possession, her baby grand Steinway.[5]

The Brockway girls were raised to honor traditional stalwart principles by guiding their "surer" road to success, perhaps a "slower and harder" path, but one "possessing the joy of achievement" by "rising by one's own efforts." Inherited from "sturdy Ohio stock," the Brockways taught their girls the "homely virtues of endeavor and the will to succeed." Ida Brockway eventually demonstrated her robust embrace of these values, which reinforced her loyalty to the Republican Party's orthodoxy of individualism. Nevertheless, Ida and her sister Phoebe first digressed from these maxims on their way to middle-class propriety. When Ida was four years old, the fourteen-year-old Phoebe ran away, ostensibly to marry the eighteen-year-old Charles Fisher of Newport, Kentucky. Her disappearance left a gap in Ida's life, who, at least for a while, was raised as an only child.[6]

Ida was an adventurous sort. When she babysat her cousin Mary, she took her on a couple of unsupervised "excursions," which inspired Mary to later affectionately recall Ida "in glowing terms" as an individual who "never backed down from anything or anyone." She had a notion that Ida was "a little on the risqué side," that she might have engaged in scandalous behavior and always seemed to be "involved in some conflict or another." It was thought that Ida and her cousin Henry Brockway sought careers in vaudeville, with Ida assuming the stage name of Laura Brockway. While entirely plausible, it is not, to date, manifestly evident.[7]

Ida "Kay" Brockway matured as an ambitious and focused young woman. Her first job was as a clerk for W. T. Eichelberger & Co., a jewelry store known for diamond settings and sports-medal manufacturing. She started out at three dollars a week, and by her mid-teens she was promoted to store manager. She taught herself bookkeeping, retail finance, and salesmanship, and soon she was promoted to "an executive of a jewelry store." She rejected the more common path for young women of her ilk of becoming teachers, choosing instead to attend business school.[8]

At the age of twenty-one, Ida landed a civil service position as a stenographer in the office of the Surveyor of US Customs. After six months of probation, in April 1898, the results of her evaluation were published. Supervisors concluded her performance "eminently satisfactory," and noted that she was an "amiable" and "efficient" worker who would be promoted to the "permanent" hire list. This came with a $120 raise, bringing her salary to $720 per year. After the next evaluation, her salary was raised to $900 per year, and by the time of the warrant, it was purported to be $1,500 per year.[9]

While Ida was creating an independent professional existence, her sister Phoebe and Charlie Fisher bore several children: Catherine, in July 1886; Stanley in 1889; Laura in 1892; and Ruth in 1896. Eventually, the Fishers returned to her parent's home, and it was an uneasy reunion. John Brockway never approved of her marriage, and he never grew to like Charlie Fisher. With good reason. Fisher turned out to be a sadistic bastard, and his son Stanley took the brunt of it, being forced to live in the cellar. When Charlie wasn't around, Stanley's siblings snuck him food. Charlie Fisher eventually left his family, either through death, divorce, or desertion, because the 1900 US Census listed a "May" Fisher as a second "head" of household, along with her recently widowed mother and her twenty-four-year-old sister Ida in Bellevue City, south of Cincinnati. When Laura Brockway died in 1903, the Brockway sisters moved to Flat #5 on 125 West 7th Street. Phoebe May worked as a clerk at 810

Vine Street. After that, they moved several times around Cincinnati's business district.

Miss Brockway maintained an active social life, attending gala events, anniversary dinners, singing soprano in a local choral ensemble, and attending the theater. Her attendance at one performance made the local newspaper. She sat just behind the orchestra enjoying a particularly rousing comedy, so that when a man sitting directly above her was "convulsing . . . in an extraordinary burst of hilarity," he fell onto the railing, causing his false teeth to propel out of his mouth and down onto her lap. Startled, she looked up to see the toothless man frantically waving to her, and the whole audience burst out laughing as they patiently waited for the usher to run upstairs to return the dentures to the embarrassed gentleman.

Her life continued to be filled with laughter and a lot of theater. But she also began to make choices that would eventually raise questions about her judgment. In 1909, as news of prosecutor Henry Hunt's warrant spread throughout the country, America wanted to know who and where she was, why she disappeared, and what she knew about the extraordinary criminal investigation that captured the attention of the nation.

CHAPTER 2

"The Other Woman"

CINCINNATI WAS AFFECTIONATELY CALLED "THE QUEEN CITY," OF THE Midwest, and it was a major transport hub. As such, Ida Brockway's office at the US Customs office was located near the magnificent Union Depot belonging to the region's biggest railroad conglomerate, commonly known as the Big Four, made up of its four lines, the Cleveland, Cincinnati, Chicago and St. Louis, and New York Central. By the end of the century, the Big Four behemoth covered over twenty-three hundred miles of track, employed ten thousand workers, and spent $10,000,000 annually.

Daily interactions of the mutual business between the railroad and the US Customs office encouraged personal friendships such as the one that arose between Ida R. Brockway and Edgar Streete Cooke, the assistant treasurer at the Big Four office. Edgar S. Cooke was a well-built man and a snappy dresser. Although not particularly handsome, he made the best of what he had by accessorizing with diamonds and fine silk clothing (and underwear), and his "flashy appearance" made lasting impressions wherever he went.[1] Edgar Cooke often visited Ida Brockway at her office in the Customs house, and even after he left the Big Four in 1902 and moved to Chicago with his wife and two children, he would stop by Ida Brockway's office whenever he visited Cincinnati. During one visit, and while waiting for her to return from lunch, he struck up a conversation with her supervisor, Frank Couden. The two men became stalwart drinking buddies.

Edgar Cooke introduced Ida Brockway to Mrs. Jeanette Stewart Timmonds Ford, and after 1902 their lives intertwined, perhaps as a way for Ida to escape the cacophony of her family in their small apartment. Mrs.

Ford's lifestyle was more exhilarating than her own, but that would eventually bear consequences neither woman could anticipate at the outset.

Mrs. Ford was twenty-two years old when she arrived in Cincinnati from nearby Portsmouth with her husband, Alfred Ford. They were happy for a while, but after the birth of their son, Alfred Timmonds Ford Jr. in 1899, the marriage began to fall apart.[2] Mrs. Ford moved into an apartment on West Fourth Street, where Edgar Streete Cooke always rented a room when he came to Cincinnati. During one of his visits, he met and then wooed Mrs. Ford.

If Ida Brockway knew her two friends were having an affair, it didn't deter the women's blossoming friendship. Ida's secretarial skills were an asset to Mrs. Ford, as were her local connections and references. To handle Mrs. Ford's divorce, for example, Ida Brockway recommended her family's long-time friend, attorney Thomas Cogan, after which Mrs. Ford retained him to handle another case following a surgical procedure.[3]

Mrs. Ford lived comfortably, thanks to the eighty thousand dollars she inherited from her father and another small fortune when her aunt passed away.[4] She was a big spender, though, and money soon became a chronic source of despair. Ida Brockway became indispensable to Mrs. Ford's peripatetic lifestyle, witnessing and enabling her increasingly erratic and irrational behavior. She was privy to Mrs. Ford's impetuous instincts and excesses of the heart, and because Mrs. Ford had such poor eyesight and penmanship, Ida Brockway wrote letters on Mrs. Ford's behalf, sometimes of the most intimate kind.

Edgar Cooke didn't hide his relationship with Mrs. Ford, who claimed she had no idea he was married. By the time Cooke made a full confession, she lamented that she could not free herself from her "devoted attachment" to him. Part of the reason might have been that their fates were permanently linked with the birth of their daughter, Jeannette Victoria Timmonds, in 1905.[5]

The child exacerbated the couple's volatile chemistry, which fueled intermittent violent confrontations. When Cooke tried to return to his ever-faithful wife, Anna, in Chicago, Mrs. Ford became enraged. She pulled a pistol out of her purse, and at nearly point blank range, she fired a bullet into Edgar Cooke's chest. It should have killed him. His miraculous survival, however, made for a great story frequently told with a dramatic finale of opening his shirt to reveal the scar imprinted on his chest.[6]

In spite of, or perhaps because of, the drama, Ida Brockway and Mrs. Ford appeared to be the closest of friends. Mrs. Ford often rented elegant hotel suites or temporary lodgings where Ida Brockway would often stay with her for weeks at a time, and when Mrs. Ford traveled, Ida Brockway helped care for little Jeannette and Alfred. During one such tenure in the summer of 1909, Ida Brockway escorted Jeannette to Chicago to visit her father, Edgar Cooke. They traveled in style, stayed at the historic Palmer House—even then thought to be one of the world's most lavish hotels— and what seemed like an innocent trip ignited in Mrs. Ford a simmering mistrust of her friend.[7]

Ida Brockway was having her own doubts. She had indulged Mrs. Ford's disturbing tendencies, until one day, she found her limit to their friendship. For years, the two women had met for lunch, but Ida Brockway began to suggest they no longer meet at the Customs office. Just as Edgar Cooke had discovered, Ida Brockway realized that Mrs. Ford could be a nuisance. Eventually, it was Mrs. Ford's otherwise innocuous request that turned into a national scandal. Mrs. Ford moved from the Havlin Hotel to a permanent residence at the fashionable Sun Building apartments, but she lacked sufficient references to establish a telephone line in her own name. She asked Ida Brockway to set up an account using her own name on Mrs. Ford's behalf. This turned out to be an unreasonable request because Mrs. Ford had only lived there a short time, but Ida's refusal led to a devastating quarrel that abruptly ended their friendship and brought down the Big Four railroad office in Cincinnati, Ohio.[8] At first, a connection with the private row between Ida Brockway and Mrs. Ford was far from evident, when on November 2, 1909, a story broke about a financial shortage in the accounts of Charles L. Warriner, head treasurer at the Big Four's Cincinnati office. Little by little, however, the disparate pieces of the puzzle began to fit together, captivating the public's attention like an unfolding dramatic serial novel.

Charles Warriner initially said the shortage was an inadvertent tabulation error. Then, over the next week, reports revealed that this was far from a typical crime of greed, and it was filled with a growing cast of characters who fleshed out a bizarre decade of blackmail and extortion and the actual damage hovering around two million dollars. Charles Warriner painted himself as a victim forced into treachery by the hotheaded Mrs. Jeannette Timmonds Ford and her lover Edgar S. Cooke, who had been bleeding him dry for the last seven years. The whole saga began soon after Charles Warriner transferred to the Cincinnati office of the Big Four, when he discovered shortages in the books of Edgar Cooke and his own predecessor, Frank Comstock, a well-respected family man holding one of the most important positions in the service of railroad.[9] But because Charles Warriner had also been stealing from the railroad in his previous office, if he reported the current losses, his own malfeasance would be discovered, so he stayed silent.

Unfortunately, Warriner would soon learn that when Edgar Cooke admitted his adultery to his lover, he also confessed his financial misdeeds, which clarified to Mrs. Ford why he could not leave his wife, because she knew and benefited from his crime. Neither Cooke's duplicity nor criminality diminished Mrs. Ford's attraction to him, and, in fact, he was even more appealing, as a sympathetic figure trapped in a marriage, so she "stuck to him all the closer." But when Mrs. Ford's patience with Cooke grew thin, and now emboldened with her own leverage, she approached Warriner and threatened to expose his thievery if he didn't help her with her lover. Neither Warriner nor Cooke could afford to ignore Mrs. Ford, so Warriner agreed to pay Cooke and Mrs. Ford hush money, and he even sent money to Cooke's family because he felt a moral obligation to assist them while Cooke ran off to New York with his mistress.[10] After a few years, though, Anna Cooke wanted her husband back, which fueled another violent confrontation that left Mrs. Ford requiring an extended hospital stay.

But Mrs. Ford still wouldn't let go, and now she enlisted the help of the other thief, Frank Comstock, Warriner's predecessor at the Big Four. It was a perilous choice. While he plied her with alcohol, Comstock listened as she poured out her broken heart. In his own inebriated state, he confessed his wrongdoing, and then what started out as a brief rendezvous became a clandestine commiseration lasting for two weeks. She eventually made her way to Cooke in Chicago, and during the confrontation she revealed her intimate encounter with Comstock, which triggered Cooke's jealous rage that left her with permanent scars. Charles Warriner was summoned, and he was able to convince Mrs. Ford not to press charges against Cooke, in part by promising to take care of her until she could get back on her feet.

It wasn't just Mrs. Ford who was obsessed. Edgar Cooke could not overcome his own fixation with Mrs. Ford, and so another round of their volatile romance ensued. This time, Frank Comstock also contributed to their cohabitation, because of his own fear of exposure as a philanderer and a thief. Over the next seven years, Charles Warriner gave Mrs. Ford over eighty thousand dollars, twenty-two thousand of it filtered through Edgar Cooke. No matter what the actual sum, however, she never had enough, and Warriner lived with the constant burden of knowing he would never be free of her.

When Ida R. Brockway and Mrs. Jeannette Timmonds Ford ended their friendship, Warriner's troubles began, and he quickly blamed Brockway as the person responsible for his current misery. As the drama unfolded, Ida Brockway was at the center of a convoluted vortex of embezzlement, blackmail, assault, and sexual impropriety. Charles Warriner knew that Ida Brockway and Mrs. Ford "had become so thick" that it was implausible that Mrs. Ford wouldn't have confided in Brockway, and thus she was the only person who could have exposed the crimes to her "intimate" friend and supervisor at the Customs office, Frank Couden, a respected citizen of Warren County and an active Republican partisan.[11]

As soon as Ida Brockway's name surfaced in the press, Edgar Cooke went into hiding until his attorney worked out a deal for him to turn himself in. Then, he spoke to reporters. He said Warriner was a "nervous, erratic little man, who had become extremely religious," who was thus incapable of masterminding the crimes of which he was accused. Cooke admitted giving Mrs. Ford money, but it had not come from Warriner. His efforts to distance himself from Warriner and Mrs. Ford were futile when his intimate letters, filled with subject matter that at that time was "not permissible in the mails," were widely published. He defended himself by paradoxically suggesting the only reason he continued to write love letters to Mrs. Ford was to try to get rid of her persistent advances.[12] No one really bought that story.

Ida Brockway tried to disentangle herself from Mrs. Ford by withdrawing her guarantor of Mrs. Ford's credit-worthiness. The store drew up a bill for the balance due and sent two constables to collect the funds. After disparaging remarks, she paid her bill. The Big Four's secret service got wind of her whereabouts, and under whatever pretense of authority they claimed, they persuaded Mrs. Ford to "remain away from everybody for a little while," as a "voluntary prisoner," and to ensure her sequester, the private detectives stationed themselves around the apartment building "to keep her from talking" to anyone.[13]

Reporters found a way around them and knocked on Mrs. Ford's door, which unleashed a flurry of Mrs. Ford's accusations against Brockway. She claimed she was being persecuted because she was a woman, and she denied blackmailing anyone. She shouted that the whole controversy was "all the fault of Ida Brockway!" and refused to answer any more questions because, "The papers have settled it already . . . ask Ida Brockway . . . she is giving out the news." She lamented that she had trusted Brockway, and cried, "I thought she was my friend," and vowed she would "never again confide in a woman friend!"[14]

Prosecutor Hunt asked Ida Brockway and Frank Couden to come in for questioning. She provided information crucial to the investigation because

Hunt hinted that a conviction could rest on her testimony. The stress was overwhelming, evidenced by Ida Brockway's disappearance soon after she met with Hunt, which inspired Mrs. Ford's assertion that Ida Brockway was "the other woman" involved in the scandal, who could impugn her moral rectitude by accusing her of collaboration in the alleged crimes.[15]

Ida R. Brockway was a "badly wanted" woman as word spread around the country announcing "Warriner Witness Missing," which inspired a round of inquiries about the mysterious "other woman" who was "the chum and roommate of Mrs. Ford." Henry Hunt issued a subpoena demanding Brockway's appearance before the grand jury in four days. He told reporters that Ida Brockway was a key witness and that his case would be seriously hurt if she could not be located. Ida Brockway's family friend, attorney Thomas Cogan, guaranteed Brockway's appearance in court, which Hunt promised would produce "a sensational story."[16]

Upon learning that his colleague at the custom's office was missing, Frank Couden tried to assuage the press's attention on her by confessing that he also had done favors for Mrs. Ford, just as he would for any friend. He said that it wasn't Brockway but himself who contacted officials in New York about the shortage, without promise of reward, immunity, or promotion in return. Couden then disclosed that he had learned of Warriner's shortages nearly a decade earlier from his drinking buddy Edgar Cooke. Whenever Cooke had too much to drink, he blathered about his troubles with Mrs. Ford and about Warriner's bookkeeping. Only when Ida Brockway approached him with what she knew and "[expressed] her opinion about the correctness of the story" did he realize the seriousness of Cooke's ramblings. He finally broached the subject with Ohio's US senator Charles W. Dick, who arranged a meeting with him and railroad executives.[17]

The press took note when Ida Brockway returned to Cincinnati two weeks later with headlines such as, "Stenographer Has Returned Summoned to tell Grand Jury about Big Four Shortages." She came back with a new attitude, donning a defensive posture, proactively shifting the narrative about herself. She said she had not run away from anything and she came back of her own accord, insisting that she had a perfect right to go anywhere she pleased. "Why shouldn't I?" she defiantly challenged, indignant at their suggestion that she sought a reward from the Big Four. Prosecutor Hunt was not taking any chances with his star witness, so he forced her to post a bond to guarantee her court appearance.[18]

People began to wonder why Ida Brockway had kept silent for so long as she deftly defended herself by pleading ignorance about whatever conspiracy had swirled around her for years. She said she had met Mrs.

Ford through Edgar and Anna Cooke when they lived in Cincinnati, and whenever Mrs. Ford and the Cooke's had trouble, she sided with the Cooke's, for which Mrs. Ford had "never quite forgiven me." What's more, the lovers' machinations that led to Mrs. Ford firing a bullet into Edgar Cooke's chest had been, she said, "well exploited" by the press.[19] But she was adamant that she never met Warriner, and knew nothing about their relationship with her friends or a blackmail scheme "levied on him." She expressed regret for the current turmoil, but she never anticipated that Mrs. Ford would be a central figure in a scandal about the Big Four.

That Ida Brockway was never implicated in any crime mattered little to the head of the US Customs office and former Cincinnati mayor, Armor Smith Jr., who was more troubled by Ida Brockway's unapproved absence from her job. He ignored how the revelations meant that the Big Four owed money to the US Customs office because they obviously took in more money than was claimed by the treasurer. And he disregarded her years of stellar service. After a meeting with prosecutor Hunt, he recommended her discharge, and his opinion carried weight. She was fired and quickly replaced.[20]

A few weeks later, just before Christmas 1909, Charles Warriner pleaded guilty to all charges of embezzlement and larceny, and he threw "himself on the mercy of the court," acknowledging that he had transgressed and "suffered considerably" already. Any hope for leniency was quickly dashed, and when the judge pronounced a six-year sentence, Warriner's body went limp, and he collapsed onto the floor.[21]

After Brockway's grand jury testimony on December 10, 1909, she was described as the one "who is alleged to have furnished the information which set the machinery of the New York Central Lines at work and discovered the gigantic shortage in its treasury." Soon after, Mrs. Ford was indicted for blackmail, and Ida Brockway, Charles Warriner, and Edgar Cooke would be called to testify for the prosecution.[22] Grand jurors had poured through hundreds of documents dating from 1905 with the couple's calculations all the way up to 1922, which provided evidence that Mrs. Ford and Edgar Cooke demanded installment payments of $150, totaling $25,000, and scores of Mrs. Ford's hotel bills ranging from $250 to $1,000 per stay. Warriner decided he couldn't drag out his blackmailer's control over him, so he returned their demand letter and tried to pay them off all at once.[23] But it turned out there was no way out of the web in which he had entangled himself.

Published letters reveal Mrs. Ford's offensive nature and relationships with Cooke, Ida Brockway, and Charles Warriner. "My own dear Pop,"

began one letter to Edgar Cooke, "I wrote W [Warriner] for more money
. . . but haven't seen or heard anything further from him." She badgered
her lover to leave his wife, whom she called "the old hag." Edgar Cooke
even urged Mrs. Ford not to expose Warriner's shortages at the Big Four
because of her own need for "the financial aid," and then he asked her to
send him "another ten spot" when she received money from "Charlie."[24]

The press had a field day portraying Mrs. Ford as a depraved femme
fatale preying on weak, vulnerable, and innocent men. Her letters to
Edgar Cooke inspired little sympathy with her sense of social superiority,
and her disdain for men beneath her station, especially bartenders who
overstepped their place, such as one who dared to flirt with her: she wrote,
"Old Cheapskate, I wonder if he thought I would even notice a common
slob like himself." When one bartender refused to sell her a drink because
she was already inebriated, she wrote, "You can bet I was up in the air
in a minute, to be turned down like that—by some damn common slob
here in this forsaken hole," because, after all, she had been to "some of
the swellest" places in New York. [25]

Jury selection began for Mrs. Ford's trial, set for January 20, 1910, six
days after Warriner began serving time in a Columbus, Ohio, penitentiary.
By ten o'clock, the courtroom had filled with spectators, including half
a dozen women during an era when women were not even allowed to
sit on juries or vote in most states. Charles Warriner took the stand on
January 31, wearing his cumbersome overcoat, a feeble attempt to hide
his prison garb. Mrs. Ford's attorney demanded he remove it, and for any
juror who might not have been paying attention, Warriner's testimony
was newly framed by the obvious symbol that he was a convicted felon.
Warriner described how Mrs. Ford's threats led to his blackmail payments
of $2,000, and then $1,000 per month from October 1902 through the
fall of 1909 when he was caught, totaling $84,000. [26]

In preparation for her testimony, Ida Brockway booked a room under
another name at the nearby Emery Hotel. One evening, her friend and
colleague Frank Couden visited with her in the hotel's second floor parlor. Deep in conversation, they were oblivious to the silent approach of
a woman who began screaming and beating Couden with her umbrella.
He struggled to block the assaults while trying to get out of his chair and
ran from the scene. Then, the enraged woman turned her "tongue and
lashing" to the terrified Ida Brockway. She was finally able to escape into
the powder room, locked herself inside and waited until she assumed
the hysterical woman had left the parlor, and then she ran up the stairs
to her room. [27]

The aggressor was Mrs. Mattie McDermott, whose attack had little to do with Mrs. Ford and a lot to do with Frank Couden who, two years earlier, had been acquitted of the manslaughter of Mrs. McDermott's son. Mrs. McDermott was now on a mission of vengeance against Couden, who had fired one of his two shots, into the back of her son as he ran from Couden's yard after trying to steal a chicken for his starving family, who were surviving on his mother's meager Civil War widow's pension.

Within days of being accosted, Ida Brockway was called to the stand on February 4, 1910. She impressed observers as she walked through the courtroom. The gallery took notice of the supposed "other woman," a tall, striking figure, dressed in a tailored gray business suit, with upright posture exuding confidence. She was sworn in and seated, and then, to everyone's surprise, she appeared a reluctant witness. Perhaps she was intimidated by the altercation in the parlor, or maybe it was because Mrs. Ford had now threatened to reveal unflattering or salacious details about what she thought had taken place during Ida Brockway's sojourn to Chicago with her daughter. Mrs. Ford said she would soon be ready to tell the public things about the proper stenographer that would shock everyone. Mrs. Ford bragged, "The eyes of many people would be opened," and, "Oh, I'm going to tell and when I do just look out."[28]

As prosecutor Hunt approached Brockway, the anticipation in the courtroom was palpable. He asked her to describe her relationship with Mrs. Ford and to relay her observations about Mrs. Ford's finances and lifestyle. She proceeded to describe how she had witnessed Mrs. Ford receiving money through the mail and during her midday excursions. Ida Brockway came to believe that, in spite of Mrs. Ford not having any visible means of support, she always had enough money to get whatever she wanted or needed. She had often observed Mrs. Ford mysteriously leave the apartment to hail a taxi for what Mrs. Ford called her "pressing engagement," and then return with her finances, and her mood, greatly improved. She also noticed how Mrs. Ford frequently mailed self-addressed envelopes to men that were returned stuffed with money.[29]

Brockway described her connection to Mrs. Ford as less of a friendship than one of a transactional nature, where she would provide secretarial and administrative services, and she countered Charles Warriner's assumption about the extent of the women's intimacy by asserting that Mrs. Ford never really confided in her. After these initial questions, prosecutor Hunt surprised the court by handing over his star witness for cross-examination, and when the defense declined, the gallery didn't hide its shock as the judge abruptly adjourned the court for lunch.

Mrs. Ford took the stand when the trial resumed, earning groans and moans from the crowd assembled to hear her describe the series of events that led to her current dire circumstances. It was a dark portrait of ill-placed and undisciplined passions but slanted by her claim of victimization by Charles Warriner and Edgar Cooke, who had exploited her weaknesses. She claimed, until Warriner's trial, she had no knowledge of the deal between the two men, whereby "Cooke was to keep his liberty as long as he kept me away from Cincinnati or people might suspect something of the rottenness that was going on in the office of the Big Four Treasurer."[30] Then, again to the utter disappointment of the gallery, the defense rested without presenting another witness.

The next day, it was time for closing arguments. Replacing prosecutor Hunt was his assistant Dennis Cash, who unleashed an unmerciful diatribe against Mrs. Ford, after first noting that he had "to *apologize* to the jury for calling Mrs. Ford '*a woman*,'" because it was an injustice to her sex, and whatever initial sympathy he had for her evaporated because such an emotion would be wasted on this creature. Then he began to laud Charles Warriner's "high moral character," suggesting that he was the "only worthy one" in this case, with the hyperbolic claim that Warriner was "whiter than the driven snow compared to the mess that has engulfed him," hoping to play to the male juror's empathy for their own vulnerability to sexual manipulation. Headlines quoted Cash describing Mrs. Ford as a demon in disguise, a human vulture preying on men. He warned the jury that everything Mrs. Ford touched had decayed or had run desolate, and if they turned her loose, she would be free to break up homes and to ruin more families. With a minister's fury bellowing from the pulpit, he demanded the jury convict her so that "the community might be spared the evil influence that she wielded." Cash's righteous indignation was met with an eerie silence as Mrs. Ford fainted and slid from her chair onto the floor.[31]

After she recovered, her attorney simply pointed out that the only evidence against Mrs. Ford came from her former lover and a convicted embezzler who admitted to stealing from the railroad for twenty-five years, while he had only known Mrs. Ford for seven. What's more, it was Warriner's admission that he had encouraged and financed Mrs. Ford's life in New York City, and it was this that led to the downward spiraling of her life that forced her to live at the mercy of men who exploited her.

Whether the jury bought this version or not, after one day of deliberations, they failed to convict by a vote of eight to four. Two jurors said their decision rested, in part, upon not finding Charles Warriner to be a credible witness, easily imagining his perjuring himself to convict the woman he held responsible for his own transgressions. The remaining counts against Mrs. Ford were finally dropped, and the judge agreed that because "Mrs. Ford already was ruined in fortune and health, . . . further prosecution . . . would put her in a madhouse." In fact, that very day, she had already "escaped from the institution" where, after some public disturbance, the police had confined her.[32]

After a number of delays, Edgar Streete Cooke stood trial in the summer of 1911, anticipated to be "the most sensational of the series" of all of the cases involving the Big Four railroad. Observers throughout the gallery were buzzing in anticipation of hearing Mrs. Ford's potentially explosive testimony. She was a celebrity of sorts, and the scene couldn't have been more dramatic, when, as if on cue, at just the right moment for dramatic effect, the courtroom doors slammed open, revealing not the femme fatale who had exuded confidence and boasted of her expoits, but rather a severely debilitated woman who as an invalid of forty, appeared to be a feeble sixty years old. Tears began to run down the cheeks of onlookers as they sat stunned gazing at Mrs. Ford's palsied and frail body being rolled down the aisle lying in a nearly prone position in a rickety wheelchair. Desperately clinging to her was her weeping daughter Jeannette. In spite of her fragility, she testified for two days, after which her physician pleaded that to continue with her interrogation would be at great risk to her life. Mrs. Ford described Edgar Cooke's visits to her flat two or three times a week, arriving with a package filled with money that she would hide in a trunk until they had accumulated $22,000 and secured a safety deposit box in New York City.[33]

The other witness was Mrs. McDermott, who used the opportunity as part of her larger vengeance on Frank Couden for the murder of her son. She agreed to testify on Cooke's behalf when he offered to help her with her civil case against Couden. When Couden was fired from the custom's office, Mrs. McDermott happily took credit. She found Mrs. Ford in a hospital, eager to speak freely about her affair with Cooke and the thousands of dollars she received from him and Charles Warriner. Edgar Cooke's faith in Mrs. McDermott was well placed. She told the court that Mrs. Ford had spoken freely, unaware McDermott was spying on behalf of her former lover, Cooke. The clincher came when Mrs. McDermott said that while Mrs. Ford said she was under the distinct impression that Cooke had stolen the money, she didn't actually know, and she couldn't swear to it, which undercut the prosecution's case against Cooke and her own previous claim that it was, indeed, stolen money. Cooke beamed that he "would not be around here long after the jury went out," and just as his often unbearable confidence had proved true, the jury came back with a not-guilty verdict.[34]

Ida Brockway's ordeal hastened the process whereby one of the nation's largest railroads established an entirely new method of conducting business, fueling a revolution described as "an upheaval" in accounting transparency and oversight. Initially refusing to believe their loyal employee had abused their trust, railroad executives finally realized Charles Warriner simply credited a smaller sum in the general ledger than what the clerks had turned into the office, which allowed him to take wads of cash on a daily basis. The whole thing could have been avoided by merely checking the clerks' remittance slips against the ledger and an occasional audit. All future cash transactions were removed from the treasurer's office, and remittances would go directly through the railroad's local bank depository with a new documentary paper trail. Cincinnati's treasurer's office was closed for good, and the whole operation was transferred to Chicago. It wasn't just a symbolic gesture then when Charles Warriner's rolltop desk was carried out, quietly destined for a lowly clerk in the freight department. Two years into his six-year sentence, Charles L. Warriner was released from prison for good behavior. He told reporters he hoped to start a new life by taking up "fruit farming in some rural community."[35]

Ida Brockway had been living close to individuals whose real lives were the stuff of a serialized melodrama, guided by obsessive passions, unbridled sexuality, and financial greed. And they were all a bit trigger-happy. It remains a mystery why she maintained her relationship with the adulterer and his unstable lover, and what led to her eventual break with them. We will never really know the actual nature of her relationship with Mrs. Jeannette Timmonds Ford, but it's possible the volatile way their friendship ended reflected a deeper intimacy between them, or at the very least, a stronger bond than Ida Brockway's public testimony suggested, as more perfunctory with few confidences exchanged between them. She was a "proper" professional woman, who was attracted to people who not only ignored Victorian moral proscriptions, but along with their illicit sexuality if not downright debauchery, were ruthless manipulators of the most corrupt persuasion.

But now, Ida Brockway felt compelled to escape life as she had lived it, and she would successfully do so beyond her expectations. Unlike Mrs. Ford, who vowed to never trust another woman, Ida Brockway went on to forge friendships and professional bonds with scores of women who were far removed from the world she had known, and they would include some of the world's most famous movie stars. In order to reincarnate herself, though, she had to make sure that "the other woman," Ida R. Brockway, disappeared forever.

CHAPTER 3

Mermaids and Matrimony

IDA R. BROCKWAY WOULD MAKE SURE THAT HER LIFE WOULD NO LONGER be dictated by the tribulations of friends and colleagues whose contorted notions of friendship, love, fidelity, and the rule of law motivated their tangled, wretched lives. Ida Brockway forever distanced herself from the Big Four railroad scandal and the notoriety of being "the other woman." While she freed herself from culpability in the assortment of crimes, she never explained her prolonged silence about what she knew or why she finally spoke up when she did. In fact, no one would ever hear anything from or about Ida R. Brockway again after a December 2, 1910, Cincinnati newspaper announcement: "Miss Ida Brockaway [sic], who helped disclose the shortage of Charles Warriner, former Big Four treasurer, was married to Oscar Koverman, a Cincinnati manufacturer."[1]

As the trials of her former friends carried on, Ida Ranous Brockway and Oscar Henry Koverman applied for a marriage license on November 10, 1910. Their romance was detailed in the local press: "Oscar Koverman, president of a manufacturing concern at Oakley, who lives at 2057 Elm Avenue, this city, yesterday admitted the truth of the published rumor of his marriage to Miss Ida Brockway in New York City on November 16." Noted as a former clerk and stenographer in Armor Smith's office with United States Surveyor of Customs, there was no mention of the Big Four railroad scandal or her dismissal by Smith; the story was merely that Miss Brockway had resigned the previous summer and moved to New York. While there, Oscar, "who [had] paid his attentions to her when she resided in Norwood several years ago," renewed their acquaintance when he just happened "to be in the metropolis on business a few weeks ago."

Only a few days "elapsed after the couple met before they were married." Apparently, Oscar hoped to stay in New York with his new bride; the *Enquirer* reported, "If a deal in which the groom was interested had gone through, he and his bride would have made their permanent residence in New York." Clearly, the deal did not go through, because Oscar remained in Ohio forever after.[2]

Ida R. Brockway's marriage to Oscar H. Koverman allowed her to erase any link to her previous life through the deliberate ignoring of custom that dictated that a married woman adopt her family name as her middle name followed by her husband's surname. She should have become Mrs. Ida Brockway Koverman, or Mrs. Oscar H. Koverman nee Brockway, but instead, she became Mrs. Ida R. Koverman. Thus, by keeping her middle initial "R" for Ranous, and by dropping her widely publicized family name "Brockway," she ensured that after her last known address at 5108 Carthage Avenue in Cincinnati, Ida R. Brockway would disappear from the historical record.

Oscar Henry Koverman was a suitable partner. According to the 1900 US Census, he was born either in 1878, or, as documented on his 1918 draft card, on September 12, 1880. It mattered little to the thirty-four-year-old Mrs. Ida R. Koverman because all she wanted was to escape any vestige of her former life. Oscar Koverman must have been a lovely fellow, tall with medium build, gray eyes, and brown hair. He was one of several siblings whose father, Henry, had passed away long before the nuptials. Family lore had it that "the marital bonds were more legalistic than emotional," and, at least according to public records, it seems that the marriage was simply one of convenience after the notoriety of the Big Four scandal.

Family members had heard various rumors, such as that Ida Brockway left town to give birth to an illegitimate child or that she married Oscar because she was already pregnant.[3] When Ida and Oscar tied the knot, he was still living with his mother and working as a clerk, and he continued to do so long after the exchange of vows.[4] It's unlikely the newlyweds ever resided in the same city, and in fact, it appears that Oscar and Ida Koverman actually led separate lives hundreds of miles and worlds apart.

Their individual existence started around the time Oscar departed for Cartagena, Colombia. His new bride might not have noticed he was gone or that he returned to New York City on December 13, 1911. Mrs. Koverman also probably never assumed her marriage would include sharing her life with Oscar, because she kept herself very busy without him. A local social column reported that she was one of the late vacationers who came to stay in one of the "unique cottages" nestled in the quaint hamlet town of Haines Falls in the Catskills. She spent her summers in Brooklyn, attending grand affairs such as the Knights of Columbus charity ball in 1913. The society page made occasional note of her activities, but Oscar was never mentioned. In 1918, he was still in Cincinnati, and his draft card listed his mother as his closest living relative, while his wife lived at 48 West 95th Street and then at 443 Grand Avenue in New York City.[5]

Another indication that Mrs. Ida R. Koverman was an independent woman, with possible ties to the burgeoning motion-picture industry, was her identification, separate from her husband, as one of three "incorporators" for United Studios Corporation, founded in August 1914 with $300,000 capital along with T. Bell and H. O. Coughlin of New York. United Studios is associated with Michael C. Levee, who was linked during his long career with Fox, Paramount, and United Artists.[6]

Mrs. Ida Koverman lived her married life as a single woman, but she rarely lived alone. In 1915 and 1916, she rented an apartment at 5 Hillside Avenue in New York City, designated as "the head of household," and she worked in various jobs as a cashier or office manager. The other resident at the Hillside address was Jessie Turner, a sixteen-year-old boarder attending high school, described as her niece. Ida Koverman and Jessie Turner were booked into the new Hotel Shelburne in Brighton Beach in the spring of 1916, and they were expected to stay throughout the summer.[7]

The Shelburne hosted guests of a different breed, when, in August, "a number of pedigree dogs" were seen "summering with their owners." Nearby, Seaside Park welcomed the "high brow" canines as they proudly paraded with their owners in tow. Some noticed how "in direct contrast" to the show of "toy dogs," there were "several bull-dogs that gazed contemptuously at their smaller brothers whenever they happen to meet." Among them was a pedigree English Bulldog named "Prince . . . accompanied by Mrs. Ida R. Koverman." A month later, Ida Koverman, Jessie Turner, sans Prince, attended a party at the Shelburne, where everyone played bridge, drank tea, and afterward were joined by "a number of men for dancing," but Oscar was not among them.[8]

Ida Koverman pursued her passions during her liberated life in Brooklyn. It wasn't unusual for married women to spend time away from their spouses while enjoying social activities with other married women friends, daughters, and relatives. Men and women tended to live much of their lives in "separate spheres," with women dominant in the private, domestic, child-centered world, and men earning livelihoods in the public world of business and commerce. Middle- and upper-class women often spent time at retreats, spas, or other venues where strong female bonds formed and subcultures flourished. Daughters of the rising middle and professional classes were more highly educated than previous generations, but they would still marry, bear children, and devote their spare time to the genteel female-centered social and community groups engaged in uplifting the world around them.

Before her marriage, Ida Koverman lived a professional and personal life that blurred the traditional demarcation of where men and women existed. As a married matron, she assumed a more traditional sphere of activities, but she still challenged proscriptions and perimeters of where and what women could and should do. Aside from attending charity balls, parties and teas, and walking Prince, Ida Koverman had a passion for swimming. The Shelburne was near the Brighton Beach swimming pool, and the hotel often hosted groups of women who delighted in aquatic pursuits.

Women's public swimming was still guided by prudish sensibilities about women's bodies and physical abilities, and beachside exposure of the female body could elicit possible arrest on morals charges. Women of Ida Koverman's age grew up wearing bathing dresses over leggings made out of wool or other heavy fabric, which when soaked with water were so heavy and cumbersome that for even the most liberated among them, it was difficult to remain buoyant, literally and figuratively.

What women wore at the shoreline was symptomatic of broader restrictions about their participation in swimming as a competitive sport. Ida Koverman challenged these traditions when she and her like-minded colleagues overcame the Victorian propriety institutionalized in the rules of the Amateur Athletic Union (AAU), which served to thwart initiatives that encouraged the legitimacy of women's competitive swimming. AAU president James E. Sullivan thought it was "an abhorrence," and women's involvement in sports generally "a morally questionable activity." The tides were changing, though, and many came to see Sullivan as "a narrow minded bigot," and finally, in 1915, the AAU sanctioned women's swimming as an official sport, paving the way for advocates to now aggressively lobby the international Olympic committee to overturn rules keeping women out.[9]

This effort was part of the mission of Charlotte "Eppy" Epstein and others, who founded the National Women's Life-Saving League (NWLSL) in 1914, spearheading women swimmers, divers, and training for national and international competition. Rumblings within the ranks, however, soon demanded more focus on the goals of dedicated competitors. Ida

Koverman helped to spur this rebellion, which in October 1917 spawned the New York Women's Swimming Association (NYWSA). Described as one of the "guiding spirits," Koverman was elected president, and she quickly oversaw the drafting of the organization's founding documents.[10]

The first event under WSA auspices was held on January 13, 1918, when the New York "mermaids" opposed challengers from Philadelphia at the Brighton Beach Swimming Pool. NYWSA promoted the skill and joy of swimming and diving for recreation and encouraged women to compete in amateur swimming on a national level. It was dedicated to bringing together the most talented among them to train for international competition.[11]

One year after the founding of the NYWSA, Ida Koverman fostered the establishment of the Brooklyn's Women's Athletic Club (WAC), and after she was elected secretary, she again headed the organizational committee to draw up founding documents and bylaws. She took charge of WAC's summer program to set up tennis classes along with swimming lessons in the Brooklyn Heights division. Vice president of the WSA, Charlotte "Eppy" Epstein, hoped the group would attract professional women and increase the number of venues where women could swim without crimination.[12]

Part of the draw was volunteer coach Louis De Breda Hanley (aka Handley), an internationally acclaimed coach who perfected the American crawl. WSA branches sprouted up all over the country after women finally won the right to compete in the Olympics, and the Shelburne Hotel became the headquarters for America's first female Olympic swimmers as they prepared for the 1920 games in Antwerp, Belgium, where they would win three gold medals.[13] As the center of American women's competitive swimming blossomed in New York, the WSA "launched America into Olympic prominence" by dominating the medal count for the next three competitions. By then, Ida Koverman had moved to California, where she brought her organizational skills, her love of swimming, and her attraction to all things spectacle to Los Angeles. The local press described her as the former president of the New York Swimming Association, "herself a well-known swimmer," who was preparing for the "Huntington Beach Plunge," overseeing "Cady's Mermaids," a group of young women coached by Fred Cady that included Thelma Darby, the national one-mile champion. Koverman was hardly a competitive swimmer, but she knew how to promote the sport for men and women, and between January and July 1922, she had a byline in the *Los Angeles Times* in which she colorfully reported on the "classy bunch" of swim meets that featured Olympic freestyle medallist Ludy Langer and the world-renowned "star of stars," father of modern surf boarding, Duke Kahanamoku, who guaranteed to "show celerity," in the upcoming rematch. A mixed team of "water stars" would entertain with "fast spins" at the Los Angeles Athletic Club's tank in a series of programs "sparkling with interest and promising many thrills." Up-and-coming swimmers appearing at the March 8 "swimfest" would perform "high and fancy" diving, and the regional champions, the Mercury Mermaids, were pitted against their friendly rivals from Milwaukee and Koverman's old haunt, the New York Women's Swimming Association. In April, "Mermen and Maids to Seek Watery Laurels" announced the championship meet, which would also premiere Coach Cady's "water shoes," designed for fencing combatants to stand up in the water. In June, the "Gala, Swimming Carnival" would move to San Francisco's Sutro Baths, as part of the entertainment for the Shriners' convention, headlined as "Local Nymphs to Go North."[14]

Koverman's coverage not only made a "splash" for women's competitive swimming, but it also raised her profile among the ranks of the city's female journalists. This might explain the attention and affection the press had for Koverman from the earliest months in the Golden State. Koverman's own life and her passion for the sport fostered the "new woman" of the post-WWI era, a woman who had the advantage of expanded political, professional, and social freedoms won by rebels and reformers alike. The more familiar image of electrified nighttime cityscapes with speakeasies filled with liberated lives perpetuated the stereotypical woman portrayed as a bobbed-haired, cigarette-smoking, heel-kicking flapper wearing a formless, corset-free Gatsby-style frock as she frenetically danced the night away. The new woman of the 1920s, however, was much more than that, and Ida Koverman ushered in her arrival as a vibrant athlete who was as "hard as nails," and who could sometimes beat men at their own games. Within a decade, the enthusiasm for training Olympic caliber swimmers and divers had spread to all parts of the country.[15]

The question of why Ida Koverman moved to California remains unanswered, but tracing the record of what she actually did counters the perpetual mythical narrative and, in fact, it provides her a more complex historic legacy and a more interesting backstory on which to rest it. While recent references suggest she first settled in San Francisco and worked for Herbert Hoover before she moved to Los Angeles, the published documents exacerbate the mystery. The 1920 Los Angeles city directory lists her as residing at 3978 La Salle Avenue, while the voter registration roll of San Francisco County has her as a registered Republican living at 929

Sacramento Avenue. What's more, the January 1920 US Census describes Koverman as the head of a two-person household living in a rented apartment at 132 Gratten Street in San Francisco's Ashbury Heights district. Her roommate was thirty-three-year-old, Wisconsin-born Myrtle G. Wright, listed as a secretary in the mining and oil business, but elsewhere noted as a stenographer at the St. Francis Hotel. Regardless of Mrs. Wright's occupation, it can't be a coincidence that Myrtle Wright is the same name as the then well-known, record-setting amateur swimmer who, along with her daughter Myrtle "Babe" Wright, broke the world record for crossing the Golden Gate channel. Both mother and daughter "made waves" in sports history and were associated with the city's branch of the California Swimming and Lifesaving Club.[16]

In 1913, Mrs. Wright and her daughter made news when they were setting up for the filming of a rescue scene. The mother prematurely fell into the sea when the wash of a passing ferryboat knocked her off her footing, and she lost consciousness after hitting her head on the side of the boat. The daughter jumped in the water, just as the script dictated she do, but only after she grasped her mother's limp body and another champion swimmer came to their aid did she learn of the seriousness of the situation.[17] Years later, Koverman's passion for swimming, pageantry, and musicals were blended in MGM's extravagant, water-based movie production numbers starring America's "million dollar mermaid," Esther Williams. Williams's charisma and skill were attractive features, but the movie of the same name was inspired by the Australian Olympian Annette Kellerman, who, on a grander scale, ushered in a new international mode of female swimwear and athleticism.

While Ida Koverman was helping to popularize swimming in and outside of the pool, she did it while constructing a new persona and deliberately compartmentalizing her previous life and any marital relationship with Oscar H. Koverman. He had merely provided the former Ida R. Brockway with a way to escape notoriety in Ohio and a platform to launch her new life of legitimacy and legacy.

Within weeks of her court appearance in the trial of her former friend Mrs. Jeanette Ford, Ida Koverman transformed herself into a middle-class matron engaged in wholesome, women-centered community activities. She no longer socialized with eccentric characters who lived outside the norms of propriety and the boundaries of the law. While her marriage to Oscar liberated her from her past, if she held any illusion that Oscar would provide financial security and a middle-class lifestyle, she quickly learned he could do neither. Happily, however, the next phase of her compartmentalized life offered new and exciting opportunities. She was primed to join the army of skilled professional men and women who buttressed America's entrepreneurial spirit and set the country on a path of unprecedented internationalism that redefined the world order for the twentieth century.

CHAPTER 4

Cathedral of Commerce

MRS. IDA R. KOVERMAN WAS WELL PREPARED TO CREATE A NEW LIFE for herself in New York. She had honed her secretarial and administrative skills during her years employed at the US Customs office, and these were marketable assets. She held many titles such as cashier and notary public, but her elevated abilities allowed her promotion to higher status and lucrative posts over the decade. America's business infrastructure had expanded exponentially, transformed by innovative technology that led to large-scale industrial production and transportation networks that not only attracted waves of cheap foreign workers to its shores but also inspired a demographic shift from the hinterland farm communities to new jobs in fast-growing cities. Complex corporate oligopolies were increasingly managed by distant directorates, which spawned new layers of management hierarchies. The rise of big business created new relationships between workers and employers, and new organizational models that integrated experts and engineers and specialized technicians of all stripes. Men moved upward into higher paying managerial job descriptions, while the more tedious administrative clerical duties drew upon a new feminized generation of stenographers, typists, receptionists, telephone operators, and secretaries. Ida Koverman had years of professional experience with which she could approach her new life anywhere she saw an opportunity.

Many years later, gossip columnist Sheila Graham told her readers that while Koverman was at the Customs house, John Hays Hammond, the "business prince . . . great engineering genius," was looking for talent, and he found it in Koverman, whom he hired as a secretary. The actual timing is vague, but the connection is credible, as Koverman hinted later that year to MGM's *Studio Club News* that she had worked as "the confidential secretary" to a group of men who oversaw large mining projects around the world. While she did not mention Herbert Hoover, even as late as 2018 the rumor persisted that Koverman worked for Hoover at Consolidated Gold Fields of South Africa (CGFSA), but at that time, CGFSA had no operations in the United States, an often-overlooked but important detail.[1]

John Hays Hammond had worked for CGFSA, but he resigned in 1903, although not completely cutting his ties. Hammond joined the colorful Baron Alfred von der Ropp to identify properties they saw as good investments for the eventual expansion of the CGFSA in the United States. Von der Ropp soon realized CGFSA had little capital for these ventures, however, so he oversubscribed stock issues to finance the new Gold Fields American Development Company (GFADC). Joining Hammond and von der Ropp was another former CGFSA engineer, Harry H. Webb, and together they launched "the beginning of a new era in the history" of the parent company.[2]

James McDougall was hired to mange the New York office of GFADC, which in 1913 moved into the new Woolworth Building at 233 Broadway, soon known as the Cathedral of Commerce. The petroleum boom of the early twentieth century transformed America and integrated transnational corporate empires. The Woolworth Building housed the operations of established and newly emerging petroleum and engineering empires, along with other big players in the international import and export trade. Frank W. Woolworth was the largest retailer in the world, and he commissioned the architectural wonder of what would be, at 792 feet, the world's tallest building. Its outer and interior design paid homage to European facades that inspired spiritual uplift, but was now blended with symbols of capitalism's modern entrepreneurial genius.[3]

Once settled in at the Woolworth Building, James McDougall hired Ida R. Koverman. Just as she had worked inside Cincinnati's massive federal office building, Ida Koverman now worked in New York's most majestic edifice. Eventually she would sit at a desk in another iconic structure, the executive building on the MGM studio lot in Culver City, which came to symbolize the historic stature of the studio within the burgeoning motion-picture industry. Ida Koverman was part of an "edifice complex" that memorialized America's expanding infrastructure of power and influence through government, business, and culture.

Every day she stepped into a bustling tower of eclectic modern neo-Gothic style. Among the twelve thousand regular personnel who walked through the wide and well-lit corridors lined with polished terrazzo marble and wainscot made of selected Italian marble, she took one of the twenty-nine high-speed elevators up to the thirty-sixth floor. During her breaks, she might have blended in with any of the fifteen thousand daily visitors who filled the galleries, visited the observation deck or the grand arcade. For a woman seeking a new identity, she found a new world.

One of GFADC's new ventures Baron Alfred von der Ropp oversaw was its Foreign Mines Company, described as the "first step into the complex field of oil investment, in the Transcontinental Petroleum Company and the Tampico oilfield in Mexico." Tampico saw its landscape resurfaced by the ferocious activity of American and foreign workers searching for black gold. Nearly all of the international oil companies had headquarters there, but the growing instability of Mexico's internecine political wars threatened operations and personnel.[4]

The civil war fueled antagonism between the US and Mexico's Pancho Villa, who led notorious raids across the border. Things deteriorated rapidly after April 1914 in the wake of General John J. Pershing's seizure of Veracruz. The US-backed forces' siege of Tampico lasted for days. Petroleum profits were threatened, and so were workers caught up in the crossfire.[5]

The situation in Mexico touched Ida Koverman's life both personally and professionally. Soon after she joined GFADC, her older sister, the widowed, divorced, or separated Phoebe May Fisher, showed up with her daughter Kathryn and son-in-law, Frank Hawkins, and their three children in tow. Frank Hawkins needed a job. Ida Koverman had the best of intentions when she helped him find work with GFADC as a machinist at the company's mining operation in Tampico. Frank Hawkins's descendants believed he was one of the remaining American workers left stranded in Mexico, and in an incident known as the Tampico Affair, Pancho Villa himself personally escorted him out of the oil fields. When Frank Hawkins finally made his way back to New York, he was ready to go home, so he took his wife and their children back to Ohio. His mother-in-law, Ida Koverman's sister Phoebe May, refused to go, so she would not see her daughter Kathryn again until twenty-three years, and a couple of husbands, later.[6]

Ida Koverman worked hard for James McDougall when he became president of GFADC's next new venture, American Trona Corporation. Its subsidiary, California Trona, was a seven-hundred-acre operation in the desolate Southland desert town of Trona that manufactured chemicals from the brine extracted from Searles Lake. When Henry Webb retired from American Trona in 1918, Amor F. Keene, a former associate of Herbert Hoover in London, joined Hammond and von der Ropp as Trona's new vice president. Amor Keene visited California in February 1920 where Ida Koverman had by then moved, still employed as McDougall's executive secretary and working in Trona's downtown Los Angeles branch office at 724 South Spring Street.[7]

It is likely that Ida Koverman first met Ralph Arnold through Amor Keene at the Trona office. Ralph Arnold was a successful engineer-entrepreneur with an interest in Republican politics. He was a great admirer of Herbert Hoover after carefully observing him while he was in London working for CGFSA. Arnold believed Hoover was a man of "obvious presidential caliber." Arnold was also a cousin, and former roommate at Stanford University, of Hoover's close friend, Dr. Ray Lyman Wilbur, the future president of Stanford University and Hoover's secretary of the interior. Arnold's admiration of Hoover was a harbinger of Hoover's broad-based appeal, which grew exponentially and internationally after World War I. Early in 1920, Ralph Arnold and Democrat Samson Lindauer formed one of the first bipartisan "Make-Hoover-President" groups that were popping up around the country, designed to test the waters of a Hoover candidacy. The earliest ties between Koverman, Arnold, and Hoover first appear in the April accounting of Arnold's Hoover club, where Amor F. Keene's name appears as facilitating an early donation of one hundred dollars to the Hoover movement.[8]

Ralph Arnold had hired Ida Koverman to oversee distribution of a questionnaire about Hoover sent to 21,210 people whose names were compiled from directories of elite institutions and blue books throughout the country. She received $650, which included travel expenses of $500. It's unclear just when she left her job at Trona, but she took a job with the Los Angeles Transfer Company, a successful trucking company that initially seemed to offer job security, but by September 25, she was out and hoping her outreach to a Mr. Kraft with an oil company would pan out. It didn't.[9]

Ralph Arnold might have inadvertently accelerated her departure from the Transfer Company, and this would inspire his acute sensitivity over the next decade about her constant financial insecurity. Arnold casually mentioned to Transfer attorney Edward Dean Lyman that Koverman was looking around for another position, after which Lyman approached Koverman and suggested that it wouldn't be "fair to hold" her if she was not willing to stay on but hoped she would break in a new hire before she left. Koverman's temporary job with Arnold resumed at some point thereafter because by June 1922, Koverman noted that she had been working in Arnold's office for the last sixteen or eighteen months, carrying out Arnold's agenda "devoted to the political work . . . in the interests of a certain cause in which [he was] intensely interested."[10] Neither of them likely realized that over the next decade, Ida Koverman's professional life would be closely allied with Ralph Arnold, and his vision for the political fortunes of Herbert Hoover would also become her own.

Although Herbert Hoover had not lived in the United States for nearly two decades, soon after the first World War broke out, he visited New York to set up the New York Commission for Relief in Belgium. His popular appeal exploded, and his "rags to riches" life story reinforced the American dream narrative. Hoover came to symbolize the strengths and later the weaknesses of twentieth-century conservative Republican Party ideology. By age forty, he held assets upwards of four million dollars. Even as the first inklings of his growing attraction as a political candidate, Hoover had never voted in a presidential election. As a registered Republican, he donated to Theodore Roosevelt's Progressive "Bull Moose" candidacy in 1912 when Roosevelt broke with the standpatter Republican Party.[11]

It wasn't until 1921, when President Warren G. Harding appointed him secretary of commerce, that Hoover lived without interruption in the United States. Ida Koverman and Herbert Hoover eventually developed a genuine friendship, but it did not start in New York, and she was never his secretary. Ida Koverman's connection to Herbert Hoover cannot, to date, be established before she met Ralph Arnold in 1920.

When Ida Koverman's life shifted from New York City to Los Angeles, her estranged husband was still living with his mother and sister in Cincinnati. Some of the Kovermans had already settled in the Golden State. His spinster sister Gertrude lived with their uncle John Frederick, a grocery clerk, and his wife Charlotte and their children. Sister Gertrude was a stenographer, as was his cousin John Alston and Mary Leila. Oscar's other cousins in the household were Howard, a railroad clerk; Katherine Isabelle, a telephone executive; and Lawrence, a salesman. Another uncle, Andrew, lived in Glendale, but the larger clan lived together at 1353 Toberman Street. Within a decade or so they spread out and some moved up. Two of them worked in the movie industry. Oscar's cousin Irby was a cameraman at Paramount Pictures, and his cousin Rita M. was an inspector at Columbia Pictures.[12]

Accounts of the family's demographics are far from tidy, and it remains unclear just how much communication Ida Koverman had with her estranged husband's family. But soon, another closer relative was living nearby. At some point Ida's older sister Phoebe had married a man named John J. Boyer, and they lived near MGM in Culver City. The last we hear from Phoebe is of her death in Santa Monica on March 18, 1944, at the age of seventy-eight.[13]

PART II

LIFE TWO— KINGMAKER AND MATCHMAKER

CHAPTER 5

"Now Is the Time for All Good Women to Come to the Aid of Their Party"

Political Operative

IDA KOVERMAN'S PERSONAL STORY ENTWINES WITH LARGER SOCIO-economic shifts taking place in America after World War I. The Golden State had already granted its female citizens the right to vote in 1911, and the victory came largely through sympathetic progressive Republicans under the leadership of Hiram Johnson, who were eager to push through an anticorruption, pro-democracy, and social-welfare reform agenda. California women voters took their new role seriously and, along with their male allies, they passed new laws and overturned those that had denied women's rights over their own estates, custody, and franchise. When New York granted women the vote in 1917, it's likely that Ida Koverman supported the suffrage movement, given her alliance with strong, proactive women leaders. Soon, with the imminent passage of the Nineteenth Amendment, women all over the country would be able to vote, and this meant that Ida Koverman could not have entered politics at a more propitious time.

The process of integrating women into the state's political parties had been well underway, but now the merging of the separate worlds of male and female politics everywhere was accelerating at an historic pace, and both political parties aggressively courted women voters in time for the 1920 presidential election. Strategies of how to do this reflected the ongoing debate about whether women should be integrated into existing party structures or enrolled in separate women's organizations. Women's divisions were set up, and recruitment plans were designed to reach down to local precincts. California employed both strategies to overcome institutional inertia and male partisans who saw women not as equal contributors to democracy but as interlopers in their tradition of exclusion. Ida Koverman had not stood out in publicly identifying herself with "women's issues" or the suffrage movement, but she was becoming a key player within the state's complicated Republican Party, now infused with the excitement over the possibilities of the anticipated success of the women's suffrage amendment and the upcoming presidential-primary campaign season.

When it came to learning the intricacies of California's unique political terrain, she was a quick study. She learned about the polarized camps identified with the progressive former governor turned US senator Hiram Johnson, and the other camp increasingly identified with the more ambiguous Herbert Hoover, who appealed to progressives and conservatives in both parties. The schism among Republicans was growing, as the party stepped up its efforts to galvanize women and Hoover supporters in an effort to take down the cranky but esteemed Hiram Johnson. Koverman and Ralph Arnold revved up their war-machine upon learning that Herbert Hoover had been a long-time "paid-up member of the Republican Club of New York," and that he was a "regular" rather than a progressive Republican, to boot.[1]

The local Hoover-for-President office opened with Ida Koverman as its executive secretary. She hoped to broaden her influence in multi-state organizing efforts, but she found that her male colleagues initially tried to pigeonhole her into a "woman's" post under the direction of Mrs. Frank (Mary) Gibson. Gibson was a well-known progressive Republican and staunch supporter of Hiram Johnson, but because her son was a US diplomat who had worked with Hoover, she advocated Hoover's presidential candidacy.

Ida Koverman ended up with a spot in the press bureau, at least a bit closer to where she thought the real action was. She even entertained moving up the state party hierarchy, and she asked Arnold to outline his "definite plans" for her as an explicit expression of support for her larger involvement. She assured him that regardless of his response, he could depend on her "being tactful and carrying out" his wishes. She raised the possibility of a trip to San Francisco, where a more concentrated effort was needed, and where she could "better investigate conditions there."[2] It's possible she took an extended trip up north, which might explain why she shows up in the 1920 US Census as a resident in both Los Angeles and San Francisco.

Over time, Ralph Arnold came to rely on Ida Koverman's observations, and she increasingly acted as Arnold's eyes and ears, especially regarding Herbert Hoover. Her letters included hefty amounts of complaining about the inadequacies of everyone around her; Arnold shared his business tribulations, and their gossipy confidences provide insight into their bigger visions and the daily grind and minutia of the early years of what was to become a near decade-long Hoover campaign. Their grand strategies and loftier goals were sometimes couched in a venomous spew borne out of disappointments or impatience with election cycles and uncontrollable circumstances that thwarted their goal of unseating Hiram Johnson and taking over the state Republican Party. This larger war required victories in smaller battles on the way to the day when, as she wrote, Johnson would "eventually reach his Waterloo." She counseled Arnold about what was going to be a war of attrition, and so "we must not fool ourselves for a minute," and "time and much work will be required" to beat him, and to call upon "some very skillful politicians to lead and direct us."[3]

Coupled with her trepidation about the scale of their mission, she was worried about her own job security. She was a newcomer to Los Angeles, and while circulating near the city's business elite, she did not share the social and economic benefits derived from a profession, marriage, or inheritance. While she was dedicated to the long road of the Hoover campaign, the path to her own economic survival remained tenuous. Often, she had to threaten Arnold with abandoning their cause in order to find a way to pay her salary. Professionals and newcomers alike contributed to a down-and-dirty primary season where warring Republican factions inspired expectations of a record turnout for the May 1920 primary. There were four hundred thousand newly registered voters in Los Angeles County alone, and it was believed that two thirds of them would actually turn up to vote on election day.

The growing affection for Hoover coincided with the last stages of ratification of the Nineteenth Amendment and the Republican National Committee's program to integrate women into the party apparatus. California party leaders needed more prodding to enroll women alongside their men. The national committee was not satisfied with the pace of the recruitment of women for the upcoming election. They urged more cooperation with Clara Burdette, Pasadena's clubwoman matriarch and passionate Hoover booster. It wasn't just a gender equality strategy, however, when the state was directed to "organize your state together—not as separate units." Women were now factored into the party's financial plan that would now reverse generations of adherance to "follow the line of least resistance," by funding from "a few thousand people located in four or five large financial and industrial centers." Because modern times inspired a "wide awake and watchful interest taken in political plans, policies, and business methods," the party coffers would now be filled by statewide organizations composed of men and women working together to build a wider financial base of support.[4]

Senator Johnson won just over 30 percent, just under a million votes; Hoover garnered around ten percent, just over three hundred thousand votes, while the eventual nominee, Ohio's Warren G. Harding, won half of that, at around 144,000 votes, less than five percent. The most important number for Ida Koverman and her future political career, however, was that Herbert Hoover carried Los Angeles County by fourteen thousand votes.[5] The primary signaled a new trend in the history of the state, in which Ida Koverman's efforts played a part, where Southern California exercised its growing stature, which reflected long-term demographic changes south of the Tehachapi Mountains that would further exacerbate the polarization within the dominant Republican Party. The north remained a progressive stronghold while the south spawned a virulent opposition to its progressive holdouts.[6] Ida Koverman would thrive in Los Angeles's trench warfare during Southern California's metamorphosis into a political giant.

Ralph Arnold was an advocate of women's partisan activism, especially their leadership in the Hoover movement. Ida Koverman was less satisfied with its male leaders, though, such as Ralph P. Merritt, the Sun-Maid "raisin king," about whose obvious weaknesses she felt Arnold and his colleagues had a blind spot. She conceded Merritt was a "fine fellow and an able chap," but, because "he lacks political knowledge," he was more valuable as an "assistant than as a leader."[7]

She was even less sanguine about Edward Lyman, who now headed Hoover's Southern California headquarters, and who had earned her disdain when she worked for his client the Los Angeles Transfer Company. Edward Dean Lyman was an esteemed member of the city's professional class, and a leader among cultural influencers and institution builders. Nevertheless, Ida Koverman found Lyman a dishonest broker, both as a man and on Hoover's behalf. She reminded Arnold that she had worked closely with him for about three months, during which time she had the "most intimate opportunity to study him and his methods at very close range." She warned Arnold that Lyman was "absolutely unreliable," because his word meant little, and "his only concern is for his own advancement." Too much was at stake, she thought, so she urged Arnold to think carefully before entrusting important matters to Lyman. She said he was so afraid of "getting in on the wrong foot" that he refused to take chances, and as a result he had disappointed both of them for his failure to follow through on recent requests. Edward Lyman might not have had Koverman's trust, but as a partner of Overton, Lyman, & Plumb, he sustained Hoover's loyalty as his legal representative to purchase land in the San Joaquin Valley after he left the White House.[8]

The Republican National Convention was fast approaching, so Koverman and her allies planned their strategy for the Chicago affair. They were going to try to influence other states' delegates to support Hoover, even if California had already pledged its delegates to Johnson. Some thought it "politically unethical," and "just not being done," but their zealotry blinded them to such reasoning. By the time Arnold arrived in Chicago, Ida Koverman had already set up shop and was "contacting delegates and getting tips on the situation." Arnold admitted they "were a very cocky group . . . a sort of political maverick group kicking around," testing their strength. Although Herbert Hoover earned "the greatest and longest demonstration" at the convention, he received only ten and a half of the delegate votes.[9]

Ida Koverman and Ralph Arnold were not discouraged by Hoover's poor showing, but Arnold needed reassurance from Hoover that it was a fight worth continuing. He visited Hoover in his Park Avenue New York apartment to inquire if his devotees were needlessly "keeping the pot boiling." Arnold left Hoover believing this was the actual moment that ignited Hoover's path to the White House, and the one that inspired Arnold to devote his immediate future to politics rather than to his own business interests. He understood Hoover to have guaranteed he would leave his hat in the ring if Arnold and his allies could take control of California's Republican Party. Arnold admitted later that he had no idea the magnitude of the challenge, but he shook Hoover's hand and said, "It's a deal."[10] He did know, however, he would need Ida Koverman to make it happen. It was going to be a war fought in the grassroots, and it was going to get ugly. Ida Koverman was ready for battle, but she would have to navigate between progressives and conservatives in the party's trenches.

She had already started by developing a bond with progressive Mrs. Florence Collins Porter, a professional journalist and well-known clubwoman whom Ralph Arnold described as the "most influential individual woman in state politics." Mrs. Porter soon launched a new women's group, the Los Angeles Republican Study Club, which unwittingly set in motion a nationwide network designed to galvanize women into the party. Ida Koverman was at Mrs. Porter's side from the beginning, and throughout the fall of 1920, they held a series of meetings to build the organization, modeling it along the lines of the local, state, and national hierarchy of the nonpartisan General Federation of Women's Clubs (GFWC). Over a hundred women attended the first Study Club meeting when it announced support for candidates Warren G. Harding and Calvin Coolidge. Mrs. Porter acted as temporary president, and Ida Koverman was its temporary secretary, about which Ralph Arnold was most proud, noting that she was "active in campaign work and now doing preparatory propaganda work." Well-known progressive Katherine Philips Edson also attended the Study Club's inaugural gathering.[11]

The Republican Study Club offered Ida Koverman an avenue to accelerate her political apprenticeship, and while aimed at recruiting women into the party, she was never personally motivated by nor ever articulated a female-centered political worldview. Rather, the focus on women was an organizing strategy to build a movement to elect Herbert Hoover, and in doing so, she created working relationships and a trajectory for her own notable influence in the Golden State. But first, there was a challenge by another woman of established historical significance, who had already earned the moniker of California's "first stateswoman," Katherine Philips Edson.

Ida Koverman and Katherine Philips Edson should have been hearty allies, even good friends. They were both from Ohio, loved grand opera, shared a desire to contribute to the cultural development of their adopted city, and were both political animals. Edson rose to prominence through the Republican progressive-feminist alliance that supported Hiram Johnson's gubernatorial candidacy, and she was instrumental in the passage of California's 1913 minimum-wage law for women and children and then enforced it as the executive secretary of the Industrial Welfare Commission for eighteen years.[12]

Ida Koverman's impression of Katherine Edson started to take shape just before the November 1920 presidential election during a luncheon to honor Mrs. Raymond Robbins, a well-known progressive-Republican and national labor organizer. To Koverman, Edson appeared to be "very much outside and badly disliked." Edson had been in California politics a long time, and she experienced the ebbs and flows of celebrity. At this time, though, Ida Koverman failed to properly glean Edson's stature, and this misreading would frustrate her own ambition. Nevertheless, she thought that Edson's unswerving loyalty to Hiram Johnson was diminishing her influence as Herbert Hoover's popularity among women accelerated. To the extent this was true, it portended how women partisans would become the most virulent actors in the Golden State's partisan divide. In fact, Ida R. Koverman and Katherine Philips Edson epitomized California's postwar ideological rivalry, and their clash personalized politics in an unforeseen, dramatic showdown.

When Ida Koverman showed up in 1920, she quickly learned about and immersed herself in the intricacies of the state's hegemonic Republican Party, where intraparty warfare reflected disrupting trends in the broader political landscape. Within this shifting climate, Ida Koverman helped to place Herbert Hoover in the state's political consciousness and set in motion a machine to challenge its turn-of-the-century progressive impulse long embedded in the Republican Party.

Once allied with Ralph Arnold, Ida Koverman began her professional political career and her lifetime of partisan influence. She not only became the main conduit for Arnold's messianic zeal for Hoover's presidential candidacy, she embraced the mission and saw Hoover as someone whose superior nature gave him unparalleled statesman-like qualities. Her approach to electoral politics was pragmatic and designed to exploit ways to promote Hoover and the conservative wing of the ideologically polarized Republican Party.

While she was cleaning out Hoover campaign material in Arnold's office, she pondered the next chance to challenge Senator Johnson's hold on the party. Although two years away, she thought perhaps California's gubernatorial race could be a stepping-stone for Hoover's presidential run, and she broached the notion with Guy Finney, political reporter for the *Los Angeles Times*, who subsequently wrote, "Herbert Hoover, I am told, is beginning to loom up on the California political horizon as a candidate for Governor two years hence." Finney reassured his readers, "I got that straight from one of his active supporters in the primary campaign," who said "the word is being passed along that Mr. Hoover is receptive to the gubernatorial idea," and because Hoover "wants to get back into California permanently, . . . some sort of semi-official announcement may be forthcoming at the proper time."[13] Mrs. Florence Collins Porter even told Ida Koverman she heard this rumor while she was up north at a state party meeting, which, she said, inspired "fear and trembling among the political gang up there that Mr. Hoover might run for Governor or something of the sort."[14]

Boasting to Ralph Arnold, Koverman said, "That was my stuff," and she camouflaged it so that it looked like it originated from the East Coast. To her, the time was ripe, so it was important "to get people thinking along those lines," but she confided to Arnold that she hoped she hadn't "gone too far . . . firing that gun too soon." The lineups for the next two years were already taking shaping, so they had to plant the seed early on for a Hoover candidacy. And because she observed "so much dissension and mistrust," it was necessary to keep Hoover's name out in front but above the political fray.[15]

Rumors that Senator Johnson might try another gubernatorial run incurred her ire, and by now it was evident that she could be as ruthless as her mentor. Before allowing Hoover into the limelight, she wrote, Arnold, Johnson "would deliberately run his head into a noose." The momentum must continue, she urged: "We just mustn't let him die out—he's too important and there are so few like him." A run for governor, she thought, meant that "the presidency would be coming along nicely." Regardless of the next step, Koverman was hankering to stay in the political game, and she told Arnold she was going to do her "best to get into the camp just to keep my eyes open," because her "interest is aroused because I can see our Chief's opportunity is right now."[16]

Ralph Arnold wasn't convinced of the wisdom of a gubernatorial run, which could belittle Hoover's national stature. Nevertheless, he encouraged Koverman to "gently stir up the governorship situation and see what reaction you can get in various quarters." Koverman realized the gamble of launching the plan and the consequences "if we are in on a losing game." Regardless of what strategy they would ultimately settle on, she began "showing" herself around the party's headquarters, reminding influential people how Hoover had now challenged Johnson's hold on "one of the greatest political machines in the country." Her lobbying effort described how when Hoover jumped into the ring for "his first big political fight," he was "was beautifully supported" by the people of California. She approached the head of publicity as a way to gain entrance to the inner circle, and she was quickly enlisted in the fundraising Dollar Campaign. Neither progressives nor conservatives were enthusiastic about Warren G. Harding's candidacy, and there was a general malaise because "everyone seems waiting for someone else to start the ball rolling." Koverman knew that "with Mr. Hoover it is so different" because with him "one has an ideal to follow." She believed California needed a new leader, and there was "no one capable of stepping into Johnson's shoes" except for her Chief, Herbert Hoover.[17]

During the fall campaign season, she had mixed feelings about Hoover making a public appearance on behalf of Harding. She thought it could either provide an excuse for Johnson to threaten the precarious unity the party needed in November, or it could turn the tide in an otherwise lackadaisical campaign. Eventually, she decided he should take to the stage because he was "the ONE man now who can swing them into line—the situation is critical and everyone realizes it—he is badly needed." But Hoover was reticent, and this trait would come to annoy even his most ardent supporters.[18]

After her first-year apprenticeship in partisan politics, Koverman reflected on their experience. She told Arnold that if the campaign taught her anything, it was that "we are as children when pitted against experienced politicians and if we ever expect or hope to do anything in this state for our Chief, we must go at it in the right way or we'll meet defeat." She still couldn't fathom how their amateurish group even made it through the primary fight, and the next round would require men "who have keen political insight and [who] are closely in the game," especially in San Francisco where the progressives had "a real machine." She also realized how "there is a long chain and each link represents certain men who hold and control certain conditions. Even if we are not in the chain, it is essential that we know the links and their particular significance and power." To her, "The situation politically is a very queer one—standpatters in the saddle and Progressive in but not in—hard to tell what is going to happen." Koverman knew that she liked the political arena, but in spite of the thrill of it, she understood an underlying truth about hardcore politics, which was "how little the ordinary person has to say as to the conduct of the state or national affairs." She concluded, "It is all wrong and should be changed, but one can hardly rebuild a house without knowing something of its construction."[19] She began to articulate a broader worldview of the political landscape and a new sense of her own place within it.

As the general election moved closer, she felt "the tension . . . getting higher every moment," and it appeared that Johnson was even losing favor among his own followers. She told Arnold how "they don't trust him and are afraid . . . because . . . he will knife anyone if it pleases him to do so." She believed that Johnson was not playing fair and she was in great fear of Republicans losing the state altogether.[20] She found the whole situation "most amusing," though, because, "there is a great mistrust among the machine gang," and "they are all afraid of one another." As to Johnson himself, she thought that "his ego demands that and so far as I can see he has dug a hole for himself and is in it with his face down scratching as hard as ever he can." Arnold concurred: "Johnson is still ranting around and will continue to do so until he is rolled off the stage by the intelligent voters of California. We must lay the foundation for putting the skids under him two years from now." Arnold believed "there will never be any truce between Hoover and Johnson." He thought "we might just as well stir up all the trouble for Uncle Hiram we can. . . . We have nothing to lose and all to gain," and it was "only through destructive tactics that we can bring down the machine and prepare the ground for a constructive program, of which Hoover can take advantage."[21] Ida Koverman and Ralph Arnold were fired up, at the ready, and prepared for the long haul.

Ida Koverman was an integral player within the overlapping networks of official party and unofficial partisan organizations. The May primary had ousted progressives and installed standpatters on the State and Central Committees, which were, ironically, "working at cross purposes" because no one trusted each other. Edward Lyman was part of the new lineup, which inspired another of Koverman's warning to Arnold that "you may be quite sure that if it came to a question of politics, his own interests would come first. If we decide to go ahead with anything for the Chief, the most essential and important thing is to get started with an absolutely loyal group so that any plans we wish kept under cover will be kept that way." Ralph Arnold listened carefully to Ida Koverman's ideas and told her he was "putting all of your little hints and suggestions in the back of my head for use on proper occasions."[22]

Koverman reached out to local power brokers backing conservative causes and candidates. She and *Los Angeles Times* publisher Harry Chandler pondered how to get Herbert Hoover to pay more attention to the politicking in his home state. By then, it didn't make a difference, though. The night of the election, Koverman stood among her allies and opponents at Republican Party headquarters waiting for the returns. She was infuriated when Johnson's supporters began "yelling and shouting 'this is a wonderful victory for Hiram Johnson!'" Stunned to hear their claim that Harding owed his election to Johnson, she told Arnold how disgusted she was at such a notion of "anything so ridiculous." She was aching for the next battle, telling Arnold, "I've learned lots in the past few weeks and if I can only land something which will bring me in sufficient to meet my expenses," she would remain steadfast in their mission.[23]

She and Arnold kept their eyes open for job opportunities, and after a few leads failed to develop, such as at a local oil company, she thanked Arnold for his efforts on her behalf. He tried to comfort her by reminding her there were other good fish in the sea and something better would come along. She was adamant that what she really wanted to do was focus her work on behalf of Hoover, "the Chief." In the meantime, Arnold tried to build up an investment portfolio for her through real estate or stocks. There were disappointments there too, about which Arnold was "exceedingly sorry," because he had hoped she could "make a turn of this kind." She authorized him "to go after some properties in California," and he would advise her further as things developed.[24]

She contemplated a trip to Sacramento to see if there were any opportunities for her during the upcoming legislative session, but she decided against it because she was "pretty well painted with the Hoover brush," and so her "pull is not very strong." Arnold didn't want her to go, and hoped "we are able to take care of you satisfactorily" in Los Angeles. He suggested she reach out to the county committee's acting chairman, a well-connected deputy district attorney named Edward Dennison, who might be able to help her.[25]

Whatever income she was able to generate, the following month she began "actively pushing arrangements" for a new springboard for Hoover. She thought it was the "psychological time" to hold a five-hundred-seat dinner reception for him because "time was short," and she advised Arnold to convince Hoover that California was being "splendidly directed" by "an entirely different breed of cats from New York." No matter what Koverman and Arnold conjured up, they were forced to reimagine Hoover's immediate future in February 1921, when President Harding offered Herbert Hoover the post of secretary of the department of commerce. Hoover initially thought a Cabinet post too narrow a platform to exercise his superior abilities, but he accepted, and for the first time in decades, he settled into a new life within the contiguous borders of the United States, while erasing any concerns about whether he was "a true Republican in every sense of the word." Ida Koverman hoped the Cabinet appointment would enhance Hoover's political prospects by doing "some big things" for his home state, such as "in the way of water power," to identify him with voters there.[26] The Golden State's water supply and the development of hydroelectric power would be a century-long crucible, and Herbert Hoover did, in fact, shape the contours of its future contests and policy perspectives.

Ida Koverman and Ralph Arnold continued to finagle on Hoover's behalf for a possible gubernatorial run in 1922. Soon, it was apparent that Hoover, now as secretary of commerce, was reluctant to give up "the safety of his position" to run for office.[27] With or without Hoover's urging,

Koverman and Arnold were determined to build a Hoover-for-President movement, and for the next eight years they pushed candidates, carried on campaigns, and courted causes that would carry on their mission. All along the way, Ida Koverman gained stature in her own right as she fought her own battles while leading an army of women to victory.

CHAPTER 6

A Woman of No Distinction

IDA KOVERMAN CAME TO POLITICS DURING A TIME OF MAJOR TRANSI-tions in women's social and political influence as the accelerated pace of demographic change altered the landscape of Southern California. Even within this larger context, Koverman's inclincation was to challenge en-trenched leadership among women's groups and to criticize traditional male politicos as they faced day-to-day skirmishes and larger ideological factionalism and personalities. After the aborted effort to win Hoover a presidential nomination, her ardor for the political game waned. She wrote dispassionately about political causes and candidates she had once promoted, now as if she had merely acted as an extension of Ralph Arnold. Her shifting mood might have reflected momentary money troubles. Unlike the fervor for Hoover and politics she expressed during the 1920 campaigns, in August 1922, two months before the state's primary elec-tion, Ida Koverman threatened a revolt and demanded accountability to force Arnold's hand.

Arnold had grown dependent on Ida Koverman's insights and counsel and her management of local affairs, in effect becoming indispensable to him. All the while, she was a rising personage in her own right. When she spoke before the Los Angeles City Council, she was described as one of the "prominent speakers" to be heard on the subject of representation. Likely initiating the news snippet herself, she took control of her public profile, even if she struggled to enhance her economic status. While she was living in an unassuming downtown apartment on 1231 West 8th Street, she was listed as a member of the prestigious Women's City Club of Los Angeles, and she appeared in the annual *Who's Who among Women in California.*[1]

Without Arnold's insider status and financing, she could not have embedded herself within the city's elite and the political trenches. The disconnect between her growing reputation and her means of financial support would remain a constant over the years, and at times she was explicit about her frustration. "Work of this nature entails considerable expense," she reminded Arnold, such as membership dues to clubs and organizations, their luncheons and banquets, and their subscriptions and fundraisers. At an average of fifteen dollars a week, she was living beyond her means. She told Arnold, "I cannot afford this expense and would greatly appreciate it if you could in some way arrange that I be reimbursed, at least for my actual increased expenses," threatening, "I certainly hope that you may be able to see your way clear to assist me in this matter, as I can no longer continue this work at my own expense."[2] Ralph Arnold financed her entrée into the institutions and associations where the elite nurtured personal friendships and political alliances. Her name increasingly appeared in Southland newspapers that kept track of such things, but the problem of finances dragged on. Arnold wrote to party insiders about her salary, noting that the salaries of two male workers had already been paid, while hers had not. Arnold's efforts on her behalf reflected his larger vision about how the County Committee should continue functioning between election cycles. The office needed to keep a paid staff, especially to handle the entertainment of prominent guests. Eventually it was settled that Ida Koverman would be paid thirty-five dollars per week, and her assistant twenty-four dollars.[3] A powerful County Committee would not only serve his efforts to build a strong party infrastructure, it would also keep Ida Koverman employed.

The immediate challenge, however, was the 1922 US senatorial campaign, seen as an opportunity to whittle away at Senator Hiram Johnson and progressive control of the Republican Party. Anti-Johnson Republicans had to find a candidate who could "carry the standard against Johnson," to open the path for Herbert Hoover. They found him in Charles C. Moore, a successful engineer and businessman with a reputation for "safeness" and "soundness," who avoided offending the financial and corporate interests being challenged by progressives like Johnson.

Charles Moore was a popular figure. He served as the director of the 1915 San Francisco World's Fair, headed the state Boy Scouts, and owned one of the biggest olive orchards in the world. Moore was reluctant to become a candidate, though, so it took a delegation of bigwig merchants, professionals, bankers, and even some labor leaders to convince him to challenge Johnson for the US Senate. Ralph Arnold saw the Moore-Johnson contest as "the biggest fight that has ever taken place in California," and he believed that "if we don't lick Johnson, we have very little chance of ever doing anything for Hoover in the bigger things," and that "No one ever gets anywhere by not taking a chance, and Hoover cannot afford to be classed as a pussy footer and one who is afraid to come out and take an open stand." He saw "nothing to be gained by his quiescence just now."[4]

Arnold's hardcore attitude inadvertently served to alienate Hoover's full engagement in the state's machinations, but Arnold continued his onslaught believing that defeating Johnson "was one of the most important fights affecting the political destinies of Herbert Hoover." Arnold's confidence was palpable as he assured Hoover that the majority of the "established power in Los Angeles was strongly behind" him. Many California women were attracted to Moore because they saw him as being above the political fray, as Moore minimized the progressive-conservative divide by suggesting that just being a Republican was good enough. In spite of Arnold's invective, however, Hoover remained silent for the rest of the Moore primary and general election cycles. Koverman now saw herself as a referee between Arnold and his peers, who were often put off by his aggressive posture. Her instinct for self-preservation found her, at times, trying to distance herself from Arnold's zealotry. Regardless, whatever political fortunes were in store for Herbert Hoover, they would not rest on Charles C. Moore, who failed to win his 1922 Senate primary run.[5]

Arnold's hyperbolic tendencies could work to his advantage, though, such as his election as chairman of the Los Angeles County Republican Party Central Committee. As his right-hand assistant, Ida Koverman's political influence rose in the process, and their formal elevation spurred them on to ensure that the County Committee was "the official representatives among the electorate of the administration."[6]

Although Ida Koverman was a relative newcomer to Los Angeles, because her talent was recognized early on, she made friends with prominent women. One of the most influential was Mabel Walker Willebrandt, appointed by President Harding as an assistant US attorney general, only the second woman to hold the post in the Department of Justice. According to documentary filmmaker Ken Burns, Willebrandt was more famous than any movie star in America, largely because as the Justice Department's key enforcer of prohibition, she earned the nickname "Prohibition Portia," who at times infused her fiery oratory with bigoted religious stereotypes.[7] Koverman and Willebrandt's friendship grew over the next three decades as they both transitioned out of formal politics to the inner circle at MGM.

Willebrandt became an avid Hoover supporter, but early on she did not support Arnold and Koverman's effort to challenge Hiram Johnson in the primary with Charles Moore. Her vocal support of Johnson inspired Arnold to suggest to Hoover that "something should be done" about her because Johnson was using her statements to create the impression that Harding welcomed his re-election.[8] The 1922 congressional elections provided the Republican National Committee with an opportunity to rally women into their ranks. But women wanted more. They wanted representation in matters of international diplomacy. Since the end of the Great War, knowledge about the unprecedented horrors of modern warfare inspired calls to limit armaments and ban weapons of mass destruction, particularly chemical agents. The Harding administration took on the challenge by holding an International Disarmament Conference, and the announcement that four women would be selected for a prestigious Public Advisory Committee inspired a fierce competition between women's groups throughout the country.

Ralph Arnold approached Herbert Hoover about nominating Ida Koverman's colleague in the Republican Study Club movement, Mrs. Florence Collins Porter. Hoover wired Arnold to explain that the selection of the delegates was limited to experts and "municipal authorities and representatives of large employers," and thus Mrs. Porter didn't qualify, but he reassured Arnold that at the "first possible opportunity" she would receive a post of "noteworthy distinction." Hoover added that the progressive leader Katherine Philips Edson had not even been invited, but unbeknownst to him, this soon changed.[9]

Arnold was well aware of Ida Koverman's ill will toward Katherine Edson, and Hoover was familiar with Edson's support of Hiram Johnson. Edson's position as executive secretary of California's Industrial Welfare Commission gave her the advantage, and when Arnold learned Edson was invited, he was infuriated. He beseeched Hoover to nullify her appointment because the reaction had been "something fierce," and supporters "take it as a slap in face." Arnold believed an Edson appointment would hinder their initiatives on Hoover's behalf and disrupt their organization's efforts unless something drastic was done to counteract her influence. He complained how "our loyal tireless workers deserve and must have recognition indicating our interest and appreciation." He urged that it was "vitally important you do something quickly." Another Hoover supporter mirrored Arnold's sentiment, writing that her "personal impression is one of great chagrin and deep disappointment," and "this mark of favoritism will greatly encourage and strengthen enemies and weaken friends." She implored Hoover to get the president to "remedy this grievous mistake."[10]

Hoover was fed up, and he told Arnold he "had nothing to do with this particular matter as it rested entirely between the president and the secretary of state." He conceded that while "there was no question of rivalry in the matter, . . . the President made up his mind solely from the point of view of securing advice of specialized character," and the bottom line was that such "appointments [were] made solely by the president and are final."[11]

In spite of Hoover's growing popularity among women voters, he had difficulty recognizing their diversity and factional schisms. Ralph Arnold continued to advise him about the matter, while perhaps stoking a brewing opposition to Ida Koverman's rising prominence as well. Hoover finally attended a luncheon sponsored by the Women's Republican Study Club, which Arnold explained to him was the most influential women's political outfit in the state, founded by Mrs. Porter.[12]

Following the nod to women at the Disarmament Conference, the Republican Party and Harding formally acknowledged their debt to women in June 1923, when the National Committee announced its reorganization included the appointment of one woman from every state as a female "associate" member to the committee. The following year, these appointments were endowed with voting power.[13] The historic process of selecting the first round of Republican national committeewomen exposed the reality that women were as ideologically divided and proprietary as their men, and in California the competition was magnified by the roles played by Ida Koverman and Katherine Edson. The task of selecting California's first Republican national committeewoman fell to William H. Crocker, the Bay Area's esteemed banker and old-guard, long-serving member of the Republican National Committee. He was "now faced with one of the most difficult problems," and the contest turned into a battle for the soul of the Republican Party.

Crocker announced three names on his short-list. Two prominent clubwoman, Mrs. Clara Burdette and Mrs. Margaret Sartori, a regent of the University of California, were obvious choices. The third, however, Ida Koverman, sent shock waves among progressives. Koverman's consideration for such a historic appointment raised vocal opposition, including an anonymous "prominent" Republican Party insider who told reporters that while Ida Koverman would "make an ideal executive worker," her selection was inappropriate. The spot "should go to a woman of more state-wide prominence, a woman of wealth or of long residence in the

State."[14] The public protest reflected the deeper ideological divide and prejudices about social status and class.

This unfettered criticism of Ida Koverman came from Katherine Philips Edson, whose identity was obvious to anyone paying attention and is supported by her private communication, which echoed the published record. Edson had written to Mrs. Harriet Taylor Upton of Ohio, the first woman vice chair of the executive committee of the Republican National Committee. Edson described William Crocker's failure to consult with her about "who the most effective woman should be." Given her experience and stature in the state, Edson thought Crocker "a most amiable gentleman" but "a political moron." Edson and Ida Koverman shared similar views about the men around them, and this might explain why many male partisans did not welcome women into their ranks with open arms.[15]

William Crocker could hardly ignore Katherine Edson, and he knew their meeting was going to be uncomfortable, even a heated exchange, so he insisted his personal secretary be present. Crocker defended his choices, telling her he would never select someone like herself who was a progressive supporter of Hiram Johnson, and that the appointment would go to a Hoover supporter who "represented the deep-eyed reactionary Republican group." Edson pointed out that he already represented the Hoover faction, at which Crocker countered that she already represented the Johnson camp. After more back and forth, Edson proposed the selection of a compromise woman who had not publicly identified with either Hoover or Johnson. Then William Crocker showed his hand. He confessed there was really only one person being seriously floated, Ida R. Koverman, and she had the backing of the "most influential group in Los Angeles."[16]

Ralph Arnold had been quietly lobbying to promote Koverman's candidacy, and she too took steps to promote herself by asking Hoover's Commerce Department for information about the Republican National Committee for "our committee work here," but apparently in order to push her name forward.[17] Arnold sent telegrams to well-placed Californians about how he was "very anxious" to have Koverman appointed, and he urged his colleagues to do everything they could to promote her by obtaining endorsements in their own districts, and sending them to William Crocker as soon as possible. Among the responses was one from Herbert Hoover's friend, Stanford University president Dr. Ray Lyman Wilbur, who said that the "idea of putting Mrs. Koverman in is certainly a good one and an important victory to gain."[18]

Katherine Philips Edson now realized she had underestimated Ida R. Koverman's growing influence in the Republican Party. Edson had perceived Koverman "merely" as Ralph Arnold's secretary, and she understood Arnold "merely" to be Hoover's local zealot. As a hardcore politico Katherine Edson saw Koverman as a "woman of *no* distinction," and the national committeewoman needed to be someone who represented leadership and standing. Edson and Crocker concluded their meeting with an agreement to seek the guidance of a neutral person "of good standing," and they settled on the former US senator Frank Flint, who along with his brother Motley was a colorful figure in local banking, business, and boosterism. Edson already knew, however, that Frank Flint would never endorse a Koverman appointment.[19] Nevertheless, Edson stormed out of Crocker's office threatening to launch a public protest against Koverman, and he knew she could cause a lot of trouble, the last thing the party needed as it struggled to recruit more women. In the end, Crocker tossed out his short list and selected Mrs. Oliver P. Clark, who he thought could bridge the party's factional divide.

Katherine Edson won the contest over the national committeewoman, but she failed to see that Ida Koverman represented the growing threat of conservative Republicanism. Edson was a sophisticated political operator, but she failed to gauge how Ida Koverman and her allies would expand their influence in unexpected ways for decades to come.

Between 1920 and 1923, Ida Koverman underwent a political seasoning where higher ups took notice of her talent and sought to uplift her status within the national party hierarchy. Ida R. Koverman and Katherine Philips Edson were iconic, oppositional figures who represented the deep divide among Republican women in the post-WWI era. Although they were the same age, Katherine Edson's politicization was honed during the earlier progressive era when women struggled to balance their commitment to women's issues and partisan loyalty. Ida Koverman never agonized over the dichotomy between partisanship and gender. Her correspondence with Ralph Arnold reveals her transition from being a temporary hired gun to a political mercenary, who at first absorbed the goals of her benefactors rooted in their belief that Herbert Hoover was a man of superior ability worthy of assuming the nation's highest office. Ida Koverman's personal ambition and dedication to Herbert Hoover would become her own as they shaped her unexpected and extraordinary reincarnation in the Golden State.

CHAPTER 7

Harding's Demise, Coolidge's Rise

Ida Koverman and Women in the GOP

KOVERMAN'S DISAPPOINTMENT AND THE DRAMA SURROUNDING THE appointment of California's national committeewoman was soon eclipsed by the anticipation of President Warren G. Harding's visit to Los Angeles as part of his historic ten-thousand-mile journey dubbed "The Voyage of Understanding." The city's familiar Republican leaders set up a special organization to handle Harding's visit. As secretary of the new general committee, Koverman would work directly with chairman Mayor George E. Cryer on the Committee for the Entertainment of President Warren G. Harding. Such opportunities with elected officials increased her visibility, and it enhanced her ability to navigate the city's volatile political terrain. She hobnobbed alongside *Los Angeles Times* publisher Harry Chandler, chair of the committee on printing and publicity, and Hoover's friend, banker Henry M. Robinson of the finance committee.

The presidential entourage left the White House on June 20, but after sixty major speeches and scores of informal talks all along the 7,500-mile journey, Harding was forced to cancel his big adventure after a day of speechmaking under a burning Seattle sun, when he exhibited what was believed to be ptomaine poisoning from a tainted crabmeat lunch. The ailing president was transported to San Francisco's Palace Hotel, where his downward spiral overwhelmed his personal physician, so Dr. Ray Lyman Wilbur, Herbert Hoover's close friend, was called in to minister to the gravely ill president. Unable to travel, financial arrangements for

Harding's convalescence fell to William Crocker, who also hosted the First Family for their unanticipated stay in the Golden State.

No matter what the plans, Warren G. Harding took an alarming turn for the worse, and on August 2, 1923, the fifty-eight-year-old head of state succumbed to "an instantaneous death due to cerebral apoplexy after a gastrointestinal infection and bronchial pneumonia." Back in Vermont, Vice President Calvin Coolidge took the presidential oath of office just before 2:25 in the morning.

Ida Koverman had little time to mourn because she had to immediately rein in her mentor, Ralph Arnold, who saw the tragedy as an opportunity to promote Herbert Hoover and to ridicule Senator Hiram Johnson. Arnold wailed that if Coolidge would not follow the policies of our "beloved president . . . then the fight will be centered for our Big Chief." He urged fundraising to begin and planned for Johnson to "get the licking of his life." Harry Chandler warned Arnold to take it slow, advising that the best policy was to avoid any suggestion that Hoover could be a presidential contender the following year. Chandler said, "We must handle this delicate situation . . . to prevent Hoover's embarrassment for subtracting anything from his usefulness to the country at this critical time." He was adamant that "when and if the right time comes we will all be on the job, but that time is certainly not yet."[1]

The day Harding cancelled his trip, he had been scheduled to deliver a much-anticipated speech about America's participation in the World Court, an issue Ida Koverman had supported as a member of the Los Angeles World Court Committee. The group sponsored a mass meeting at the end of August under the auspices of the local branch of the American Peace Award of New York City. Among Koverman's colleagues on the committee were Harry Chandler, John R. Haynes, Henry M. Robinson, Louis B. Mayer, and Koverman's former nemesis, attorney Edward D. Lyman.[2] Koverman's appearance alongside the city's renowned leaders outside of the strictly partisan arena meant that she was no longer "merely" Ralph Arnold's sidekick, no longer an outsider or interloper, but rather she was in the big league of Los Angeles's historic influencers.

The 1924 campaign season reinvigorated her optimism, if not her financial security, and it tightened the threads weaving women's participation in Republican Party politics with the prospects for Herbert Hoover's political future. Ida Koverman's central place within the diverse local and statewide groups reflected her growing prominence and it spawned friendships with northern Californians such as San Francisco's Marshal Hale, who served as president of the statewide League of Coolidge Republican Clubs, and its vice president, Santa Paula's Charles C. Teague. Locally, Ralph Arnold was a member of the League's executive committee, which meant that Ida Koverman was doing most of its work while she continued to oversee the office of the County Committee. Her colleagues on the County Committee were also members of the Coolidge League, including William M. Garland, a realtor and head of the Los Angeles Athletic Club, Mrs. Florence Collins Porter, and George B. Bush, who served as secretary.

Early on, the ill-defined demarcation of the diverse Coolidge groups created tensions over their missions, methods, and monies. William Garland warned Arnold and Koverman that the local League would soon run out of funds at their current rate of expenditures, and there were conflicts over mixing local needs with state and national campaigns, forcing him to threaten to take over all of the financial affairs of the League's headquarters.[3]

Another League member threatened to quit if Arnold continued his "present methods of incurring expenses." E. P. Clark complained he would no longer "act any longer as a dummy treasurer," being particularly bothered by the paid employment of salaried workers, suggesting that Ida Koverman should make around seventy-five dollars per week, while he recommended that a male precinct worker be paid one hundred dollars a week.[4]

On top of the local stresses, state party chair Mark Requa feared there was a general apathy about the election that would lead to failure at the polls.[5] As Koverman and Arnold struggled to keep operations afloat, she found other rewards in glowing reports about her contribution to the party's electoral success. Arnold enumerated his praise of Koverman as the one who was in charge of headquarters, and as someone with the combined qualities of tact, ability, and generalship as a constant source of respect and admiration from all. These attributes would serve her well, but for now, accolades couldn't pay the bills.

Ida Koverman and Ralph Arnold turned their attention toward the 1924 presidential primary campaign season and the upcoming national nominating convention. Koverman and Arnold recognized how important women were going to be in the upcoming campaign. Toward this end, they joined the concerted effort to promote Mrs. Florence Collins Porter's selection as a second nomination speaker. It would become a historic moment, with such an honor preceded only by the renowned reformer Jane Addams who, in 1912, seconded the third-party presidential nomination of Theodore Roosevelt, followed by Katherine Philips

Edson, who seconded Hiram Johnson as the vice presidential nominee. Republicans recognized women voters, and they sought to capture more of them. Koverman also knew how important the involvement of professional women in high places would be for the fall campaign. She made sure Arnold introduced Helen Matthewson Laughlin to both Coolidge and Hoover. Laughlin was a dean at the University of California and a vice president of the statewide League of Coolidge Clubs.[6]

When Koverman lobbied for the slot of secretary to the Coolidge convention delegation, state party treasurer Charles A. Johnson committed to doing everything he could to help her, since he was "happy to learn that she is willing to go." Southern California's growing brand of Hoover Republicanism was finally making inroads into the hegemony of the "invincible" Hiram Johnson.[7]

Katherine Edson summarized the present political situation as "a choice between two conflicting philosophies of government," by which she meant "between liberalism and conservatism; between progressivism and reaction; between a government for the people and by the people, and government by those who wish to exploit the nation's natural resources." She said Hiram Johnson had always been the champion of the people, while Coolidge was the "spokesman for special privilege and conservatism." Southern California gave Coolidge his margin of victory in the state's primary, which earned kudos for Ida Koverman. Acknowledging Arnold's contribution, Hoover wrote him, "You have won a great victory by hard work and devotion. I owe you much personally for it." State chair Marshal Hale suggested the Southland was more entitled than the north to what he called a "jollification" meeting. In fact, during the intense last ten days of the campaign, Arnold was recuperating in the hospital with a fractured hip after his car skidded into a truck. Arnold never shied away from praising Koverman, even sending word to Coolidge that credit should go to her and another colleague, who he described as the most important two people in charge of the "wonderful organization that developed the big majority in Los Angeles."[8]

The Coolidge victory also ensured the survival of the county committee headquarters, and so Koverman decided to run for the official post of secretary to the Republican County Central Committee. She had mistakenly believed another member, bank vice president Willis Baum, was after the spot, and before he informed her he was running for a different seat in his 65th District, he aired his grievance toward Koverman. Baum told Arnold that he felt mistreated by her, and was offended by what he saw as her lack of cooperation. Now that her personal ambition "had announced itself," he understood he was merely an "innocent party" in what he called a recent altercation with her.[9]

Such local squabbles soon faded as everyone focused their attention on the upcoming Republican National Convention in Cleveland. Koverman approached the event with dread and optimism. She feared potentially disastrous arrangements beyond her control, particularly the publicity surrounding the journey and arrival of the special Coolidge train she and the southern delegates boarded in Los Angeles on June 3. It traveled north to pick up Bay Area delegates, including William Crocker, and then it sped eastward to pick up delegates from Nevada and Utah.

She was anxious that the whole enterprise would be "an entire failure from every standpoint," when it should be a noteworthy spectacle, if not "the biggest thing at the convention." She failed to realize, however, that regardless of the publicity, no one would be able to ignore the clamor of their arrival on June 8, because the entire clan booked sixty hotel rooms, and their wildly boisterous group drew attention in and outside of the deliberations. Before the formal opening of the convention, Californians elected new state party officers, and after a moment of uncertainty, they re-elected chairman William Crocker. Ida Koverman and Ralph Arnold had hoped Charles C. Teague, vice president of the Southland's Coolidge League, would pose a real challenge, but when Crocker was re-elected, they tried to be optimistic that everything "perhaps will turn out all right."[10]

By 1924, the legacy of the progressive era was carried forward by the growing bipartisan attraction of Wisconsin senator Robert La Follette. Californians were enthusiastic about La Follette even though he had to run as a Socialist, and the Republicans had to fight "a two-headed campaign" primary. During the convention, US Attorney General Harry M. Daugherty sounded a clarion call to women to challenge La Follette's left-leaning appeal. "Never before in the history of the party has there been a greater need for Republicans to be Republicans," he declared, and he insisted that Robert La Follette's brand of Republicanism was not the real thing, but rather was "making trouble with its interest in communism," and the party's destruction. He said, "The hand that used to rock the cradle in the home now rocks the cradle of the world," and now women "have come to be not the better half of American home-making, but the better half of America. As long as women play their part in party politics and hold their party ideals, America will never be Russianized as it would be under La Folletteism." Daugherty pleaded for "women as women, [to] re-establish the ideals of the Republican Party and be Republicans now if they never were before in their lives."[11] Ida Koverman and her allies would draw on this theme of impassioned anti-communism to recruit female partisans.

The repeated clarion calls of alarm about the impending threat of Bolshevism didn't keep anyone from having a grand time in Cleveland, and for the first time, radio broadcasts reached dozens of states to listen in on the proceedings. Calvin Coolidge was uncontested, but it wasn't until after twenty-three rounds, and just before midnight on the last day, that the delegates finally settled on Charles G. Dawes for his running-mate, which was immediately followed by a stampede to the depot where all the departing trains were being held.

Koverman learned a few tricks at the 1924 RNC that she later adapted for the gala Hollywood affairs and star-studded political rallies. For now, though, it was time to gear up for the November election. She was being considered for the post of the executive secretary of the Southland Coolidge campaign, which, along with her duties as executive secretary of the county Central Committee, raised concerns for the state party treasurer Charles A. Johnson, who had doubts about her ability to handle both challenges. He wrote to Arnold that "our playmates strongly suggest" a substitute be named in the event that Ida Koverman's name could not be secured for this important role, which, in effect, was intended to assure "control of the situation in the south."[12]

Charles Johnson worried too much. Ida Koverman became the executive secretary of the 1924 Southern California Coolidge campaign, now directed by attorney Mendel B. Silberberg, and this was the beginning of her close friendship with Silberberg, which would, decades later, transition to MGM, and explains how they were both present in Louis B. Mayer's office after the death of Paul Bern in 1932. By October, the Koverman-Silberberg launch of the Coolidge-Dawes campaign was in full swing, with Koverman employing her creative instincts, such as enlisting a local Flying Squadron club and arranging for Hoover to send "a telegram of inspiration" to new converts of young Republican businessmen.[13]

This was around the time she also forged a friendship with Lawrence Richey, Hoover's trusted assistant, about whom many believed he saw serving Hoover as his single purpose in life. For years, Koverman and Richey's frequent exchanges were both professional and familiar. But, sometimes they were among the strangest correspondences between Koverman, Arnold, and other Hoover's supporters, with encrypted messages decipherable through a secret code. The reason for the subterfuge is unclear, but it made for amusing texts, such as one telegram that read, "John *Smelt* has wired *sardine* endorsing *elephant* if *sardine's* first choice cannot be appointed." [14]

Decoding such messages was as important as paying attention to political polls. One summery of the 1924 campaign included a reference to the motion-picture industry: "The moving picture theatres seem to give La Follette a much better 'hand' than the President. However, those of us who are studying the situation here have nothing to fear as we appreciate the type of people who attend these cheap moving-picture shows." [15] Just four years later, Herbert Hoover's presidential campaign brought legitimacy to the media and its moguls, and Ida Koverman facilitated this process with her elevated professional profile within the motion-picture community.

La Follette remained a source of annoyance, garnering almost 26 percent of Los Angeles votes and nearly 45 percent in the Bay Area. Calvin Coolidge won California by 57.2 percent, and all of its thirteen electoral votes. In conservative Los Angeles County, however, Coolidge won 65.16 percent, while the more liberal San Francisco County gave him 47.75. Following the vote tallies, Ralph Arnold told Herbert Hoover that, once again, Ida Koverman and her colleague Fred Frank were the ones to whom "we owe more" than any others for the perfection of the organization. The election validated the rising importance of Southern California and the Los Angeles Republican County Central Committee, but more importantly, it sealed Arnold's view that with Mrs. Ida Koverman in charge as its executive secretary, "We expect to make the County Committee a real factor in everything pertaining to the Republican Party." [16]

CHAPTER 8

"A Peculiar Business"

KATHERINE PHILIPS EDSON AND HER POST ON THE STATE'S INDUSTRIAL Welfare Commission (IWC) personified the continuity of California's pre-World War I progressivism, while Ida Koverman epitomized the conservative challenge to it. Just as they had in 1923, when Edson thwarted Koverman's ambition to be national committeewoman, Koverman and Edson once again represented larger tensions within American feminism, now in its role in guiding public policy in general and for women and children in particular. The exponential growth of the motion-picture industry offered new opportunities for workers both male and female, adult and child, and as such, it attracted the attention of Edson and the IWC. By 1925, Louis B. Mayer had reconstituted Metro-Goldwyn-Mayer Studios in Culver City, and he had become active in local Republican Party politics, where he made the acquaintance of Ida Koverman.

At first, the triangulated relationship between Ida Koverman, Louis B. Mayer, and Katherine Edson appears unrelated and independent of Koverman's expanding influence among Los Angeles elites. But a closer look reveals an interconnectedness of players and politics as Ida Koverman's story eventually became intertwined with Edson's. But, for the moment, Mayer found himself negotiating with Koverman's progressive nemesis, a central figure in both the crossroads of the women's historical paths and the state's oversight of labor relations in the motion-picture industry.

During the 1920s, hundreds of thousands of migrants flooded into Los Angeles seeking a shot at stardom in the movie business. To the extent that studios kept records, approximately 2.8 million extras were employed in the movie industry between 1926 and 1936, averaging around 250,000 a year or 788 per day, and earning an average daily wage of $8.75.[1] Sixty percent were female, including young children and teenagers with their mothers, and most came without having secured a position, making them all particularly vulnerable to con artists who financially duped or sexually exploited them. Only a small fraction of the Hollywood hopefuls who moved to Los Angeles ever saw a movie set, and if they did, most of them were drained by agents' fees and other hidden costs that came with being anonymous, temporary studio day hires.

Even after extras were hired, problems continued and were even exacerbated by an industry accountable to no one. The state's labor commissioner began investigating, and in 1925 Edson called for public hearings to investigate and set rules and regulations for all full- and part-time female workers in the motion-picture industry. Louis B. Mayer and other studio executives showed up for the first IWC meeting in a room packed with extras. The IWC-hearing transcripts provide a unique window into Kate Edson's and Mayer's negotiations to address state oversight about wages, hours, safety, and working conditions, all of which were complicated by the studios' shift to large-scale industrial operations. Ideologically, state intervention was anathema to Ida Koverman and her conservative ilk, and the movie industry would soon face ardent efforts to fend off government-sanctioned unionization. But in this pre-New Deal first round of public IWC hearings, Mayer had yet to ally with Koverman's political network, and the industry took initial steps to address the growth of a new labor force of movie extras.

The preliminary goal of the IWC hearings was to determine just what the movie studios were actually doing in terms of hiring extras. They sought existing employment records, but once they learned no such documentation existed, the goal was to develop an industry-wide method for data collection along these lines. The second goal was to determine a fair number of hours to consider one full day's work, and when overtime hours would begin. Given the unorthodox nature of filmmaking compared to traditional industrial production, the IWC's goals posed monumental challenges, both practically and politically.

Katherine Philips Edson knew the complexity of setting policy in a new industry was a daunting task. The hiring of extras in Hollywood was unprecedented in its scope and diversity. There was no standardization among the various studios, and the parameters that came with the centralization and division of labor, repetitive motion, and assembly-line and conveyer-belt processes that created the economies of scale in mass-production manufacturing offered little guidance. The overall nature of filmmaking included scenes shot either on a sound stage in a studio or out on location, and the theatrical demands of extras to wear costumes and makeup were all exaggerated by the number and variety of non-salaried, day-to-day hires in number, character, and location on a daily basis. So many factors determined the length of the workday, and whether production was on or behind schedule, and whether an extra would be working on the same production the next hour, day, or week, and it was difficult to systematize it all into a calculated formula.

Three hundred extras listened to Louis B. Mayer articulate the enormity of the problem. MGM had been in the midst of a firestorm of problems plaguing the overseas filming and then local refilming of the epic spectacle *Ben-Hur*, slated to open by the end of the year. Whatever difficulties had existed with the casting of extras before, *Ben-Hur* finally clarified the situation for Mayer by the time he showed up at the IWC hearing on November 18, 1925, held at the Los Angeles Chamber of Commerce. Mayer described the motion-picture industry as "a peculiar business," explaining how "after all it is a new industry, and it takes time to develop and perfect it, the same as anything else." Some of the challenges were that "there are so many details to be worked out for each new set, and each new scene," and that the movie business was "not like a factory, where they employ practically the same number of people day after day and week after week. No, ours is a peculiar calling."[2]

Louis B. Mayer has been described as many things, and often as a sympathetic, even paternal figure. It's worth noting, then, that during the decades before the American Civil War, the most enlightened and beneficent of slave holders, and their supporters, justified slavery as "a peculiar institution" because of the nature of ownership and the dehumanization of their human property while ensuring its productivity. Mayer's testimony and interaction with the participants, both on the IWC and the audience, portray him as an empathetic, beneficent landlord slaveholder. That side of his temperament and public persona came through his expression of how sorry he felt "that any of the artists here have to apologize for being extras, because they are just as important to us and to the picture as the star or the director." He reminded the audience, "It was not the generals or the captains or the lieutenants that won the World War."[3]

Mayer was both pandering and practical in his response when a member of the audience complained that Mayer was inaccessible. He suggested that a "reasonable person" would understand that because "we are handling several thousand people on a set, it would be pretty hard for me to see each one of them individually." But, he added, he "would rather see that lady than a millionaire walk into my office, because I know her problems. And if I have nothing else good about me I think I am at least human." Ultimately, Mayer's ambivalent pronouncements revealed a more threatening, patronizing persona. When the meeting focused on setting hours and pay for extras, the gist of Mayer's argument echoed those who had fought interference with the shibboleth of the free-market determination of wages. He argued that if the IWC established an eight-hour workday while disallowing women to work overtime, it would be a "hardship on the women as well as on us, because many of the women will lose a day's work, as we will have to substitute others in their place." He instructed IWC commissioners, however, "if you set the hours at eight," and allow women to work overtime, then "in regard to making us pay overtime, I am for it." He said he didn't "want to abuse them," and suggested that the IWC penalizing abusers would "stop those that might otherwise take advantage." Before such punitive measures, though, he thought, "The spirit should be one of coordination and cooperation." He was optimistic because he saw "improvement in this respect has been very notable in the last year or two."[4]

Mayer took a more defensive tone in case his cooperative gestures were misinterpreted. "People talk about the 'poor extras' and the burdens imposed on them by the moving picture studios, but if the studios left the state tomorrow," he said, "you would hear a terrible wail go up." He earned applause when he added, "The thing to do with the pictures is to try to make them better. If there is anyone here who can suggest any way to help out the extras, and make it possible to conduct our business more efficiently, I vote for him."[5]

Among the more difficult tasks was to reach an agreement on the maximum number of hours in a workday, about which the discussion lasted more than a few. Mayer again earned applause when he claimed, "I have shaken up our casting departments—not the principals, but I am going to fight with all the power I have to see that they do not treat those extras as I am afraid they have sometimes been treated in the past." He seemed caught up in the exuberance the public discourse inspired, perhaps envisioning his ability to correct any injustices that had been exposed by the scrutiny of industry improprieties toward extras. Mayer promised, "We are to reconstruct the entire building," where "every provision is going to be made for their comfort and convenience." He said his "sympathies are with the women first, and the men second," because of "the way they have been treated in the past, at times." To him, the issue was not so much of the details about "the half hour or even the hour these women have to wait," but rather "the long hours they have to work under those lights." Nevertheless, Mayer argued that some women wanted to work as extras because "they like it," and then he perpetuated the fantasy driving most of them, that "some of them make great progress." He said, in fact, some of those who started out as extras were now "very important people on our payroll." Mayer compared his own experience with the dreams of extras: "I myself started in a very humble position in the business. If I had not, I would not be much of a success now." Whether the response from IWC Chairman Dohrmann was patronizing or sincere, he remarked to Mayer, "That is no doubt why you understand their needs so well."

Months before the November IWC hearing, Fred Beetson, head of the Motion Picture Producers Association (MPPA), was already concerned about the hiring of extras. He wrote to MPPA members about the "vast amount of complaints" made to the state Labor Bureau regarding women's overtime hours working both as extras and in wardrobe departments. He advised members that after a meeting with the deputy labor commissioner, Walter G. Matthewson, he was optimistic that "in a very short time" permission would be granted for women extras to work overtime through "an arrangement" worked out between the bureau and the Industrial Relations Committee. He was informed, however, that under no circumstances could wardrobe employees work more than eight hours in a twenty-four-hour period, and violations would result in prosecution.[6]

In the shadow of the growing interest of state labor officials, Beetson and the MPPA developed a multi-studio plan to institutionalize the hiring process, which would be paid for by producers who used the system. They came up with Central Casting, and Beetson was eager to introduce the concept to the IWC commissioners at their first public hearing. Beetson said, "There have been all kinds of rumors about it and all kinds of questions being asked." He reassured the commissioners that they didn't "have to ask anybody about it" because he was there to speak on behalf of the MPPA to tell them all about how it would be a nonprofit office and a free service for extras. There was "no trick, no catch, no anything," because producers would minimize the victimization of extras by agents who charged exorbitant fees. Another topic covered was the lack of documentation of hiring practices, which continued to the next meeting.[7] Mayer confirmed they "just give them checks." Edson wasn't surprised because until now, the industry had "perhaps never felt the necessity for regulation," as employers did elsewhere. She said the IWC would provide criteria to document hiring practices, to which Mayer urged simplicity in their design, but he then reassured her that "whatever you feel should be done; we will consent to it . . . whatever rule you lay down—I do not think it will burden us so very much, but anyway whatever it is we will accept it."[8]

The hearing went on to address the "weather permitting" clause, and what to do about extras who showed up on rainy days, as well as costume fittings and then, perhaps historically the most familiar and most sensational aspect of the casting process, that of the casting couch and the sexual exploitation of studio hires. The problem of the "personal influence with directors" was one Fred Beetson believed Central Casting would eliminate, declaring that with the new hiring office, "the sheik will not exist."[9] When Central Casting opened its doors on Hollywood Boulevard on January 26, 1926, Katherine Edson's longtime assistant on the IWC, Marian Mel, was hired as director of Central Casting's Women's Division.[10] In the first six months, the agency processed over 113,000 extras, and the following year the number tripled to 330,000.[11]

In order to establish a standard workday and payment for overtime, Edson asked if the standard workday should be more than eight hours. Everyone agreed that it should be eight hours with overtime after that, but whether this was based on "the ground of ethical, moral, or health standpoint" was one of the biggest challenges the IWC faced. Edson argued it was largely due to "the health standpoint," and there was a consensus that eight hours was accepted "as an ordinary thing" in other occupations. The problem was that extras often did not work a full eight hours in one day, even if they worked on multiple movies at the same time. It appeared a nearly impossible task to regulate the hours and overtime of each extra on every set in every studio, about which Mayer suggested, "We should be penalized in some way, so as to safeguard the women against those who maybe show a tendency to be avaricious, and will not hurt those who want to be fair anyway. Some are fairer than others. Temptation gets the best of some," he said, and suggested that there was a need for compromise, noting that on some days, the extra would lose some hours and on other days they would gain them back. Just what constituted the start and end of a pay period was even more complex because of the question of the time it took for an extra to pick up and to put on their costumes and make up, especially for historical films. Edson acknowledged that standardization wasn't going to be easy. Mayer reasoned that the extra would "put on at one end and take off at the other," to which Edson responded, "It seems to me that that end of it is tremendously important." To her, the establishment of strict guidelines would lead to a "tremendous cleaning up process," where everyone would "have to make an effort—artist and employer—to get things harmonized. . . . They cannot just lally[gag] along."[12]

Mayer brought up more variables such as the difference between fast and slow workers, "mean directors and some human ones," and then he struck a nerve with Edson when he added, "Let us not compare these girls with those who work in factories. I would not want to do it myself." He said, "A woman should not have to work in a factory," to which Edson simply replied, "They can't starve to death can they?" as Mayer sat speechless.[13]

When the conversation shifted to compensation for the time spent putting on costumes, Mayer was more rational, and then after wondering how much a fair wage was, he compared the challenge before them to his own personal experience. He said this was "the same thing that happened on the legitimate stage," where an actor would "rehearse four weeks, play one, and be paid one week's salary." For now, though, and possibly sensing labor strife ahead, he added, "That is what brings revolution, and we don't want revolution in our industry." Louis B. Mayer left the IWC hearing and headed for a banquet at the nearby Biltmore Hotel.[14]

By December 11, 1925, the IWC announced its plans to remedy conditions of employment for extras, and over the next few years, the IWC and the motion-picture industry worked out details for guidelines for the hiring practices, and Central Casting emerged as a viable tool in the process. As of October 1928, however, it was reported that film studios were going to be hauled before the state Department of Industrial Relations because of their alleged violations, such as the rule that an extra should be paid if the day's work was cancelled without an immediate dismissal, and the failure to pay overtime wages beyond the established eight-hour day.[15]

During this period, MGM grew into an enormously successful studio under the management of Louis B. Mayer, and it would become the premiere model for early twentieth-century movie production, both in its organizational structure and in its development of on-screen talent. Koverman began to forge her own relationship with Mayer while Katherine Edson continued her work with the IWC, including hearings with Mayer and industry representatives. As Ida Koverman and Louis B. Mayer moved up in the state Republican Party, neither of them realized their futures were destined to create a lasting partnership in both politics and pictures. And they would realize how important it was to have allies on the IWC, which would in effect usurp Edson and turn back the policies she had established and enforced. In the interim, Ida Koverman looked optimistically ahead to forwarding Herbert Hoover's presidential as well as her own political ambitions.

CHAPTER 9

Federation, Finances, and Fried Chicken

THE REPUBLICAN PARTY'S PRO-HOOVER FORCES TARGETED WOMEN
voters on a breathtaking scale, unprecedented then and rarely achieved
since. One of the ways Ida Koverman and her allies did this was through
the rapid, steady growth of Republican Study Clubs in collaboration with
the County Committee, which won accolades for "the everlasting team
work of every blooming soul that wins the day." The County Committee's
"willingness and steadfastness" was carried out by its "efficient executive
secretary." The victory of Calvin Coolidge inspired the creation of a permanent, statewide organization of the Republican Women's Federation
of California (RWFC), formally announced at the downtown Alexandria
Hotel on January 20, 1925, to serve as an educational resource and to
promote "womanhood, working obediently to conscience . . . to build an
organization that will be ready to work together in harmony in a national
campaign."[1]

Ida Koverman sat on the new group's executive board and within a
month, she helped to accelerate the establishment of four new clubs that
would form the basis of the Federation's "firm, permanent foundation."
The vastness of the Golden State demanded its division into a northern
and a southern division, with Mrs. Florence Collins Porter serving as
acting president of the south, which inspired Ralph Arnold to claim that
this was "in reality the inception of a new political era for women in the
United States as well as in California." Its mandate was unprecedented
in its explicitness: "to cooperate with the Republican State and County
Committee in campaign work for the election of Republican candidates

70

for office" and to serve as a political machine to counter progressives by institutionalizing conservative Republicanism. [2]

Not coincidentally then, the Federation's southern branch set up its office in the Hellman Building, the same address as the Republican County Central Committee, where Koverman already worked. She joined Mrs. Porter's and Mrs. Clark's travels throughout the Southland holding weekly recruiting meetings, such as when the women checked into San Diego's affluent U. S. Grant Hotel for their organizing meeting the following day. Within three months, thirteen clubs with two hundred founding members were established. Each new group selected delegates to attend an upcoming convention where permanent officers would be elected. A newcomer from Washington, DC, joined them on the circuit, Miss Nellie E. Kelley, and after that, almost everywhere Ida Koverman went Nellie Kelley accompanied her to rally the crowd. [3]

Originally, from Minnesota, Nellie E. Kelley worked for the Republican National Committee in Washington, DC. She moved to California in 1920 and, as a spinster, was always escorted by one of her two brothers after her fiancé died during the Great War. By October 1924, she was already addressing gatherings in San Pedro and in Eagle Rock.[4] Nellie Kelley assisted Ida Koverman to galvanize an army of women citizen-soldiers, earning praise from Koverman, who thought she was an "exceptionally capable" person "doing excellent work" and producing "gratifying results." Southern California's growing population and Los Angeles County's increasing dominance accelerated the need for women's integration into the party, and everyone knew their numbers could weigh heavily in future electoral outcomes.

Ida Koverman became an advocate for Kelley's services, noting how she revisited new clubs in every community, facilitated speakers, and strove to ensure these smaller groups would continue "working along conservative Republican lines." Koverman's view of the Federation's mission apparently contrasted sharply with another founder, Mrs. Clark, who thought it was necessary to reach out to women of all ideological persuasions, while Koverman explicitly eschewed efforts to recruit progressives. In part this was a strategy and in part it was an ideological commitment to conservatism, and the ambiguity was rooted in the challenge of appealing to women who already felt over-organized, so "it was necessary to appeal to women's patriotism," defined, at least by Ralph Arnold, as an oppositional philosophy that fostered fear and repulsion of "unwholesome political conditions" that were "largely due to the well-meaning better class of citizens who" neglected their civic duties, or who were only in politics "for their own selfish reasons, to control public affairs."[5]

Conservative Republican Clara Burdette had employed Red Scare fear tactics for years, but historically, women's clubs had been nonpartisan associations. Now, Ida Koverman and Nellie Kelley fostered a new legitimacy for promoting a conservative ideological group with the agenda of recruiting Republican women. Nellie Kelley's speeches were explicit, telling women that the Federation was "being carried forward on the basis of organization against Radicalism and Socialism in all its various forms," and this massage would continue to frame women's conservative Republican domestic- and foreign-policy party platforms. Nellie Kelley told eager listeners about the dangers of socialism, Bolshevism, and other forms of "political disintegration" and urged them to take a more active role in political and civic affairs.[6]

Koverman and her allies' efforts paid off. By the middle of May, plans for their first regional convention were underway, with an invitation to Mrs. Herbert Hoover to speak as recognition of the "culmination of Republican women's work." Ralph Arnold admitted that it had been "done at the suggestion of the Chief and largely in his behalf," but Mrs. Hoover declined to participate, much to Ida Koverman's disappointment.[7] No matter. In fact, Koverman and Arnold believed, rather than being discouraged, they were just getting started.

Two days before the Federation convention, a banner *Los Angeles Times* headline announced, in all caps, "REPUBLICAN WOMEN OF STATE IN CONVENTION." The article was written by Myra Nye, who would become a longtime watcher and fan of Ida Koverman. Nye's subtitle announced, "Politics Summon Women: First Partisan Conclave Here Next Tuesday to See Entire State Represented." Accompanying her story was a collage of sixteen portraits of the city's leading female politicos. Ida Koverman's photograph was prominently featured at four times larger than the others, and it remains a singular image of her as a mature, elegant, and attractive woman with dark round eyes, full lips, and high cheekbones. Her dark brown hair parted to fall just over her left brow, accentuating her oval face. No one noticed, however, that Ida Koverman was at the time a matronly forty-nine years old, so the photograph was likely taken a decade, or more, earlier. It continued to represent her for years regardless of the obvious discrepancy with photographs taken a mere three years later. More importantly, though, the placement and size of the portrait symbolizd the magnitude of esteem she had already inspired among the local press and the city's female leadership corps.[8]

Similarly, the first evidence of the blossoming friendship between Ida Koverman and Herbert Hoover appeared in July, when Hoover asked Ralph Arnold to arrange an in-person conference for himself and Koverman at his home in Palo Alto.[9] Undoubtedly, the success of her Southland organizing inspired Hoover to recognize Koverman's contribution to his own and the larger Republican cause.

The convention for the Federation's Southern Division was held on June 23 at the Alexandria Hotel, with the theme of "Patriotism, Republicanism, and Active Citizenship of All in a Representative Government." Educational literature was provided, including a pamphlet on the need to reduce government spending, which Ida Koverman had received from Herbert Hoover's Department of Commerce. Faux butterflies decorated the hall, and fashion models wearing designs by Maxime meandered throughout the luncheon.[10] Attendance beat all expectations. The grand ballroom seated one thousand diners, but the overflow crowd sat at tables in the halls and mezzanine. There was much interest in the administrative business meeting for the election of permanent officers; Ida Koverman was elected secretary to a standing-room-only crowd. Koverman's colleague in the Coolidge campaign, Mendel Silberberg, had a plum spot introducing the keynote speaker, which confirmed his rising popularity among women's groups, and among the speakers were Buron Fitts and Ralph Arnold, who heralded the convention as a "wonderful Republican women's meeting, . . . the best one probably ever held in the state." To keep the momentum going, Arnold argued that the group required donations in order to hire an "efficient, paid organizer," and he proposed a five-thousand-dollar fund to prepare for the next primary election and to expand their efforts into surrounding states.[11]

Ida Koverman contributed more than her organizational skills and fighting spirit. The platform allowed her to showcase her creativity as well. Singer Karl Brandenburg, known as the "Whispering Tenor," performed a song composed by Ida Koverman, with lyrics by nonprofessional Edward H. Sharpe, called "Darling," a waltz-ballad for voice and piano, and a rare example of Koverman's romantic side. The first line read, "Darling, darling moonlight is beaming," and the chorus, "Darling, darling, my arms waiting." Koverman and Sharpe's friendship grew out of their mutual love of music and their sojourns driving around the Southland accompanied by former Assistant US District Attorney Albert K. Lucas on a double-date with Ed Sharpe and his wife to the Inland Empire's Orange festival.[12]

Along with the musical interlude, Ida Koverman promoted the Federation in a radio broadcast over local station KHJ, owned by *Los Angeles*

Times publisher Harry Chandler. She or Ralph Arnold read the script, entitled "Friends of Radio Land and of the Republican Women's Federation of California," focusing on the declining role of political parties in government and lamenting the rise of nonpartisan elective office. The remarks were directed to "the patriotic and self sacrificing women who are carrying on this great work" and who were helping "to bring the state of California back to old-time party lines and party responsibility." The importance of the political party was that "individual responsibility to the people is a very hazy and obscure thing," while "party responsibility, on the other hand, is very real." The Republican Party had the responsibility to put "good men into office," and "self-preservation, . . . if for no higher reason, is bound to nominate the best man," to elect partisan candidates "to every office in the gift of the people, from councilman, to president." Organized Republican women were creating a "stronger union for offensive and defensive purposes," and they were being called on to "throw your influence toward getting more people registered." It closed with a vision for the future where women would find their rewards in politics getting "stronger and stronger."[13]

The statewide Federation of Republican Women was less than a year old, but it was so successful that, in late October, fifty-three statewide affiliates held its first annual convention in Santa Monica. The group passed resolutions affirming loyalty and support of the Republican Party ticket. There was some opposition to such endorsements, but the president of the Los Angeles branch, Mrs. Josephine Winn, countered with, "You cannot serve God and Mammon. You cannot serve the Democrats and the Republican Party at the same time," after which the endorsing resolution passed. The purpose of the statewide Federation was summed up: "We believe that by learning to be good Republicans, we make ourselves better Americans." Ida Koverman provided some of the lunchtime entertainment, including the Junior Auxiliary of Young Republicans who sang her composed parodies of the era's most popular songs.[14]

By the fall, Ida Koverman was exhausted and once again feeling the brunt of financial insecurity that plagued the very survival of the committee's office. Ralph Arnold had avoided burdening Herbert Hoover about local troubles, but now he was compelled to approach him because, in effect, he reasoned they were Hoover's troubles too. Arnold bluntly stated that "Mrs. Koverman had a serious breakdown last week. . . . She is so discouraged and is only hanging to the job because of her loyalty to you and me." He wasn't sure if she could continue because of a failure to honor what she had been "promised," by way of the "assistance as would enable her to live comfortably." She had not been paid in three weeks, and all other funding arrangements had fallen through.

Arnold had sung Koverman's praises before, but now he painted a dire picture by emphasizing the vital role she played in Hoover's ambitions. If finances forced her resignation, Arnold feared devastation of the entire Los Angeles Republican Party operation. He warned Hoover the situation was so bleak that if she did not receive the $500.00 owed to her by the end of the week, she would carry out her threat to close down the office, "store our effects" and "seek other employment," which he believed "she can easily get."[15]

There was more to it than Ida Koverman's salary, though. There were lingering challenges by their old nemesis Edward Lyman and a "small coterie" who wanted to close the office. The financial obligations were taking a toll on Arnold, and he could no longer assume "the technical side of the fight and finance it too." He asked Hoover to apply his "strong arm" on the men who should be contributing, and he insisted "it must be done immediately," or he would be forced, once again, to try to raise the money for himself.[16] If Herbert Hoover ever had a chance to win a presidential nomination, it would be from the efforts of individuals like Ida Koverman, so it was crucial he attend to the matter.

During his more frequent business trips, Ralph Arnold pondered Hoover's predicament. He knew that without the "hard work in political channels by his admirers," like Koverman, his "personal popularity with the people" alone would never "secure his nomination."[17] As Arnold leaned on Hoover, Koverman leaned on Arnold to return to Los Angeles to assert his authority over the County Committee that she nearly single-handedly was running. Disparate, routine, day-to-day and unexpected matters confronted her, and when she could, she acted on Arnold's behalf, but this wasn't enough, so Ida pleaded with him to resume his role as county chairman. She was pressed to arrange and attend meetings without his prior knowledge and to report the business or resolutions passed without his authorization or consideration. There were conflicts over endorsements and appointments for local and federal offices, and she warded off bigger crises until he finally returned to Los Angeles. Years later, this dynamic would characterize her job at MGM when Louis B. Mayer became preoccupied with matters beyond the studio. Now as then, she handled a relentless flow of multifaceted minutiae according to how urgent she perceived it to be. Each decision involved one or more individuals, and most issues were imbued with unanticipated or unforeseen implications. And of course, there was always the problem of paying the bills.

After November's rent, salaries, and incidentals were secured, more serious matters arose with the realization that there were no funds left for Nellie Kelley, even with the odd jobs Koverman had been able to find for her. Koverman feared the worst if Kelley could no longer recruit women for the Federation, especially in light of the competition from other groups reaching out to women voters, who would exploit the inroads made by the Federation because women, she surmised, were "greatly stimulated through the Republican [Federation] administration work." Koverman couldn't carry both Arnold's work and Kelley's as well because, as she said, the days were simply "not long enough."[18]

Ida Koverman was a take-charge kind of person in her professional and her social life, especially when things were going wrong. She could even turn into a pretty good handyman. During one of her gatherings at "a seaside venue," the guests enjoyed themselves while chaos broke out in the kitchen. The chef was overwhelmed with the renovation work going on while he was preparing his masterpiece. Construction workers hammered and turned the gas and electricity off and on. Ida swooped in and "not only soothed this chef, but sliced miles of bread and helped fry the chickens." After the guests were fed, some of them ran cheerily into the surf. "Behold Ida again amongst the enterprising and courageous." The reporter added, "Incidentally, she swiped the handsome life saver's bathrobe—with excellent effect."[19]

CHAPTER 10

Petroleum and Partisans

WHEN JOURNALIST ALMA WHITAKER ANSWERED A RHETORICAL QUESTION about who California's women leaders and "bright feminine minds" were, she counted Ida Koverman among them, "a woman of brains and efficiency."[1] By 1926, Whitaker recognized Koverman's central role in Southern California's rising presence in national politics, aided to a large degree by women citizens flexing their political muscles. The successful organizing of the southern branch of the Republican Women's Federation now demanded that women get more than a passing glance by their GOP counterparts.

Herbert Hoover's growing friendship with Ida Koverman, separate from Ralph Arnold, signaled that this was indeed the case. She was now a direct conduit between Commerce Secretary Hoover and Los Angeles partisans. When Hoover made plans for a Southland visit, Ida Koverman provided the "first definite information" during a luncheon where she was identified as "one of the valuable aides on the official staff" of the Federation, as chair of the speakers' committee and a seat on the resolutions committee.

Hoover's appearance at the luncheon was one of the rare concessions he made to publicly acknowledge women's growing importance in his political fortunes while also validating Ida Koverman's influential stature. This was an important milestone for her as she sat at the head table, right next to Mr. and Mrs. Herbert Hoover, before three hundred and fifty guests in the grand hall of the San Bernardino Women's Club building. Mrs. Florence Collins Porter was re-elected president of the Southern Division, Mrs. Edith Van de Water became second vice president, and Koverman's ally Nellie Kelley was elected official organizer. Another upcoming ally of Ida

Koverman was there: Mrs. Josephine Winn, president of the Los Angeles branch, along with the largest contingent of the Federation at the convention. Local candidates in attendence s were "doing a little campaigning," including Assistant District Attorney Buron Fitts, who was running for lieutenant governor and who "made a splendid impression as he always does" talking about the "obligations of public service."[2]

The Federation passed resolutions in support of or in opposition to pending Congressional bills, emphasizing to legislators their need to thwart any "socialistic attempt" that could undermine the Volstead Act, legislation that enforced the Eighteenth Amendment's ban on the production and imbibing of alcohol. The Federation resolved that prohibition had "brought increased happiness into the homes of our country, increased deposits in savings banks and increased efficiency in the workshops of the country." Whether Ida Koverman had ever aggressively supported prohibition is unclear, but in anticipation of the upcoming convention of the Women's Christian Temperance Union, Mabel Walker Willebrandt encouraged her mother to network among the city's locals, including Ida Koverman, about whom she said, "whatever her differences on other subjects may be, [she] is a loyal prohibitionist."[3]

The Federation also called on all Republicans to support their party's candidates in the primaries because they wanted to ensure "no radical candidates."[4] The energized partisans were readied for the final battles of the campaign season, and by now Ida Koverman was a recognized leader of the troops. Ralph Arnold didn't hide his increasing dependence on her, but on the local level the city's shifting power alliances and permeable loyalties tested her in new ways. Navigating the treacherous waves of local politics raised a concern about her ability to tread in perilous waters closer to home. Little did they know that Ida R. Koverman was an expert swimmer.

Mabel Walker Willebrandt remained a controversial figure for Ralph Arnold, who told Hoover in 1925 that he wanted the new Coolidge administration to remove Willebrandt from her post in the attorney general's office. He was unequivocal, and to support his view, he sent extracts from Ida Koverman's letter to Hoover's secretary, Lawrence Richey, in which she stated, "I think I have explained to you the reasons why Mrs. Willebrandt should give way to our candidate, Miss Vere Radir-Norton." Arnold implored Hoover, "I shall depend on your pressing this matter very hard, as there is no reason why those office holders should hold over indefinitely, when others who deserve their places are left waiting." Radir-Norton was a well-connected state inheritance tax appraiser, who, when studying law at USC with classmate and future Superior Court Judge Georgia Bullock, founded the local branch of Phi Delta Delta.[5]

Arnold opposed Willebrandt's interest in a local judgeship because she had failed to support Charles Moore's Senate race. Arnold was aware of her efforts to counter his opposition, suggesting she was now "paying the price for the company she picked." He wired President Coolidge to suggest Willebrandt's appointment would "materially weaken" Coolidge's support in Southern California because the County Committee was "practically unanimously" against her.[6]

Ida Koverman allied with scores of politicized women, but her relationship with Mabel Walker Willebrandt was ambivalent from the start, in part because of Koverman's growing identification with conservatives and Willebrandt's association with progressives. It isn't that surprising, however, that Ralph Arnold and Ida Koverman would seek to promote a local figure over the more distant Willebrandt. Willebrandt did not get the coveted judgeship, so she stayed at the Justice Department.

Ralph Arnold kept Herbert Hoover informed about local affairs and never missed an opportunity to talk about Ida Koverman. In the spring of 1926, he said there was an acute crisis that could affect Hoover's long-term political survival, which rested to a large degree on Koverman's persistence and goodwill, and the help of her colleague George Bush. Echoing his earlier pleadings, Arnold reminded Hoover that "If it were not for the loyalty of Mrs. Koverman to you, our fighting legion would long since have folded up its tent and departed." It wasn't just the fear of a diminishing influence of the County Committee, but the entire state apparatus could be threatened because "the business men and the better element are thoroughly frightened" about recent trends. Just as Ida Koverman had counseled, Arnold was convinced that Edward Lyman's opposing faction sought to topple Arnold and close the entire office.[7]

Arnold's recognition of Koverman's near-singular importance did little to ease her continued anxiety about her salary. He had cajoled small contributions from notables like *Los Angeles Times* publisher Harry Chandler, but it was Hoover's close friend, business attorney Henry Mauris Robinson, who ultimately "saved our bacon." Robinson specialized in corporate consolidation and mergers and helped to found the California Institute of Technology in Pasadena after working closely with Hoover during the Great War.[8]

County Committee member John Booth had little faith in Ida Koverman's influence to push back on even more corrosive forces, especially Los Angeles Mayor George Cryer and his hired gun, the notorious police chief Edgar "Two-Gun" James Davis, who ran an unofficial squad to aggressively and violently support the anti-union business elite. Koverman's stature "did not amount to a snap," Booth thought, because she had already "done all she could," while the real problem was that the County Committee as an "organization is not feared."[9]

James W. Everington saw broader challenges facing the committee, such as the "rapidly increasing numbers of dissatisfied voters, radicals, Klansmen . . . and youngsters," who threatened the Republican Party by gnoring so-called reformer types, such as "the Veterans, the Women, the Wets, the Drys," and the corrupt, de-facto mayor, Kent Parrot, who opposed Arnold's faction. Everington blamed the press for cynically convincing the public that "everything which pertains to politics is inefficient or crooked" so that no one ever expects committees like theirs to bring significant change. He suggested using the psychology of salesmanship and "crowd psychology" to "put over . . . the right sort of leaders," to win recognition for the County Committee as the dominant "organization to which all other Republican organizations look for guidance," and as "the coordinator of all activities and elected by the people," to "be in a position to disarm our radical critics and opponents . . . use our heads and our knowledge of mob psychology . . . to frame up a program . . . and to sell to the man on the street."[10] Ida Koverman and Nellie Kelley had already been using such techniques by exploiting the real or imagined threat of communism to promote the patriotic recruitment of women into the Republican Party.

Koverman's immediate challenge, however, was the survival of the County Committee. One avenue toward this end was to advance the visibility of MGM's Louis B. Mayer, who, soon after making his partisan debut, took a prominent place among the local elite. Over the next few years, during Ralph Arnold's increasing absences, Ida Koverman shepherded the rising influence of the County Committee. Louis B. Mayer's political stature was also rising, as MGM was becoming the most successful movie studio of that era and beyond. Initially, both Koverman and Arnold facilitated Mayer's entrée into party affairs enabling Mayer to further his own business interests. Arnold described Mayer as "one of the most active and influential members of our committee, and a great booster for the Chief," on whose behalf he asked Hoover's secretary, Lawrence Richey, to send Koverman information related to a Federal Trade Commission investigation into the aggressive theater expansion of Adolph Zukor.[11]

Mayer's interest in politics wasn't unique among movie moguls, and some of them attended an affair held on behalf of the re-election of

California governor C. C. Young, sponsored by the well-known local banker and movie financier Motley Flint. After Young's primary victory, Arnold invited Mayer to dinner at the prestigious Jonathan Club to meet Secretary of the Navy Curtis D. Wilbur, but it's unclear if Mayer accepted the invitation to an establishment where Jews were banned from membership. Attributions of Mayer's partisan posts include the notion that Herbert Hoover anointed Mayer as treasurer of the state's national committee, but this appears not to be a post that Mayer held, and Hoover paid little attention to details of local affairs. More accurately, perhaps, was that Arnold and Koverman were quick to realize they could tap a new source of funds in the movie business, and because of Mayer's particular interest in getting more involved, Arnold's invitation might have signaled mutual interests. Regardless, Mayer gained traction, and he did become chairman of the County Committee's finance committee.[12]

In spite of the appearance of service to the party, Mayer's closest friend and advisor, San Francisco financier Louis Lurie, suggested that "for all of his intimacy with various Republican power brokers, there is a strong sense that Mayer was more interested in proximity to power than he was in actual policy." Lurie also noted that Mayer was "never a large contributor and never did any work on the organization level." What's more, even after Ida Koverman and her allies lobbied to overcome opposition to Mayer's later election as chairman of the State Central Committee in 1932, Lurie recalled how "unfortunately, L. B. did no work."[13] Mayer's standing within the state party actually reflected the growing influence of Ida Koverman and her network. In fact, in both Arnold's and Mayer's case, because she actually did much of their work, she survived long after both men left their respective perches.

In the meantime, Ralph Arnold drew on his influence to promote women in politics and in their careers. In one instance, he approached Lawrence Richey to assist a Mrs. M. J. Jury in getting a job in the Bureau of Investigation (later the FBI) under the direction of J. Edgar Hoover. J. Edgar Hoover personally responded to Arnold, informing him that the department had "not had occasion to utilize the services of any women in connection with our investigative work." Specifically, he said, "Appointments in this Bureau are limited to men between the ages of twenty-five and forty, who have either had legal training or are expert accountants." Up until then, only two women had served as special agents, and after J. Edgar Hoover became the director in 1934, one of them resigned, and he forced the other one out. The Bureau hired only one other woman during his controversial forty-eight-year reign, but one month after his death in

1972, two female special agents were hired. How well Ralph Arnold or Ida Koverman knew Mrs. Jury is hard to discern, but they were likely paying attention to her private investigations into the sale of fraudulent stock in the city's booming oil market, which would soon implode. Mrs. Jury was a private dick, but she did her sleuthing without a license, so she was arrested in a sting operation while working for victims of one of the many stock con games fermenting in the City of Angels.[14]

The motion-picture industry helped fuel the city's phenomenal growth, but petroleum extraction attracted big money oil interests, new settlers, investors, and innovators. Both oil and movies spawned technical and creative opportunities employing thousands, and they gave rise to great wealth, wonder, and whole new worlds, real and imagined. When the Julian Petroleum stock scandal hit the city like a jolt from the San Andreas Fault, no one saw it coming, except maybe Mrs. Jury, but movie moguls and oil magnates felt the impact along with scores of vulnerable wage earners.

The financial meltdown came after eager investors willingly handed over their money, and sometimes their life savings, in order to get in on the quick riches of gushing black gold. Chauncy C. Julian had begun to attract smaller investors as a way to rival corporate dominance in oil speculation. His wells produced enough oil to support the value of his company's stock certificates, but when he resigned from his company, things got out of hand. Groups of individual investors were brought together to form larger entities called "pools," with colorful names like the "Million Dollar Pool," or the "Tia Juana Pool," and each one overseen by a trust or pool manager. This allowed bigger investments among disparate people while minimizing the overall risk. At first, the pools were made up of the city's most reputable citizens who could afford to lose, but soon they were attracting investments from every social stratum. Little did anyone realize that dividends were paid with money that came in from new investors rather than from profits earned. As long as no one kept track of the actual number of stock certificates sold, and they remained unredeemed, everyone was happy. Such financial manipulations became known as Ponzi schemes, and like most of them, this enterprise soon morphed into a labyrinth of winners and losers, victims and perpetrators, and a cast of characters that ranged from individuals and families to those at the center of local, state, and national politics, many of whom circulated in Ida Koverman's world.

Some of these investors had shared interests in petroleum, politics, and motion pictures, such as Louis B. Mayer and First National Bank vice president Motley Flint, who, along with their oil investments, were allies in support of Hoover's presidential ambition. Under auspices of the bank, Flint had set up the Cinema Finance Company to fund Hollywood studios when their East Coast executives refused to open their wallets. Flint joined the Million Dollar Pool and brought Louis B. Mayer into it along with an "impressive cross" of the city's most prominent "men of wealth and power." Attorney Mendel Silberberg, Ida Koverman's close ally in the 1924 Coolidge campaign, also invested over $585,000 in the Tia Juana Pool, along with "representatives of a powerful political machine, wealthy Main Street pawnbrokers, and Tia Juana concessionaires."[15]

By May 1927, when the enormity of the losses from the Julian Petroleum stock fraud surfaced, it sparked an investigation that led to indictments and prosecutions. Forty thousand Southern Californians had bought five million dollars of worthless stock, and as the price of the stock fell, the market was flooded with the over-issued certificates. No one really knew where all of the invested money went, but some thought a lot of it went into the presidential campaign of Herbert Hoover.

Ida Koverman's partisan associate, attorney Joseph Scott, had "reluctantly accepted" an appointment as trustee of the receivership of Julian Petroleum. Joining Scott as co-trustee was H. L. Carnahan, who had served as the state's first commissioner of corporations.

Quick action by Mendel Silberberg's Tia Juana Pool divested its holdings, and he removed himself from any financial interest, which enabled him to soon act as defense counsel to a Julian company official, Ed Rosenberg, being prosecuted by District Attorney Asa Keyes. Motley Flint, who had overseen the "Million Dollar Pool" with money from Cecil B. DeMille and Louis B. Mayer, left the country, but he later returned to testify in another case involving RKO studio's David O. Selznick, Louis B. Mayer's future son-in-law. Compounding the misery of victims of the Julian debacle was the stock market crash of October 1929. For one individual it was all too much, and on July 14, 1930, when Motley Flint finished his testimony, Frank D. Keaton pulled out a gun and killed him. When news spread of the tragedy, producer Jack Warner said that Flint "was the first Los Angeles banker to recognize the value of the fast-growing motion picture industry," and, "we have lost a great friend and benefactor." Flags flew at half-mast at Warner Bros.[16]

Louis B. Mayer's first $65,000 investment had earned a $50,000 profit, and when Mayer inadvertently received $39.50 less than what he was due, he forced the pool manager to write him a personal check to cover it. In June, along with the indictments of fifty-three others, Mayer and director Cecil B. DeMille were charged with "conspiracy usury" for the unlawfully high interest rates they earned when they provided loans to purchase Julian stock. Bank presidents, former judges, and attorneys were also targeted. By September, District Attorney Asa Keyes decided to accept reparations from the defendants, and the charges were dismissed against Louis B. Mayer after he returned his illegal profits to help compensate victims. After a public outcry, the grand jury reinstated the charges. Keyes' replacement, Buron Fitts, would later earn a reputation as Mayer's pawn, but now he reissued the indictment against Mayer, who appeared before Judge Stephens on June 14, along with his colleague, Motley Flint, and ten others. He would have to reappear in September.[17] Hollywood's celebrated defense attorney, Jerry Giesler, came to Mayer's rescue, and once again the charges were dropped.

Ida Koverman held shares of oil stock, facilitated by Ralph Arnold, but her five hundred shares were for Montana Pacific Oil. As the Julian scandal was unfolding, she was "anxiously waiting" for the sale of her shares because, as she wrote to Arnold in the summer of 1927, she could not start her vacation until the sale went through. Arnold sent her a check for $625.00 along with another five hundred shares and an apology. He said he was sorry she had to sell, and hoped "the loss can be recovered in some other way a little later." At the same time, she said Herbert Hoover would be in Los Angeles on July 27th, or "so Mayer tells me," and therefore, "unless I get away pretty quick, I'll not go as I feel I should be here when Herbert Hoover is here, especially with you away. Kay."[18]

Through Koverman, Mayer established a friendship with Hoover, and he unabashedly nudged Koverman to "get busy with Chief." He was eager to enter the blossoming broadcasting industry, so he urged her to "see what his attitude is and what can be done" while she was in Washington, DC, for the upcoming International Radio Conference chaired by Secretary of Commerce Hoover.

Mayer wired her the text of a telegram from Roy D. Keehn of Chicago, a prominent attorney involved in major publishing concerns including those of William Randolph Hearst. Keehn wired Mayer, "If your friend Hoover has any influence with the radio commission we now want his help." He explained they were establishing a *Herald Examiner* radio unit as the head one of the Hearst chains and asked Mayer if he thought he could "help us not only with Hoover" but with other commissioners as well. Mayer then told Koverman, "This [is] very important as [it] will give me just the ammunition I need to enlist their support and friendship. Drop

[the] matter of publishers until I arrive[, and I] will give [the] list then. Kindest regards, Louis B. Mayer."[19]

Louis Mayer's confidence in Ida Koverman was well-placed. She quickly worked her influence, after which Hoover reassured Mayer, "Strictly confidential to your self. In accordance with my promise, I am now working on a plan to arrange a satisfactory wavelength for your proposed station in a general readjustment. Do I correctly understand that this is a joint license for yourself and the Hearst interests?" According to author Scott Eyman, Hoover told Mayer that after much string pulling "pending the construction of your station and assuming its completion within a reasonable time this wave length will not be assigned to any other Los Angeles station but will be held for you when ready.'"[20] Ida Koverman had now confirmed her value to both Mayer and Hoover, and if karma was a real thing, she would soon realize the fruits of her efforts in her next extraordinary and unexpected reincarnation.

Ralph Arnold appeared to have been far removed from the Julian scandal and Mayer's growing reliance on Koverman and Hoover. But one day in October of 1928, after he visited Hoover at the Commerce Department, Arnold met with Mabel Walker Willebrandt in the Justice Department. He "told her the whole story of Julian Petroleum," and whatever he confided, he did so because, while he had his political differences with her, she was actually one of the few people he trusted. His tantalizing tidbit offered no details, but two years later, on May 14, 1930, seventeen defendants went on trial for charges related to the Julian case. Mabel Walker Willebrandt was the defense attorney for one of them, Albert Lane, the head of Progressive Financial Corporation, and she would go on to represent Lane in other cases down the line.[21]

Herbert Hoover was unscathed by the Julian Petroleum scandal, but his connections with the oil industry and his enormous wealth raised questions during his presidency. Lawrence Richey said he thought they were being pushed for "infamous political purposes," sparked by Hoover's "tremendous efforts" to promote the interests of American independent oil producers. After Arnold inquired about the rumors, Richey emphatically stated "that the President has not one dime invested in any country outside of the United States, much less in any foreign oil business," and he hasn't had any such interest or investment since he entered public life fourteen years ago.[22]

Louis B. Mayer overcame his own problems with the oil industry, but to handle the legal trouble of his brother Jerry, he called on Mabel Walker

Willebrandt and Buron Fitts. Fitts's change of heart toward Mayer was profound, and Sam Marx later claimed that Fitt's reputation as a tough guy allowed him to set a high price for "favors," such as those on Mayer's behalf. But it was more complicated. Willebrandt and Fitts were able to get Jerry Mayer out of the country and sent to Shanghai, China, when authorities in Baltimore, Maryland, initiated his extradition for the selling of fraudulent stock shares to finance movie-short subjects. While oil stock fraud was more notorious, such stock scams were rampant in the movie business. Jerry Mayer was ordered to pay back the victims with the largest losses, but it was Louis B. Mayer who made good on the claims.

Ida Koverman had spent the last seven years building friendships and alliances diversely borne out of the trenches of political campaigns, financial mayhem, and familial entanglements that would soon morph into an inner circle in MGM. Among the disparate cast of insiders was Blaney Matthews, a former FBI agent turned city detective assigned to protect Jake Berman, a defendant turned informant in one of the Julian cases. Matthews was sleuthing around at pivotal moments during the twists and sometimes deadly turns of the scandal. Buron Fitts and Blaney Matthews were allies inside the district attorney's office, and at times they worked with MGM's chief of police, Whitey Hendry, to clean up after some of the sordid messes involving the studio's heavenly stars. Blaney Matthews would go on to become the chief of security for Warner Bros., where he earned a reputation as a bully in the studio's labor wars.

Just about everyone Ida Koverman knew was directly involved or affected by the largest Ponzi scheme the nation had ever seen. The convoluted web of vultures and victims were connected in a "world of confidence men, promoters, and boosters and business leaders, politicians, and public servants" that ensnared them, wittingly or not. And these members of Ida Koverman's network made up part of the financial backbone that supported Herbert Hoover's political ambition. As Hoover's presidential mission gained momentum, Louis B. Mayer's reputation within the party would suffer from his engagement in "a fair amount of investment wheeling and dealing" that led him straight into charges of criminal transgressions.[23] By the time of Herbert Hoover's 1928 presidential nomination, neither Ida Koverman nor Mabel Walker Willebrandt could remove the taint on Mayer and, in spite of assertions to the contrary, his ascendancy on to the national arena was sidetracked until the renomination of Hoover at the next Republican national convention.

Nevertheless, the courtship between MGM and the Republican Party facilitated by Ida R. Koverman was well underway and along with

Koverman, Mendel Silberberg and Mabel Walker Willebrandt would become part of Louis B. Mayer's virtual family administering to the needs of the MGM Empire. But first they had to win a presidential election.

CHAPTER 11

Kingmaker, 1928

"Koverman wanted what loyal party workers everywhere wanted: a chance for the local powers to mingle with the president-to-be in the bright glow of triumph. . . . Koverman's appeal carried more weight than most . . .she was an old friend."[1]

AFTER YEARS BATTLING IN THE PARTISAN TRENCHES, IDA R. KOVERMAN was a seasoned, hardcore political operative who increasingly garnered respect, and in 1928, a backstory framing her rising acclaim began to emerge, published in the first issue of the *California Elephant*, a newsletter mailed to the three thousand members of the Federation of Republican Women of California, Southern Division. The newsletter was an unabashed vehicle for the Federation's "devoted adulation" of Herbert Hoover." Koverman contributed a "sparkling and interesting article" about Mrs. Hoover, apparently implying a nearly lifelong friendship. This Koverman portrait explained that after she moved to Los Angeles, she became known for her "ability and devotion," and she had "a pronounced genius for leadership," which quickly made her "a force in the political activities in Southern California."[2]

As Koverman's political cachet rose, Louis B. Mayer ascended to his throne at MGM. By 1928, the courtship between Hollywood and national politics was ready to be consummated, largely through the efforts of their matchmaker Ida Koverman. In anticipation of California's May 1 presidential primary, the frenetic energy inside Republican Party headquarters at the Alexandria Hotel was palpable. The driving force was Ida

Koverman, who supervised the clerical staff, directed the machinery, and accelerated the momentum of the campaign while adjusting to all of the "intricacies and difficulties" of the enterprise. One observer noted that "if it is true that in America the men ostensibly rule . . . the real power behind—the real living power—is in the hands of the women," and the real "chief of the organization is Mrs. Ida R. Koverman, or 'Kay' as she is popularly called." As the auditor of the Republican Study Club, and secretary of both the statewide and Southern Division of the Federation, her multiple talents were extended, but her networking ability was second to none. "She has the advantage of personal acquaintance with thousands of ardent Hoover supporters," which came about as a result of her concerted effort, "for she has been taking part during the past eight years in a campaign that is responsible for sending twenty-nine California delegates to Kansas City next June to nominate Herbert Hoover as president of the United States."[3]

Now, more than at any other time in American history, Ida Koverman and millions of other women voters were viewed as the lifeblood of the body politic, and for her, the Hoover campaign nourished her identity and defined her public persona. The larger political and cultural changes evidenced in the 1928 presidential election were, for her, also fought in more intimate, personal ways. Even as a hardcore partisan working on behalf of a higher calling to elect Herbert Hoover, she still had to fight for her own financial security. She needed to keep her post not only to ensure the influence of the County Committee, but to cultivate relationships for her own survival.

Shifting cycles of alliances repeatedly threatened Ralph Arnold and Ida Koverman's control of the County Committee. Some of Ralph Arnold's tactics came under increased scrutiny, putting more pressure on Koverman, who served as the executive secretary for the local Hoover-for-President Club, an extra-party organization filled with many of the same people working at both the party and County Committee headquarters.[4]

A statewide conference during the first week of April welcomed the newly formed Hoover-for-President Clubs, and for a while a rapprochement prevailed, inspiring local Hoover Club president, Charles Teague, to offer kudos for the "remarkable harmony prevailing among all elements of the party," in large part due to Mendel B. Silberberg and Ida Koverman. The collaboration between Koverman and Silberberg and Louis B. Mayer was growing, and Mayer introduced the keynote speaker, Stanford president and Hoover friend Ray Lyman Wilbur, at a gala held at San Francisco's Palace Hotel. Mayer's rousing speech impressed Wilbur, particularly his

warning, "The only opposition to Herbert Hoover is from the politicians
. . . the same back room clique that acted up in 1920. We will have none
of that in Kansas City!"[5]

Ida Koverman and Mabel Walker Willebrandt successfully finagled to
get Mayer elected as a delegate to the upcoming national convention,
representing Culver City even though Mayer's home address was in Santa
Monica. Koverman and Willebrandt then promoted Mayer for an even
more spectacular opportunity. They had high hopes for Mayer to second
Hoover's nomination, but, contrary to previous accounts, the Julian Petroleum scandal detoured Mayer's visible role at the 1928 Republican Party
convention. "At the last minute," Koverman and Willebrandt's "careful
groundwork was sabotaged by adverse publicity." Even after the convention, Mayer's activities were played down because he "was considered too
tarnished to be publicly linked with the candidate."[6]

Ida Koverman "won the admiration of her own delegation and the
national Hoover campaign leaders," columnist Kyle Palmer noted, "by
her personal sagacity and her ability to solve problems which demanded
clear thinking and keen judgment." She was neither a delegate nor an
alternate, but her facilitation in "building acquaintances and making contacts" was "valuable to our cause."[7] Koverman helped build a lattice of
mutually interested powerful people, and she ensured they stood ready
for action when the time was right. For Ida Koverman, politics was not
only serious business; it was downright fun. Conventions were always a
time for big celebrations, and she was a big party girl.

Nearly a century later, a photograph of the hearty, fifty-one-year-old
Koverman radiates her broad-grinned, unbridled joy as she prepared
to head off to the Kansas City convention. She was giddy with delight
anticipating the climactic finish to her long fight to elect Herbert Hoover.
Accompanying her in the photograph is Marion Fitts, wife of District
Attorney Buron Fitts, just before they boarded the Santa Fe Chief. After
a stop in San Francisco, they would travel with the usual band of state
notables, including Mr. and Mrs. Louis B. Mayer. The two women were
standing with a huge drumhead bearing Hoover's portrait publicizing the
special train.[8]

It was a time of excitement and jubilant merriment. Several thousand
people were expected to bid farewell to the delegates at the Alexandria
Hotel, followed by a torchlight parade to Central Station. Los Angeles
Mayor George Cryer gave them an official goodwill sendoff. The train
would make whistle-stops all along the American Canyon route. Upon
their arrival in Kansas City, as usual, the Golden State delegates "stirred

the pot," supplying "nearly all the visible evidence of political enthusiasm." They "lost no time letting Kansas City know they had come and why," aided by the band roaring out "California, Here I Come," and long lines of decked-out automobiles blasting their horns, "oozing through the downtown streets." Red, white, and blue Hoover hat ribbons and armbands were flaunted everywhere. San Francisco's Mayor James Rolph toted the state's Bear Flag, leading the parade through the streets toward the great convention hall for a boisterous Hoover rally. The famous hotelier Mark Hopkins sprinkled poppies and Hoover buttons. Because the westerners were unaccustomed to Kansas City heat, however, they caused a stir when the men showed up in "ice-cream trousers" and "sport shoes," with Louis B. Mayer "not the least conspicuous" among them.[9]

The golden-poppy-badge-wearing California delegates brought a splash of color to the affair. Ida Koverman and Mabel Walker Willebrandt managed the delegation's "charming and attractive" headquarters and later, at the bonfire Hoover rally, a golden-yellow poppy glow radiated in every direction. The city turned into a temporary Mecca for devoted followers, and the $100,000 they were spending was welcomed by Hoover supporters and opponents alike. Unfortunately, along with the heat, the humidity rose, and a morning torrent drenched delegates as they straggled in on opening day, June 12. While excitement filled the hall, behind the scenes the internecine battles began. Mabel Walker Willebrandt sat on a number of committees, more than any other woman, and in recognition of her national stature, this included chair of the Committee on Credentials. As was often the case, that committee was soon embroiled in a volatile, eleven-hour fight over the selection and recognition of delegates from Texas and another kerfuffle over delegates from Georgia.[10]

California's Hoover delegates could not be ignored as they sat prominently in the front rows, bursting into rowdy demonstrations at the mere mention of Herbert Hoover's name. Ida Koverman had worked for eight long years for this moment, and the exuberance heightened when Alabama immediately yielded to California, which sparked more cheering. John L. McNab struggled to deliver his introductory remarks as a collective euphoria exploded in a thundering, uninterrupted cacophony for the next twenty-four minutes, spurred on by delegates carrying huge photographs of Hoover through the hall. McNab filled his speech with the usual praises and reminded the partisans that the "millions who make up the womanhood of America" needed "to heed the tremendous power of that spiritual force upon the affairs of today." This inspired California's delegation to lead another jubilant, twenty-two-minute march. When

McNab repeatedly pounded his gavel for order, revelers shouted even louder over his appeals.[11] When Herbert Hoover finally formally won the nomination with a vote of 1,089 to 837, Ida Koverman was showered with accolades such as from columnist Kyle Palmer, who wrote that Ida Koverman and Mabel Walker Willebrandt played a substantial part in the victory. Ralph Arnold later wrote that Koverman and Willebrandt were "two women politicians [who] stood out, as of importance and strength, equal to that of any man," and were most credited with securing the nomination of Herbert Hoover.[12]

Once the celebration subsided, Koverman and Arnold offered advice to the nominee about how to run his campaign and how to handle his loyal supporters. Koverman established a rapport with Hoover's aide, George Akerson, who would soon become the nation's first presidential press secretary. After he left the White House, Akerson joined Paramount Studios and then 20th Century Fox. In a sense, George Akerson's career is another example of the growing courtship between Hollywood and Washington.[13]

This new connection between politics and pictures was not lost on popular New York Mayor Jimmy Walker. He observed how the motion-picture industry "had been delivered into the camp of the major political parties," and that if the industry allowed its neutrality to be violated in the 1928 presidential campaign, it must expect the consequences of such partisanship if it guessed wrong. In fact, Walker threatened that "so long as the organized motion picture industry sticks to its function of entertainment it has a right to expect the cooperation of public officials, regardless of their political affiliations, in the development of the industry's legitimate business. But if it departs from its own field to enter the field of partisan politics, it must accept the consequences of partisanship." Walker said that he preferred to believe that the individuals who made up the motion-picture industry "are not so enslaved that they can be handed over," nor were "two or three men prominent in the industry" strong enough to swing the political influence of the screen in one direction or the other. His remarks were inspired by the visible activities of movie moguls Louis B. Mayer, producer Joseph Schenck, and MPPDA chair Will Hays. Moviegoing audiences paid little attention to the political machinations of movie moguls, and they hardly noticed how the courtship of American politics and motion pictures was moving closer to consummation with the ultimate election of Herbert Hoover.[14]

The glow of the convention soon faded, and by mid-July, Ida Koverman was once again "thoroughly disgusted" with intraparty tensions that were accelerating just as the imperative of unity was upon them. Ralph Arnold was in Montana while Koverman prepared for the bloodletting. Members of the County Committee's eastern Ninth District had gnawed at them for years, and now both her and Arnold's seats were up for re-election. She reassured Arnold that their opponents would fail in "their brag of keeping us both out," but she had her unspoken doubts. She was "not only willing to quit . . . and . . . would give anything under the sun if we could both get out," but she assured that they were not going to be forced out, telling Arnold, "Let's finish the job and then quit in our own way" and make "a determined effort to re-elect both you and myself to the positions we now hold." She determined, "We are going to be successful," but ultimately, this would be true for only one of them.

Arnold retained his loyalists who, she told him, were "very much interested in retaining you as chairman." As for the troublemakers, "They are due for a whipping and they know they are going to get it, so one by one they are gradually climbing on the bandwagon." She said he still had some control over the situation, and defeat was far from the only outcome. "We have been doing a little whip cracking ourselves and it is reaching home," she said, and thus if he was approached, she urged, "Now don't say 'no,'" and "let's get through with our job and then kick them." Finally, she cautioned, "So far as you are concerned you know nothing about this move to re-elect you and you have no comments to make on the next group of officers to be elected . . . that's your story—now stick to it."[15]

Soothing Arnold's ego was only part of her job dealing with the anxiety permeating party headquarters, once again facing financial distress. Hoover's friend, banker Henry M. Robinson, wrote to Arnold about the committee's deficit and the salaries of Koverman and Nellie Kelley, which he understood to be more of a problem of distribution of current funds rather than raising more. Arnold contacted another potential donor to say, "We are indebted to Mrs. Koverman and Miss Kelley in a very considerable amount for back salaries over the last two years," and so to him it was incomprehensible how they carried on their wonderful work without compensation. Nellie Kelley, in fact, he said, was more responsible than anyone else for the success of women's Republican organizations.[16]

August was a particularly busy month, and Koverman again worked alongside Mendel Silberberg, director of Southern California's Hoover Campaign Committee, and state chair Mark Requa. Hoover's acceptance speech was scheduled for August 11 at Stanford University's stadium. Koverman happily told the press how quickly the tickets were being snapped up. She arranged the Los Angeles contingent's trek up north, while she stayed in Los Angeles to listen to Hoover over the radio. She offered Hoover feedback, telling him it was enthusiastically received and even inspired favorable comments from previously unfriendly sources.[17]

Acting Los Angeles Mayor William G. Bonelli extended an official invitation to Hoover, but his failure to respond forced Koverman to tell George Akerson the "Mayor's office very much disturbed," and requested an immediate official acceptance. After her prodding, Hoover's acceptance quickly followed, and she began planning for his arrival, including an inquiry about who would be in the entourage, important details for VIP accommodations of the group that ultimately numbered over fifty. Back-and-forth communications handled details about the press corps following Hoover's motorcade, which noted that at least "two cars should be set aside for the moving picture people" and that the police were required to follow Hoover's car because they were responsible for his security while in the city.[18]

In preparation for this campaign season, the years of Ida Koverman and Nellie Kelley's organizing efforts to build a Hoover army through the network of Republican Study Clubs was now going to bear fruit with the launch of its mission "to begin one of the most important seasons of its entire history." In spite of the momentum for the national presidential campaign, however, ongoing local simmering tensions came to a head regarding the September elections for members of the County Committee. Ralph Arnold decided that because he had fulfilled his promise to Hoover to loosen Hiram Johnson's grip on the state Republican Party, it was time for him to step down, and so he withdrew his bid for re-election as committee chair. Even though Ida Koverman's cheerleading had accelerated as Arnold's influence declined, it was still a disappointment that Arnold's decision came so close to the projected Hoover victory. The true import of her supporting role becomes clearer when it is viewed within the larger context of her entire life and her next incarnation at the side of Louis B. Mayer.[19] For now, though, she had to fortify her own survival against a power grab by the Ninth District. Party post elections within local fiefdoms rarely attract attention, but the call to elect new officers brought three hundred partisans downtown trying to cram into a courtroom, forcing them to move to newly built City Hall across the street.

Col. William Eric Fowler was elected to replace Ralph Arnold as chairman of the County Central Committee, after which he read Arnold's farewell message to the increasingly boisterous crowd, which included Arnold's fulsome endorsement of Ida Koverman's re-election as executive secretary. "There is one whose close association with the details of our work has been such that I would be an ingrate indeed if I did not mention her," he said, and so "to her belongs much of the credit that has come to me for the success of our work . . . that indefatigable, unselfish, constructive stateswoman, Mrs. Ida R. Koverman." Attorney Joseph Scott jumped up to enthusiastically nominate her, and then all hell broke loose.[20]

The gathering turned into a melee "distinguished for tumult, disorder and disregard of a semblance of parliamentary rules," when attorney Ralph S. Armour challenged Ida Koverman's candidacy. After a heated debate, he lost 108 votes to Koverman's 180, which inspired another revolt. The whole meeting was a big mess, but Chairman Fowler tried to quickly push through his agenda; the newly elected members kept "the meeting in noisy disorder for more than two hours," his shouts for order being ignored amidst "pounding with sticks and boards on tables and floor." When anyone tried to enter their reports for the record, they "became entangled in a maze of technicalities and shouts of objection," until Joseph Scott's "stentorian voice" rose above "the medley of scrapping chairs" and disparate heated arguments and won hearty applause in praise of Hoover as the nation's greatest leader.[21]

Ida Koverman's fortitude overcame the auspicious start of her fourth term as executive secretary. In spite of "certain enemies" who tried to defeat her, Arnold later explained how "she swamped the opposition and there was no question in anybody's mind as to who was still the political boss of Los Angeles County."[22] She also had to counter rumors that she "had run [Arnold] out of politics." She chided him about how "the disgraceful organization meeting of your county committee . . . would have made a good mob scene," and that she was happy she wasn't responsible "for the exhibition they made of themselves." The incident also inspired deeper feelings about the necessity of "forgetting so far as possible the opposition of some of my old friends. It is all in the game of politics and we must look at it that way and not too personal . . . I shall certainly be most happy when I can walk out of the office and say 'finis' to politics and this I most certainly intend to do at the close of the campaign. I am thoroughly sick of the whole thing and only a sense of loyalty to the Chief keeps me until November 6."[23] Signaling a future incarnation, she gave no hint of what she imagined a new life away from politics would be.

George B. Bush became the official chair and treasurer of the local Hoover campaign committee, but to her the post of secretary was the preferred one because there she could "get things done," rather "than standing out front, taking the honors as chairman."[24] Over time, one task would increasingly become part of her day-to-day job description, the getting and gifting of autographed photographs, now of Herbert Hoover for his key supporters, and later the sharing of politicos and movie stars for each other and fans of both. Her correspondence with Hoover's secretary, Lawrence Richey, included scores of requests for autographed photos, and often they took turns boosting each other's mood as election day neared. After she saw Richey at the movies, she wrote, "You surely looked tired—just the way I feel. Never mind, we will celebrate after November 6! If we live that long."[25]

She was renting Studio 26 in the historic Granada Shoppe at 672 South Lafayette Park Place, alongside the Vegetarian Tea Room, the lingerie shop, the Valmedine Studio that offered Mental, Oral, and Physical Harmonie, and other specialists who offered book reviews, osteopathic medicine, furs, and interior decorating. More meetings and rallies brought together party leaders. Republican Federated Women held a Hoover rally when campaign chair Mendel B. Silberberg introduced Mrs. Florence Collins Porter, who introduced Ida R. Koverman, who called for local reports, including one by Nellie E. Kelley. Koverman reported that ten thousand copies of "How to Win Votes for Hoover" were distributed throughout the region, and a few days later, the southern wing of the Republican Federation held its fourth annual convention with Koverman in charge of local arrangements, and where she easily won re-election as state secretary. Four days before the November presidential election, Ida Koverman and Nellie Kelley were honored at a party thrown by the Southwest Women's Republican Club that featured the famous Blues Chase Orchestra.[26]

Targeted appeals were made to the polyglot citizens who hailed from foreign lands, with KNX radio airing "outstanding musical-political pro-grams" in eleven languages, reminding everyone that Americans were drawn from diverse nationalities. Women voters were courted with appeals echoing the "unique" female attributes of "the fairer sex." These efforts paid off. Herbert Hoover won 444 electoral-college votes to Democrat Al Smith's 87, with Hoover's 59 percent popular vote to Smith's 41 percent. The total vote for all candidates combined beat the 1924 presidential election by almost eight million votes, and Ida Koverman and her allies could be proud of the more than three hundred thousand plurality for Hoover, a greater number than found in entire states.[27]

Within days of Hoover's victory, Lawrence Richey sent Koverman a questionnaire to analyze the election. She was just too exhausted, so she gave the task to George Bush, who was happy to report that much of his pre-election suppositions were borne out, including that "women played a much more important part in this campaign than in any other campaign with which I have been connected, and I likewise believe that the Chief [Hoover] benefited more by the participation of women in this campaign than did [Al] Smith." Richey responded to the news about Koverman. He was "sorry she had so much campaigning! It was a big fight though and everybody was pressed pretty hard."[28]

Ralph Arnold later described how "the primary and election of 1928 was again handled locally by our committee with Mrs. Ida Koverman in control," so the victory was a joyous climax for her devoted, near-decade-long efforts. Koverman simply explained that "it was our job to translate Hoover's popularity into votes," and they successfully fulfilled their mission.[29] But for her, the more important moment came midway when Hoover won the nomination. After that, her activities multiplied, the internecine warfare grew exponentially, and Ralph Arnold's business interests pulled him away until his opponents finally pushed him out. After the general election, when it was all over, she could not avoid facing the looming question about what she was going to do next and how she was going to support herself.

The existential problem meant she needed to find employment that would not only secure a steady income but would also draw on her extraordinary professional skills and experience. She had worked with the biggest names in politics, fought and negotiated with idiosyncratic personalities and polarized factions, raised the political cachet of the County Committee and women operatives within it, and built up legions of voters in the party's ranks. Where could such an influential politico go, especially one with a passion for opera and an uncanny sensitivity for assessing popular taste?

It is possible that, as was casually rumored somewhere in the Koverman ether, Ida Koverman really did decline a post in Hoover's administration, but if she did, she might have already had her sights set somewhere in particular. It would have likely been a job with an unusually diverse job description in a high-stakes operation. Whatever it was, she faced an unknowable future, and possibly another bout of despair. So, while the victory was sweet for Hoover supporters everywhere, for Ida R. Koverman it must also have been a frightening scenario.

CHAPTER 12

Matchmaker

Politics and Pictures

Louis B. Mayer's "real entrée was a middle-aged bulldog of a woman named Ida Koverman."[1]

REPUBLICANS EVERYWHERE WERE ECSTATIC AT HEBERT HOOVER'S 1928 victory, and in California, women partisans were beside themselves. Credit for Hoover's success went to the women's vote, and in Southern California, Ida Koverman and her allies all but assured the outcome and thus reveled in proportionate measure. The election proved that women were central to the courtship and now marriage of Hollywood and American politics, and Ida R. Koverman was their matchmaker. Her role continued long after the wedding reception, more commonly known as the presidential inauguration, and for decades to come she re-emerged as a sort of mother-in-law to both Herbert Hoover and Louis B. Mayer.

A victory banquet at the Biltmore Hotel, hosted by MGM director Fred Niblo, celebrated the consummation of MGM and the Republican Party. Louis B. Mayer directed his "high compliments," to the notable women in the audience, inspiring Niblo to jump up, grab the microphone, and proclaim he now understood what Louis B. Mayer's middle initial stood for—"Bologney! [sic]" The less colorful but popular attorney Joseph Scott also praised women's efforts in the campaign, and he advised the less than attentive men there to not let "the women think they did it all," even if it was the truth.[2]

Ida Koverman was unable to attend the celebration, still "suffering from the reaction of an extremely strenuous campaign." She was not overlooked, though. It was clear that everyone was "most proud" of her because at the mere mention of her name, the crowd "bubbled spontaneously and joyously" and repeatedly gave "hats-off" to Ida, and all agreed that as their leader, she was the "one woman with whom men like to work shoulder to shoulder." Her colleagues knew "she will play the game straight, knows the finesse of politics, keeps her eye on the main issue, is downright, forthwith," and every other synonym for such high praise.[3]

Congratulatory galas were held throughout the country, while the president-elect decided to embark on a goodwill tour of South America. The trip extended Hoover's role as the secretary of commerce and his promotion of a global network of international corporate finance. Ida Koverman coordinated plans for the local leg of his journey, including arrival to and departure from San Pedro harbor, just south of Los Angeles. There were concerns about local security and the public relations needed to deal with the anticipated hordes of fans that would try to get a glimpse of the new commander in chief. She suggested a series of "meet and greets" and the use of a microphone, fearing there would be great disappointment of the throngs if they could not see or even hear him. After the decision to forgo a formal reception at the dock, they arranged for a group of school children to greet Mrs. Hoover before the entourage boarded the barge that would take them to the battleship anchored out in deeper waters.[4]

Ida Koverman was clearly an expert in the realm of politics and partying. She was a featured speaker at one Republican Study Club meeting on the subject of "Political Entertainment," and over the next few weeks, she used her connections with Louis B. Mayer and MGM to promote Herbert Hoover. A red carpet premiere was held at the Criterion Theatre featuring a new "talkie" about his life. All of the city's Republican elite attended, and they were "led by the always languid, lovely lady Ida Koverman." Soon enough, it was time to arrange the state party's pilgrimage to Washington, DC, for Hoover's March 1929 inauguration. She suggested ideas about proper protocol to Hoover's secretary, Lawrence Richey, and in particular about Hoover's need to quickly recognize California's Republican Party leaders for their role in the campaign. She emphasized Hoover's need "to throw a bone" to leaders of his California campaigns, his longtime friend and fellow mining engineer Mark Requa from the north and the Southland's Louis B. Mayer.[5]

Mayer biographers have used Koverman's suggestion to Richey as evidence of Mayer's deep-seated insecurities. Because of their focus on the mogul, they miss the larger import of Koverman's observation that actually tells us less about Louis B. Mayer than about her own understanding of powerful men, even top-tier political figures, who needed nurturing and overt acknowledgement for a job well done. What's more, her letter to Richey suggests that without her personal lobbying, their invitations to the inner circle of inaugural activities might not have been forthcoming.

Writing to Richey, Koverman said that it was imperative for Hoover to invite Mark Requa to the Washington inaugural or to Florida, where the president-elect would be staying before heading to the capital. Requa really wanted to go, but he didn't want to appear too eager. Koverman explained, "We all have tender feelings and an old mortal mind does make us feel sad and neglected at times," and this might be particularly true for Requa, who had recently retired, and, she said, if he wasn't kept "extremely busy," he would become very nervous and unhappy. She came to view Hoover's loyal servants in sympathetic, maternal ways, and Requa reminded her "of a very loveable little boy," so she wanted "to see him made happy for he certainly is a wonderful man."[6]

Then she shifted her attention to Louis B. Mayer, prefacing her comment with a bit of self-reflection: "You know, Larry, everyone isn't as 'hard boiled' as you and I," and after years of laboring in the party's trenches, she noted "personally, I can be neglected and even mistreated and still come back and put my nose in the door as of old." But, she said, men like Louis B. Mayer cannot be overlooked, and reminded Richey of a previous conversation about Hoover "making a gesture" toward Mayer, perhaps an invitation to Florida. The next line of her letter is the oft-repeated quote, removed from the larger context that included Requa. She described Mayer as just "another small boy—new at the game, and used to a great deal of attention. I know he would strut around like a proud pigeon," just the recognition Mayer needed at this particular moment due to the recent effort by William Fox to buy MGM. She wrote, "People closely allied . . . with whom he is intimately associated . . . sort of 'rub it in' that his efforts are now a thing of the past," and his fear that he is "more or less in the discard." Koverman need not have worried. When Mayer's invitation came, it acknowledged his special status in a way he could not have imagined. But his name, contrary to repeated claims, was not being floated for a diplomatic post in Turkey. In fact, as early as February 1929, Ida Koverman had sent Lawrence Richey samples of newspaper clippings about Mayer's denial that such an offer was made or even considered. A few weeks later, Ida Koverman, and Mark Requa boarded the California Hoover inaugural train along with Mayer's entourage, made up of his wife and two daughters, Irene and Elizabeth, and his secretary, Margaret Bennett.[7]

Herbert Hoover took his oath of office on March 4, 1929, on a drab and gloomy day, but it was the first one to be recorded by a talking newsreel capturing a mood that looked more like a day of national mourning than a day to celebrate a hard-fought victory. After the initial hoopla, the Mayer family left for New York, while Koverman stayed behind to enjoy the fireworks and parties where she mingled with state delegations. Partisans from across the country, including women of national stature, such as Mabel Walker Willebrandt, attended luncheons and dinners hosted by the First Family. The Mayers returned on March 12 to Washington, where Ida Koverman joined them for an intimate "family dinner" in the White House. After tours and conversation, the Mayers were Hoover's first overnight guests, which Mayer later savored as a reaffirmation of his great success in America. He was an "immigrant boy, born in Russia," who was a house "guest of the President of the United States."[8]

Louis B. Mayer's stay in the Lincoln bedroom symbolizes the consummation of the marriage between Hollywood and the Republican Party, and Ida Koverman's significance as matchmaker. Historian Steven Ross noted Ida Koverman's importance to Mayer, but when he argued that Mayer was "the first Hollywood figure to obtain direct access to the president and his cabinet," he ignored Mayer biographer Scott Eyman's conclusion that "the true bond seems to have been between Hoover and Koverman."[9]

MGM producer Samuel Marx explained why Ida looked out for her "old boss," as he unintentionally perpetuated the notion that she had worked directly for Hoover. Marx admitted, "Well . . . let's face it," the president "wasn't exactly a barrel of fun when they put a microphone in front of him. He was well read, he knew books and could quote from the classics, yes . . . he was very accomplished in many ways, but he was also a colossal bore."[10]

Throughout the months prior to the inauguration, Koverman made recommendations to Richey for posts in the new administration. Some authors have suggested Louis B. Mayer exercised a new level of influence in the selection of Hoover appointments. When it came to a new regional tax collector, neither Koverman nor Mayer had much sway, and Mayer failed to "throw his weight around" like a political boss, "meting out patronage appointments." Mayer opposed the reappointment of Galen H. Welch, and even recruited Mark Requa and Mabel Walker Willebrandt to promote Brainerd B. Smith, the current register of the land office. Galen Welch had faithfully carried out his duties, among those involved in the Julian stock scandal, the dismissal of a tax lien against the Rudolph Valentino estate, and going after theater mogul Alexander Pantages for claiming as a deductible business expense his defense attorney's fees in his prosecution for raping a young girl. Whatever Mayer's opposition, Welch retained his position at the IRS until 1933. Ida Koverman set up a meeting through Richey, after initially forgetting about Schenck," but urged Richey to "arrange for him [to] see Chief . . . suggested not later than Monday," and then she wired Schenck to contact Richey upon arrival in Washington.[11]

During the transition and early months of the administration, there was widespread speculation that Hoover would appoint a woman to his cabinet, but ultimately, that historic choice came with his successor. Nevertheless, because women had used their vote "to considerable effect in the election of Mr. Hoover," men were now "gloomily" realizing that "something certainly must be done for the ladies." An obvious choice was Mabel Walker Willebrandt. Ida Koverman threw a luncheon in her honor where columnist Alma Whitaker noted, "Mabel was looking a little tired—she had done her share so ardently to elect Hoover, and it hasn't spoiled her dimples yet." Whitaker's keen observation hinted at something deeper. In spite of Willebrandt's vigorous efforts on Hoover's behalf, she had been losing influence with him.[12]

Willebrandt was never even considered for a cabinet post or the logical choice of attorney general. Contrary to the repeated assertion that she had been appointed by Hoover, she had already served a nine-year tenure in the Department of Justice, and she actually submitted her resignation to Hoover on May 15, 1929, effective the following month. One of her last acts before leaving office, however, was assisting Louis B. Mayer in obtaining nullification of William Fox's attempt to buy MGM from the Justice Department. Ida Koverman was glad that Willebrandt resigned because Willebrandt "would be crucified" if prohibition was overturned, and even if it was not, just "as she has been in the past no matter which way it goes." Koverman told her audience, "It is time for some man to take on the big job."[13]

When Louis B. Mayer retained Willebrandt as counsel for MGM, it was hardly surprising. Throughout the 1930s, she advised Mayer and MGM stars such as Jean Harlow, Clark Gable, and Jeannette MacDonald, all coincidentally close friends of Ida Koverman. Willebrandt would later ally with Mendel Silberberg to formalize industry-wide anti-communist policies, and she urged the FBI to investigate German-born actress Marlene

Dietrich for communist or fascist subversion. After agents looked into it, the case was dropped.[14]

Koverman stayed on at Republican Party headquarters during the first year of Hoover's administration, working alongside Mrs. Buron Fitts and Mrs. Florence Collins Porter in the Republican Study Club, and after one trip to the White House in early June, she told the Study Club members that there were "terrific battles in terrific heat being fought in Washington and President Hoover needs every ounce of support we can give him." Described as a "woman politician," she said Hoover's job "is one of the greatest any President has had." The three main challenges confronting the president and Congress, she told the audience, were "reapportionment, farm relief and prohibition enforcement." Reapportionment was an increasingly important issue for Southern Californians, with its rising population and political influence, and shifting congressional representation was crucial. She said, "We will have five or six Representatives from Los Angeles County," and in this, she noted, "the singular thing about the fight is that California and New York are together." Koverman's stature continued to rise, and her name was on a list for a post in the US Housing Corporation in the Department of Labor. Apparently she had an interview for some position, but when Mark Requa mentioned it, he failed to reveal with whom or what it was for, but it clearly indicates that she was pursuing leads for securing a new job, even returning to the capitol, staying at the Hotel Mayflower."[15]

Ida Koverman turned fifty-one years old within weeks of Hoover's election. She was a "zaftig," full-figured matron, with cropped white hair framing her round eyeglasses, and no matter how energetic and zestful, she was still a grandmotherly figure, albeit one with extraordinary, seductive, professional capabilities. It turns out that Louis B. Mayer was well aware of her talents, and he wanted them exercised on his behalf. Neither of them realized, however, that she wasn't just a kingmaker, but a star maker as well. With their formal alliance, they would ensure that the love affair between MGM and the Republican Party and women's groups would continue long after Hoover's election. Just exactly when Koverman joined Mayer at MGM remains unclear. As biographer Bosley Crowther explained, the two first met during the 1924 Coolidge presidential campaign, but that it was through a man named Rasty Wright is less clear. Wright supposedly introduced Mayer as a "willing worker" to Koverman when he was told to find a movie projector for her to view recent footage of the campaign. Rasty Wright's name appears on a handwritten organizational chart for the statewide Coolidge campaign, identified as the head of the "Non-Partisan Get Out the Vote Committee," which was just one of several divisions Ida Koverman oversaw in her role as executive secretary of the Southern California campaign. Charles Higham suggested the later, formal MGM-Koverman association began sometime between March 1929 and December 1930, during MGM's shooting of the movie *Trader Horn*, when "Mayer made a very important decision" to offer Koverman the position of executive assistant. No matter when she joined the payroll of MGM, or what her title, it was clear from the start that she would be "far more than a secretary," and soon many believed Ida Koverman was "considered the most important person in the studio next to Mayer and [Irving] Thalberg."[16]

Signs that the historic partnership between Ida Koverman and Louis B. Mayer was forming came during the winter of 1929, when her correspondence with Lawrence Richey on December 28, written on MGM letterhead, thanked Richey for an autographed picture of Hoover she could forward to a local constituent. Such requests would become commonplace and a valued commodity she brokered over the next two and a half decades. She later explained to a reporter that her transition from politics to pictures came when Mayer simply "offered her just a part-time position and a chance to help out wherever she saw an opportunity to be of service." Mayer instinctively trusted that her skills would serve him well on and off the studio lot. He gave her a desk "and told her to make a job for herself," and so, as she said, it began "with little jobs [that soon] became big jobs."[17]

Once ensconced at MGM, the cycle of political campaigns and the scathing intramural warfare would no longer dictate her life and financial security. And even though a December 26 news item reported that "Ida Koverman . . . has forsaken politics for screenland," there was never a clean break, intentionally so.[18] "Although Mr. Mayer's chief interest, outside of the new car, lies in the business of making motion pictures, . . . he devotes no little time and effort backing his favorite political candidates for office." The author explained that Mayer now "employs continuously a political expert in the person of Mrs. Ida Koverman, whose sole duties are to keep Mr. Mayer advised politically." Her credentials matched the job description perfectly, because "Mrs. Koverman knows everyone worthwhile in the civic and political world, and on the walls of her office hang personally autographed portraits of President Hoover and former Presidents Wilson, Harding and Coolidge."[19]

She now sat at her new desk just outside of Louis B. Mayer's office on the second floor of the old colonial-style wardrobe building, connected by metal walkways to MGM's other senior personnel. A few years later, when the new executive-office Thalberg Building was finished, she worked in yet another iconic, now historic, edifice. Throughout her professional life, she had existed close to the centers of power, in symbolic constructions that had extended the hand of the federal government at the US Customs office and then later celebrated the wealth and rise of America's titans of commerce in New York's Woolworth Building. Now, she sat at the center of power at MGM in a new industrial order, and she would draw on her established administrative expertise and enjoy new expressions of her artistic passions as a cultural influencer during Hollywood's Golden Era and beyond.

Once safely charting a new course, it was time for Koverman to settle up with the Los Angeles Republican Party's County Central Committee. She had been receiving a steady paycheck of $50 through the end of November 1925. By the end of the following year, while she and Ralph Arnold struggled to keep the County Committee office up and running, she received erratic weekly payments of between $100 and $150. Throughout the spring, there were semi-regular $50 checks totaling $1,100, averaging $157 per month, or just over $39 per week, which was quite a good salary compared to the national average of $14.60 per week or $750 per year. The problem was its inconsistent nature. After the election, the County Committee still owed Ida Koverman $5,200, so she presented Arnold a bill for services at $50 a week for November, 1925, through March, 1928. She received just over $2,000 of the debt from an assortment of donations between $10 and $100, and one for $562.50.[20]

Nellie Kelley also reached out to Arnold, and the back and forth about the particulars went on for quite a while—for another two decades, in fact. She made claims for as far back as the 1924 Calvin Coolidge presidential campaign and up through various campaign seasons to 1928. Arnold initiated a subscription list from Ida Koverman's inner circle—longtime leaders within the party, women's clubs, and Hollywood. Some of them balked, with complaints ranging from the expenditures not being appropriate for the committee given that Ida Koverman said Kelley's organizing efforts were in collaboration with the Republican Study Club. Nevertheless, this one critic concluded that because of the magnitude and importance of Kelley's "first class" and "thoroughly successful" work, he would gladly contribute $100 and lobby the RNC for more contributions.[21]

Others remained skeptical, and suggested that Kelley had already "been well taken care of." Her work was amply rewarded when she landed a plumb job in the office of District Attorney Buron Fitts. Over the last few years, Ida Koverman and Louis B. Mayer had developed a mutually beneficial relationship with DA Fitts, and now their able colleague had a high-profile position with his office. As Buron "Fitts's Attaché," Nellie Kelley was an invaluable asset to Koverman and Mayer's interests, while she continued speaking to women's groups about the DA's office and "good citizenship." Years later, when Kelley renewed her efforts for compensation, Ralph Arnold forwarded her letter to Ida Koverman at MGM because "she has kept up with the political situation much more than I have and might be able to interest some of the present party leaders in your case."[22]

Fitts was a popular figure, except in 1930 when he decided to run for governor. No one thought it was a good idea. Koverman suggested Herbert Hoover refrain from commenting, which was great advice because the party's displeasure was widely known, and the press described how his "high strung and tempestuous" demeanor rendered "him unfit" to survive a rigorous campaign.[23]

Louis B. Mayer had an ambivalent relationship with Buron Fitts, but their bond was strengthened by Koverman's teaching that politics required ongoing nurturing. Koverman's friendship with Mrs. Marion Fitts also blossomed, and Mrs. Fitts's ambition brought personal success while she promoted the same for her husband.

Midway through Hoover's presidential term, a newly established body, the United States Board of Parole, oversaw the parole process for those convicted of federal crimes. One of the names floated for a seat on the board was Ida Koverman, which inspired Mabel Walker Willebrandt to write to Hoover. Just as Katherine Philips Edson had argued six years earlier, Willebrandt also suggested that although "Koverman would do the work in an outstanding manner and miss no opportunity for loyalty and effective service," there were other more qualified women "who have outstanding names" and who were directly involved in penal matters, along with devoted service to the Republican Party.[24] Whether Koverman was aware of or cared one way or the other about the possibility of the appointment didn't matter at all, because by then, her political prowess was morphing into a new incarnation, calling on a kind of talent in the moviemaking business, and the local press wanted everyone to know about it. Newspaper columnists had their eyes on Ida Koverman for a decade, and professional writers adored her. Soon after joining MGM, industry related groups sought her out, such as her recruitment to the Women's Association of Screen Publicists (WASPS), also identified as the Screen Women's Press Club, and two years later, she was elected director. Ida Koverman's ability to maintain the relationship between MGM and local women's clubs was by now a well-honed art. Louis B. Mayer also followed Koverman's advice and joined numerous civic, business, religious, and political groups.[25] Like Herbert Hoover, Mayer needed to pay attention to women's groups because of their increasingly influential politicized, partisan organizations.

With the marriage of politics and Hollywood, Louis B. Mayer's political cachet and MGM were magnets for candidates and elected officials from around the country and beyond. Under Koverman's continued guidance during the Rolph-Merriam gubernatorial campaign, Mayer joined Koverman and their allies Buron Fitts, Nellie Kelley, and Joseph Scott at meetings of the Women's City Club, the Women's Breakfast Club, the Republican Federation of Women, and local branches of the California Federation of Women's Clubs. After the state election, Mayer and his family hosted a luncheon for Governor Rolph at the Ambassador Hotel, clearly an Ida Koverman event but reportedly merely assisting Mrs. Mayer and her two daughters, Mrs. David Selznick and Mrs. William Goetz. On his own Louis B. Mayer attracted the A-list of guests, but now his affairs reflected the years of Ida Koverman's coalition building and hardcore politicking.[26]

In turn, women's groups acknowledged Mayer's attentiveness. When the Woman's Breakfast Club honored Mayer, it was an MGM affair. Pete Smith of MGM's publicity department served as "the genial master of ceremonies," the studio's orchestra and singers entertained, and producer Harry Rapf spoke. Mayer was seated on a spotted wooden horse on the stage for the highlight of the night, his initiation as a "pal" of the Breakfast Club, presided over by Mrs. Haele Freeman. As the target of the jibes and jokes, Mayer endeared himself to the audience as he seductively told Mrs. Freeman he would make her a star. She responded in a slow, sultry voice, advising Mayer to "just relax," as if he were about to be examined by a chiropractor. She made him promise to give screen tests to all of the club's members, and then he rose to speak, posing as if he were confiding his deepest secrets to each and every one of them. He told them that even though he was no longer young and "no longer has ardor for the opposite sex," he could still make them all stars, and promised free passes to any MGM show. Mrs. Freeman coyly remarked that Mayer certainly understood "the club's 700 members even if their husbands did not." Mayer flirted with the audience and confessed that he had always been a little jealous of director Cecil B. DeMille. But now, he could boast of at least seven hundred platonic lovers, and now "having just turned forty," he joked, he was of "the dangerous age," which delighted everyone. Pete Smith closed the program with the presentation of MGM's iconic lion,

Leo, who unfortunately frightened many of the ladies, as one observer said a well-trained lion should do.[27]

Ida Koverman's new preoccupation with the studio didn't preclude her from being an asset to Hoover's secretary Lawrence Richey, and she asked for favors, too, such as for the use of live ammunition for a motion picture, which elicited a personal response from the secretary of war, Patrick J. Hurley, informing her that such a purchase was impossible under current law.[28]

She secured letters of introduction at American diplomatic offices for director Cecil B. DeMille and his wife Constance during their trip to Europe and the Soviet Union, scouting potential projects. Koverman passed on Mayer's suggestion that Hoover "might be interested in meeting Mr. DeMille" during his stopover in Washington, DC. She thought the president would find the director "a very interesting guest." Koverman also wrote to Richey about a US visa for Valentin Kataev, which was sent on to Secretary of State Henry Stimson with a request "to be good enough to advise Mrs. Koverman, what, if anything, could be done."[29]

In the fall of 1930, Ida Koverman's eight-year tenure as the executive secretary of the Los Angeles County Central Committee finally came to an end, but as she was invited to sit on diverse political and cultural committees and participate in numerous causes, her network and influence expanded. In the spring of 1931, she supported the re-election of municipal court judge Frederickson, alongside Mrs. Leiland Atherton Irish, who became a lifelong ally in their mutual passion for classical music and the Hollywood Bowl. Koverman's name was included with high-powered professional and organized clubwomen who wholeheartedly supported a $6 million bond issue to improve the city's sewer system, for which Koverman was planning an event where the governor and "many film stars" were expected to attend. She hosted a luncheon at MGM for Mrs. Irish and the Citizens' Traffic Safety Committee launching the city's Safety Week, featuring movies designed to promote the cause.[30]

Epitomizing Louis B. Mayer's relationship with Ida Koverman, Mendel Silberberg, and Mabel Walker Willebrandt was their promotion of his election to vice chair of Republican State Central Committee in 1930. And while this kind of politicking was part of her legacy, it reflected the threads of her personal and professional efforts as well as the larger fabric of regional political change and the movie industry's place within its rising economic power. But, as her new incarnation evolved, none of these colleagues ever imagined she would continue to shape the course of MGM and American popular culture for decades to come.

PART III

LIFE THREE— MOVIE STAR MAKER

CHAPTER 13

Friends in High Places

Ida Koverman was "proudly acquired by L.B. not only as a sign of class but as a means of moving up the Republican ladder to the lofty appointments for which he panted."[1]

IDA KOVERMAN MIGHT NOT HAVE REALIZED KATHERINE PHILIPS EDSON was responsible for her loss as Republican national committeewoman in 1923, but Edson was well aware of Koverman's alliance with Louis B. Mayer and her role in promoting his stature within the party, coincidentally paralleling her growing interest in the motion-picture industry. Kate Edson knew her tenure on the Industrial Welfare Commission was threatened after the 1930 election of California Governor James "Sunny" Rolph, who was "obligated to a group of political women in Los Angeles who supported him," including Ida Koverman. Edson had already established a rapport with MGM's Louis B. Mayer, but once he became vice chair of the state Republican Party, she knew it was unlikely he would "make the personal application" on her behalf for Rolph to retain her post. More IWC hearings were planned for the movie industry, which meant approaching Mayer was inappropriate. Nevertheless, in what can only be understood as Edson's desperate fear for her financial survival, she reached out to Ida Koverman to rally support for her plight. Koverman explained to Edson the realpolitik of her predicament. Opposition to Edson came from the influential network of Republican Study Clubs because of Edson's longtime, vocal support of Hiram Johnson. She reminded Edson "the Clubs" were known enclaves of Hoover loyalists.[2] Koverman confirmed that the Club's real mission was to serve one master, not the party, all along.

Edson had naively believed that Koverman was "big enough" to respect Edson's loyalty to Johnson, while rationalizing that it was "smaller
women" who narrowly viewed her as "a Johnson politician." It remains
doubtful that Ida Koverman thought Edson actually believed her when
she told her "she would get busy with Mr. Mayer and other people in the
industry and get an endorsement immediately," and that she would rather
visit with Hiram Johnson in Washington than anyone else because he was
"by far the biggest man there." Edson didn't buy it, but optimistically told
Johnson, "Whether she means it or is just being agreeable to me I do not
know, but she has always seemed to me perfectly sincere."[3]

Governor-Elect James Rolph announced on January 3, 1931, that Mrs.
Mabel E. (Thornton) Kinney would replace Katherine Philips Edson at
the end of her term in June. The press described Mabel Kinney as "active
in women's work in Southern California and was a preprimary campaign
worker for the new Governor."[4] Mabel Kinney was also a close friend of
Ida Koverman, and her selection to replace Edson reflected the ongoing
ideological divide within the Republican Party. Rolph signaled a shift in
policy affecting women workers within the motion-picture industry and
everywhere else. During the final months of her eighteen-year stint on
the IWC, Katherine Edson did her best to prepare Mabel Kinney to take
over her role administering the commission, including its oversight of
the motion picture industry. At the time, few, if any, knew then, or now,
of Mabel Kinney's close ties to Ida Koverman, which would affect public
policy and personal piety.

Mabel Kinney's appointment to the IWC crystallized the ideological
schisms within American feminism that accelerated in 1923 with the
introduction of the Equal Rights Amendment, which threatened hard-
fought, gender-specific workforce regulations. Ida Koverman and Mabel
Kinney supported the ERA like many organized professional women's
groups, who were beyond the reach of IWC oversight. One of the most
vocal groups seeking to overturn gender-based social and labor legislation was the Business and Professional Women's Association (BPW). Ida
Koverman and Mabel Kinney were members, but Mabel Kinney was a
prominent leader in the local branch.

Mabel E. Kinney and Ida Koverman shared political perspectives, a
passion for music, similar religious beliefs, and their interest in motion
pictures and the business of making them. Born Mabel E. Cohen in February 1886, Kinney came to California in 1910 and filled her life with music,
piano, and song. But her interest in religion was historic. She joined with
brother pastors Ernest and Fenwicke Holmes to establish their Venice

Union Congregational Church, but soon after, the brothers embraced the tenets of New Thought and successfully converted their flock while they dabbled in local politics, initially in a campaign to ban prizefighting in Venice. Their new venture was the 1927 founding of the Church of Religious Science, later in 1954, renamed as the Science of Mind. Mabel Cohen married Thornton Kinney, a son of Abbott Kinney, the renowned entrepreneur and developer of the Venice community and its historic canals. Mabel Kinney soon became a leader in the local women's club network and Religious Science community, and as the motion-picture business flourished, she chaired the Motion Picture Committee for the Women of the Golden West, and another for the Wilshire Women's Club, and the Better Films committee for eight different local parent-teacher associations. She taught classes on "The Art of Previewing," and for years she lectured, sometimes up to four times a day, seven days a week, about both films and faith.[5]

Koverman and Kinney's public lives and private faiths often over-lapped, as did their memberships in local and statewide women's groups like the Hollywood Studio Club. Koverman was a member of the advisory committee of the motion-picture department of the California Federation of Women's Clubs, and Mabel Kinney sat on the same committee of its Los Angeles branch.[6] In February 1930, MGM producer, director, and overall nice guy Paul Bern talked to clubwomen about "Problems of the Motion Picture from the Producers Standpoint," and when the CFWC sponsored a motion-picture luncheon, Louis B. Mayer was a featured speaker. Guests of honor included Mrs. Mayer, Ida Koverman, the mother of actress Myrna Loy, and journalist Alma Whitaker, and the toastmistress was Mabel Kinney, described as "the past district state chairman of motion pictures," who currently sat on the Industrial Welfare Commission. The group was again featured together at an CFWC event held at the Ambassador Hotel.[7]

Viewing Ida Koverman and her circle of friends in high places provides a window into previously unexamined networks of conservative women in business and public office who aggressively sought to overturn the policies of their progressive counterparts. And it highlights unnoticed connections between Ida Koverman, Katherine Edson, Louis B. Mayer, and Mabel Kinney that illustrate how individuals representing conflict-ing social, cultural, and economic interests navigated through the layers of private advocacy, partisan politics, and public policy. Now that Louis B. Mayer was at the top of his game, with his political prowess and con-nections well established, during the next round of IWC hearings held near the end of Edson's tenure, his testimony took on a more adversarial posture and at times even a threatening tone.

In November 1929, Katherine Philips Edson issued a report to put the public on notice that the problem of movie extras had yet to be solved. In an article,"Movie-Struck Girls Warned," she outlined the problem of how "more than 10,000 'extras' are pounding the pavements of Hollywood, jobless, penniless, hungry, the figures reveal." There were already 11,000 signed up with the new Central Casting office, but only 133 men and 87 women were hired on movie sets for more than two days a week. On average, only 756 extras were employed per day. Edson broadcast these statistics in hopes of encouraging "would-be movie stars" to "consider all angles before embarking" on a venture to Hollywood.[8]

A few years later, during the last months of her IWC tenure, Louis B. Mayer explained that the movie business was "a creative thing," and that great productions were possible "because we have had a liberal attitude to work under, and I am willing for the industry to do everything that is possible so that Mrs. Edson and the members of the Commission feel that we shall do the right thing." He conceded that overtime was necessary, and "anybody working in the studios and is honest about it will realize that you don't know what moment or hour something is going wrong, going to break you." Nevertheless, standardization was rapidly coming, Mayer said, and it was much better than it had been a couple of years ago.[9]

But then Mayer's tone became more threatening. He said that while he wasn't opposed to overtime, there could come a point "where there will be no script girls, but script boys, and the regulation ceases." Mayer reasoned that "if the cost becomes prohibitive . . . if the industry found it to its advantage in having men because of discriminatory rules and regulations—if you say no overtime for script girls—we love the girls, but what do you think we would do if that same rule applies to any other work that becomes oppressive," And then, as he was prone to do, he applied the general principle to his personal experience. He said, "I am thankful none of my family has to be an extra because of the uncertainty of earning a living," to which Edson pointed out that many girls had been afraid to ask for overtime pay due them because of their fear they would be laid off. Mayer said there needed to be a rule, and he would "love to see the studios operate from a humane standpoint," but "boys do it right along fine. We had for a short time no girls, gave up the girls entirely and there was no yelling about overtime or fussing." Edson asked how long that lasted, and Mayer had to acknowledge that it "drifted back" from "pressure all around."

One month before Edson retired from the IWC, she described how the recommendations she was about to make were the result of the opposition of the Business and Professional Women because of their position that such legislation was "a handicap in obtaining higher paid employment in competition with men," and Edson feared the BPW would injure current legislation designed to protect workers in manufacturing and other hourly waged jobs. Salaried workers were not included in existing regulations, but Edson had to reinforce that they would also be exempt from future codes because there appeared "no real need for including them." Edson noted that the ideological divide between organized women's groups was now affecting women in the motion-picture industry.

She said she believed that reasonable regulations would be "honestly supported by the industry," and she praised Mayer's influence in the industry for accepting "our regulations with so fine a spirit." She could be threatening as well, though, adding that she had every reason to believe the regulations would be strictly adhered to, and if not, an order to include "all women" would be forthcoming. She said she would not seek this alternative, nor would she "care to be a party to it for fear either would result in the elimination of many high salaried women." Nevertheless, she raised the possibility.

Soon after Katherine Edson's departure from the IWC in July, she believed Mabel Kinney was purposefully thwarting IWC's mandate. Kinney failed to publish announcements for public wage-board meetings and did not inform the public about cost-of-living updates; she eliminated investigators, and she ended payroll calls, making it nearly impossible for women to collect thousands of dollars in back pay. Edson understood there was "a complete breakdown of labor enforcement" because of Kinney's leadership, and to her, "The gradual disintegration and degeneration of this work is worse than an actual repeal of the law—it could have at least died clean!"[10]

Then, another blow to Edson's vision of the IWC came at the end of the year, when the mother of comedian Harold Lloyd, and a close friend of Ida Koverman, Mrs. Elizabeth Lloyd Smith, was appointed to the IWC. Harold Lloyd biographer Tom Dardis believes Mrs. Smith's appointment was a reward for her work with the Columbian Society, a short-lived conservative group.[11] The Lloyds' familial relationship was a troubled one, but Ida Koverman provided a shoulder for Mrs. Smith, an apparently troubled person in her own right, who lived in the shadow of her famous son. Mrs. Smith's genuine interest in labor relations remains unclear, but conservatives everywhere and the movie industry in particular now had two sympathetic seats on the IWC. Mrs. Smith would go on to spearhead radical anti-communist, pro-Nixon events during the Cold War era, but for now, the nexus of Ida Koverman, Mabel Kinney, and Mrs. Smith and the IWC provided an institutionalization of the conservative agenda Koverman and the BPW fostered and was allied with the motion-picture business.

The IWC never existed in a vacuum, and as a new presidential administration revolutionized labor relations on the federal level, Mabel Kinney found herself under attack, even requiring guards around the clock because of anonymous threats to her safety. She tried to balance her vision with new mandates of Franklin Roosevelt's National Recovery Administration (NRA) of 1933. When the NRA drew on state level officials to form a committee to find ways to reduce the number of extras already listed through Central Casting, Mabel Kinney was among the members. The news sent shockwaves through the industry, inspiring one columnist to write that "an official mob 'execution' looms in Hollywood," as "that great throng of hangers-on, people who live from hand to mouth and day to day waiting for extra work in films," would be whittled down from 25,000 to a figure somewhere between 3,000 and 10,000. The whole process was a nightmare, and because of various complaints and complexities, the plan to reduce the number of extras registered in accordance with NRA guidelines was dropped in April 1935. In an otherwise excellent study of the IWC's efforts to address the employment and oversupply of extras, Kerry Segrave mischaracterizes Mabel Kinney, in her association with the NRA, as someone who "had no film industry connection whatsoever, and no axes to grind." Mabel Kinney clearly had connections to MGM and an ideological perspective opposed to New Deal principles. Leigh Ann Wheeler suggests that Kinney was appointed because she was "the Hays Office nominee," and "not one suggested by organized women," but Kinney was deeply embedded within California's organized women's groups.[12] Will H. Hays, a longtime Republican heavyweight who appealed to progressives and conservatives became, in 1922, president of the Motion Picture Producers and Distributors of America (MPPDA). Hays and the MPPDA oversaw the industry's efforts to address myriad problems, including extras. His name is mostly associated with the morals production codes of 1930, popularly known as the Hays Code, but it was Hays's successor, Joseph I. Breen, who reigned for two decades rigidly enforcing the codes as the public's censor, while holding unequalled power over the nation's media empires and the cultural icons they fostered.

In spite of her connections to Ida Koverman and Louis B. Mayer, Mabel Kinney's IWC did take one action against MGM during its production of the 1936 movie *Riff Raff*. She charged the studio with negligence when it failed to compensate women who lost work after being drenched during the filming of rainstorm scenes. Forty female extras were ultimately paid $15 for their work on location at Fish Harbor in San Pedro, California.[13]

The opposition continued to grow against Kinney, even from the state Business and Professional Women's organization, which eventually found that "Mrs. Kinney had no comprehensive grasp of her work [and] that she was 'just a political appointee.'" To others, it was clear that Kinney was instrumental in getting Elizabeth Lloyd Smith appointed because the movie interests wanted another body on the commission. According to the San Francisco Chapter of the National Lawyers Guild (NLG), "Mrs. Kinney does just what they [the moving picture companies] tell her." California Assemblyman Gardiner Johnson believed Kinney maintained her position "with the full support of Louis B. Mayer and his famous secretary, Ida Koverman . . . because she would not enforce the eight-hour law against the motion picture industry."[14] The NLG incorrectly identified Kinney as a cousin to Ida Koverman, who also worked at MGM, but it made the connection that Kinney and Koverman, as the personal secretary to movie mogul Louis B. Mayer, helped to carry Venice for Rolph as part of "the local Mayer political machine." Within three years, IWC hearings had stopped, and Kinney ordered investigators to soften the enforcement of IWC policies. California's attorney general insisted that "Kinney did not have a broad conception of the work before her." Others reported that she had taken steps to create a political machine of her own to bolster her standing with Governor Rolph. In October 1939, the Congress of Industrial Organizations called for Kinney's resignation because of her "alleged assistance to employers in their attempts to sabotage the minimum wage law." When the new Democratic governor Culbert Olson assumed office in 1939, he replaced Mabel Kinney with Mrs. Marguerite O. Clark, who quickly reversed Kinney's rulings.[15]

Ida Koverman and Mabel Kinney were political and ideological opponents of Katherine Philips Edson. Their opposing worldviews about women and feminism shaped public policy and the lives of women wage earners. As the Great Depression dragged on, with the encouragement of New Deal policies, the motion-picture industry experienced violent battles over efforts to unionize the industry, which exploited fears about communist infiltration. One outcome of anti-union sentiment was Louis B.

Mayer's promotion of the establishment of the Academy of Motion Picture Arts and Sciences and its sponsorship of the annual Academy Awards. While Margaret Herrick is credited with naming the statuette "Oscar," it's worth noting that Ida Koverman was always at Mayer's side, and she had been married to a guy named Oscar, and she, as the studio's premiere stargazer, found the brightest stars in the MGM heavens.

CHAPTER 14

Secret Meeting, Part II

"For hers is the unseen hand that pulls the strings that make the puppets dance and her name is spoken softly and with some degree of veneration. There's a great deal that goes on in this town that Miss Koverman knows about and, with the carte blanche she enjoys in the matter of executive decisions, she has a lot of pretty important gents tiptoeing around her with devout respect."[1]

AS THE VICE CHAIR OF THE STATE REPUBLICAN PARTY, IN JANUARY 1932, Louis B. Mayer sounded a clarion call for the re-election of President Herbert Hoover. At his side were Ida Koverman, Governor James Rolph, and the Southland's Republican Party leaders. Koverman and Mayer trekked to San Bernardino to rally support for Hoover in the upcoming May 3 presidential primary. Mayer told his audience at the California Hotel that voters needed to show Democrats they didn't have a chance in November. Finding his stride, he called Hoover's re-election even more important than the decision to re-elect Woodrow Wilson to keep us out of war. Now, he said, the question was "shall we reelect Herbert Hoover to keep our families from starving?"[2]

After Hoover handily won the California primary, Ida Koverman prepared for the Republican National convention in Chicago, where she would serve as an alternate delegate.[3] Louis B. Mayer was now free to play a more visible role than the Julian Petroleum scandal had allowed him in 1928. He threw a luncheon and oversaw the special effects of the entertainment, even personally tending to the projector that shined gigantic images of Hoover in the cavernous hall. As usual, there were kerfuffles over delegates from Northern and Southern California, but eventually Mayer was given the honor of officially conveying the formal nomination to Hoover, and Mabel Walker Willebrandt informed Vice President Charles Curtis. Members of Ida Koverman's inner circle were featured players on the national stage, and as usual, the California delegation was the most boisterous clan parading around behind Governor Rolph and William H. Crocker. Seventeen orators seconded Hoover's renomination, and Mayer timed huge movie lights to switch on just in time to record the climactic speech of Joseph Scott as he described women and children being thrown to the lions if Hoover failed to win, reminding the crowd how Hoover had stood "at the helm . . . and steered the vessel through fog and hurricane, and passed the terrors" of windy shores.[4]

American political observer William Allen White was not impressed, describing the affair as anticlimactic, "synthetic, even mechanized," with Ziegfeld Follies gaudiness, and overplayed with "marching robots and whooping morons."[5] Nevertheless, Koverman and her allies were inspired enough to head home prepared to fight what was their last battle on behalf of their Chief, and their grand vision to cast the final death blow to the progressive impulse couldn't survive the crucible of the Great Depression.

No matter. Ida Koverman focused her attention on the August 30 state primary and the re-election of District Attorney Buron Fitts. She served as toastmistress of a gala luncheon held in the ballroom of the Alexandria Hotel, where even after overflow crowds were accommodated, more than two hundred had to be turned away. She introduced Joseph Scott, and her political allies at MGM, actors Wallace Beery and Marie Dressler, came in a show of support for Fitts. Another friend and MGM actress, Hedda Hopper, also spoke, as did Koverman's longtime ally Nellie Kelley, who was still working in the DA's office. Hopper had recently appeared in MGM's *As You Desire Me* (1932), about which she thought the "kindly Paul Bern" had given her a role to ward off being dropped by the studio.[6]

Labor Day served as the formal launching of presidential campaigns in the days before primaries, and the day when national nominating conventions provided a climactic moment in deciding a party's candidate. The day after Labor Day 1932, however, found a somber Ida Koverman and her inner circle gathered inside of Louis B. Mayer's executive office in Culver City. Their attention was not on Herbert Hoover, but on actress Jean Harlow who, with the tragic, untimely death of her new husband and the investigation of its mysterious circumstances, now might be feeling a similar anxiety about her future that Ida Koverman felt under threat of a warrant all those years ago. Koverman also understood the pressure Mayer was feeling, exacerbated by his anticipation of the launch of Hoover's re-election campaign, as it was no less than her own.

Always aware of what was going on with MGM employees, Ida Koverman was often "as powerful as her boss," in large part because she was "the only living soul in Hollywood Mayer would listen to." Joining Koverman and Mayer was the studio's public-relations director, Howard Strickling; studio attorney and longtime Republican Party ally, Mendel Silberberg; Jean Harlow's annoying stepfather, Merino Bello; and Whitey Hendry, the head of MGM security and former police chief of Culver City. Hendry was now a loyal servant to MGM's stars and executives, known as "the man who guarded the gate" from overzealous fans or the occasional "crackpot" who tried to sneak onto the lot.[7] Because of Koverman's friendships with Whitey Hendry and Nellie Kelley in the DA's office, she was kept well informed when MGM's sometimes troubled stars interfaced with law enforcement. She already knew that Louis B. Mayer and Howard Strickling were the first to arrive at the Harlow-Bern home after their housekeeper discovered the body. Hendry knew to contact Mayer's office before calling the police, and now Mayer knew to call Hendry, who joined him and Strickling at the house. Hendry quickly surmised he was looking at a murder scene, after which he and Mayer began rearranging things to make it appear that suicide was the cause of Paul Bern's unfortunate demise.[8] Guiding Mayer was his impression that Paul Bern was really a homosexual, and the self-inflicted wound must have reflected his failure to satisfy the supposedly hypersexual Harlow.

While at the Bern house, Whitey Hendry called a colleague who then called MGM producer Sam Marx, a close friend of Bern's. Marx quickly drove to the Bern house, where he saw fellow producer Irving Thalberg talking to the gardener, Clifton Davis. Davis recounted how he first found a broken piece of delicate crystal glass by the pool with blood on it, and, thinking it expensive and repairable, he went inside to rinse it. Only then did he see Paul Bern's body lying motionless on the floor. As the three men stood talking, neighbor filmmaker Slavko Vorkapich approached them. He said that earlier that day, during his regular early-morning walk, he had noticed a limousine coming down the hill with a woman wearing a black veil sitting inside. [9]

When Sam Marx learned that Hendry and Mayer were inside of the house, it confirmed his later notion that they had designed a conspiracy to cover up a murder. Ida Koverman's account reaffirmed his view. So did Whitey Hendry, who later boasted, "I made that guy's murder look like a suicide! I put the gun in his hand!" It was Mayer's idea to move the body; he wanted Bern to appear as if he had been standing in front of the mirror, rather than in the less dignified manner lying inside of the closet, perhaps avoiding the symbolism of such a placement. It was only a few feet, Hendry bragged, so he had little difficulty dragging the body. Hendry and Mayer shared many secrets, but this was one of which Hendry was especially proud, later telling a friend, "He wished they'd given him an Academy Award."[10]

When the police arrived, they found two more smashed brandy glasses and an overturned crystal bottle at the edge of the pool, and footprints in the muddy grass leading to the end of a hidden driveway, where tire treadmarks looked like someone had left in a hurry. Two hours later, the newswires began to spread the word, and national and international outlets had a free-for-all, with or without Howard Strickling's press releases. DA Buron Fitts began to sift through the evidence, and initially he concluded that Jean Harlow had "found Bern with another woman and shot him," and ordered a warrant for her arrest.[11]

These were the concerns of Ida Koverman and the clique who met in Mayer's office twice on the day after Labor Day. The first meeting focused on Bern's purported sexuality and impotence, with details about Bern's anatomy from Bern's physician given to Mayer, who was also his patient. Mayer informed the police and the press that Bern's death was motivated by his humiliation about his undersized penis, which made him unable to consummate his marriage to one of the sexiest women on the planet.[12] The press had no compunction about reporting this juicy speculation.

The second meeting that day focused on what to do about Buron Fitts's suspicion that Jean Harlow had murdered her husband. Ida Koverman said Mayer was more "composed and completely in charge," unlike the "manic power" he had at the previous meeting. He even suggested the studio might throw Jean to the wolves because "this may be one scandal too many." He warned that the studio "could end up with federal intervention into our operations," that had been kept at bay by the Hays Office. In the end, Mayer decided to take matters into his own hands.[13]

Ida Koverman watched Mayer ask Whitey Hendry to "make the first move." She saw Hendry pick up Mayer's private telephone, the one that didn't go through the studio switchboard, and he dialed Blaney Matthews, head of the Bureau of Criminal Investigation in Buron Fitts's office. Koverman listened to Hendry explain, "First of all, Blaney, a matter of some public interest has arisen of which you must be aware." After a "short interchange" in a "jargon the two men understood and instantly interpreted," Hendry said, "I want to promise you there will be full and complete cooperation on the part of the MGM studio in any investigation into those recent matters of concern." Koverman studied Hendry as he listened to Matthews, and she saw him gesture "OK" to everyone in the room, as he closed with, "I knew I could count on you." She knew this meant an arrangement for a bribe for Buron Fitts to squelch the investigation into Jean Harlow's possible involvement in her husband's death. In case there were any doubts about what had happened, when the meeting broke up, Koverman heard Mayer tell everyone that he would follow up with Fitts who, he reassured them, was "never a problem."[14]

Suddenly, as far as Buron Fitts was concerned, there was nothing more to investigate. LAPD Detective David A. Davidson was not convinced, however, as he tried to reconcile conflicting versions of events immediately after Bern's body was discovered. Davidson announced he was going to reinterview witnesses, including Jean Harlow, at a coroner's inquest scheduled the following day, Thursday, September 8.[15] The only hard evidence supporting the suicide theory was a supposed "note" written by Bern, but there was no way of knowing when it was written, though it appeared to have been torn from a guest book or diary found in the bedroom. It was an apology for an offense, but of what or when it occurred was unclear. If Harlow knew, she never told anyone.

Ida Koverman said that Mayer felt a need to protect Harlow, and she told Sam Marx that Mayer had found the note in the diary while searching for a way to distance Harlow from the cause of Bern's death. Mayer removed it from the book and placed it conspicuously near Bern's body. Howard Strickling confirmed that Mayer found the note, but it was already near the body, so he picked it up to hide it from police until Strickling convinced him to turn it over to them. However the police got the note, newspapers all over the country reproduced it as evidence of Bern's suicide. The note was later delivered to Mendel Silberberg on September 15, 1932, never to be seen again.[16]

Mendel Silberberg, who was signed to represent Harlow, was among the entourage with her when she met with the police. Her mother and stepfather, Mama and Marino Bello, were there, along with Louis B. Mayer, and in spite of Jean Harlow being a devout Christian Scientist, a studio physician. Detectives realized Harlow was so despondent she was in no condition to testify at the inquest the following day.[17]

The police could not officially close the case until they established a motive for Bern's suicide, so they revisited the house, and based on what they saw and the information provided by Slavko Vorkapich, they now determined that someone else could have been involved. A few days later, Silberberg told the press that he was urging Harlow and her brother-in-law to make a public statement about Bern. Silberberg also protested the inquest, suggesting there was no reason for it "in view of the fact the police and public are satisfied that Bern took his own life. There is no mystery about the matter; nothing further to be gained." The coroner disagreed, however, and he wanted to know what the motive was and to "find out, if possible, why studio executives from MGM were at the suicide house in Benedict Canyon more than 3 ½ hours before authorities were notified that Bern had killed himself." The next day the press reported "there was tension galore at the studio, where Mayer vigorously denied that Paul Bern's lovely and spectacular bride is 'through' as a star there." It was no surprise that Silberberg presented Harlow's petition to be excused from the inquest because "she was so weak from the collapse she suffered" upon learning of her husband's death. He pleaded that if it was "humanly possible" she would attend, but he didn't want to jeopardize her, and if her physician determined that she shouldn't go, she would not.[18]

Ida Koverman told Sam Marx she believed Louis B. Mayer or his allies pressured everyone who was set to testify at the inquest to present his unified storyline. Irving Thalberg thought this too because he also told Marx "LB" was "writing the script."

Bern's funeral drew nearly two thousand people to Inglewood Park Cemetery who were eager to see the mourning stars as they walked into Grace Chapel. Ida Koverman arrived with Jean Harlow in their closed limousine, along with her mother and stepfather. Louis B. Mayer, Eddie Mannix, and writer Carey Wilson, were among the few others who were allowed into the service.[19]

A contemporary in Buron Fitts's office was confident that whatever Ida Koverman said about the Bern affair was accurate, because it was well known that the studios knew that in times of trouble, Blaney Matthews "was the one to call." Ida Koverman's revelation to Sam Marx about Mayer's belief that he had to protect Harlow was because, she said, as "keen as [Mayer] was about politics, the studio and its people came first." She was convinced Buron Fitts initially suspected Harlow of murder, and he shelved the investigation because Mayer had bribed him to drop it. Koverman knew Fitts loved publicity, so any incident involving a movie star guaranteed his name in the paper. "Fitts had the studio over a barrel," she told Marx, and he was "a sly one" who, by putting his hand out every so often, had done quite well for himself over the years.[20]

Ida Koverman offered no clue about who she thought was a suspect in what might have been the murder of Paul Bern. She didn't bring up the mysterious woman who might have had a motive, in part perhaps because she brought back her own memories of the notoriety she drew, described as "the other woman" during the Big Four railroad scandal all those years ago. It turned out that Paul Bern had a common-law wife, the forty-six-year-old Dorothy Millette, who showed up at his home just hours before his body was found. Her disappearance set off a statewide search, and soon she was found up north, floating in the Sacramento River. Like Koverman, Dorothy Millette was a former stenographer who had married briefly, moved to New York from her Midwest home, and briefly pursued an acting career before she met Paul Bern. A few years later, Millette suffered from mental illness and was confined to a Connecticut institution. Paul Bern had been sending her money ever since, and Jean Harlow knew all about Millette and the arrangement. Upon learning of Millette's death, Harlow directed Mendel Silberberg to notify the Northern California mortuary that his client wanted to ensure that Millette "was properly cared for," paying for her burial and tombstone. [21]

After the Bern-Harlow sensation died down, the public and the MGM clique turned their attentions to the presidential election. They needn't have really bothered. Herbert Hoover lost in an electoral and popular landslide to Franklin Roosevelt, after which Ida Koverman's life resumed its new rhythm of varying cycles of parties, politics, and pictures. She threw one Sunday tea, with Clark Gable and Jean Harlow among the guests. Jean Harlow went on to became MGM's first female representative to Washington when she and actor Robert Taylor, another of Koverman's pets, attended the annual March of Dimes Birthday Ball celebrating Roosevelt's fifty-fifth birthday in January 1937. [22]

At the time of the trip, Harlow was engaged in a heated salary negotiation with MGM, so Koverman thought a break was needed. She encouraged Harlow's ambassadorship, and as Harlow biographer Irving Shulman wrote, "Politics, philanthropy and publicity demanded the truce," with the studio even paying the expenses for Mama Jean and Merino Bello to accompany their now well-established movie star. Six months later, Jean Harlow was dead. The whole world mourned "the blond bombshell," and for Whitey Hendry, who had seen everything, the funeral was the toughest of all his challenges, especially making sure the "whole army of newspapermen who'd been promised $1000 for a picture of Jean in her coffin" wouldn't stand a chance. [23]

Herbert Hoover's defeat signaled that a new era had begun for the nation and for Ida Koverman in particular. Her daily life shifted to a new universe of richness, of star making and cultural passions. Her influence spread across America's moviegoing masses. While still riding the political merry-go-round, she guided the MGM starship full speed ahead.

CHAPTER 15

Water and Politics

"Years ago, Virginia Woolf wrote: 'Woman has served all these
centuries as a looking-glass possessing the magic and delicious
power of reflecting the figure of a man twice its natural place.'
Such a woman was Ida Koverman . . . known to all of us as
'Mrs. K.'"[1]

AS PART OF THE PREPARATIONS FOR THE 1932 LOS ANGELES SUMMER
Olympics, Ida Koverman was appointed the previous year to head the
newly formed women's division of the Chamber of Commerce. Her connection to the president didn't hurt, so when Hoover was invited to kick
off the ceremonies, she extended an invitation for him to speak at a local
Town Hall meeting. Hoover's trip was aborted because, as Lawrence Richey
told Koverman, for the president "to be away from Washington for three
weeks would be a national disaster," particularly during a re-election
campaign. Vice President Curtis and his wife came instead.[2]

Louis B. Mayer joined the formal celebrations by hosting a luncheon for
"200 Olympic champions, officials, visiting nabobs, together with MGM
stars . . . where all sorts of naughty gags are being planned for the delight
of guests." Ida Koverman's hand was everywhere, but Mayer earned accolades as one of Hollywood's most eminent party makers. Reporter Alma
Whitaker said Mayer appeared "benignly internationally godfatherish" as
he told the crowd how "some people thought the success of MGM pictures
was due to its array of stars, its clever writers, or Irving Thalberg's bright
producers." No, he confessed, "it was really due to these luncheons."[3]

The international sporting event provided an unanticipated opportunity for Koverman to exercise her instincts as a talent scout, when she spotted the sixteen-year-old high-school student whose prize for winning a local poster contest was a spot on a float in the Pasadena Tournament of Roses parade. Koverman learned it was Lois Stephanie Green, and she telephoned her at home to tell her she was arranging an audition for her at MGM. Nonplussed, the girl replied, "I can't come tomorrow. . . . I'm going on a bike ride." Koverman wasn't sure if she was being impertinent or if she genuinely didn't realize the opportunity she was being offered.

At least this is how the story went, and however it really was, an audition was arranged, and Ida Koverman immediately liked her and said if the test went well, she could join MGM under contract. Miss Green said she didn't want a contract because she had two more years of high school. She said she wasn't an actress and wasn't that beautiful, and anyway, she was going to be a commercial artist. Koverman was persuasive, because within twenty-four hours, the renamed Miss Green became Jean Parker, and she was immediately immersed into the world of star-making, taking acting, voice, and dance lessons, and within months, she landed a bit part in the Jackie Cooper film *Divorce in the Family*. The following year she made seven movies, and became known as the "Cinderella Girl." The *Hollywood Reporter* noted how "Ida Koverman is getting plenty of handshakes and backslaps for her discovery of Jean Parker who looks like a cinch star." Jean Parker made more than eighty films in her thirty-five years in the movie business. She later explained that it was because of the encouragement of Ida Koverman, to whom she owed everything, and "mostly grateful for her tremendous faith, which made me forget fear and inspired me."[4]

Another opportunity for Koverman came with the 1932 Olympics. After helping to launch the decade of "twenty thousand novices," some of whom went on to become future champions, in 1933, Koverman established the Los Angeles Women's Swimming Association (LAWSA), a local branch of the group she helped found in Brooklyn, to foster "youthful talent for the 1936 Olympic Games." Membership would be open to "all qualified Los Angeles women." The *Los Angeles Times* announced, "Women's Swimming of Los Angeles Organized by Local Aquatic Stars," with the subheading, "Ida Koverman Made President," with the a goal to develop talent to compete in the international arena. Her longtime friends joined her at the press conference, including Marion Fitts; bank executive Grace Stoermer, Hedda Hopper, Mabel Kinney, and the wife of MGM casting director, Mrs. Ben Piazza.[5] Infusing a bit of East versus West

Coast competition, the new group would be modeled along the lines of the New York club, and she predicted the Los Angeles group would rival its predecessor to "achieve greater prominence." In fact, both groups welcomed each other's swimmers and nurtured the camaraderie of friendly competition. Eventually a clubhouse and a pool were built, but in the meantime, the Los Angeles Swimming Stadium, the Los Angeles Athletic Club, and other local public pools were used.[6]

Fred Cady, the former director of Cady's Mermaids, signed up as the official coach. Los Angeles Mayor Frank L. Shaw blessed the group, and the city's playground commission pledged support with the understanding that the LAWSA would recruit professional women and juvenile swimmers as well. This was important because Koverman and many of her allies, such as Mabel Kinney and Grace Stoermer, were members of the local Business and Professional Women's group, which would be a key vehicle to promote swimmers drawn from the ranks of successful women.[7]

The Los Angeles Olympic games and the nation's growing enthusiasm for female swimmers provided an incentive for Hollywood to link swimming and movies, beginning with California's three-time gold medalist Helene Madison, who appeared in two films, *The Human Fish* (1932) and *The Warrior's Husband* (1933). She was the body double for Maureen O'Sullivan in an underwater nude scene for MGM's *Tarzan and His Mate* (1934), subsequently deleted from the original version. Madison had no idea that her shift to the silver screen meant she was no longer an amateur, and she could not compete in the 1936 games.

Warner Bros. signed 1932 gold medalist Eleanor Holm to a four-year contract, and she also appeared in the Fox film *Tarzan's Revenge* (1934). She then married Billy Rose, whose aquatic spectacles inspired the next decade of MGM's swimming musical extravaganzas. Exemplifying the studio's evolution that furthered the creative translation of the many passions of Ida Koverman, the genre grew from its ability to technically execute and creatively exploit the extraordinary skill and charisma of swimmer Esther Williams.

When Esther Williams joined MGM in 1941, she had no idea Koverman's interest in her was not limited to what she believed was Louis B. Mayer's desire to find MGM's answer to ice skater turned movie star Sonja Henie. Williams noted that Koverman "had her own secretary and two assistants," and that "L. B. relied on her judgment," and she quickly learned that it was Ida who encouraged Mayer to feature classical artists in the movies, a decision that had paid off handsomely for the studio. Koverman was instrumental in bringing opera stars Ezio Pinza, Helen Traubel, and Lauritz Melchior to MGM. Soon, she also learned that Ida could be a sympathetic person in whom to confide as part of her particular support for younger actors. Williams believed a friendship with Koverman was a distinct advantage, although her own began as a tug of war, when Williams quickly learned that because she was the "power behind the throne," you didn't say no to Ida Koverman.

When Koverman called Esther while she was doing laps, Esther whined, "Mrs. Koverman, you can't imagine what I look like right now. I'm a sight. I'm dripping wet. I have no makeup, a wet head, a pair of old sloppy slacks and a baggy old sweater. Couldn't we do this tomorrow?" Koverman reminded her, "When Mr. Mayer says 'come,' you come right now." Koverman scowled when she saw Williams, admonishing her, "My God, you look like a drowned rat! You can't go to see Mr. Mayer like that. Fix yourself up. Fast!' Koverman opened her drawer, handed her a lipstick and a comb, and demanded, "Pull yourself together and make it speedy. . . . He's waiting!"[8]

Without her glasses, Williams couldn't see who was also waiting in Mayer's office, but out of the corner of her eye, she noticed a man with unusually large ears and quickly realized it was Clark Gable. She learned that Mayer was seeking to punish Clark's costar, Lana Turner, for marrying bandleader Artie Shaw, a move he saw as insubordination. He was going to set up a screen test with Williams and Gable to see if she could replace Turner. For three days, Williams anxiously imagined herself with Gable, but upon her arrival, Dan Dailey was standing in for Gable, who showed up later. Dailey apparently called her "mermaid," and the knickname stuck.[9]

Mayer soon told Williams he wanted her to costar with Gable in *Somewhere I'll Find You*. Instead of being elated, Williams argued that her contract stated that she would have nine months to prepare before being cast, and after only three, she hardly felt ready. Mayer's pleasant mood turned to outrage, and because, as Williams said, "Ida Koverman had very acute hearing, . . . as soon as she heard me say the word legal, she pulled out a copy of my contract," to inform Mayer that Williams was correct. Winning that round, she walked out, and as she made her way down the long hall, she could hear Mayer still yelling at Koverman the whole time.[10]

Koverman took Williams under her wing, and the two women developed a strong rapport. One time Williams confided she was having trouble with an acquaintance who was encouraging bad habits that countered the image of the wholesome, all-American girl. Koverman suggested she observe other actresses and set up lunchtime viewings of films to demonstrate different styles and methods of the studio's biggest stars. When Williams and Koverman discussed the specific attributes of Myrna Loy, Ingrid Bergman, Irene Dunne, and Claudette Colbert, Williams was happy that "Ida was pleased," and said she would pass her comments on to Mayer.[11]

Williams and Mayer eventually came to an unspoken understanding, but there were skirmishes throughout their collaboration. Williams was eager to appear in a Cole swimsuit advertisement, but when she told Mayer there would be no MGM tagline, Mayer "hurled himself to the floor." She said the image of Mayer, a "grown man, with his white-on-white tie and his beautifully tailored suit, rolling around on the rug . . . kicking his heels and actually foaming at the mouth," stayed with her for decades. Now, with more confidence, she handed him a tissue and scolded him like a child, reminding him that everyone up and down the hall could hear him, but she felt bad for Koverman, who had to listen to his theatrics. Mayer quickly composed himself to unabashedly reply, "Ida Koverman has heard it many times before."[12]

The Olympics didn't interfere with the fact that 1932 was also an election year, and while no one challenged President Hoover's renomination in California, his odds in the general election were diminishing by the week, including from what Louis B. Mayer recognized as voters' growing attraction to the charismatic Democratic candidate, New York governor Franklin Delano Roosevelt. Many believed the "deadly calm within the Republican Party forecast the overthrow to come." After the momentary distraction of Paul Bern's death, it was time for Ida Koverman and her MGM clique to turn their attention back to the Hoover campaign. California appeared to be headed toward a Roosevelt victory, and by October the campaign was described as a "home fight" to be waged by Mayer, Mark Requa, Joe Scott "and the rest of the old guard spouters." Hoover's reputation as the "great engineer" was irreparably damaged, and it would be decades before scholars revisited his achievements, which had been shrouded more by his abject inability to instill hope or, unlike Roosevelt's natural ability, to exude a sense of public empathy. No matter what Hoover did, though, he couldn't win, as one columnist summed it up: "Outside of Soviet Russia no man has ever put so much government in business as President Hoover, and all the while he talks rugged individualism and the American plan."[13]

After serving as vice-chairman of the Republican State Central Committee, Louis B. Mayer's future role in the party would be decided in the upcoming party elections on September 24th. Historian Steven Ross argues that party leaders had been so impressed with Mayer's work, they appointed him chair of the state party, which "signified that Hollywood celebrity and money had dramatically changed American politics." It wasn't quite that simple, and in fact, the fight over the chairmanship reflected not just the state's perennial regional schisms, but also the cultural divide they spawned. Actually, his success rested on his longtime inner circle, Ida Koverman, Mabel Walker Willebrandt, and Mendel Silberberg.[14]

Herbert Hoover's supporters and many elected officials supported Mayer, but for others, their first choice was William Eric Fowler, Ralph Arnold's successor, and current chair of the Los Angeles Central Committee. Another candidate, Leo V. Youngworth, vowed he would "fight to the finish" against Mayer. Initially, California governor James Rolph gave Mayer a lukewarm endorsement for merely retaining a seat on the State Committee. But when Youngworth surprisingly withdrew his name one day before the election, Rolph formally nominated Louis B. Mayer, citing his loyal service over the previous four years, and, "If ever the Republican Party needed leadership of a man of courage, it is now, [and] Mayer is that man of courage." Steven Ross is correct that Mayer's election reinforced the marriage between Hollywood and American politics, but it also signaled the historic influence of Ida Koverman and her allies on Mayer's team. The *Los Angeles Times* ignored the details of the contentious rivalry, announcing the "unanimous election" of Mayer "presaged unanimity of thought and action in the general election campaign." Mayer hoped such harmony would make "sure of electing every Republican from President Hoover down."[15]

Others were not so optimistic about Mayer's abilities, and blamed party stalwarts for promoting him, even though he was not as popular among the party's ranks, the "scores of Republican warhorses [who] were going to avoid the front line trenches in the presidential battle."[16] This was a biting rebuke to Koverman, but the reality was that Herbert Hoover never had a chance and voters had had enough of the GOP's utter failure to uplift the economy or their spirits.

Encouraged by Koverman, Hedda Hopper launched an aborted political career with a run for a seat on the County Central Committee. Koverman saw Hopper was a vibrant voice who would have broad appeal beyond party insiders. Unfortunately, Hopper "didn't realize it meant a fight" among eight candidates, but she rallied supporters and "became politician pronto," by raising "an army of young men," to pass out fifteen thousand handbills within hours. She had twenty "pretty girls" hand out "snappy literature about herself," including slogans such as "Hop to It for Hedda," and "Hopper ahead by leaps and bounds," as they stopped motorists and pushed doorbells. One observer noted that Hopper was winning support with her campaign pamphlets with their fetching pictures. Ida Koverman hoped Hopper would be her successor on the committee and, like others, she believed she was "a grand representative of the motion picture industry as it should be."[17]

The *Los Angeles Times* endorsed Hedda Hopper and Louis B. Mayer and Mendel B. Silberberg, along with the slate of Koverman's colleagues vying for seats on the County Central Committee. MGM star Mae Murray endorsed Hopper with a charming speech that included a bit "of Christian Science grace" and hinted at the importance spiritual faith had in Koverman's inner circle at MGM. Hedda Hopper and Murray appeared together at the Biltmore Hotel, where Hopper linked her politics with her sex, single status, and self-sufficiency. She said she "was present as a mother, wage-earner and head of a household," and declared this was a time "when every woman must work for her country and her convictions." Aside from her own candidacy, she said if Hoover wasn't elected, "We shall be very, very sorry for the next four years." She appeared at the Republican Study Club along with the district attorney's wife, Marion Fitts.[18]

Hopper lost the election, but she realized she liked politics and soon began to appear as an emissary for Mayer, at times admonishing audiences that "it will be an everlasting disgrace to the women of California if Hoover is not re-elected. . . . The country will backslide a century." This was part of Mayer's effort to counter what would be Hoover's inevitable loss, along with a series of radio spots and other strategies to excite the electorate. It was too late, though, and both state chair Mark Requa and vice chair Mayer were easy targets to blame for the fiasco. It wasn't entirely fair, but someone had to be held accountable for Roosevelt polling two to one in a predominantly Republican state.[19]

Koverman did what she could to improve Hoover's popular appeal. She offered feedback on his speeches, sharing tricks of the trade, such as when she sent him blotting papers to paste his typed-out radio addresses, which would keep the microphone from picking up the sound of his ruffling notes. She would continue to comment on the performance and substance of Hoover's speeches. She was particularly enthusiastic after one performance, writing to Lawrence Richey that it was "the finest speech he ever made on the radio." She said Hoover's talks were "always very meaty and constructive," but often they "were over the head of the ordinary person." This time, though, she said, it was filled with "words of one syllable . . . was clear and understandable by anyone with just barely average intelligence," and "his delivery was such that it was hard for me to believe that it was the Chief talking," because "he spoke with a great deal of fire and really stirred one's emotions which has not always been true."[20]

In the final weeks before the 1932 election, Koverman reached out to Hoover's Washington office on behalf of studio matters big and small. During the filming of the movie *Eskimo* on location in Alaska, not yet a state, she asked for advice about how to ensure the film crew who were quartered at "Camp Hollywood" would be able to vote for president. She learned that voting was not a federal matter but was handled through individual offices of the secretary of state. Losing a few votes wouldn't have mattered to the ultimate outcome, but the continuing love affair between Republican politics, women, and MGM survived during the dark days of the Great Depression, and was on full display three days before the election. Mae Murray and dozens of movie stars entertained during a gala luncheon for Koverman and the wives of her allies Mendel Silberberg, Buron Fitts, and Louis B. Mayer. MGM's ten-year-old child star Jackie Cooper chimed in that he would vote for Hoover if he were old enough to do so.[21]

Following Franklin Roosevelt's inauguration, Herbert Hoover and Law-rence Richey took a transcontinental flight back to California, after which Richey was amazed at how they departed DC Sunday at 3:30 pm and ar-rived in San Francisco at 11:45 Monday morning. After Richey enjoyed a fishing trip at the exclusive Northern California Bohemian Grove, he hoped to "have the pleasure of seeing you and Louis Mayer and some of the other folks" at the studio, eager to observe "the mechanics" of a live set.[22]

Maintaining her leadership posts in local women's clubs was part of her job description at MGM, including the influential Women's Breakfast Club, where Mayer had become a "pal" and charmed the audience. Koverman and her now close friend and district attorney's wife Marion Fitts launched a revolt in May 1933 to defend their legitimacy as elected officers after a challenge by Mrs. Harriet Mason Sunday, a radio minister of spiritual science and daughter of the well-known evangelist Billy Sunday. Mrs. Mason argued that because a small group of stockholders installed Kover-man and Fitts, they did not represent the vote of the thousand members in their ranks. A court date was set for October 18, but in the meantime, Koverman and Fitts demanded recognition and the club's books, cash, and records. After a few court continuances, the case was dropped, but the brouhaha had ruffled feathers, which were finally calmed when "all the hatchets and stilettos were honorably buried," and the presidential gavel was officially passed to Mrs. Fitts. Louis B. Mayer "paid flattering tribute" to her and "expressed the hope that there were more women gathering like this," for "these are times when we need a steady hand and a steady mind."[23] If Buron Fitts was corruptly in the pocket of Louis B. Mayer, it grew out of his and his wife's rapport with Ida Koverman, Nellie Kelley, and Louis B. Mayer and their battles forged in Republican Party trenches. Their mutual interests were served by their persistent politicking, and they firmly rooted their stake in Southern California, as the region saw demographic shifts that exacerbated its right-wing tendencies and Los Angeles fostered an urbanized liberal oasis during the post-WWII era.

Hoover's 1932 loss to Democrat Franklin Roosevelt marked the end of conservative Republican dominance in national politics and the resurgence of a half century of a Theodore Roosevelt–Woodrow Wilson, bipartisan style of progressivism. In California an indigenous Democratic movement would grow, electing Governor Culbert Olson in 1938, but thereafter, for two decades, Republicans maintained a conservative stronghold in Golden State politics. Ida Koverman continued to harness partisan allies, but now her gaze searched for new discoveries that would bring the brightest stars to MGM's heavenly sky.

CHAPTER 16

The Other Widow

WHEN MARIE DRESSLER, MGM'S RISING STAR AND A RECENT ACADEMY Award winner, was diagnosed with terminal cancer, she was only told she had anemia and low blood sugar. Louis B. Mayer was one of five people who knew the truth, and Koverman was another, allowing her to better navigate the actress's frustration at what sometimes seemed to her the studio's arbitrary limits on her activities. One Dressler biographer explained Koverman was in the loop as "Mayer's matronly and well-liked executive secretary," whose association with former presidents meant that her "credentials were impeccable," and "she knew how to keep secrets."[1]

Perhaps the biggest secrets Koverman kept were about her sexual proclivity and her marital status. There is no porthole into her intimate life, private romances, sexual affairs, or loving partners. Her avid followers didn't hide their curiosity about her, but just as she had successfully hidden her past, she shrouded her present private life. When she attended a garden party with Marian and Buron Fitts, Grace Stoermer, and the Clark Gables, journalist Alma Whitaker hoped there would be a "romantic announcement . . . but, no," Whitaker wrote. "Ida insists she is not even in jeopardy." As she was now known as "a party expert," her guests were "nicely represented" among the "film, political, educational, literary, musical, and business realms."[2]

When director Robert Vignola escorted Koverman to an affair in 1933, Whitaker "decided it was a case we should look into." Vignola took her to a party hosted by Harold Lloyd's mother, filled with "a nice sprinkling of political nabobs." Another reporter soon assumed that Koverman was married when she referred to the charming hosts as "Mr. and Mrs. H. C. Koverman." It's possible the reporter was referring to Howard O. and

Jennie Koverman, parents of Howard Charles Koverman, who, in 1937, at the age of seventeen, was a college student in Los Angeles, and it suggests Ida must have been in closer contact with Oscar's family after his death than is readily apparent. Charles recalled visiting the home of a friend at that time, whose father inquired about his possible relationship to Ida Koverman at MGM, and clearly conveyed she was an esteemed executive who commanded respect on and off the lot. Howard "Bud" Koverman also had an inkling about Ida and Oscar's relationship through family lore passed on through his father and aunt. [3]

Whitaker was there too, inspiring her to ask, "Now just what has Ida Koverman, who we thought was an indubitable widow in reasonably good standing, been up to?" Whoever the mystery man was, Whitaker reminded her readers that Robert Vignola was "the most enthusiastic aspirant we know about for the position of 'Mr. Koverman.'" Whitaker concluded, ironically, that "we cannot imagine him letting Ida pull an extreme 'Lucy Stone' on him . . . even for the honor of becoming an MGM executive," referring to the women's rights activist who maintained her maiden name after marriage.[4]

Little did Whitaker realize that Ida Ranous Brockway had married Oscar H. Koverman precisely to assume his last name. Robert Vignola was an Italian-born silent filmmaker, who, at the time of his death in 1953, was described as "never married, devoting his entire interest to directing and writing." It's unlikely Whitaker suspected Vignola was gay and in need of Koverman to create a façade of heterosexuality. It's even less probable that Whitaker or anyone else ever suspected that Koverman and Vignola's mutually beneficial companionship might have also served as a cover for Koverman's sexuality. Whatever her proclivities, one writer noted that Ida Koverman "knows her masculinity," revealing that she found actor Otto Kruger, a versatile actor and musician, to be "a champion adept at the gentle art."[5]

Koverman and Vignola shared many friends, such as MGM's Benny Thau and Eddie Mannix, and one night they all showed up at Jean Harlow's hilltop home to mix with Gloria Swanson, William Powell, and Louis B. Mayer's daughter and son-in-law, Irene and David O. Selznick. The same group again showed up at Edgar Allan Woolf's grand farewell for Broadway vaudevillian composer Anatole Friedland. Woolf, most well known for his collaboration on the screenplay adaptation of *The Wizard of Oz* was, according to Sam Marx, "a wild, red-haired homosexual," who was a meticulous, charming man and a superb cook. He kept an immaculate kitchen and held regular Saturday-night dinner parties attended by directors and writers. On Sunday mornings, Woolf sometimes drove to Louis B. Mayer's beach house to prepare brunch for his guests.[6]

Robert Vignola also attended gatherings at Koverman's home, and in the late 1940s he lived a couple of doors down from her on Whitley Terrace in the Hollywood Hills. Boxing was popular among the Hollywood crowd, who often set up makeshift portable boxing rings on their manicured lawns. One night, Koverman and Vignola apparently sat a bit too close, because she kept "closing her eyes at the hectic moments in the fistic battles."[7] Robert Vignola wasn't the only man to escort Koverman around town. She enjoyed the company of a succession of good-looking young men, especially those whose movie careers she was promoting, who accompanied her to parties or nightclubs. Whether they were gay or straight hardly mattered to Koverman or to the press accounts about who she showed up with and never had reason to ponder who she went home with.

During the near twenty-five years she lived in the Golden State, and in the decades since her death, the assumption that Mrs. Ida R. Koverman was a widow, and thus a heterosexual female, has persisted in the absence of evidence to the contrary. There is no evidence to support conjecture about an alternative sexual orientation, but it isn't altogether implausible that she married Oscar for another reason than to escape the Ohio railroad scandal. Perhaps Koverman and Mrs. Jeannette Ford had been more than friends, and Oscar was the respectable rebound after their devastating breakup. There are a few clues to suggest Koverman might have been a lesbian. She lived her adult life as a single woman living with a succession of female housemates, and she associated with single women whose professional lives allowed them financial independence and thus the freedom to sleep with whomever they pleased. Whether Ida Koverman was gay or straight, a little of both, or none of the above, she existed behind a façade of widowhood in a town that both went to extreme measures to hide the breadth of human sexuality while at the same time it enabled its fuller expression. As a mature, matronly woman, she lived most days and a colorful nightlife in public places with little time or space for secretive seclusion, solitary or otherwise.

More than her sexuality remained shrouded in deception. Whomever she slept with before or after she married Oscar in 1910, she was not a widow in spite of repeated references from the 1920 US Census to her death in 1954. The 1943–1944 *Who's Who in California* lists her as "Married: Oscar H. Koverman," and twelve years younger than her actual age of fifty-two, and married to Oscar eight years earlier than their vows.

While she might have merely finessed the details in non-legally binding publications, Oscar appears to have lied to the Selective Service and census takers, which identified him as a single man living with his mother and sister in Cincinnati, Ohio, in 1920. The truth is Ida Koverman could never have been a widow because she and Oscar were divorced on July 6, 1923. Oscar died eleven years later on July 20, 1934, just before Koverman's June 30 sailing to Hawaii on the popular Lurline, quickly followed by a trip to and from Ensenada, Mexico, by August 5. She traveled again over the Memorial Day weekend, missing an invitation from Herbert Hoover during his visit to the Southland.[8]

Other than Oscar's 1924 pilgrimage to a Shriners' ceremony amidst the rain and cold at the Cincinnati zoo with sixty-two others seeking to wear the red fez, there is little to draw a portrait of his life except for the extraordinary news that, along with surviving brothers, there was a *widow*, Mrs. Jessie Price Koverman. While Ida was reincarnating herself in New York and then as a political powerhouse in Los Angeles, Oscar and Jessie Price Koverman were living comfortably near Loveland, Ohio, with a plot of land in the nearby Symmes Township.[9]

Oscar had worked at one of the biggest meatpacking companies in the country, the Chicago-based Armour & Co., gorily depicted in the 1906 muckraking novel *The Jungle* by Upton Sinclair, which led to the consumer protections in the Food and Drug Act. The Armour Company was a huge international corporation, and among its diverse interests was a booming commercial waste by-product, fertilizer industry like the one in St. Bernard, Ohio, where Oscar Koverman worked.

On July 20, 1934, Oscar climbed up a giant, sixty-foot-high scaffold near the top of a huge crane standing high above a mammoth cauldron filled with a foul brew of decomposing organic matter. His grasp faltered and he lost his footing. There were no safety harnesses or ropes to catch him, and in a matter of seconds, as he fell six stories, he smacked up against the scaffolding, breaking his neck and fracturing his skull, and then he disappeared into the fecal sludge being transformed into manure. What was made to nourish life now took it.[10]

The irony of Oscar Koverman's death in 1934 at the fertilizer works is that this was the same time that author Upton Sinclair launched his "Campaign of the Century," when he ran for California governor, and the campaign against him became known for establishing a new relationship between motion pictures and dirty politics.

As late as May, the ailing Governor James Rolph was still undecided about seeking re-election, but soon after that he withdrew, and when he died in June, Lieutenant Governor Frank Merriam assumed the office and ran for the post in his own right. Louis B. Mayer had been traveling in Europe, and his return was indefinitely delayed when his wife Margaret became seriously ill in Paris, forcing them to miss the birth of their first grandchild. Mayer missed the September party elections when Alameda County District Attorney Earl Warren succeeded him as chairman of the State Committee.[11]

Mayer's absence until early October made it difficult for him to follow, let alone to engage in, any direct challenge to Upton Sinclair's campaign momentum. When he returned to the States, he said he was going "to organize the fight of the movie industry against Upton Sinclair's candidacy." While later denying he said so, he even threatened to move the studio to Florida, along with other Hollywood moguls who toyed with relocating to Florida before Sinclair announced his campaign.[12] A decade before, Ida Koverman and Nellie Kelley recruited new members to the Federation of Republican Women by exploiting fears about the threat of communism. Now, employing the same message against Sinclair, who was actually a Socialist in Democratic clothing, the 1934 gubernatorial race introduced MGM propaganda in a series of movie shorts designed to defeat Sinclair.

During the 1930s, many former progressive Republican women joined the liberal Democratic ascendancy, but Koverman and her allies tried to fight the seepage. One of them was Mrs. Elizabeth Lloyd Smith, who aggressively campaigned against Sinclair, in part by setting up the California Constitutionalists, to combat communism in Los Angeles. As its president, Mrs. Smith mobilized more than a thousand women, including Ida Koverman, to parade to a rally at the Carthay Circle Theatre. Sinclair was not a communist, but Mrs. Smith's incendiary speech railed against radicalism threatening "the safety of our homes and the continuance of the present form of government." Another Koverman friend, Mrs. Leiland Atherton Irish, also spoke about how she was "appalled by the growth of many 'isms' that threaten our land," so it was "up to the women to assert themselves against such movements . . . for they will be the greater sufferers should such a movement cause an upheaval in their present state."[13]

Louis B. Mayer tried to get his employees to help finance Merriam's campaign. Katharine Hepburn, Jean Harlow, Will Rogers, and Franchot Tone were listed as employees who, as "threatened workers," were "sandbagged" into donating to the Merriam campaign, by being threatened with dismissal if they didn't do so. Studio personnel were asked to donate a day's pay, which could range from one hundred to five hundred dollars depending on their job categories. Some employees were handed blank checks already made out to Louis B. Mayer, so all they had to do was fill in the dollar amount. Such intimidation didn't work on James Cagney or Jean Harlow, who refused to contribute to Mayer's political fund.[14]

Following the general election, Ida Koverman was among the scores of Hollywood luminaries attending a huge party hosted by director W. S. Van Dyke for Los Angeles Sheriff Eugene Biscailuz, for whom she and actress May Robson had campaigned. Sheriff Biscailuz liked to be around movie stars, and they liked him, evidenced by Mae West's visit to inspect the city jail.[15]

The 1934 campaign was Louis B. Mayer's last hurrah in the limelight of the state Republican Party. For Koverman, it was a year when her MGM living legacy was on the rise, and the following year, although women were losing ground to men in the movie business, one author noted how, when it came "to women executives, Ida Koverman seems to stand alone."[16]

It was also around this time that Koverman's ten-year-old grandneice Mary Hawkins came for an extended visit. Her grandmother was Koverman's older sister, Phoebe, who now lived nearby with her fourth husband, John Boyer. Eventually Mary's mother and father, Katherine and Frank Hawkins, also moved to Culver City, where Frank worked briefly as a machinist at MGM. Mary's older brother, Bruce, had already come earlier when Phoebe and Jack Boyer still lived in North Hollywood. Mary's recollections about her great-aunt Ida are invaluable, but it is possible they are blended with later encounters, family reminiscences, or published accounts.[17] Through a child's eyes, however, Mary observed Ida's lifestyle, and only later understood they reflected Koverman's prominence at MGM. Koverman's friends demonstrated their esteem for her by welcoming Mary, such as actress Billie Burke's candy gift basket, and a doll from actress Marion Davies.

Mary's activities included dance classes at the renowned Meglin Dance Studio, and she spent time at a beach house in Santa Monica, which might have been a now mysterious address at 237 Palisades Beach Road, described as a Cape Cod–style dwelling. First permitted in 1922 to the son of major developer Moses Sherman, the address is located on the thin strip of ocean-front-facing land filled with elegant beach homes designed for entertainment-industry luminaries. Dubbed the Gold Coast, with custom-designed residences by the "architectural aristocracy of Los Angeles," with interiors imagined by the "art departments of the movie studios." Although one 1933 directory notes a "Mrs. I. R. Kooerman [sic]" residing there, and a 1934 city building permit indicates Louis B. Mayer as the owner and occupant who altered the property with interior work and a garage, subsequent city directories of the late 1920s and 30s have no listing for a 237 Palisades Beach Road. The property was later listed as vacant or owned by a physician and then by aluminum mogul Leo Harvey. It's possible that Mary remembered visiting with her Aunt Ida at Louis B. Mayer's residence at 625 Palisades Beach Road.[18]

Mary is very clear about how Mayer sometimes showed up in his limousine at her aunt's apartment on Sunday mornings, and he and Ida would ride around for a couple of hours discussing whatever couldn't wait until Monday morning. She learned firsthand that her Aunt Ida was well ensconced at the center of power at MGM, and that she was an indispensable partner to Mayer. Soon thereafter, columnist Louella Parsons acknowledged that Ida Koverman had a new aspect of her job description, telling her readers that, "Ida Koverman, executive secretary to Louis B. Mayer, is a female Christopher Columbus when it comes to discovering talent."[19] No one would ever doubt that, indeed, Ida Koverman's explorations opened up a completely new world of creativity for the silver screen.

CHAPTER 17

"Tiffany Trademark"

Ida Koverman was the "biggest woman in this movie industry, political power and chief aide to Louis B. Mayer," who had "discovered more big stars than any other person in the world." In other words, "approval from *La Koverman* is like a Tiffany trademark."[1]

MOVIE STUDIOS WERE BECOMING HUGE INDUSTRIAL ENTERPRISES WITH a finished product made from a blend of technology, craftsmanship, and artistry—writers, directors, actors, photographers, and supporting personnel that turned parts of Los Angeles into industrial zones now called the Entertainment Industry Support Services Planning District.[2] Out of this complex process came a sometimes magical experience, but like other big businesses, the motion-picture industry "rationalized" itself in assembly-line productions, distribution networks, theaters, and marketing outlets throughout the globe to promote their brands. Similar to other consumer products, a studio's success rested on the tastes of the moviegoing public, so publicity departments methodically launched campaigns to ensure fan loyalty rather than risk the whimsy or fickleness of audiences. As part of the need to sustain the appeal of movie stars who supported the entire behind-the-scenes ensemble, often the lines between their public professional lives and their private personal lives were intentionally blurred, and characteristics were cultivated that would most likely elevate an actor to enduring movie star status.

Although stories about how Koverman's ability to discover talent from a photo or an incidental notice were common, she dispelled such expectations by explaining that she never found "motion picture talent behind soda fountains or looming up suddenly before her on a street corner," or while stopped at a traffic light. She said she found potential movie stars where one would expect to find singers, dancers, or actors where they performed in venues all over town.[3] Ida Koverman knew that charisma and talent were the foundations on which to build a movie star, but she also realized that packaging performers was part of the movie-production process. Early in her tenure at MGM, she made creative hiring decisions, and because she seemed to know what appealed to movie fans, especially women, her opinion was highly regarded.[4]

As part of Ida Koverman's chosen mission to bring fresh talent to MGM, she tapped charismatic musicians and singers who embodied the fundamental traits necessary to create "the rule of illusion," and who could capture "daydreams on celluloid" and convince "the public that Hollywood was paradise on earth." She believed that "a star must have an unattainable quality," achievable by their adhering to the minutia of day-to-day lives, such as the rule that a movie star could "drink champagne or nectar, but not beer."[5]

Movies and marketing went hand in hand, and how a movie star smelled created the illusion of stardom. In 1935, Koverman's diverse hats included her role as the director of Vimay, Inc. perfumes, a Mayer venture designed to link box-office returns with a line of exotic scents. This little-known connection, one of the many between Ida Koverman and Louis B. Mayer, becomes visible in a rare photograph of Jean Harlow posing with a glass bottle of a Vimay fragrance called "Emotion" (autographed after her death by her mother). Ida Koverman's grandniece, Mary Troffer, suggested that a distant relative of the Brockway-Koverman clan might have been the manufacturer of glass bottles, so it's possible the connection stretches further into her great-aunt's mysterious past. Nevertheless, under the brand of Prince de Chany, Vimay fragrances included the sensual fragrances Mystery Gardenia, Lost Orchid, Sins of Hollywood, and other titillating names.[6]

In spite of the countless look-alike actresses in Hollywood's stable, Ida Koverman believed that the true secret of a star's success was "individuality," and "the art of being yourself," from which genuineness emanated and translated onto the big screen. She said that it distressed her to see the copycat tactics because "to succeed you must never copy anyone else in looks or habits," and instead it was necessary to "work hard . . . be sincere," and "never be afraid to take a stand for something you believe in." She said, "Above all, be yourself!" Those who learned to "develop unusual personalities" were so attractive to the public that they were "willing to pay to see them on the screen." [7]

Ida Koverman's reputation as a talent scout gained momentum with her aggressive posture and sympathetic columnists, who were always looking for colorful backstories. One of her early finds, in 1933, was eighteen-year-old Pancho Lucas, who was initially promoted along the familiar narrative of overnight success, "From Office Boy to Film Celebrity." The story was that after "studio scouts tested hundreds of olive-skinned, dark-eyed boys," Lucas, who already worked at MGM, was spotted by Kover-man, who just happened to see him as he crossed the lot. A screen test showed he had "a good speaking voice and natural acting ability," so he was hired as the young Pancho Villa in *Viva Villa!* (1934), starring Wallace Beery as the adult Villa, and he was sent to join the production already filming in Mexico.[8] The movie career of young Pancho Lucas, however, was thereafter very short lived.

When publicist Robert Vogel joined MGM in 1930, he quickly learned to navigate around "the whole damn" place, so he felt the need to create his "own mental All-American" with Ida Koverman having two positions, one on "the line," and one "in the backfield." He eventually became one of her close friends, and he surmised that long before she left her post at Republican headquarters, she had designs on a plum perch in Culver City. He said she "had stars in her eyes and wanted to work in Hollywood." Given Koverman's matchmaker role in the marriage of politics and motion pictures, this is a reasonable notion, even if his assertion that "Hoover let her go and Mayer took her" is not. Nevertheless, Vogel clearly understood that "she, as I say, pretty jolly well ran the studio," and she was "a very brilliant woman."[9]

Vogel saw her as the facilitator-in-chief, moving people inside the huge studio operation with a strong but empathetic hand. He observed how every morning a mélange of visitors greeting her outside of Louis B. Mayer's office. Her authoritative yet maternal demeanor ensured that everyone would be tended to, and the whole ritual ran smoothly because she swiftly discerned who should be sent where and the real or imagined urgency of the diverse matters to be handled. She set appointments either for Mayer's calendar, or for the sound department, or any other fixer with the appropriate expertise. She determined who would see Mayer, so Vogel decided to send her notes rather than just show up at her door. He wrote them to realistically reflect how quickly he needed to see Mayer, such as,

"I'd like to see Mr. Mayer . . . any time in the next ten days," or "I'd like to see Mr. Mayer . . . in the next three or four days." His strategy paid off. When he had a pressing matter, his meeting was expedited because she knew he wasn't cheating.[10]

Adrian A. Kragen, a former lobbyist and later law professor, said that dealing with Ida Koverman was not easy or very friendly compared to the various secretaries of the studio executives he had to "get through" during his nine years working in the industry. Koverman's role as gate-keeper headed her job description, and it is underscored by the rare in-stance when her skill at it worked against her. In 1933, George Donald Smart moved to Hollywood and landed a job as a technician at MGM, where he "saw people in the studio throwing money around like water." He was determined to meet Louis B. Mayer, but Ida Koverman refused his approach, which inspired his belief that, "If I could have seen him once, I would have gone to the top." Instead, George Smart had the bril-liant idea to hatch a criminal scheme to pose as a confidential agent to Mayer. It worked for a while. He pretended to be authorized by Louis B. Mayer on behalf of MGM's high profile actors to find investors to fund a convoluted secret contract arrangement outside of traditional sources. Mr. Smart would receive a 10 percent commission for successful transac-tions. He forged Mayer's name on promissory notes, and in one case he induced a banker to buy a note for $10,000. He was finally caught after kiting three notes totaling $50,000. George Smart explained that the problem started when Ida Koverman refused to set up a meeting for him with Mayer, and this is what launched his criminal endeavor. This might have eerily reminded Koverman of Charles Warriner, who also blamed her for his downfall rather than his act of malfeasance in stealing from the Big Four railroad. George Smart said, "If a Hollywood secretary had let him see Louis B. Mayer . . . on just one occasion, . . . he would be famous and wealthy today." But because Koverman "refused him admittance," he was "going to prison."[11]

Along with guarding the star galaxy gate, part of Koverman's job was to keep an eye out for pending legislation in Sacramento, and to lobby for or against it on behalf of the studio's interests. Entertaining lawmakers, including many familiar with her pre-MGM career, was another of her duties. Singer Eadie Adams (not the wife of Ernie Kovacs) accompanied Koverman on one trip, "getting out their best finery" to "attend the gov-ernors dinner in honor of the legislature." Adams had been singing ballads at the Cinegrill in the Hollywood Roosevelt Hotel, a popular spot of the movie crowd. Koverman believed Adams "was going places" when she signed with MGM in 1935. Louella Parsons called Adams "something of a pet project" for Koverman, and another reported that Adams was getting her first role in the movie *Mob Rule*. It wasn't a smashing career, but she did go on to dub the voice of Jean Harlow singing "Did I Remember" to Cary Grant in the film *Suzy* (1936), Harlow's last movie. She appeared as an extra in the Three Stooges film *Restless Knights* (1937), but soon after, her physician ordered her to rest her voice. After a few more stints performing with Les Parker, she moved to Palm Springs and launched her more profitable and lasting career as real estate agent to the stars.[12]

Leatrice Joy Gilbert was another Koverman hopeful, even though she already had connections as the daughter of MGM star John Gilbert and actress Leatrice Joy. Nevertheless, Koverman was the first to promote her for an upcoming project, the 1944 classic *National Velvet*. Louella Parsons reported that Ida Koverman had found "the perfect Velvet" when Miss Joy showed up at the studio "all done up in riding togs to prove her contention that here at last was the youthful heroine for the best seller." Koverman immediately took her to producer Hunt Stromberg, who found her charming. Unfortunately, World War II interrupted moving forward with the production, but Joy made her movie debut in 1938 in the Walter Huston production *Of Human Hearts* starring James Stewart. Two years later, Leatrice Joy's mother and Koverman hosted a World Affairs Council Forum talk on the subject of "Paul and John, Two Apostles in a Troubled World."[13]

After hearing one of her recordings, Koverman met the twelve-year-old Susanna Foster and her mother at the train station in 1940. Foster was considered a contender for *National Velvet*, and as a possible replacement for Deanna Durbin, who had moved to Universal. Foster's voice was so spectacular that a film called *B Above High C* was probed as a perfect vehicle for her, but the project failed to pan out. She was "dubbed a tremendous singing 'find' and cast, pronto, as the daughter of Mary Martin and Allan Jones in *The Great Victor Herbert*." Regardless, she soon "got a big fat envelope from the studio on Christmas morning," informing her "they no longer needed her services." No matter; Universal signed her up, where she starred with Nelson Eddy in *The Phantom of the Opera* (1943).[14]

Ida Koverman operated within the symbiotic spheres of Hollywood parties, performance, public personalities, and publicity as she circulated in a world filled with creative, gifted, and beautiful people. Her mentoring didn't guarantee stardom, but her efforts never went unnoticed, and it wasn't at all odd for her to be seen around town on the arm of a handsome young man, such as Jay Lloyd Brubaker from Amarillo, Texas, whose good looks resembled a combination of Cary Grant and Clark Gable. Brubaker, according to one columnist, was a "personality boy, . . . a salesman [who] could have sold shoe-hooks to mermaids!" The story was that Brubaker simply went into Ida Koverman's office to sell her tires, but instead of buying a set, she said, "We can't use your tires, but we might use you," and, "that's how a tire salesman crashed the movies." Louella Parsons suggested, given her nose for talent, "Ida must be 100 per cent right" about Brubaker.[15] Jay Lloyd Brubaker dropped his last name, and he got a screen test in February 1934. Later that year, Jay Lloyd's and Ida Koverman's evening at the Riviera Country Club inspired kudos to Koverman for launching his MGM career. While Lloyd "remained as a player," over time, however, this really meant only in local theater productions.[16]

A more successful aspirant was the handsome pianist Dalies Frantz, already known as "Titan of the Keyboard." After his 1934 appearance with the renowned conductor Leopold Stokowski, Frantz won a touring contract with Columbia Concerts Corporation. When Ida Koverman heard him a few years later, she promoted him around Hollywood. His first opportunity came in a 1938 piano solo when he replaced José Iturbi in the movie *Sweethearts*. Koverman threw a party to showcase his "art and musicianship," which impressed everyone, including Joan Crawford, Nelson Eddy, Edward G. Robinson, Rosalind Russell, Frank Capra, and Hedda Hopper. Ida and her new protégé attended a party with José Iturbi hosted by good friend and opera singer Rosa Ponselle. The *Los Angeles Times* noted that Frantz was making a screen test with Joan Crawford, and "It is believed that he has screen personality as well as musical ability." Even though this transition was "very unusual for instrumentalists, among musicians, to succeed," Frantz's movie career looked promising. He was slated to portray Franz Liszt in *The Life of Frederic Chopin* starring Robert Donat, but that film later turned into Columbia's *A Song to Remember* (1945), without Dalies Frantz. It didn't matter because Frantz continued his scheduled concert tours across thirty American cities.[17]

Ida Koverman took Frantz on a tour of MGM, and columnist Sheila Graham said the "blond concert pianist" Frantz was Ida Koverman's "latest protégé," who was making his film debut in the 1938 production of *Balalaika*, costarring Nelson Eddy and Ilona Massey. Graham pointed out that as Louis B. Mayer's "right and left hand," Koverman "is doing for Dalies what she did for Nelson Eddy when he was a Hollywood unknown." That is, she was "showing him the ropes, telling him which actors to study, which executives to play ball with." Graham hoped that "Mr. Dalies will be as grateful as Nelson Eddy, who last year presented Miss Koverman with a mink coat."[18]

Dalies Frantz's appearance with conductor Arthur Rodzinski at the Hollywood Bowl was preceded by a party attended by Koverman and her friends, opera stars Lawrence Tibbett, Jeanette MacDonald and her husband Gene Raymond, Nelson Eddy, and Lily Pons; actors Beulah Bondi and Mary Pickford; and writer Frances Marion. Frantz quickly won over the Hollywood crowd, but his Bowl performance received mixed reviews. Columnists remained optimistic that Frantz was "on the high road to a movie career to all intents and purposes," but his screen career never took a grand leap. It was just enough to join the ranks of celebrities, however, who bought property in the San Fernando Valley to raise horses and thoroughbred dogs. The press still kept track of him, and, in 1940, he had a part in *I Take This Woman*, and his name was included in an occasional fan magazine.[19]

Like many in Koverman's circle, the Second World War also took its toll on Frantz's health and for the most part ended his Hollywood career. He served briefly as an intelligence officer, but medical problems forced an early discharge and continued to plague him for years. He joined the music department at the University of Texas, and he remained in touch with Ida Koverman. In 1949 he visited Los Angeles, where, the press noted, Ida Koverman accompanied "the illustrious American pianist" to the Hollywood Bowl for the Koussevitzky-Rubinstein concert.[20]

Nineteen-year-old William Albert Henry was another Koverman discovery, and he was actually cast in 1934 as a young lieutenant in *Operator 13*. Henry grew up around the stage and studied acting in Pasadena. His love of swimming likely enhanced his appeal to Koverman, who arranged acting lessons for him at MGM. His big break came with his being cast as the round-horn-rimmed-glasses-wearing bookworm Gilbert Wynant in the 1934 classic *The Thin Man*, starring William Powell and Myrna Loy. Then, he joined Koverman's other "discoveries," Jean Parker, Robert Taylor, and her friend Betty Furness in the 1934 *A Wicked Woman*, playing the adult son of a troubled woman who murdered her lowlife husband and fled with her family for a life on the run. As the film was about to wrap, Henry suffered an attack of appendicitis. He was rushed to the hospital where, according to Hollywood lore, Henry's last scene was partially filmed with the real sounds of the hospital because it coincided with his character recovering from the brutal attack. Henry's next part was in *Society Doctor*, a film designed to showcase MGM's contract players. At first, he feared he would suffer from typecasting, but he happily went back to work because it would be "duck soup," an easy way to earn money while lying down on the job.[21]

Henry didn't have to worry about being typecast. In February, he was listed as "idle" in the MGM weekly stock talent report, but cast as Rockwell in the 1935 *China Seas*, starring Clark Gable, Jean Harlow, and Wallace Beery. He then moved to Fox and, later, other studios. In 1940, he earned top billing in *Emergency Squad* with Anthony Quinn. By the time he died in 1982, Henry had appeared in 117 movies and countless television shows. Only one other mishap threatened his life. In 1943, during the filming of a torchlight parade scene for *Johnny Come Lately*, a frightened horse headed straight for actress Marjorie Main. He raced toward her and pushed her aside, but he was knocked to the ground and nearly trampled in the process.[22]

Society Doctor didn't catapult William Henry to star status, but it did wonders for one of Ida Koverman's most famous protégés, Spangler Arlington Brugh, whom she rechristened as Robert Taylor when he signed his MGM contract in 1934. She proudly told a reporter he was just a kid of nineteen when he showed up in her office, apparently after being spotted by an agent in Pomona, and she "helped him along and gave him some advice," because he had little confidence in his acting ability. He almost cried when he was asked to play Romeo because he'd never even read the play.[23]

Their friendship grew out of a kinship of political persuasions, German heritage, and family backgrounds. She immediately "began grooming him for stardom," and the studio launched "the most extensive and expensive public relations effort" to introduce America to Robert Taylor. His extraordinary good looks made him an easy sell, but even after appearing with MGM's most popular stars, it was playing opposite Greta Garbo in *Camille* (1936) that established him as a consummate ladies' man.[24]

As Robert Taylor's star was rising, so was Koverman's, aided by the stories about her intimate relationship with Taylor. "Louis B. Mayer's confidential super-secretary and one of the most brainy and popular women in Hollywood" was the one Taylor sought out "as his confidante anytime he feels his fan mail and press notices may make him swell-headed." During a dinner at the Bel Air home of Jeanette MacDonald and Gene Raymond, Koverman spoke to a reporter about how Taylor "has asked her to serve as his personal conceit mentor," to tell him "whenever she noticed his cranium was beginning to expand."[25]

Publicity fodder aside, evidence of Koverman's personal intimacy with Taylor while serving as Mayer's watchdog is exemplified in the surprise elopement of Robert Taylor and Barbara Stanwyck. The Taylor-Stanwyck relationship had irritated Mayer, but eventually he assisted Taylor with

planning the sequence of events on Saturday, May 13, 1939. After a lei-
surely dinner with friends Zeppo and Marion Marx, they headed to the
Hollywood Palladium. Suddenly, Taylor abruptly announced he had an
appointment in San Diego, and said to his lover, "Lady, you have a date
with the man who is going to marry Barbara Stanwyck." They had talked
about marriage and had a license, but the moment was a genuine surprise
for Stanwyck. He had hired a judge, arranged to hold the ceremony at
the home of friends, and upon their arrival, Stanwyck's godfather, Uncle
Buck Mack, Ida Koverman, and Dalies Frantz greeted them.[26]

Socializing around the Southland provided opportunities for friendships to blossom among young and old who circulated in Koverman's
world. Sometimes, romances blossomed among them, however varying
in depth or duration. She became friends with Jackie Cooper's mother,
Mabel Cooper, who shared Koverman's interests not only in promoting
Jackie's career, but also as a pianist and an actress, who even appeared in
an MGM short with her son. In 1933, Koverman was a matron of honor
for Mabel Cooper's nuptials to Charles J. Bigelow. The women stayed
friends and in 1936, along with Jackie, they took a trip to Palm Springs
for a vacation at the B & H Ranch. Joining them at the popular dude
ranch was Koverman's close friends Horty (Hortense) and Bill Levy and
actresses Betty Furness and Irene Hervey. Hervey had earned some press
with Koverman's other protégé, Jay Lloyd, when he carried her across
a flooded street, for which he was dubbed "the Sir Walter Raleigh of the
movie colony."[27] Along with Lloyd, she was romantically linked to Robert Taylor, but, in 1936, she married singer Allan Jones. She appeared in
movies and television for two decades while their son, Jack Jones, went
on to a highly successful singing career.

Ida Koverman sealed her reputation as a premiere talent scout with her
promotion of Clark Gable, who was initially shunned by others at MGM.
Irving Thalberg whined, "Look at his big, batlike ears," and Ben Piazza
said, "With those ears he looks like a giant sugar bowl." The ridicule was
relentless, and Gable was sensitive about them, but Ida Koverman saw
something in him, as did one studio photographer who equated Rudolph
Valentino's nostrils to Clark's attributes, suggesting, "If nostrils can become
sex symbols, so can ears."[28]

Koverman's lobbying efforts apparently included her initiative to prove
that Gable had sex appeal. She filled a Glendale movie theater with MGM
messenger girls and secretaries to view his screen test and, just as she had
anticipated, "the audience sat bolt upright whenever Gable appeared."
Based on the inquiries and rave reviews scribbled on the comment cards,

Gable was signed the next day. Louis B. Mayer was away at the time, but Thalberg immediately lined up several projects for Gable before Mayer even realized who he was.[29]

When Mayer did pay attention to his contract players, he exercised a great deal of control over their on- and off-screen lives. He "developed a technique . . . that guaranteed the imposition of his will," which became known as "Louis's swoons," and it was Ida Koverman who repeatedly resuscitated him, for which others believed Mayer showed little appreciation. Learning about Gable's affair with Joan Crawford, for example, Koverman knew Mayer had taken another "elegant slide into the twilight zone," when she heard a loud bang from inside his office. She rushed in with soda water, a moist towel, and some ammonia, and asked what was wrong. He held up his hand and nodded his head, which in Mayer sign language, meant to "buzz off."[30] Nevertheless, she remained a loyal servant on behalf of Mayer's interests, which intertwined with her own.

She was instrumental in deflecting potential scandals and putting out hotspots before they turned into infernos. During the shooting of *Honky Tonk*, Gable's wife, actress Carole Lombard, became concerned about rumors he was involved with the newly hired teenager Lana Turner. After all, her own adulterous affair with Gable while he was married to his first wife Ria meant that her fears were not unfounded. Photographs from the set only fueled her anxiety, and she confided her concern to Louella Parsons, who decided to see what was going on. She phoned Koverman to say she was coming to the studio, and quickly hung up. Koverman had just enough time to call over to the set to learn that they were just starting to shoot a love scene. Director Jack Conway laughed as he reassured her there was noting to see, but Koverman argued that it wasn't very funny, because Louella was out for Lana's blood.

Koverman learned that Parsons's real motive was to protect Lana Turner, who, at seventeen, was "vulnerable and unschooled," because Parsons knew the studio could "make them grow up overnight," and she feared Turner could unintentionally "cause Gable and Carole a lot of harm." Koverman intercepted Parsons as she walked to the set, where it was clear to both women that Lana Turner was hardly the "Lolita" Parsons had feared. In fact, Turner appeared to be intimidated and standoffish toward Gable rather than charmed by him. Parsons left the studio convinced the studio actually planted the rumors to create a buzz about the movie.[31] The two costars went on to make three more films together. Sadly, three months after the release of *Honky Tonk* (1941), thirty-three-year-old Carole Lombard died in a plane crash returning from a war-bond drive.

Examples of how Koverman navigated the studio's chronic crises and her own living legacy are scattered throughout decades of testimonies by MGM and Hollywood contemporaries. Often from fleeting images, it is possible to glean some of her interactions with those she befriended and those she promoted. One of them was with one of the most beautiful, brilliant, and controversial women MGM ever hired, Hedy Lamarr. The relationship between Mayer and Lamarr was a difficult one, but she "remained in good standing" even when they stopped communicating directly during negotiations over her contract. Ida Koverman had become her supporter and friend, recognizing there was something to her that Mayer had taken a little longer to realize. Koverman acted as Lamarr's intermediary, and so they frequently had lunch together. Lamarr finally settled with Metro for a new salary of $2,500 a week, and she gave up plans to appear in the stage production of *Salome*.[32]

Ida Koverman's personal tastes reflected social and cultural changes, and she became a leading force in bridging older and newer musical genres. The creative tension between classical and modern music was noted in Maxine Bartlett's 1940 column describing an upcoming "musical hash" of vocal and instrumental selections that ranged from traditional classical to "the latest 'hot' swing." The concert of "symphony and swing," would feature Leopold Stokowski versus Benny Goodman, with fans such as Clark Gable preferring the Goodman style, while his wife was drawn to "the soothing strains of the classics."[33] Koverman earned accolades during her early years at MGM, and she helped to enrich the studio's coffers, but her more significant contributions to the studio's heavenly star power were still to come, as would her broader influence throughout the industry and to the wider cultural evolution of Los Angeles.

CHAPTER 18

Troubled Tenors and Superstar Sopranos

"Ida Koverman—the first-class helper of Louis B. Mayer, boss of
MGM studios . . . known as his jack-of-all-trades . . . carried a lot
of weight with Mayer."[1]

THE METRO-GOLDWYN-MAYER STUDIO WAS A BEHEMOTH ENTERPRISE
located outside the perimeter of Hollywood proper, and its reach into the
adjoining communities was profound, as the motion-picture industrial
base expanded its footprint with its surrounding environs serving as play-
grounds and nurturing fields. Ida Koverman was one of many conduits
through which cultural transfusions circulated through the city's veins and
flowed from local to international arenas of popular entertainment. Just
as she had facilitated relationships between politicians and partisans, she
cultivated musical talent for the movies while more broadly promoting
the performing arts throughout the city.

Her first love was opera, however, and as she explained to MGM vocal
coach Arthur Rosenstein, she was "just a disappointed soprano at heart,"
which was why she was so interested in, and thankful for, so many young
singers in Los Angeles. The advent of motion-picture sound technology
in 1929 inspired new opportunities for her to exercise her ear for talent
and to persuade the studio to upgrade its audio-recording system.[2] MGM
was hardly alone, or even the first, in exploiting the natural music-movie
symbiosis, but Koverman helped to shape the studio's star-studded roster
of its upcoming Golden Era.

It seemed as if Koverman were everywhere, and wherever she was, she "made a point of hunting for fresh talent to keep the wheels turning at MGM." Creatively unconstrained and unbound by tradition, she often saw potential or imagined greatness in unconventional people. Robert Vogel attested to Koverman's skill, believing it derived from Louis B. Mayer's unconditional confidence in her. To him, the point was, "In effect, she was everything." She used her extensive influence generously, and as Garland biographer David Shipman understood, she was so close to the seat of power that her contemporaries assumed she was "the conduit of ideas, schemes and projects," so that "pictures could be made or abandoned according to her sensibilities."[3]

Attesting to this was MGM singer-actress Marion Bell, who noted that Koverman "had a big hand in shaping the classic MGM musical style by quietly encouraging her boss to sponsor musical talent like herself."[4] Bell had a long career after her brief stint at MGM, where she appeared in cameos in such films as *Ziegfeld Follies* (1946). She left for Broadway to appear in *Brigadoon*, composed by Alan Jay Lerner, to whom she was briefly married.

New York Metropolitan Opera star Lawrence Tibbett was the world's highest-paid baritone when Koverman envisioned him as the perfect vehicle to couple her style of movies and music. She initiated his 1930 hiring for *The Rogue Song*, which later inspired Tibbett's son to say that Koverman was not just "an opera buff," but also "the reputed 'brains' of MGM." She "had been the first to imagine the possibilities of the Tibbett voice" and his good looks on the big screen. Tibbett Jr. was convinced that because Koverman "just loved opera [and] she loved" his dad, this is what really launched his movie career, and not because Louis B. Mayer had any hand in it.[5]

Overseen by producer Paul Bern, *The Rogue Song* was MGM's first Technicolor sound film. Koverman had hoped, and many agreed that it was a great vehicle to expose mass audiences to the "high culture" of opera. It was a big gamble, though, so in order to hedge their bets, the studio included scenes with Laurel and Hardy, and in some places promoted it only as a comedy. Nevertheless, Lawrence Tibbett's role earned him an Academy Award nomination for best actor. He went on to make several more films, and for many years, he continued his concert tours. While his personal life would be plagued with problems, he remained friends with Ida Koverman and joined her in the promotion of the city's musical culture.[6]

Tibbett was just one of Koverman's early "discoveries," and the press followed her every initiative, big or small. In 1933, for example, she held a luncheon in the MGM commissary, where "social, musical and other guests" listened to Metropolitan Opera diva Maria Jeritza. Two years later, Jeritza finally made a screen test, greeted with great anticipation that she was about to fulfill "her much-prophesied film career" with the role of Carlotta in *Johann Strauss*.[7] It didn't pan out, but to her it didn't matter, because she was happily married to film executive Winfield Sheehan, and until his death a decade later, she joined Koverman and Tibbett to promote opera and the musical arts.

Encouraging established musicians and singers to transition from the concert stage to the movies was only one avenue for Koverman to find talent. She often promoted lesser or completely unknown talent by hosting well-attended private salons or studio events to introduce a new find. Her guest lists reflected her diverse networks floating between creative, cultural, and political circles. Over her quarter century at MGM, she sat on dozens of boards and committees, such as the Los Angeles Philharmonic and the Opera Guild and even Christmas concerts featuring regional folk music portraying "mountain and plantation music, songs, and character delineations" at the Beverly Hills Hotel.[8]

Before Jeannette MacDonald joined MGM in 1933, she enjoyed a successful singing career, moving back and forth from the stage to film in America and abroad. Once settled in at MGM, she was "Hollywood's undisputed queen of song." She knew that Koverman had been a major force in California's Republican Party, and now MacDonald felt "freer to cement" their friendship, which grew as Koverman became MacDonald's devoted ally and trusted advisor, even if on occasion Koverman's counsel ran counter to her own instincts. Koverman thought MacDonald's paramour, press agent Robert G. Ritchie, was "a schnorrer, or parasite," and told her she "would do far better to depend on her and L. B. when trouble threatened," which apparently it often did. MacDonald eventually fell in love with the handsome actor Gene Raymond, and in 1936 Koverman attended their engagement party at the Beverly Wilshire Hotel, their wedding in June the next year, and for decades she was a frequent guest at the MacDonald-Raymond home.[9]

Most baby boomers recognize the title song from MGM's 1935 classic *San Francisco*, with a story line about colorful characters and the major 1906 earthquake. MacDonald lobbied the studio to cast Clark Gable as her costar, and finally after overcoming his schedule and resistance, he reluctantly took the role of the saloonkeeper and gambler Blackie Norton, a similar persona he captured again as Rhett Butler in *Gone with the Wind*. Gable didn't like that the script required him to stand silently with his back to the camera or merely smiling at her while she sang to him. Off-screen, he ignored her. During her efforts to recruit Gable for the film, MacDonald asked Ida Koverman for advice about how to handle Gable if he wanted to know why she wanted him so badly for the part. Koverman advised her to cozy up to Gable rather than tell him the truth—that she thought he was a great actor and perfect for the part. Gable did ask, and MacDonald immediately regretted how she "looked him square in the eye" and told him it was because he had sex appeal. The minute she said it, she "could have cut out my tongue," as she saw he was "repulsed and insulted" and "grunted and walked away." She believed she lost a chance to make a friend.[10] Rumors about Gable's macho reputation suggests she would have been disappointed no matter what she said, and it's hard to divine Ida Koverman's logic or if MacDonald interpreted it as Koverman intended.

Nevertheless, it is probable that Koverman's experience with powerful men led her to believe that Gable was like them, who, in spite of their charisma and success, needed constant reassurance about their virility. Perhaps she thought MacDonald could build up his confidence, a trait he so easily projected to the outside world, but which Koverman felt he lacked internally. Koverman later revealed how she believed "Gable always thought less of himself than anyone else," and "his success was a great surprise to him." She thought his success was, in part, because of the very quality she had advised Hollywood hopefuls to embrace, an "individuality and charm."[11]

The Gable incident hardly affected the lifelong friendship between the two women. Perhaps this was, in part, because Koverman was largely responsible for forging Jeannette MacDonald's most profitable and enduring legacy as a costar to baritone Nelson Eddy. Nelson Eddy was an established opera singer when, in February 1933, he stepped in for German soprano Lotte Lehmann at a sold-out concert at the Los Angeles Philharmonic Auditorium. This unscheduled audition exceeded everyone's expectations, including Ida Koverman's, who, along with the cheering crowd, gave him eighteen encores. Instantly smitten with his good looks and resonant voice, she immediately began lobbying Mayer, emphasizing how he was the total package of good looks, genuineness, and beautiful voice. "She demanded and got a screen test," after which he was offered a contract at twelve hundred dollars a week, with accommodations for his concert commitments. It took another eighteen months for the studio to figure out what to do with him, but the 1935 operetta *Naughty Marietta* launched what would become his iconic partnership with Jeannette MacDonald. It almost didn't happen, though, and after negotiations stalled with the popular singer Alan Jones, Koverman and MacDonald made clear their preference for Eddy.[12] Deemed one of the year's biggest hits, the movie's memorable song, "Ah! Sweet Mystery of Life," earned Eddy his first gold record.

Child actor Cora Sue Collins had a part in *Naughty Marietta,* and she recalled a colorful incident during the filming. She and her mother were sitting in Ida Koverman's office outside of Mayer's executive suite. Suddenly, they were startled by Norma Shearer abruptly backing out of Mayer's door screaming, "Don't tell me that, L.B., I fucked all those bastards on my way up!" Shearer turned toward the door and, although surprised to see the young girl, she didn't skip a beat and mumbled, "Oh, hello, Cora Sue, how are you?" as she rushed out the door. Cora Sue innocently turned to her mother to ask, "What does fuck mean?" who continued to sit shocked and stone-faced, as did Koverman when asked the same question. The fearless child walked into Mayer's office and asked him, and without a flinch, Mayer simply replied that someday someone would explain it to her.[13]

As "America's Singing Sweethearts," Nelson Eddy and Jeannette MacDonald were among the studio's most popular singing duets of all time. They made seven more films for MGM until they both left in 1942. Nelson Eddy was never a regular on the Hollywood party circuit like most of Koverman's finds, save for one notable exception at one of Koverman's buffet dinners, where he performed a classic Greek dance with a water pitcher on his shoulder, and sang for the rest of the evening.[14] Nelson Eddy became the highest-paid singer in the world, and one of most successful of Koverman's crossover stars to bring their operatic skills to the movies.

Always on the lookout for charismatic singers, Koverman also had a keen sense of who would appeal to movie audiences. When she first heard Mario Lanza, she knew she had found another box-office wonder on the scale of a Rudolph Valentino, who spawned an international hysterical fan base of the later magnitude of Frank Sinatra, Elvis, and the Beatles.

After a promising incipient opera-stage career, Mario Lanza was encouraged to make a sound test for RCA Victor records, after which executive Mannie Sachs sent his vocal samples and photographs to Ida Koverman in anticipation of his appearance at the Hollywood Bowl.[15] In a surviving audio-recording interview, however, Lanza attributes Art Lash with sending the recordings to Ida Koverman, and yet another suggests that she played them for Louis B. Mayer, who was equally impressed, and then persuaded the Hollywood Bowl to book Mario Lanza for its 200th concert on August 28, 1947.

However it evolved, Ida Koverman and Louis B. Mayer attended Lanza's Hollywood Bowl debut. Another MGM star, Kathryn Grayson, and her husband accompanied them, and the next day at the studio, she and Lanza sang together. Everyone agreed they were perfect partners. Lanza recalled how, "I fractured 'em. . . . Ida Koverman, Louis B. Mayer's right hand assistant, was at that party too, and she lined up all the producers. What a night. Why, even Louis B. Mayer had tears in his eyes." Hedda Hopper heard him and wrote that he was the only man to play Caruso.[16]

Koverman "was deeply impressed with his singing and his striking good looks," and that she found in him "an unusual combination" for an opera singer, but Lanza biographer Derek Mannering suggests it actually required "a little bit of arm twisting" for her to set "a plan in motion that would forever change the course of Mario Lanza's career." Lanza was hardly the first singer Koverman had identified with the combined attributes, and, in fact, he was part of a succession of charismatic singers Koverman turned into movie star idols.[17] Lanza's 1947 contract allowed for filming, recording, and live concerts, so his first film, *That Midnight Kiss* (1949) with Kathryn Grayson, was his first chance to infuse the operetta genre with a new vibrancy. The *Toast of New Orleans* followed the next year, and *The Great Caruso* in 1951. His last MGM film was *Because You're Mine* in 1952. Lanza was RCA Victor's first classical artist, singing *Be My Love* to sell more than one million copies in 1951. Chroniclers of American popular culture rarely include him in the catalogue of major stars, but Mario Lanza was among the most famous, biggest stars of the post-war era. Mario Lanza was an "international sensation," who made millions of dollars for MGM. His fans literally accosted him, tearing at his clothes, forcing him to wear protective padding in order to keep their fingernails from scratching his skin. Contemporary opera stars even credit Lanza with their inspiration to combine popular ballads and opera in their repertoires.

Lanza was a big man with a big personality, a big appetite, and a big ego. His career was short-lived, and even before he was removed from the 1954 production of *The Student Prince*, reports surfaced that Ida Koverman was "pitching a Met tenor, Brian Sullivan, to play the prince," perhaps because she thought the role was not the right fit for Lanza's voice and personality. Lanza's voice was dubbed for his eventual replacement, Edmund Purdon.[18]

Tenor Brian Sullivan, a local boy, was another of Koverman's picks, but his movie career hardly began before it ended after he came to MGM in 1943. After watching and listening to Sullivan, Koverman decided he was wasting his time. She candidly told him he was much more of a singer than an actor, and advised him to go east, and offered a prestigious letter of introduction. She later described Sullivan as having "a magnificent voice [who] made good on the concert stage" as a "regular member of the Metropolitan Opera Company," adding that "he never forgets to say 'hello' when he comes back to Hollywood."[19]

During Lanza's difficulties, rumors floated that Cuban-born Manola Alvarez Mera was kept in reserve to ensure that Lanza sustained his interest in finishing the movie *Seven Hills*, filming in Rome. He had already had a two-year run with Billy Rose's 1948 New York production of *Violins over Broadway*. Koverman, who had already "picked the best of them, . . . [now] says the greatest tenor she's heard in years [Mera] is the sensation of Las Vegas, singing at the Flamingo with the Freddie Martin band." She threw him a party where one observer believed, "If he's as good as some of her other finds—Mario Lanza, Jane Powell, Kathryn Grayson—he's in for a long career." After a few bit parts and appearances, he returned to Cuba to perform until the revolution, after which he lived in exile, performing throughout the hemisphere known as the "Caruso of South America." For another decade, he sustained his "popularity singing in operettas, musical reviews, radio, television, vaudeville, and major nightclubs."[20]

As one of the "denizens of the Bowl," or the Philharmonic or grand opera, the start and end of the concert seasons was always a great time for Ida Koverman and her friends to gather, and often an opportunity for her to promote a new singer or musician. In August 1948, she attended the Lehmann-Strauss-Ormandy concert with Frank Vitale, Wynn Rocamora, and Patricia Morison, who were among the "real music lovers" she associated with among the Hollywood crowd. In November she dined at the Bowl with her fellow board members Joseph and Hortense Levy and was "proud as punch over film tests of new basso buffo Italo Tajo," described as "her new protégé."[21] Unfortunately, his movie career failed to launch.

In spite of lingering skepticism about bringing more opera stars into the movies, Koverman pushed MGM to sign Metropolitan Opera star Ezio Pinza, who had a successful Broadway starring role in *South Pacific*. She thought he could easily transition to the big screen because he "was the only person for the lead" in the 1951 production of *Mr. Imperium*. Unfortunately, in spite of costar Lana Turner, the film did little for Pinza's movie career or MGM.[22]

Ida Koverman helped to guide MGM's embrace of the sound revolution by fostering the infusion of the classical musical arts, big business, and celebrity on an unprecedented scale. Some of her "discoveries" struggled to navigate the personal and professional perils of movie stardom, some had fleeting success, and others found the limelight elsewhere. But as she secured her own destiny inside the Culver City enclave and the broader industry, her hand also shaped the contours of twentieth-century American popular culture that has endured for generations.

CHAPTER 19

Swing versus Opera

"It was Koverman who codified the star system, . . . and Koverman had a real nose for talent."[1]

DURING THE EARLY 1930S, AMERICA'S CLASSICAL-MUSIC TRADITION AND its modern sensibilities coalesced and cross-fertilized.[2] When Ida Koverman facilitated MGM's hiring of two equally gifted and precocious young female singers, their contrasting vocal styles epitomized this cultural shift. Koverman inadvertently fueled a contrived musical rivalry that fostered the careers of two movie-musical legends while bringing millions of fans and their dollars into movie-industry coffers. Deanna Durbin was a cultivated, angelic operatic soprano who sang traditional opera. Contralto Judy Garland soulfully belted out swing arrangements of the emergent big-band era. Their friendly competition began when, around the same time, they joined MGM's catalogue of young performers. While Judy Garland ultimately stayed on to usher in a new genre of movie musicals, Deanna Durbin moved on to Universal International, just in time to keep its star system from imploding.

Deanna Durbin loved singing and she was very good at it, but she thought acting was an altogether different aspiration. Nevertheless, when MGM began preparations for a movie about the acclaimed contralto Madame Ernestine Schumann-Heink, the exuberant Durbin realized she might have more options.[3] The elder opera singer would play herself, but the search began for a singer who could play her as a young girl. Ida Koverman had already heard Durbin sing, so she called her agent to set up a meeting with Louis B. Mayer and Schumann-Heink. Unfortunately, the audition was postponed when Schumann-Heink became ill.

Ida rescheduled the meeting while Louis B. Mayer was away in New York. Durbin performed *Il Bacio* (The Kiss), after which Koverman abruptly stood up, asked Durbin to wait, and then disappeared into another room. She rushed back in to say that Mayer was holding on the line eagerly waiting to hear her sing. Surprised but unruffled, Durbin sang into the phone. The brilliance of her voice transcended time and space, instantaneously impressing Mayer as fast as the current caried the sound. He told Koverman to offer Durbin a contract at fifty dollars a week, which she did, and before Durbin even left the studio, Mayer wired her a congratulatory telegram.[4] *Il Bacio* would become Durbin's signature aria.

While Durbin had been honing her skills, it was becoming increasingly obvious that the youngest member of the Gumm Sisters trio, Judy, known as "Baby Gumm," had a charismatic stage presence and a unique, compelling voice fueled by an equally vibrant ambition. After the singing siblings became the Garland Sisters, their mother Ethel Gumm, like countless other stage mothers, began slogging her daughter to auditions around Los Angeles in hopes that someone would "discover" her youngest songbird. Hedda Hopper was openly critical of mothers like Mrs. Gumm, wondering "if there wasn't a special, subhuman species of womankind that bred children for the sole purpose of dragging them to Hollywood?"[5] The reality is that while there were and still are untold numbers of mothers and coaches who nurture protégés, it was the powerful men running the industry who turned some of them into Hollywood stars. Ida Koverman was one of the most influential women to facilitate this process, and in doing so, she fully realized that mothers and musical children came as a package. They came with adult actors as well. Koverman befriended the mothers of Jean Harlow, Jackie Cooper, Harold Lloyd, and Marni Nixon, and so when she took an interest in Judy Garland, it was also the beginning of her relationship with Ethel.

Koverman also knew that some parents abused and exploited their children, and the industry eventually took notice when she and Hollywood Assemblyman Kent Redwine sponsored the 1939 California Child Actor's Bill, more commonly known as "the Coogan Bill," to protect child income earners. It was prompted by the lawsuit filed by former child actor Jackie Coogan, who learned that his mother and stepfather had squandered the millions of dollars he had earned as a professional actor. The Superior Court already oversaw contracts of high-salaried minors, but now the court had to ensure that parents put fifteen percent of their child's salaries into a trust, ensuring it as separate and not community property.[6]

Not only was a child actor's income vulnerable, but so was the legal and financial rewards that came with divining legitimate claims of "discovering" an actor. Ida Koverman's role in bringing new talent to MGM was an extracurricular part of her job description. She circulated among informal and professional networks filled with individuals who eagerly sought untapped talent. Sometimes staking out who deserved credit was a convoluted, cutthroat journey that required mapping out in court.

Such was the case with Deanna Durbin, when a screenwriter took her case to court arguing she was responsible for "opening the gates of Hollywood" to Durbin and sued her agents for a share of their commission. She won compensation up to the date of the decision, but put off a decision about future earnings. When Ida Koverman initiated Durbin's audition at MGM, she didn't get a cut of Durbin's earnings there or from Universal when Durbin became the highest-paid movie star of the era.[7]

Koverman didn't receive bonuses for the box-office success of Judy Garland, but she figures prominently in most of the accounts about how Garland came to join the MGM repertory. With so many variations about Garland's origin story, they are a genre unto themselves. Just when Koverman became part of Judy's audition process remains inconsistently described in a sequence of events that are frequently melded into one neat storyline. Rarely is Koverman slighted or omitted altogether, such as in Hugh Fordin's *MGM's Greatest Musicals: The Arthur Freed Unit.* Not only does Fordin inexplicably leave Ida Koverman out of the Garland-MGM origin story (except for mention in a footnote about her advice for Garland to sing "Kol Nidre" for Mayer), but he inexplicably ignores her in an extraordinary photograph, the caption of which identifies a white bobbed-haired woman as Louis B. Mayer's sister Ida Mayer Cummings. Cummings had dark hair, worn parted and pulled back in a bun. It is Ida R. Koverman standing with Mayer, Judy Garland, and Deanna Durbin who is also mistakenly identified as Mayer's adult daughter Irene, but who by then was a grown woman married to David O. Selznick, who is seen standing in the background.[8] The artifact visibly symbolizes Ida Koverman's singular place alongside three iconic figures of Hollywood history, and yet it is a startling reminder of how Koverman has remained, until now, invisible in front of our eyes.

Ida Koverman's interest in Judy Garland started when she first heard her sing in December 1934, during the Garland Sisters' performance at the renowned Wilshire Ebell Theatre in Los Angeles. So moved by Judy's voice, Koverman rushed backstage in hopes of arranging for Judy to "test at the studio." She was skeptical if Mayer would respond favorably to Judy's modern style, but she told Judy's mother she would arrange an audition anyway.[9]

It's very likely that accompanying Ida Koverman that night was Joseph Mankiewicz, a twenty-something, recently hired MGM screenwriter turned producer. He was a friend of Judy's family friends, Dr. Marcus and Marcella Rabwin, and it's likely he had already heard Judy sing at their home. Dr. Rabwin, in fact, delivered "Baby Gumm" into the world back in June 10, 1922, when they all lived in Grand Rapids, Minnesota, and coincidentally Marcella was the executive assistant to Mayer's son-in-law, David O. Selznick.

Judy Garland was about half Mankiewcz's age, half his size, and she internalized half of his confidence, hardly adequate to support her fragile ego. Joe Mankiewicz had a powerful inner strength and equally obvious and diverse outward talents. He went on to a career recognized for his literary sensibilities and craftsmanship in moviemaking, winning four Academy Awards and accolades as one of Hollywood's most intelligent filmmakers. Garland and Mankiewicz's initial friendship gave no hint of the blossoming romance they would later share.

Mankiewicz had little "faith in Mayer's ability to spot talent," and he believed that Koverman was "one of the most influential people at Metro." He was certain that MGM's most successful stars were there because of what MGM British producer Michael Balcon had described as her "eminence grise," suggesting that she exercised great influence in spite of her rank or title. Mayer biographer Charles Higham supports this view, especially after the death of the wunderkind Irving Thalberg in 1936, writing that "Mayer successfully bluffed his way through the rest of the thirties and into the forties," while he both hoped for and yet feared the rise of another Thalbcrg. Mayer and Ida Koverman and the other geniuses worked behind the scenes, and even if "Mayer could also rate a strong A average in picking stars," the reality is that Ida Koverman picked most of the stars that illuminated MGM's Golden Era.[10]

Columnist Sheilah Graham also acknowledged Ida Koverman's importance in her article headlined, "Take A Look Behind the Scenes at Women Who Make Film Wheels Spin." Describing her as the "white-haired confidential executive secretary to Louis B. Mayer," Koverman was included among the "important and powerful," women who worked "in the shadow of the mighty film land thrones." But Koverman stood out in how she "wields a scepter of power second only to that of her employer," and "in Mayer's absence from Hollywood, Miss Koverman takes over the reins of office."[11]

Mankiewicz believed Koverman understood the hired talent was of "primary importance" to MGM, unlike other executives he perceived as having "a chilling, impersonal attitude toward the studio's stable of stars." Koverman also realized Mankiewicz was not one to give way to "extravagant judgments," and he was more "inclined to cynicism and caution in many movie matters." After Koverman listened to Mankiewicz's exaltation of Judy Garland, she agreed to check out the Garland Sisters.[12]

It took a while, but eventually the momentum on Judy's behalf gained steam because of Koverman's "particular interest in the child." She kept in touch with her mother and recruited producer Sam Katz in the pro-Judy campaign. Garland's three separate auditions are usually morphed into one spectacularly tidy event, where Judy sang for Mayer, who immediately signed her up and then paraded her around the studio lot. During an early interview about her movie contract, Judy summed it up with a simple storyline saying that her manager had taken her to sing for MGM music publisher Jack Robbins, and then "she sang for Miss Koverman and Mr. Mayer," who had her sing for Mr. Katz, and then she got a contract. However succinct, Judy Garland already knew Ida Koverman was crucial to the narrative, noting that she was "a very important person," and urged the reporter to "put that in capitals, please."[13]

For what turned out to be the first two of three auditions, however, Judy's mother took her daughter to the Culver City lot. Koverman reassured them that Louis B. Mayer was very interested in hearing Judy sing. They walked to the studio's state-of-the-art sound stage at Studio I, where producers Arthur Freed and Jack Cummings were waiting.[14]

Actress Ethel Merman's former pianist, Roger Edens, soon became an unquestionable, creative influence on Garland's artistic evolution. He had joined MGM through the recommendation of silent-film actress Carmel Myers, who told Koverman about him, and she told Arthur Freed, who was quick to recognize Edens's ability to enhance his own work, and he hired Edens. Edens claimed he was the first to hear Garland sing at her first audition, arranged through her agent. Undoubtedly, he "really flipped" when he heard Judy's voice, recalling that he fell in "love at first hearing," and it was "like discovering gold" where none had been expected. But his recollection is that he then called Ida Koverman, who called Louis B. Mayer, who called the lawyers, and then she was signed. But to Garland, when she joined MGM, Edens "was, at the time just a pianist . . . who got sort of dragged in to hear this little girl."[15]

During the third audition, Judy's father, Frank Gumm, escorted her to the studio and accompanied her on the piano, the usual task of her mother, who was ill or out of town that day. It wasn't going very well, so Koverman called Edens to step in, a move everyone agrees made all the difference in the outcome. For Judy, it was even more significant, because two months after she signed with MGM, her father died suddenly in November 1935. Garland is purported to have "forever clung to the memory of their association" at that decisive Metro audition. "It was the first time he had ever personally entered into any business arrangement," but she was "so glad he did come, because I feel like he brought me back. . . . I know he watched and helped me get my screen start."[16]

One view is that Mayer still needed what turned into relentless lobbying from his nephew Jack Cummings, Ida Koverman, and Arthur Freed, and only then did he agree to give Garland a contract. It's probably true that Mayer was reluctant to hear or hire another adolescent singer, but it's also likely that he showed up to the audition after Koverman assured him that Judy's voice "will stun you." [17]

Edens suggests he knew Judy could make "Mayer's eyes glisten," with the right song, so he and Koverman selected *Eli, Eli* (My God, My God), in the original Yiddish. Hedda Hopper believed Ida Koverman coached Garland on the rendition, while others suggest Judy already knew it because she performed it at Jewish venues. With or without Edens's or Koverman's direction, everyone knew the impact it would have on Mayer, who, for dramatic effect, got down on his knees and performed the song of mourning, as he did for Jeanette MacDonald and Ida Koverman during her contract update.[18]

Frances Marion recalled Koverman advising Judy to learn to sing *Eli Eli*, after which Mayer told Koverman she could decide whether or not to hire Judy. It is possible that Mayer was indifferent so he "tossed the ball right back to Ida," telling her, "If you want her, sign her up." Hedda Hopper said Koverman's strategy to bolster her instinct to hire Judy included support from Jack Cummings because she feared that if Garland failed, Mayer would never let her forget it. Koverman "was too knowing about the foxy ways of Mayer," and as Hopper said, after Cummings heard Garland sing, he told Koverman, "Let's sign her up."[19]

Judy Garland's contract was approved by the Superior Court on September 27, with a starting date of October 1, 1935. Her mother hired a new agent for her, but a few years later, Ida Koverman advised her that she needed to work with Frank Orsatti, who, in spite of his "unsavory" reputation, had already represented many of MGM contract players, because

Koverman believed he could "get Garland proper remuneration for the hard and important work she was now doing."[20]

Judy Garland now joined Deanna Durbin on the lot, where they took singing, dancing, and acting classes, along with the required educational curriculum, and they recorded sessions and made public appearances. Durbin loved performing at venues such as the Breakfast Club, especially when broadcast over the radio. The biographic production was cancelled because Madame Schumann-Heink failed to rally, and then died of leukemia in November 1936, inspiring Durbin to lament that "there was nothing else but to abandon the picture," and to her this meant that "the world lost the story of a life that was inspiring and full of beauty and great music."[21]

In the meantime, friendships grew, as did an esprit de corps among the youthful actors. Garland and Durbin shared their joys and impatience, and Koverman reassured them that their efforts would pay off. Deanna Durbin became part of the studio family, but she would fail to find a permanent home there. Just before both Durbin and Garland's contracts were due to expire, MGM featured them in the 1936 movie short *Every Sunday*, billed as "A Tabloid Musical." The homespun small-town storyline symbolized the larger context of America at a cultural crossroads, and in spite of one advertisement that promoted it as "the miniature musical of swing and rhythm," Durbin sang opera in the climactic duet.

Ambiguous rumors persist about what Mayer said after he viewed *Every Sunday*. He either issued a dictum to get rid of both girls, or to keep them both, or to "get rid of the fat one," but, at the time, some weren't sure which girl he meant, even though it is purported that he said unkind things about Garland's weight and physique. *Every Sunday* fails to inspire a sense that Garland was the "fat" one or inferior to Durbin in any physical way. Both of the girls are wearing similarly unattractive puffy-sleeved dresses with flowers pinned to curvy collars, and both hairstyles were unflattering, parted in the middle, pinned back to frame their faces, and both sets of eyebrows needed tending. Throughout the final musical number, sloppy editing or continuity captures Garland with and without lipstick, the absence of which emphasized her less contoured bone structure compared to Durbin's more refined features, but hardly enough to warrant exaggerated comparisons. What's more, over time, as both girls matured, makeup couldn't overcome Durbin's softer features, which faded on the big screen and paled next to Garland's dramatic beauty and charismatic expressions.

Various interpretations of why Durbin left and Judy stayed at MGM ignore how the timing of the release of all three films might have played a bigger role in the decision than which one was the fat one. After filming *Every Sunday*, both girls were loaned out to other studios, Judy Garland to 20th Century Fox to make *Pigskin Parade*, which was released on October 23, 1936. *Every Sunday* was finally released on November 28, 1936, after Durbin's contract had expired. She had already been loaned to Universal for Joseph Pasternak's *Three Smart Girls*, released on December 20, 1936, touting Durbin as the "greatest soprano since Jenny Lind," who had the "screen presence" of Greta Garbo. Universal picked up her contract, and movie audiences loved her, netting the studio a much-needed $1,250,000.[22]

Judy was inconsolable in her belief that her chance for stardom was unalterably eclipsed. Ethel took her to Koverman, the only person who she thought could comfort her daughter. Judy threw herself onto Koverman's lap, sobbing, "I've been in show business ten years, and Deanna's a star and I'm nothing!" Koverman knew how to sooth bruised egos. She had bolstered businessmen and politicians, and now she was buttressing movie actors, such as when Greer Garson "came to her rather desperately asking, 'Why won't they let me work?'" She told Garson to be patient because "she would have plenty to do before long, and—sure enough—not many months later, she was asking for a vacation." Koverman now told Garland, "You just wait. . . . you're going to get your chance, you'll be starred, and you're going to have your footprints in Grauman's Chinese—you'll see."[23] Before Hollywood Boulevard's Walk of Fame honored the industry's iconic figures, planting one's hand and footprints in the wet cement in the theater courtyard was proof that a motion-picture actor was indeed a movie star.

Ida Koverman continued to keep an eye on Judy inside and outside of the studio. "Make no mistake about it," a daughter of a family friend said, Ida "was a tough lady," and "as much as she could care about anybody," she "cared about Judy." Koverman became concerned that Mayer showed little enthusiasm for Judy, and she told screenwriter Frances Marion that whenever she brought up Judy's name for a small part in a musical, Mayer ranted, "Stop bleating! I'm running the studio, not you!" Eventually, Koverman figured out how to inspire Mayer to see the potential star-power of her young ingénue.[24]

The opportunity came during Mayer's thirty-sixth surprise birthday celebration for Clark Gable in 1937. Koverman suggested that Judy sing at the party. The audience would be a small but select group of MGM's top executives. Roger Edens quickly wrote new words to a song Judy had sung the day before, which would become the first of her signature melodies, "Dear Mr. Gable." Robert Vogel was among the group assembled that night, and after subsequent meetings, including a distributors' convention, it was clear Judy and her new song were a guaranteed moneymaker for theater owners and exhibitors, who showed their enthusiasm by banging on the tables and shouting roars of approval. Nevertheless, many found Garland unappealing and their failure of imagination is epitomized by Robert Vogel's crude observation of his first encounter when Koverman invited him and other executives to observe Garland's screen test. He said he saw "a little (girl)," who "looked almost humpbacked, very short neck, ugly little thing, fourteen, twelve, I don't know." It wasn't just men, however, who held starlets to a uniform standard of beauty. Writer Frances Marion remembered Garland was a "strange contrast to the others . . . drably dressed, short, and too plump," but "what attracted me to her was the beauty in her expressive eyes when she smiled at Ida Koverman in passing." Koverman beamed when she told Marion, "We've just signed that youngster," and "just wait until you hear her sing."[25]

After his honorable discharge from the army, and nearly a decade later, Clark Gable appeared at a birthday party for Judy Garland, where he read her a poem by Robert Nathan, to wish "her all kinds of good things." However, a few years later, in 1949, Gable was so sick of hearing Garland's signature song "at every major gathering of his barony," he whined, "Goddamn brat, you've ruined every one of my birthdays. They bring you out from behind the wallpaper to sing that song, and it's a pain in the ass."[26]

After filming *Everybody Sing* (1938), Garland and Roger Edens went on a promotional tour. She wrote to Koverman, "Dear Mrs. Kay, My goodness, here I am in Cleveland! . . . I'm having a perfect time, and I know I'm a bad girl for not writing long before this. Please don't be mad at me. New York was as wonderful. . . . I'll tell you all about the fun we had when I get home. Give my love to Mr. Mayer. Mom, & Roger send theirs—and you know send mine—Judy," with hugs and kisses, "xoxoxoxo."[27] Eventually, Garland's obvious affection expressed toward "Mrs. Kay," would be tested. But during these early years, as Garland's fame skyrocketed, so did her problems with diet and sleeping pills, and Koverman would attempt to minister to her psychological and physical needs as she transformed from an adolescent to a mature, independent woman.

Young and old, male and female, actors in Hollywood worried about their weight because the camera added pounds. Garland quickly lost weight, and while Koverman saw that she photographed and danced better, she knew this came at a cost. She felt that Judy was no longer a cheerful, young girl, but a slim, more sullen girl who was nervous, and who cried herself to sleep at night. The pressure was unbearable for Judy, who confided to Koverman, "They're starving me to death. . . . Please make them give me more to eat." Koverman pleaded with Mayer, "You can't do this to her. You can't destroy this girl's childhood," but he apparently told her to mind her own business. Hedda Hopper believed that Koverman's advocacy created a deep divide between Koverman and Mayer, but if it did, it would pale in comparison to the internal battle Koverman was waging with herself.[28]

Koverman was Garland's main ally inside the studio, but she was also an extension of her employer, and so she had to balance the studio's expectation of its actors to perform on demand with her sensitivity to the idiosyncratic nature of the "moving parts" of human talent within the star machine. Rather than directly challenge Mayer's directive to the studio commissary to keep Judy on a strict diet of tomatoes, light chicken broth, and a two-ounce hamburger patty, she called upon her good will among the staff to enlist their help and to keep it secret from Mayer and Judy's mother. Every night, Koverman whipped up thick vegetable soup and prepared thin, top grade steaks, and then she snuck the food into Judy's dressing room. Judy still lost weight, but not at the speed that endangered her health, and no one learned of the subterfuge.[29] Judy devoured the offerings as they likely bonded talking about the day's events and future possibilities.

Hedda Hopper believed Mayer's "suspicious brain came upon the idea that Ida had too much influence over Judy." He feared "she might be tempted to think of what was good for the girl before she thought of the studio," and Hopper understood that Mayer flatly told Koverman, "You've got too much work to do to look after the Garland," and to her, this meant, "by order, the old intimacy" between them was over.[30] The Koverman-Mayer alliance remained strong because of Ida's value to their mutual interests, and until bigger historical forces intervened in and outside of the studio.

Koverman needed to balance competing interests of the studio and its starlets that often blurred the lines of their personal and professional lives in the marketing of their pictures in the name of profits. Real and contrived off-screen romances were a common way to promote movies and movie stars. Koverman thought that actor and then enlisted man Robert Stack was a good match for Garland because she thought they looked good together. When Stack came home on leave, he made a date with Garland. That he showed up an hour late only confirmed their mutual lack of attraction. While the romance scheme failed, it did seal their friendship. Stack later joked that the Judy fix-up was because, as friends, she was the only one who would stop whatever she was doing to see him because she was the only one who remembered who he was. Another Judy publicity-romance snippet reported that she "put in a belated appearance" at Koverman's party where "Jackie Cooper was on pins and needles" waiting for her.[31]

Judy Garland's movie career gained momentum with the release of *The Wizard of Oz* in August 1939 and *Babes in Arms* in October. By then, Koverman's reputation as a talent scout and majordomo of the industry was incontrovertible. Although *Oz* was not an immediate box-office success, Judy's iconic performing of *Over the Rainbow* won it an Academy Award for best song, and the film would become an American television classic for generations.

Basking in the glow of Judy Garland's starshine was bittersweet for Koverman, however, because she knew the toll it was taking on the new star. Weeks before production began, Mayer asked Koverman to send a memo to Judy's mother ordering her to get a prescription for sleeping pills from the studio doctor because Judy was reporting to the set so tired that she can't work. Ida wrote down the words, but she sat and debated whether to deliver it. Mayer returned to her desk and added, "While she's at it, she can also lay in a supply of that stuff they use to pep you up in the morning." Koverman couldn't hide her disapproval, so Mayer told her, "By the way . . . I'll tend to the rest of Judy's diet. You let it rest."[32]

The local premiere of *Babes in Arms* on October 10, 1939, at Grauman's Chinese Theatre provided Garland the opportunity to plant her hands and feet in the wet cement in front of hordes of her adoring fans. When Judy arrived with costar Mickey Rooney, when she saw Koverman, instead of walking over to the display set up for the ritual, she rushed over, threw her arms around her, kissed her, and exclaimed, "I've got you to thank for all of this, Kay!" Hedda Hopper told her readers how Koverman and Garland "lived to enjoy the thrill," but added, "I should say the three of us lived to enjoy it—for I knew the story and knew how much those footprints meant to both Ida and Judy."[33] A few months later, they would celebrate the Academy's recognition of Judy Garland, who was awarded its Juvenile Oscar.

Judy Garland's appreciation of Ida Koverman's prognostications about and contributions to her career were reinforced when Koverman and

Hopper attended the November 1939 premiere of Deanna Durbin's movie *First Love*, which ironically costarred Robert Stack, who was at the other end of Deanna Durbin's first on-screen kiss. Koverman knew that Garland would be there, and so she arranged to have "Over the Rainbow" play over the sound-system as the audience filed out. "As we walked out of the theater," Hopper wrote, "it was Judy's voice that followed us," and when Judy saw Ida, she again "ran to her, threw her arms around her neck and lovingly said, 'Thank you darling. I know you did this for me.'"[34]

Ida Koverman's advocacy of both Deanna Durbin and Judy Garland transformed all of their careers and motion-musical history. Garland biographer David Shipman, however, argues that after *Every Sunday*, "all Koverman's efforts were in vain," because the studio had already decided it "did not have room for two young singers." Shipman fails to see Koverman's legacy within the broader arch of the industry's fortunes. When viewed with a wider lens, she helped to launch the enduring fascination with Judy Garland's life and career, and the extraordinary success of Deanna Durbin, without whom Universal likely would not have survived. Largely unknown today, Deanna Durbin was one of the most famous movie stars of her time. Her likeness was one of only three toy dolls resembling megastars Shirley Temple and ice skater turned actress Sonja Henie. International Deanna Durbin film festivals and fan clubs continue to thrive, and it is understandable that Louis B. Mayer "was reported to have almost torn out of his hair at the mere thought of what his studio had lost."[35]

CHAPTER 20

Party Girls

"His [Mayer's] long-time secretary, a marvelous little old lady named Ida Koverman, always put together a huge party in the commissary that everyone on the lot was commanded to attend."[1]

THROUGHOUT HER QUARTER-CENTURY CAREER AT MGM, IDA KOVERMAN'S salary never reflected the full measure of her value. And while Louis B. Mayer might have failed to articulate his appreciation for her or to financially compensate her, it appears that he found a variety of ways for the studio to support Ida Koverman's lifestyle among the rich and famous. She likely enjoyed a hefty expense account and per diem to finance the endless round of attending or hosting pricey parties and talent searches, and repeated access to prime real-estate residences while indefatigably circulating among the city's cultural, political, and Hollywood elite. After all, Ida Koverman was a party girl in every sense of the word.

Unencumbered by a husband or children, Koverman was free to do as she pleased and not only to get very important things done but to also throw a great party. Wednesday evenings were the optimal time to demonstrate the art of hosting an A-list cocktail hour or buffet dinner. High-society watchers all over the world kept track of the best of them, filling their columns with endless lists of celebrity guests, décor, menus, fashions, and clever costumes, and especially historically or culturally themed affairs, such as Koverman's party decorated in "Chinese splendor."[2]

The press kept track of where she was and with whom, cataloguing her after-hours life as a blend of social, political, and cultural merrymaking.

During the long reign of Democrats in Washington, she attended bipartisan affairs, including a Warner Bros.'s birthday party for President Roosevelt and an event for New York congressman Hamilton Fish Jr. Always nearby were her longtime Republican friends, Bank of America's Grace Stoermer and cultural matriarch Mrs. Leiland Atherton Irish, who joined well-known Democrats Louise Ward Watkins and matriarch Mrs. Mattison Boyd Jones.[3]

Her nebulous job description included her oversight at events on and off the lot, in private homes and in public spaces. She tended to details big and small, and even assisted studio teacher Mrs. Caroline "Muzzy" McPhall in holding birthday celebrations for child actors in the bungalow Green Room schoolhouse for studies and recreation. The sticky "candy pull" turned out to be a disaster, but the tea service and electric grill were always a big hit. Koverman paraded a *Who's Who* of guests to the schoolhouse, among them renowned singers, musicians, conductors, dancers, writers, government officials, and social notables from the US and abroad. Conductor John Barbirolli, pianist José Iturbi and his sister Amparo Iturbi, Mabel Walker Willebrandt, Frances Marion, and an occasional representative of America's royalty, such as Cornelia Vanderbilt, were among those visiting the classroom.[4]

As an official liaison for the studio, Koverman arranged banquets for visiting celebrities, and she orchestrated "the private life entertainments of her boss." In January 1937, Koverman invited nearly one hundred guests to a shindig at her home on Mulholland Drive in honor of Florence Browning, Louis B. Mayer's first secretary when he worked out of his office on downtown's West Seventh Street, who was later replaced by Margaret Bennett.[5] Koverman represented MGM at the June grand opening of China City, the brainchild of Mrs. Christine Sterling, who had successfully fostered the still-thriving historical and cultural landmark Olvera Street nearby. MGM even donated to China City its artifacts from the acclaimed film *The Good Earth*, adapted from Pearl S. Buck's novel and, sadly, Irving Thalberg's final production. Koverman attended the movie's premiere gala at the Carthay Circle Theatre along with local, state, and Chinese dignitaries.[6]

When she wasn't in the public's eye, Koverman worked to maintain MGM's image as "a relaxed yet luxurious studio." This included a lot of singing by opera stars or modern stylists. Koverman's parties reflected Los Angeles's evolution as a mecca for diverse artistic talent. At one of her musical soirees, Metropolitan Opera's Lucille Norman sang, and José Iturbi and his sister played piano duets. Jeannette MacDonald and Rise

Stevens were there, and so was Hedda Hopper, who quipped, "That Ida Koverman can get more music at her parties." Director Joe Pasternak attended one gathering hosted by former opera singer turned actress Irene Manning, where among the guests were Hedda Hopper, Walter "Pidge" Pidgeon, and Ida Koverman, who was, he described, "for many years Louis B. Mayer's invaluable assistant, and a brilliant judge of talent and personality in her own right."[7]

Whether she directly planted stories or made sure someone else did, Koverman's activities were a constant thread in meandering newspaper columns, and sometimes in larger stories in fan magazines. One anecdote about her lunch with actress Gloria Swanson and screenwriter Frances Marion offered readers an inside look into the studio's famed commissary. All of a sudden, Koverman shouted, "Come sit with us, Soph," and turned to her friends and said, "Do you know Sophie Tucker, girls?" Tucker later described her as "a swell gal," and claimed to have known her during her days on the Orpheum Theatre circuit in San Francisco in 1910. It's highly unlikely, but whatever the connection, Tucker went over to sit with Koverman as she continued to try to sell tickets to a charity event by abruptly grabbing potential buyers, and interrupting the chatter at the Koverman table. "After the tenth interruption . . . Koverman remonstrated, 'can't you eat in peace and sell your tickets later?'" to which Tucker replied, "The food's got more patience than the customers." Meanwhile, Frances Marion sat transfixed, staring at Tucker. She had just completed her 1937 homage to the recently deceased Marie Dressler, entitled *Molly, Bless Her*, and she now realized she had found the actress to play the lead character, Molly Drexell, for the screenplay. She whispered to Koverman, "Tell Mr. Mayer there's Molly, and nobody else can play her." Sophie Tucker had mixed feelings about the publicity campaign billing her as the next Marie Dressler, and wanted to be promoted as herself. She had just finished filming *Broadway Melody of 1938* and *Thoroughbreds Don't Cry*, both with Judy Garland and other MGM notables, but even before their release, the studio already tied the name of Tucker and Dressler together in copy about the future production. MGM bought the screen rights to Marion's novel with Sophie Tucker in mind, in what would be her third film with Judy Garland. Unfortunately MGM dropped the Marion production, but in 1945, 20th Century Fox picked it up and released it retitled as *Molly and Me*, starring Monty Woolley. By then, Tucker was disillusioned with Hollywood and had moved back East.[8]

Sometimes, Ida Koverman's name even appeared in more than one social column on the same day. She and other MGM executives, and screenwriter Virginia Kellogg and husband, director Frank Lloyd, attended a fete in honor of Nelson Eddy and Llona Massey, who were costarring in the film *Balalaika*. The same day, Koverman was listed among scores of guests enjoying the terrace views and canyon breezes at the Bel Air home of Jeannette MacDonald and her husband, Gene Raymond, along with Mrs. Leiland Atherton Irish and Mrs. Joseph L. Levy, chair of the Hollywood Bowl Hospitality Board. Another Koverman double entry in March 1941 reported her attendance at "the small, gay parties" at the opening of the Barbara Stanwyk–Gary Cooper movie *Meet John Doe*, hosted by the president of the Beverly Hills First National Bank, Richard L. Hargreaves, and his wife Helen Ferguson, a former actress who by then had established herself as a premiere public-relations professional. A few columns over, on the same page, was a snippet about Koverman with her protégé, Dalies Frantz, attending a buffet dinner hosted by actor Pat O'Malley to honor composer and satirist Alec Templeton. A few years later, Alec Templeton entertained at Koverman's party, where he created musical parodies of all the guests and launched into an impromptu "chance experiment" with actor Eddie Arnold that at least one guest believed surpassed the act they were already performing at the Bohemian Grove.[9]

Ida Koverman and her friends bridged the worlds of entertainment and politics. She consciously facilitated this cross-fertilization. Her political allies and movie-star friends held barbeques and backyard parties, and one is memorialized in an extraordinary photograph that offers another example of Koverman hiding in plain sight. The image depicts a joyful but unidentified Ida Koverman kneeling down with her arms around two handsome but unknown younger men sitting in front of her. Mabel Walker Willebrandt is standing behind Koverman, and to her left is "Mama Bello," mother of Jean Harlow, misidentified as Lela Rogers, the mother of dancer-actress Ginger Rogers. It's possible that a youthful Ginger Rogers is the blond woman to Willebrandt's left. Director W. S. Van Dyke stands behind them. Sitting front and center among the nearly two dozen smiling guests is a beaming Jean Harlow, wearing a white puffy chef's hat and apron and holding a frying pan resting on the lap of another smiling blond, possibly actress Constance Bennett or Mary Carlisle. Jackie Cooper's mother, Mabel Cooper Bigelow, is standing in front of her husband C. J. Bigelow. Sitting to the right of Harlow are directors William K. Howard and Wesley Ruggles, and standing behind them is Jeannette MacDonald and cinematographer Harold Rossen, Harlow's then husband.[10]

The worlds of sports, opera, politics, and movies seamlessly blended in Koverman's social circle. Whatever kind of gathering Ida Koverman hosted or attended, the press took notice, especially if it was on behalf of Louis B. Mayer. She oversaw a luncheon for Katherine Spellman, the niece of New York's Archbishop Francis Spellman, Mayer's houseguest at the time. The annual Pasadena New Year's Day Rose Bowl parade and football game always brought diverse people together, like the party she attended hosted by W. S. Van Dyke.[11] Foreign notables enjoyed Koverman's entertaining flair, such as Olga Revillion-Masarykova, daughter of Czechoslovakia's first president, after which event she gave a guided tour, including visiting a live set to introduce actors Maureen O'Sullivan and Peter Lorre.[12]

Indian Banker Jamshed Dinshaw Petit was part of a network of international promoters of MGM's interests. During his visit to Los Angeles in 1935, he got "the royal treatment" at every stop, including Koverman's arrangement to visit the famed Trocadero nightclub, where Petit presented elegant handbags to the female guests in the entourage, a common choice among the Hollywood jet set. Betty Furness, Maureen O'Sullivan, and Jean Parker were recipients of the "startlingly graceful" gesture. During the same trip, Koverman hosted a private affair in her Santa Monica home, where everyone played cards, tennis, ping-pong, swam, and ate a delicious dinner buffet designed "to satiate ravenous appetites induced by the sea breezes and exercise."[13] It was likely held at Mayer's beachfront home, but the reporter assumed it was Koverman's residence, further indicating that she and Mayer were sometimes interchangeable.

Koverman and her clique gathered at smaller, private, but well-publicized events, some of which turned into annual traditions. Her May 15 birthday was the perfect excuse for a party. Hollywood agent and fellow music lover and artistic director of the Hollywood Bowl, Wynn Rocamora, threw her a "delightfully intimate affair" with actress Jeanette MacDonald and actress-aviatrix Ruth Chatterton among the guests. Koverman used her friendship with Rocamora to promote Ken Curtis when she heard him sing with his group Cats n' Jammers. By then, Rocamora was head of talent for NBC. She suggested an audition for Curtis, who soon signed as a contract staff singer. Later, he replaced Frank Sinatra for Tommy Dorsey's band, and then he performed with Johnny Mercer, after which he signed with Columbia Pictures. Curtis appeared in several Western feature films, and he starred in the television series *Ripcord*. His television legacy, however, was his role as Festus, a staple of the long running *Gunsmoke*, which is still syndicated. Koverman's hand continues to reach into America's homes.[14]

As the perennial Koverman booster, Hopper described Ida Koverman as "the confidante and friend of young and old on Metro lot. . . . In fact, she's the people's choice." She was always a guest at the annual birthday party Jeanette MacDonald threw for Koverman, with 1941 being the best kind of party, with board games and simple, homespun pleasures rather than "the usual 'intimate' Hollywood party for 150 of your closest friends." Hopper must have been right about Koverman, because as the chair of the MGM Studio Club in 1937, she could proudly boast that after a recent recruitment drive, membership topped two thousand, and was cause for another celebratory breakfast.[15]

Opera singer Rosa Ponselle and her husband Carl Jackson were in town for Ida Koverman's sixty-seventh birthday in 1938, which was the more usual kind of Hollywood party of extravagant decorations, this time with amusing posters hanging on the inside of a tent set up on the huge front lawn. A maypole centerpiece overflowed with flower garlands, and blue and salamander-shaped lights on the trees created an exotic mood. Birthday cakes were works of art, and on this night, scoops of ice cream sat inside flower- and basket-shaped cones, making their serving easy and amusing. Guests mingled beneath caricature sketches by MGM's set director Ed Willis, which Hopper described as "brilliant cartoons of Ida . . . who can find her way around any political rally without the aid of a searchlight." One portrait depicted Koverman as "hot-footing it to the White House," but Hopper chided, "That should have been in reverse." Another "gay and amusing" birthday party Koverman attended for screen-writer Leon Gordon included gag telegrams sent by famous people and an amusing miniature birthday cake cut into miniscule pieces.[16]

Columnist Phyllis Powers wrote about that night as one when "all of the MGM crowd and many of film land's favorites came to wish Kay many happy returns." Powers described Judy Garland as "looking as beautiful as a magazine cover girl" and overheard her tell actress Virginia Bruce that she always found herself saying "the wrong thing at parties" and feeling out of place. In this case, it was because "everyone here is an opera singer and they sorta [sic] look down on just a blues voice . . . [and] wouldn't it be awful if they all started to sing at once?"[17]

Judy was more at ease in her own milieu and on her own turf, such as the wrap party she threw for the 1940 *Strike Up the Band* at her Stone Canyon home. A photo essay captured the frenetic dancing at the let-your-hair-down bash along with the matronly, sixty-four-year-old Ida Koverman and the other older folks sitting in a row of folding chairs against the wall, just behind Garland jitterbugging with dance champion Ray Hirsch. Mickey Rooney wildly played the drums, and others jumped into the pool.[18] Aside from this intergenerational affair, Koverman was a guest at a game-night party thrown by Garland's longtime family friends, Dr. Marc and Marcella Rabwin, along with other adult MGM personnel such as Sam Marx, Benny Thau, Ben Goetz, Frank Lloyd, and Mayer's brother Jerry.

The Garland party photo-feature story included the notion that Mickey Rooney preferred his friends with musical talent over "the famous actors and actresses" at MGM. Nevertheless, he soon married the studio's newest, glamorous actress Ava Gardner, who thought Koverman "was always the studio's first port of call in an emergency when they didn't want to disturb" Mayer. Koverman looked out for Gardner, who on one occasion complained to Koverman, "You know, Ida, I come here, work on movies I don't even understand, and then go back home to have dinner with my mother. I read the script, go to bed. The next day it starts all over again." Again, Koverman sympathetically advised how "this can all be a lot of fun if you let it. Don't take it home with you and don't believe your press releases." The next time came with Gardner's visit to Mayer's office after her marriage to Rooney. While "scared half to death, waiting to meet 'Uncle LB,' . . . Ida was giving me the silent treatment." Finally, Koverman said, "You know, young lady, a leopard doesn't change its spots," referring to Rooney's womanizing. At the same time, Koverman defended Rooney to Mayer, suggesting that he was just a young man who had to grow up, to which Mayer quickly replied, "But not this fast and certainly not with that girl."[19] The marriage lasted eight months.

Koverman frequently dined with Jeannette MacDonald and Gene Raymond, Nelson Eddy, and Hedda Hopper, but it wasn't always public or pricey. One evening, everyone "ate scrambled eggs, sausages and bacon, and waffles made by Jeannette herself," and then they "played the silliest game," a precursor to modern board games where "you're given a title, quotation, name—anything, which you draw, the members of your table guessing." Afterwards they headed over to Edgar Bergen's hilltop home, where some of his guests were in the pool and others were playing on his nine-hole putting green.[20] So much for simple, down-home cooking and word games.

Labor Day 1938 spawned a cornucopia of parties among the Hollywood crowd at Malibu beach houses, on yachts, and ran the gamut of huge affairs, formal and informal, with Koverman joining familiar Hollywood Bowl devotees Judy Garland, Eleanor Powell, and Mrs. Irish. In a rare mention of Ida Koverman as "Kay," the nickname reserved for her closest friends, she was seen at the wedding-anniversary buffet supper of talent agent Frank Orsatti, of which the highlight was a thirty-pound cake. Koverman was friends with the four Orsatti brothers, and Ernie, a former Major League baseball player, married opera singer Inez Gorman, who was a protégé of Koverman's friend Rosa Ponselle. Koverman and Ponselle were attendants at their wedding.[21]

Koverman was just one name on the list of seven hundred guests attending Elizabeth Taylor's wedding to Conrad "Nickie" Hilton Jr. Koverman's friend, MGM police chief Whitey Hendry and scores of LAPD officers kept the thousands of fans in line. A smaller, impromptu wedding reception for singer Ilona Massey and Alan Curtis brought Koverman to Brentwood, and she hosted the ceremony and wedding reception for another of her discoveries, actress Jean Parker to her groom Doug Dawson. The marriage didn't last, and three years later, her nuptials to Dr. Kurt Grotter were conducted by Superior Court Judge Stanley Mosk. Stanley Mosk was a rising star in another universe of Jewish liberal Democrats, and he allied with Koverman's longtime friend Mendel Silberberg for numerous nonpartisan civic, charitable, and Jewish-centered causes. Later, Stanley Mosk and Koverman's protégé George Murphy would change the course of California and US political history.[22]

Koverman's favorite parties were the costumed or themed parties that ranged from guests being asked to show up as a "brand of advertised product," or at Edward G. Robinson's affair, as their "childhood aspiration." More like their adult fantasy, Koverman came dressed as a "pierrette," French parrot, and she was photographed with Robinson and the comedic team of George Burns, who came as a streetcar conductor, and Gracie Allen, who was dressed as a French maid. [23]

Newspaper mogul William Randolph Hearst and his mistress, actress Marion Davies, loved themed parties, and held them in all of their homes in Northern and Southern California. Ida Koverman and Louis B. Mayer attended a 1940 gathering at Hearst's 67,000-acre Northern California estate called Wyntoon, on the McCloud River. The rustic, lush environment inspired Mayer to reveal his inner poet, and Koverman wanted everyone to know he had a softer, sensitive side, or to showcase his literacy to counter rumors that she had tutored him in elocution and public speaking.[24] She sent Mayer's poem to a columnist who assumed it meant that Koverman promoted aspiring poets along with talented actors and musicians, but it was likely written during one of Mayer's "less lucid intervals."[25]

The most historically significant party in Ida Koverman's career at MGM was the one she hosted for her friend Hedda Hopper. Not only did it transform Hopper's life, but also it changed the course of the gossip industry. Koverman thought Hopper was "one of the wonders of Hollywood," and although she looked like "a flapper," Koverman told another friend, the acclaimed artist Kathryn Leighton, that along with being a "clever actress," she believed Hopper had "a very brilliant mind," and there was "never a dull moment wherever she happens to be." Hopper had been an MGM bit player, but as her career waned, she needed to find ways to support herself and her handsome son, William Hopper, who became an actor most known for his role as the silver-haired private detective Paul Drake on the longrunning television series *Perry Mason*. Hedda sold real estate and appeared in radio spots, and she published gossipy articles about the movie business. One of MGM's publicity agents recommended Hopper to the Esquire Feature Syndicate, and soon *The Los Angeles Times* and a dozen other newspapers featured her column. After that, her momentum stopped.[26]

Meanwhile, Louis B. Mayer was increasingly annoyed by the popularity of the Hearst-syndicated gossiper Louella Parsons, so Koverman suggested that Hopper might serve as a foil to Parsons. Mayer liked the idea and began to promote Hopper's journalistic career. Part of Hopper's problem, Koverman thought, was that Hopper needed to enhance her credibility, and toward that end, Koverman decided, of course, to throw Hedda a party, a "hen party." She turned her patio into a barnyard with satirical props and party favors, with a sign greeting guests, "No Cats Allowed Here." Hopper was less impressed with the buzz-saw prop, and the inclement weather required some strong men to hold up a giant canvas to hover over the crowd, but it didn't detract from Hopper's enjoyment. She told her readers, "Did I go to a party!" and what a "shindig" it was. "The roosters just couldn't stay away," so the "husbands and boyfriends trooped in around midnight." Koverman wore a makeshift costume combining "Little Eva" and "Rebecca" with a wig of blond curls and a sunbonnet. Hand-painted and enlarged photographs caricatured Hopper's signature oversized hats, with one portraying a spring bonnet with hydrangea trees growing out of the top.[27]

Hopper was already a Hollywood insider who made her own friends, many of whom she shared with Koverman. Exemplifying Koverman's crossover networks, the guest list was drawn from the city's *Who's Who* of judges, lawyers, doctors, writers, and some of Hollywood's biggest stars. The group represented the breadth of professional women Koverman had cultivated for a decade or more in music, journalism, law, and politics. Some of Koverman's "discoveries" were Norma Shearer, Jeannette MacDonald, Joan Crawford, Sophie Tucker, Anita Loos, Frances Marion, Kay Mulvey, Eleanor Parker, Rosa Ponselle, Sheila Graham, Helen Ferguson, Ruth Waterbury, Jauna Neal Levy, Marion Fitts, Grace Stoermer, Mrs. Mendel (Dorothy) Silberberg, and Judges Georgia Bullock and Oda Faulconer. Conversations ranged from world affairs to diets, while another Hollywood hostess, Mrs. Edgar G. Robinson, contemplated ideas for her next party, and, as usual, Mrs. Leiland Atherton Irish got everyone to sign up for the Hollywood Bowl. Eadie Adams sang "Thanks for the Memory," which Hopper said inspired "tears as big as kernels of corn popped out of the eyes of us old hens."[28]

Hedda told her readers that "Ida, a swell egg, had hatched one of the best parties ever given in Hollywood. And I'm thanking her." Along with the party, Koverman gave Hopper some advice. She told Hedda to start telling the truth. She said Hedda had been too nice to people and they were laughing at her. Hedda later recognized the party and the advice were the turning point in her life and career.[29]

Ida Koverman and Hedda Hopper's personal friendship spawned a mutually beneficial professional relationship as they both had their unique and overlapping access to the public and private lives of scores of movie-industry personnel. Hopper biographer Jennifer Frost asserts that Koverman hung around Hopper in order to get the inside scoop on movie stars. It is more accurate that, as writer George Eels noted long ago, when Hedda's movie career was grinding to a halt, Koverman did what she could to help because of her own prominent influence in MGM, the industry, and the city's elite.[30]

Just as Koverman and Mayer designed, Hopper's growing popularity fueled her historic rivalry with Louella Parsons, and on a grander scale it reflected Koverman's skill as a matchmaker for Hollywood and politics. The Koverman-Hopper bond was part of Koverman's larger network of professional women in powerful places who promoted their ideological worldview. Hopper's blended commentary of politics and pictures, eagerly devoured by millions of readers, was a mesh of innuendo and ideology, a weave of fact and fiction, and it removed any pretense of a wall between popular entertainment and the rabid brand of conservative Republican politics.

CHAPTER 21

Comrades, Candidates, and the Canteen

"Everyone must have a lot of confidence in Miss Koverman's judgment." Presented with "all sorts of scenarios—good, bad, and indifferent. She estimates the value of various performers and performances. She reviews finished products. She bestows rewards and recompense."[1]

IDA KOVERMAN'S PERIPATETIC LIFESTYLE CONTINUED THROUGHOUT HER MGM years. Just as she always had when living in Ohio and New York, she moved around a lot, and she is associated with numerous addresses in Los Angeles. Tracing her mobility finds the usual discrepancies, but also some curiosities. The 1940 state voter-registration file has her living at 1840 Camino Palmero Avenue, the former home of the recently deceased director Oscar Apfel, located on one of the streets in the upscale Las Colinas Heights built by the "Father of Hollywood," C. E. Toberman, as a streetcar suburb designed specifically to cater to the entertainment industry. The 1942–44 *Who's Who in California*, however, has her living a few doors down, at 1810 Camino Palmero Avenue, and that same year the US Census details Koverman as a sixty-five-year-old widow, who completed four years of high school, renting a house on the pricey Encino Avenue, just south of Ventura Boulevard in the San Fernando Valley. Grace J. Weyworth was her live-in housekeeper, who Koverman paid six hundred dollars a year. It is interesting to note that Koverman's salary, as of December 1939, was $5,000, well below the rumored two hundred and fifty dollars per week, or $12,000. Regardless, it was an exceptional

184

salary, over four times the amount of all but two of the other residents on the same street, famed songwriter Bert Kalmar and performer Ben Blue.[2]

Wherever Koverman lived that year, Hollywood's ideological divide solidified, and the GOP institutionalized itself as the opposition party throughout the decades of Democratic dominance in Washington. When 186 members of the Hollywood for Roosevelt Committee took out a full-page advertisement in the *New York Times*, Ida Koverman and 167 other "motion picture folk" signed their names in another advertisement, entitled "The Truth About Hollywood," to correct the impression that everyone in Hollywood supported President Roosevelt's re-election. The text read, "Somebody made a mistake."[3]

From her desk in the Thalberg Building, Koverman kept up her correspondence with Herbert Hoover and his secretary, Lawrence Richey. They exchanged favors, such as arranging studio tours for Hoover's friends, or Koverman's introducing Richey to New Jersey congressman Charles Wolverton, whom she thought Hoover would find "a very active worker if you need him." Coincidentally, just a couple weeks before Jack Bryson and Will Hays would feverishly lobby to forestall a federal antitrust case against the studios, Koverman passed on contact information about Bryson to Hoover. She described him as a well-connected partisan who now "looks after the interests of the picture industry at Sacramento and . . . a very capable man . . . and very well-posted." Jack Bryson would become a familiar face in Washington, DC, as the representative of the Motion Picture Producers Association.[4]

Closer to home, Koverman had been frustrated with the "hot" political situation brewing in California during the brief interregnum of the Democratic administration of Culbert Olson. She lamented to Hoover that "if our crowd would just get together and work like they used to, we could easily get this state back in the Republican column." Locally, she joined Louis B. Mayer and Fred Beetson to promote the election of Lester W. Roth, former Superior Court judge and recent associate of Mendel Silberberg. Roth represented actress Hedy Lamarr, who was being sued by seven lawyers involved in her divorce from writer-producer Gene Markey. Roth stayed in private practice until liberal Democrat governor Edmund G. "Pat" Brown appointed him as a justice to the appellate court.[5]

World War II provided Ida with unanticipated opportunities to search for new talent for the MGM star machine. She was too old to don overalls to work on an assembly line like millions of other wives and mothers, but she served the unified homeland war effort with hundreds of members of the motion-picture industry to entertain the troops who passed through

Los Angeles. The Hollywood Canteen opened in 1942, and when it closed its doors three years later, thousands of on-screen and behind-the-scenes talent had volunteered to serve free food, to host dances, and to perform for all members of the allied armed services who showed up in uniform. Jules Stein, president of the Music Corporation of America, was the early financier, and actress Bette Davis is credited with initiating the Canteen, which she considered her proudest achievement.[6]

A 1943 feature about the Canteen acknowledged there was no satisfactory yardstick by which to calculate the measure of the services provided by "Mrs. Ida Koverman, long Louis B. Mayer's secretary," and Hedda Hopper, Louella Parsons, Ginger Rogers and her mother Lela, and Mrs. Basil Rathbone for their contribution to the Hollywood Canteen." Koverman is seen in an accompanying photograph while she compliments musician Carroll Hollister on his part in making the opening of the Canteen a success.[7] During her years at MGM, Koverman garnered the respect of the musicians' union which they demonstrated by their turnout at her funeral service.

Koverman found Janis Paige singing at the Hollywood Canteen, after which MGM signed her to a one-year contract. After a brief appearance in *Bathing Beauty* (1944), starring Red Skelton and Esther Williams, Paige left MGM, but the same day Warner Bros. signed her up, where she made several films until she moved to Broadway. Her breakout role came as "Babe" in *The Pajama Game* (1954). Another find was junior hostess Florence Lundeen; the day after Koverman saw her dancing, MGM signed her up. African American singer Lena Horne entertained one night, and soon after the story broke that "the biggest news of recent years is the signing of Miss Lena Horne to a seven year contract" by MGM, largely credited to Koverman. Twenty-one-year-old serviceman Louis Nigro had just spent twenty-seven months in the South Pacific when he visited the Canteen in February 1945. He asked Koverman if he could sing with the band, promising her, "You won't be ashamed of me." She wasn't, and Koverman arranged a screen test with director Joe Pasternak. After Nigro's discharge, he landed an MGM contract under the stage name Louis Noble. Andy Williams was just twenty years old when he and his three brothers sang at the Hollywood Canteen. He described the night as "one of those life-changing chance encounters that could never have been predicted by anyone." This was because Ida Koverman just "happened" to be there, after which "she went back and told her boss about us, and within a week we were signed to contract by MGM."[8]

Koverman also used the Canteen as a way to promote the talent she had found, such as Jane Powell, whom she felt needed to come "out of obscurity into the spotlight . . . [because] she was such a shy youngster." Koverman "had to take her night after night to the Hollywood Canteen to sing—just to give her confidence." On New Year's Day 1944, Koverman "whipped up" a show that Hedda Hopper said "was a honey," headlined by Jimmy Durante, Marion Bell, Eddie Cantor, Orson Welles, Lucile Bremer, John Conti, and so on from there. Hopper told her readers that "Ida has never asked for a hand for the work she's done, but I think it's about time she had one."[9]

Judy Garland was part of the homeland army of talent who lent a hand to raise money for the war effort. In January, she and Bing Crosby entertained on a radio broadcast featuring California governor Earl Warren, who urged citizens to participate in the Fourth War Loan campaign. A few months later she sang while "José Iturbi played boogie woogie . . . just to make the boys at Hollywood Canteen happy on Sunday night." She joined the cast of entertainers at a Hollywood Bowl bond-drive gala just days after she turned twenty-one on June 10, making her eligible to vote in the upcoming presidential election. In the fall, the invitational dinner hosted by the Hollywood for FDR Committee announced Judy Garland and Humphrey Bogart among the stars on the program. Reviews cheered the show as "a triumph from the opening notes—the big band rising behind Garland as she sang in a voice infectious with its unclouded enthusiasm . . . here's the way to win the war . . . you gotta get out and vote," and joyfully imitated candidate Dewey's brand of doubletalk.[10]

The public display of Judy Garland's political persuasion would put her increasingly at odds with Ida Koverman and Louis B. Mayer. It portended a deeper divide between them that paralleled the Cold War years. Koverman was Judy's guardian angel; she provided a shoulder and a reassuring voice for the ambitious but insecure youngster.[11] She was an auxiliary or surrogate mother to Judy, and their relationship was similarly vulnerable as mothers and their daughters in tumultuous teenage and young adult years.

Everything that was typical for other young women was exacerbated by the combination of Judy's stardom and her inferiority complex. There were times, though, when she even saw the humor in how the press had pitted her against Deanna Durbin, as when one reporter thought, "It looks like a first rate feud again" after they had married, divorced, and then remarried around the same time. Both of them had "switched from

singing to high drama," and "now they're both to have babies." When
Judy heard about Durbin's "date with the stork," she moaned, "Gosh,
can't I do ANYTHING by myself?"[12]

Judy's efforts to establish her independence from those who had guided
her career were sometimes problematic. Judy began to publicly assert
her own political inclinations, and it signaled a breach with Koverman
and the rest of her flock. It has been suggested that Koverman and Judy
grew more alienated over a series of Judy's romantic choices that began
when, in 1941, at the age of nineteen, Judy married composer and band
leader David Rose. The marriage was short-lived, and Judy's subsequent
relationships were leaving new scars on layers of unhealed wounds. But
her alienation from Koverman should also be viewed within the larger
context of both of their lives and how Judy Garland came of age during
the heightened, polarized political climate within the motion-picture industry and Koverman's leadership in what would be an opposing camp.

Since the 1920s, anti-communism had long been a fundamental tenet
of the aggressive strategy Koverman and her allies had used to increase
membership in the Republican Party ranks. She had built a coalition of
like-minded female partisans, and by the 1940s, many in Hollywood who
credit her with influencing their careers might have been influenced by
her or were already inclined toward her brand of politics or religion or
both. Ava Gardner knew that Koverman and Louis B. Mayer actively
promoted their worldview. Gardner knew, "If L.B. dropped dead tomorrow," Koverman "could have run the whole show," but "it was Mayer
who made me realize that I could never be a Republican." She said, "He
would call you up if you voted the wrong way, or went to the wrong rally.
God knows how he knew but he always did."[13]

Mayer's political arm-twisting was well known, but Koverman's more
intimate relationships with the studio's precocious young charges were as
powerful as they were invisible. According to Koverman's friend, screenwriter Frances Marion, when Mayer heard that Garland had voted "for
some Democrats," he felt personally deceived and reproached Garland
during a contract negotiation. "You, who I trusted," he whined, "they
tell me you voted for some Democrats." Garland stood her ground. "Look
here, L.B.," she reprimanded, "I think ethics are more important than
politics, and I'll always vote for the man I admire most. I don't care a
hoot what party he belongs to." Mayer ordered her to "get out of my
office . . . you two-face, you . . . you Communist."[14] This aspect of the
relationship between Ida Koverman, Judy Garland, and Louis B. Mayer,
offers an unexplored factor that contributed to Garland's alienation from

her mentors. Most of Koverman's personal relationships had grown out of a symbiosis of her professional and political interests. As Hollywood's ideological divide grew during the 1940s, Koverman's Hollywood and political identities were firmly cemented in the public's eye. For Judy Garland, her own sensibilities increasingly clashed with Koverman's, and the tension would become palpable.

The unified front at the Canteen served as a façade distracting from Hollywood's hardening partisan lines. In February 1944, the founding of the Motion Picture Alliance for the Preservation of American Ideals signaled the formal articulation of conservative outrage, and among MGM employees in particular, who made up 200 of the 225 inaugural memberships. Zealous anti-communists set designer Cedric Gibbons and director Sam Wood were in the vanguard, and Koverman's friends sat on the executive committee, including Mr. and Mrs. Gary Cooper, Walt Disney, John Ford, Ronald Reagan, John Wayne, Hedda Hopper, Clark Gable, George Murphy, Ginger Rogers, Irene Dunne, and Cecil B. De Mille. Robert Taylor was overseas, so his wife Barbara Stanwyck shared news of MPA meetings.[15]

The MPA wanted the public to know that Hollywood was not "a hotbed of sedition and subversion," and that the movie industry was "a battleground over which communism is locked in death grips with fascism." The MPA sought to "block the use of motion pictures for antiracial propaganda"; to "enlist the cooperation of religious, nonpolitical and fraternal organizations"; and "to encourage groups such as the B'nai B'rith, Knights of Columbus, and Masonic orders" to join in their crusade.[16] The MPA soon lobbied Congress to bring its House Committee on Un-American Activities (HUAC) to investigate in Los Angeles. They did, and Hedda Hopper vehemently defended the MPA's tactics, later writing, "Sure, MPA attacks petty parlor pinks and all fellow travelers. When they accused some picture writers of being 'Commies' they didn't mince words." Hopper became a second vice president when John Wayne was elected MPA president in 1949.[17]

The 1944 presidential primary season captured Ida Koverman's attention, but by April, she lamented that Wendell Wilkie had "succeeded so beautifully in talking himself out of all possibility of being a candidate." Attention turned briefly to Ohio governor John W. Bricker, who had a brother working at another studio and who was trying to "line up the picture business" behind him. Hoping to boost his popularity, the governor and his wife embarked on a promotional tour. Koverman hosted a luncheon for them at MGM attended by, among others, Jerry Mayer, Esther

Williams, Frances Marion, and Mrs. Edwin Knopf. Although Bricker made "a decidedly favorable impression," his timing was too late to win over delegates who had already decided their preference.[18]

Two months later, she told Hoover about a conversation she had with Charles Skouras, "head of the Fox West Coast Theatre Chain." Skouras told her about a reputable straw poll of forty thousand Northern California moviegoers in the "laboring districts," indicating that while the vote there was an unsurprising ten to one for President Roosevelt's re-election, it was "very alarming" to learn that the white-collar districts were voting for Roosevelt five to one.[19]

As Bricker's momentum faltered, Koverman told Hoover she was happy to see the rise "by leaps and bounds" for the dapper New York governor Thomas E. Dewey, who many, including "newspaper people," believed would win the nomination on the first ballot.

Whatever the outcome, Koverman headed for Chicago to serve as an alternate delegate at the Republican National Convention. Arriving on June 27, her friends Hedda Hopper and Grace Stoermer stayed with her at the Stevens Hotel.[20] To some observers, the convention was such a "huge bore" that it took the elder statesman Herbert Hoover, who had "absolutely no crowd appeal," to "arouse the first outbursts of enthusiasm." Hedda Hopper said even though director Cecil B. DeMille and producer David Selznick were roaming among the crowd, it was "the damnedest convention [where] the Republicans made less noise than a good mob scene on a movie set." A couple of bright spots were California governor Earl Warren's keynote speech, and after Dewey won the nomination, he picked Bricker as his running mate.

Soon after the trip, Koverman joined the Hollywood for Dewey Committee. Along with the traditional campaign galas, the biggest event was the September 22 Dewey rally held at the Los Angeles Memorial Coliseum and produced by Cecil B. DeMille, which attracted over ninety thousand partisans and Hollywood luminaries both in the crowd and on the stage.[21]

The 1944 campaign provided opportunities for a deepening of the friendship between Ida Koverman and Hedda Hopper. They took their politicking on the road, and they made a great team. They appeared in the Northern Division of the California Council of Republican Women at San Francisco's Palace Hotel, where they informed their sister partisans about Southland campaign activities. Koverman's introduction portrayed Hopper as a political neophyte, suggesting that her friend "had always been far too busy to be interested in politics to any degree." Koverman said that Hopper "was not a person to talk unless she really had something to say," but now that her son was in the army, Hopper "was cutting her 'eye teeth' in this campaign," and wherever they went, "listeners were 'all ears' to hear that 'something.'" Hopper's political persuasiveness was on the rise, with proclamations such as "we are not merely electing a president . . . we are reinstating a form of government [and] this is an election of political principles." Ida Koverman and Hedda Hopper repeated their act in San Diego, where Hopper chided, "So many barnacles already have accumulated on the ship of state under the Democratic administration that another four years will leave it greatly weakened and full of holes."[22]

Koverman's relationship with Hopper echoed the symbiotic friendship she once had with Ralph Arnold and now with Louis B. Mayer. Her matchmaking was now manifest in Hopper's growing popularity, reflecting Koverman's hand in the creation of a vehicle for her cultural hybrid of movie-star fan base and partisan politics. Hopper biographer Jennifer Frost claims that Koverman gravitated toward Hopper because of her access to "juicy gossip about film stars."[23] Their mutual gravitational pull was far more profound than that, and more accurately, Ida Koverman was a well-established personage inside of MGM while Hopper was struggling to survive there. Although Koverman remained behind the scenes, she was the guiding hand that shaped the universe where both women circulated in separate but overlapping spheres.

Aside from their politicking, Ida Koverman and Hedda Hopper loved to attend concerts at the Hollywood Bowl. It takes months of planning and promotion to carry off a concert season, but following America's entry into World War II, the nighttime Bowl concerts posed a challenge for military authorities charged with ensuring national security. At first the Bowl was told to cancel its upcoming season. Then they authorized a limited schedule and a downsized number of tickets to be sold and a limited time in which to sell them. Koverman's able ally, Bowl board member Mrs. Leiland Atherton Irish, worked with Los Angeles supervisor John Anson Ford to address the "Herculean task" of launching a program within the new parameters. Mrs. Irish feared the vacant seats would not only be bad for appearances, but would make it difficult to make financial ends meet. The predicament, however, also inspired innovative arrangements to broadcast Bowl programs to "swing shift" personnel in the army, and even when some performances were moved inland to Pasadena, thousands of servicemen were admitted without charge. By the end of the season, Mrs. Irish was pleased to report to supervisor Ford that in spite of attendance cut nearly in half, the season ended with a balanced budget and a small profit.[24] It wouldn't be long until such concerns would engage Ida

Koverman, who would not only join the board of the Hollywood Bowl but would work closely with Mrs. Irish and John Anson Ford promoting the musical arts while building her legacy as a powerful figure within the city's political and cultural elite.

Evidence of her standing in such circles are her communications with the city's historic figures, such as Los Angeles mayor Fletcher Bowron. After his election in April 1945, she wrote, "You know how very pleased I am over the result of yesterday's election." Hardly coincidental, on the same day, Louis B. Mayer also wrote to Bowron how "very happy" he was at the result of the election yesterday, but he was "not at all surprised, just pleased." With a little variation, they signed their letters "my very best wishes to you," with Koverman adding, "as always," while Mayer wrote, "to you for your continued success."[25] Nevertheless, even as a rising personage in her own right, she still acted on behalf of Mayer and MGM, and often their seemingly separate overtures were indecipherable from each other's.

Around this time, one extraordinary moment provides insight into Koverman's personality. Visiting from the United Kingdom, Lady Mary Behrens toured Los Angeles and MGM just days before the dropping of the first atomic bomb on Hiroshima. Behrens and her group "were received in an oak paneled office by the matriarchal secretary to Louis B. Mayer, a father of the industry," and "although seated behind a hectare of walnut desk, looked like an Edwardian hostess." Koverman told Behrens's group "many scandalous tales concerning the misdemeanors of the famous, peppering her sentences with the slang considered 'racy' by her generation." Behrens said she "was perfectly pleased" with Koverman's jokes about Sir Thomas Beecham," whom she called a "massive figure in the musical world." Just then, Judy Garland's mother called "about some escapade of that tempestuous young star who was just about my own age." She left the studio thinking she had been, for a brief moment, at the center in the world of filmmaking.[26] She was.

The night the second atomic bomb dropped over Nagasaki on the "balmy evening of August 9, 1945," a record-breaking crowd of twenty thousand attended the Hollywood Bowl to hear the now-legendary actress and soprano Jeannette MacDonald. Leopold Stokowski conducted, and the night proved a personal victory for MacDonald, who hoped to continue to captivate a broad fan base. MacDonald was unlike Koverman's other opera-singing friends, such as Lily Pons, Lawrence Tibbett, and Maria Jeritza, who made regular concert appearances and were considered "highbrow" singers with Hollywood ties but not "really of

These Ladies Are All Supporters of Herbert Hoover

These women are all supporters of Hoover—Mrs. James F. Curtis, Mrs. Willebrandt, Mrs. Bina M. West, Mrs. Ida R. Koverman (l. to r., front), Mrs. Reginald Baker and Mrs. C. Montague Irwin (back row), at Hoover headquarters in Kansas City.

(By Pacific & Atlantic)

Ida R. Koverman with Mabel Walker Willebrandt and others at the Republican National Convention in 1928.

Ida R. Koverman as a young girl, likely photographed by her father John R. Brockway, later published in *Studio Club News*, November 14, 1938. USC Cinematic Arts Library.

Ida R. Koverman photo portrait August 5, 1930, signed to Charlotte Greenwood and her husband Martin Broones. USC Cinematic Arts Library.

Ida R. Koverman sitting with
Mark Requa at the Republican
National Convention in 1932.

Ida R. Koverman with Jackie Cooper
and "Aunt Ruth Williamson" (as identified by Mary Troffer), early 1930s.
(Courtesy of Mary Hawkins Troffer)

Ida R. Koverman, Louis B. Mayer, Judy Garland, and Deanna Durbin around 1936 during filming of *Every Sunday*. (As appeared in Hugh Fordin's *Greatest Musicals*)

Jean Harlow holding bottle of "Emotion" by MGM's Vimay, Inc., signed, after Harlow's death, by her mother. Date unknown.

Ida Koverman with friends at B & H Ranch, Palm Springs, January 16, 1936. Standing: Betty Furness, Jackie Cooper, Bill Levy, and Ida R. Koverman. Seated: Horty (Hortense) Levy, Irene Hervey, and Mabel Cooper Bigelow (Jackie Cooper's mother).

Ida R. Koverman, bottom right, sitting with her right arm around Hal Roach (other man unidentified); Mabel Walker Willebrandt standing second from far right; Jean Harlow's mother Mama Bello to her right; director W. S. Van Dyke standing behind Willebrandt. Jean Harlow, center wearing chef's hat; to her left Constance Bennett looking toward director William K. Howard. Laughing behind him is director Wesley Ruggles; standing behind Ruggles, Jeanette MacDonald; to her left, Jean Harlow's second husband, cinematographer, Harold Rossen. Brown, *Mabel Walker Willebrandt*, and various websites.

Ida Koverman. Undated, but same as published in *Studio Club News* 1938. Core Collection Biography: Margaret Herrick Library, Academy of Motion Picture Arts and Sciences.

Ida R. Koverman and actors Clark Gable and Robert Montgomery. *Chicago Tribune*, March 14, 1963, p. 55, captioned "with her outstanding discoveries," and Hedda Hopper's *The Whole Truth and Nothing but the Truth*.

IRK and Mario Lanza cartoon featured in digitalcomics.com.

Ida Koverman at Judy Garland's house party, *Look Magazine*, October 8, 1940.

IRK with Roy Rogers and Dale Evans. (Courtesy of Darrell Rooney)

Ida Koverman, Hedda Hopper, and Anita Louise campaigning for presidential and vice presidential candidates Dwight D. Eisenhower and Richard Nixon. Koverman wearing ribbons and buttons of the "Women's Brigade for Ike and Dick." 1952. Hedda Hopper papers, Margaret Herrick Library, Academy of Motion Pictures Arts and Sciences.

Ida Koverman at her MGM desk. Signed, "Hi yah Hedda, here's me crying for you!"
Date unknown. Metro-Goldwyn-Mayer production and biography photographs (Warner
Bros.).

Ida Koverman, Louis B. Mayer, and his daughter Mrs. Edith Mayer Goetz. July 1945.
Core Collection Biography: Margaret Herrick Library, Academy of Motion Pictures Arts
and Sciences.

Hollywood." If her Bowl debut was successful, it would signal MacDonald had earned a new level of prestige for Hollywood to bask "in the reflection of her increased glory." Ida Koverman similarly enjoyed the bawdy gossip and the basking glow.[27]

After the war, in December 1945, thousands of America's servicemen were still on the West Coast, most of them awaiting transport to official separation centers located throughout the country. Koverman heard that GIs were going to be away from home for another Christmas holiday, so as head of the Volunteer Army Canteen Service, she and her friends decided to entertain them. She directed the Christmas show at Fort MacArthur, housing 1,200 soldiers, featuring Kay Kyser, Jane Powell, and Celeste Holm, among many others.[28]

One by-product of war is the inevitable investigations of munitions profiteering. Murray Garsson was the subject of a 1946 US Senate inquiry, a controversial figure who a decade earlier had been the subject of an FBI investigation for his aggressive extortion scheme targeting "alien" Hollywood actors under the auspices the Department of Labor. Garsson had surfaced on the edges of Koverman's life in New York and California through, for example, his service as a special assistant to Herbert Hoover's secretary of labor, William Doak. Garsson had other movie industry connections, including 20th Century Fox's Joseph Schenck, who had loaned Garsson 130,000 shares of the corporation's stock valued at two million dollars.[29]

During Garsson's prosecution, he claimed that Ida Koverman and Louis B. Mayer could vouch for his good character. He said he was very friendly with them, along with Norma Talmadge and George Raft. Garsson had circulated in the movie industry in New York where, in 1920, he founded Garsson Productions, allied with the distribution network of Metro Pictures Corporation. He produced a few movies before getting involved with mobsters during the Prohibition years.[30]

Garsson then went on to a series of despicable career moves, including blackmailing individuals and studio heads by threatening to deport foreign actors in an effort to "force the industry to hire him to keep him quiet." He talked with District Attorney Buron Fitts during a dinner at MGM about "cleaning up Los Angeles," and when he initiated action against an Australian citizen, attorney and Koverman ally Joseph Scott served as his initial counsel. Garsson got around. He also imposed himself into the Lindbergh baby kidnapping case, proclaiming he could solve it in record time by suggesting the famous aviator murdered his own son.[31] By invoking Koverman's name, whatever his real relationship with Ida

Koverman was, it demonstrated that her renown sometimes attracted not just the talented but the con-artistic alike.

World War II interrupted many Hollywood careers, but for the highly acclaimed Lew Ayres, the war was particularly hard on his reputation when he claimed conscientious-objector status. MGM's public dispute over Ayres's status contributed to the controversy, but after some soul searching and analysis of box-office returns, the studio backtracked on pulling his contract. Four long years later, however, the public finally learned he had actually served overseas as a noncombatant, and he recaptured his box-office appeal until he transitioned to a long career on television. Ayres appears to be one of the rare lasting friendships Ida Koverman maintained in spite of his liberal politics and controversial notion of patriotism, and she was among the first to resurrect Ayres's image. When he first returned to the studio, they had lunch in the famed commissary, where the studio made sure he could talk to reporters. He humbly told them he had no immediate plans to resume acting, and in his self-effacing manner he said he was going to take time out to do "an awful lot of thinking," and he had little of value to talk about except how deeply moved he was by what he observed during the war while working in hospitals and interacting with psychiatric patients. They talked about their children or their own childhoods, which made him realize that "we hear so much about the atomic bomb," but "we forget that the greatest atomic energy in the world is a child. Isn't it our job to control that energy and guide it?"[32] Three years later, Ayres appeared in *Johnny Belinda* alongside costar Jane Wyman, who won an Oscar for her role. During filming, Wyman, also known then as Mrs. Ronald Reagan, fell in love with the liberal Ayres, supposedly out of her growing boredom with Reagan or her disdain for his growing conservatism and obsessive politicking.

Many of the prominent actors during the thirties and forties have faded from the popular collective consciousness, but during the height of their movie careers, they were wildly successful Hollywood stars. Fans of the 1960s hit television series *Dr. Kildare* starring Richard Chamberlain might not have realized that Lew Ayres had played their beloved doctor in a nine-part film series three decades earlier. Lionel Barrymore played the elder mentor Dr. Leonard Gillespie, a role assumed by Raymond Massey as his television counterpart. Lew Ayres, a strict vegetarian, had been married to Ginger Rogers, whose mother, Lela, was a fellow Christian Scientist and a staunch anti-communist and political ally of Ida Koverman.

Echoing Joseph Pasternak, one journalist described Koverman as one of the few people who "knows what Louis B. Mayer is going to do with his day before L. B. does." Koverman was "the lady who does exactly that," and she was the "confidential advisor and beefeater-in-chief for the Metro production head. She's been there a long time, her executive latitude is vast, and there's very little taking place on the lot that she hasn't exerted some influence. . . . She has a lot of pretty important gents tiptoeing around her with devout respect. . . . She is actuated by a sense of knowing instantly what the boss man would do in a given instance; who he'll want to see, instantly, and who can be seen next day, next week—or never." Women like Koverman were rare, but where they surfaced, they were "operating up ahead of the ball while clearing away debris, the trivia, the unnecessary and the unwelcome—the buffers before whom Fate itself might recoil. In fact, buffing neatly and quickly done, while you wait. And wait. And wait."[33]

CHAPTER 22

Moral Crusader

"Public Relations for the Good Christ."[1]

MAE WEST WAS WEARING HER PINK NEGLIGEE WHEN A PHOTOGRAPHER captured the image of her sitting next to Dr. Frank N. Buchman, leader of the international Moral Rearmament movement (MRA). The flamboyant, hypersexualized writer-actress-comedienne was endorsing Dr. Buchman, the world-class proselytizer of a new collective moral vision that would spawn global peace. Mae West told reporters in 1939, in her characteristic double-entendre style, that she hoped Dr. Buchman would meet with her costar, W. C. Fields, before they started filming *My Little Chicadee*, released the following year. She wanted Dr. Buchman to tell Fields all about Moral Rearmament; and, in fact, she said, "I want him to be full of it."[2]

As word about the MRA spread throughout America, Hollywood beckoned, and Frank Buchman answered the call. Ida Koverman's attraction to the MRA stemmed from her instinctive understanding of a connection between public morals and motion pictures. She and others had long pondered ways to exploit the medium to promote spiritual uplift when she attended and spoke at a 1933 Motion Picture Symposium held at the Biltmore Hotel. The Symposium resembled similar efforts designed to shape public morality through mass entertainment, as it sought to be "the voice and vision of the world in motion pictures." The 1933 event provides a direct link between Hollywood and the MRA through Ida Koverman, and an early proselytizer for the Oxford Group, silent film actor Alec B. Francis, who sought a combination of the spiritual with the practical in the production and marketing of movies. The Symposium's goal was to influence what movies were made by advocating the incorporation of specific content and to "share information . . . with clubs, schools and other groups for the purpose of benefiting spiritually, artistically and intellectually," and to discuss "the problems of motion-picture production from many angles." Among the attendees drawn from civic-minded "producers, actors, educators, society and clubwomen, business men and women," was Mrs. Thomas G. Winter, who was the former head of the largest women's group in the country, the General Federation of Women's Clubs, and the current, controversial head of the public relations department of the Motion Picture Producers and Distributors Association.[3]

Alec Francis told the audience "purely religious pictures will not pay," frankly admitting the solution was "a fifty-fifty division with the spiritual side, so subtly interjected [that] the audience will scarcely be aware of its presence until they think about it afterward." He said the Oxford Group reminded us that "Hollywood had forgotten God's guidance," but he now saw a "new trend in that direction." If a motion picture was "truly dramatic and alive," it would foster an uplifting spirit, but because movies depicted lawlessness by offering "hokum to the public," with "stupid portrayals, [and] false people," they were guilty of "disintegrating the brains and the morals of the American People."[4]

The spiritual message crossed political lines. Liberal Democrat B. P. Schulberg, who represented producers at the Symposium, explained that just because Little Red Riding Hood and Macbeth both wore red capes, you couldn't make pictures about them with the same appeal to the same audience. He said, "The problem of the producer is to make a picture of such wide appeal that the adult, the child, the moron, the intellectual all will find something in it to enjoy." Schulberg's assessment resonates with contemporary producers who have "first to pay the big salary to the actor, and then along comes the director asking even more, and now the author is clamoring. The picture must pay all of them. So it must have a great audience not of thousands, but of millions." Schulberg declared, "We really are trying to produce the cleanest, finest, most uplifting pictures that the public will let us," and then he challenged the women in attendence to solve the problems of the producers.[5]

By the time Mae West expressed her support of the MRA in August of 1939, heightened tensions around the globe had inspired citizens to embrace charismatic leaders of all stripes in their hope of warding off another catastrophic world war. Dr. Frank Buchman offered peace through universal spiritual uplift. The MRA had been officially christened on May

29, 1938, when Dr. Frank Buchman revamped an earlier grassroots organization, the Oxford Group, whose believers spread Christian principles with messengers drawn from a wide spectrum of individuals of high social standing in politics and business. Dr. Buchman believed the MRA would become a great hope in the midst of dangers threatening civilization.

Just how familiar Mae West was with the tenets of the MRA movement is unclear, but the publicity helped to boost the organization's visibility and its local membership. Like the sultry movie star, Buchman also had a special kind of charisma that attracted followers abroad, and when his message spread to America, he won endorsements from a broad swath of business leaders and elected officials. Ida Koverman and MGM publicity man Howard Strickling welcomed Frank Buchman and the MRA to Hollywood, where thousands flocked to hear his clarion call for good over evil, and the two of them fostered Louis B. Mayer's friendship with Buchman.

Anxieties about movies and morals were now embedded within brewing fears about mounting international crises, and the MRA offered a glimmer of hope about the possibility of maintaining world peace and personal salvation through individual actions that could affect a collective result. The rapid growth of the Moral Rearmament movement came during the decline of the world's economies, the rise of aggressive despots, and fears about the failure to enforce disarmament treaties signed in the wake of the First World War.

Until recently, the MRA has received little attention from historians, and until actress Glenn Close disclosed that her family had been devoted followers, most Americans had never heard of the Moral Rearmament crusade. The MRA flourished long after World War II, and its adaptability and creative versatility has enabled it to survive well into the twentieth century, albeit with a downsized real-estate footprint. Initially, membership recruitment "house parties" grew their ranks, but by the late 1930s, grandiose pageants were the mainstay of its organizing strategy. Combining techniques of old-time evangelical camp meetings with those eerily similar to Nazi-style spectacles, the MRA employed live theater productions, popular music, and radio broadcasts in their long-term outreach agendas.

The MRA launched a three-month US tour in 1939, but their venture turned into a seven-year residency. Great fanfare greeted Buchman and his entourage before its inaugural Madison Square Garden extravaganza in New York. Manny Strauss, public relations director for Macy's department store, told Buchman about his friend Louis B. Mayer who had provided "wonderful cooperation" in preparation for the MRA's visit to Los Angeles.

Mayer hand wrote a note to Buchman. He said, "I am delighted that I am to have the pleasure and honor of entertaining for you at [the] luncheon on Friday," and he was "looking forward to a most interesting and enjoyable meeting with you and your group." Some pundits were openly skeptical of Buchman's "road show," as it was about to take on "Hollywood to make an impression on the movie world."[6] And it certainly did.

Aside from the well-publicized meeting between Mae West and Frank Buchman, the highlight of the MRA's Los Angeles visit was a spectacular rally at the Hollywood Bowl on July 19, 1939, just six weeks before Adolf Hitler's invasion of Poland. Promoted as the largest gathering in the "world war against selfishness," Ida Koverman's friend and Bowl board member, Mrs. Leiland Atherton Irish, was in charge of the MRA arrangements.[7] MGM hosted a two-hundred-seat luncheon for MRA delegates with a guest-list drawn from the city's studio executives, on-screen talent, business leaders, and public officials.

Forty-five thousand people tried to get tickets to the Hollywood Bowl that night. The gala was heralded as a call to the world's nations to learn how to live together. There were hundreds in the international delegation, which included travelers from Asia, India, Australia, and South America, with Canada sending the largest contingent of nearly four hundred.[8] The pageant was dramatically staged, especially the four giant klieg lights shooting high into the night sky. Each beam of light represented one of the four pillars or "absolutes" of the guiding principles of the Moral Rearmament Movement: Absolute Honesty, Absolute Unselfishness, Absolute Purity, and Absolute Love.

By then, the MRA had attracted the attention of America's leaders, some of whom sent messages of goodwill to be read out loud. Among them were President Roosevelt, Herbert Hoover, Henry Ford, and governors near and far. Will Hays served as the master of ceremonies, and local businessman George Lockwood Eastman formally opened the ceremonies. Modern dancer Ruth St. Denis told the audience she was convinced that "the only war to end war is the war of the Moral Rearmament membership to bring world peace." Koverman's old ally attorney Joseph Scott praised the crowd for their "wholesome, intellectual and spiritual" qualities, and Louis B. Mayer read a message on behalf of British film executives who pledged to help the MRA by acting as its "celluloid ambassadors." Mayer advised the industry to "take inventory of ourselves as business men do with their businesses," because "MRA is a spiritual, common sense philosophy." Canadian born Cecil Broadhurst, who would become known as the "singing cowboy," said he had never seen such a roundup before and performed "You and Me." As an actor, artist, and songwriter, Broadhurst went on to write and to star in MRA productions during the postwar decades. Welford Beaton, editor of *Hollywood Spectator,* believed that the MRA could be the inspiration "for a great motion picture" to tell a "human story about ordinary people" whose "desire to live in a tranquil world," free of war, would come to pass by the sheer will of their collective beliefs. The MRA had, in fact, already inspired one Broadway production, but Rachel Crothers's *Susan and God* (1937) was a parody of the movement, soon turned into an MGM screenplay written by Anita Loos, starring Joan Crawford and directed by George Cukor, which, ironically, included a cameo appearance of the MRA's singing cowboy, Cecil Broadhurst.[9]

George Lockwood Eastman was president of the Hollywood Athletic Club, and his attraction to Buchman and the MRA was, in part, its implicit anti-union and virulent anti-communist agenda. George Eastman and Ida Koverman worked together in 1932 in the Chamber of Commerce, when she headed its Women's Division to promote the Olympic games. Eastman now spearheaded the MRA's local publicity campaign, and for years afterward he unabashedly held a daily morning ritual with his employees to ask for God's direction as a way to show his workers he had their interests rather than his own at heart. The irony, however, was that on the day of the July 1939 Hollywood Bowl MRA gala, workers around the country held massive strikes and walkouts.[10]

Louis B. Mayer said the meeting was "the most inspirational thrill of my life," and he and Ida Koverman were integral to the MRA taking root in Los Angeles. It set up its headquarters in downtown Los Angeles in the Women's Athletic Club on South Flower Street, and perhaps it was just a coincidence that the Bank of America, where Koverman's friend Grace Stoermer was a vice president, financed the acquisition for $500,000. Louis B. Mayer incorporated tenets of the MRA when he spoke to an audience in Detroit about distribution of *Gone with the Wind.* He issued "a plea for racial and religious tolerance, and the elimination of hatred," and he stressed Moral Rearmament while talking about another MGM movie, *Young Tom Edison,* in which he saw a picture that "will perhaps inspire our young men and discourage them from communism." A few months later, and likely with Koverman's prodding, Mayer sent birthday greetings to Frank Buchman, acknowledging MRA's second anniversary with, "I hope the years to come will find more and more of our people interested in this splendid work. I wish you all the success in the world and send you very kind regards."[11]

The MRA entourage moved up the California coast, holding conferences and rallies with speakers drawn from politics and Hollywood, including Tallulah Bankhead's father, Democratic Speaker of the House William B. Bankhead. Hedda Hopper and Los Angeles County Supervisor John Anson Ford also "spread the message." Ford said, "We need to refresh our understanding as to the true meaning of Democracy," and "public officials must learn to utilize the power and understanding that come from God's guidance."[12]

Buchman appreciated how Mayer was "giving pleasure" to the widow of Thomas Edison when he threw her a luncheon. Mrs. Hughes was the widow of the beloved inventor Thomas A. Edison, who came to Los Angeles to participate in the MRA's national unity program. She was also an enthusiastic participant in MGM's biographical productions about Edison, as was Frank Buchman, who cheered the March 1940 *Young Tom Edison*, starring Mickey Rooney, and then its May sequel, *Edison, the Man*, starring Spencer Tracy as the mature inventor.[13]

Others were more dubious about the message and methods of the MRA. Renowned progressive attorney and journalist Carey McWilliams found MRA's finances curious and its real estate a subject of concern. McWilliams explained how the MRA had no dues or membership fees, and their meetings were free to all who attended. Rather than an organization held accountable through bylaws and trustees, McWilliams saw the MRA as an "organism" that it was impossible to belong to, or to join, or to resign from, and unlike most volunteer groups, there were no officers and no elections, but there was a great willingness to accept contributions. Buchman cultivated devotees across a broad economic spectrum all over the world, including family members of America's richest icons of the Gilded Age.[14]

Whether Louis B. Mayer ever wrote a check to the MRA remains unknown, but contrary to assumptions that he only had a passing interest in the group, Koverman and Mayer were long-time supporters of Buchman. Clearly, Buchman saw Koverman and Mayer as friends, but both the mogul and the matron were also conduits to their networks of contacts and colleagues who had deep philanthropic pockets. In Buchman's New Year's greeting to Mayer, he made a point of mentioning that Manny Strauss, a friend of Mayer, told him about a "heartened visit" he had with Mayer and Mayer's closest friend and financial consultant, Louis Lurie. According to Buchman, they all offered "favorable constructive cooperation in the program" to defend America and his group's "sagacious and farseeing vision."[15]

The post–World War II, Cold War era accelerated the MRA mission to contain communism and popular-front movements in Europe. In Los Angeles, advocates of the MRA continued their efforts, such as Koverman's ally, Los Angeles Board of Education member Mrs. Eleanor B. Allen, who had for years worked "to expand the Moral Rearmament program throughout the school system." Nevertheless, a decade later, when the MRA held a celebration for Buchman's seventieth birthday at the Hollywood Bowl, it drew an audience of a mere fifteen thousand—still sizeable but hardly the overflow crowd on the eve of the outbreak of war in Europe. After the "speechifying," the MRA now launched its first musical revue, *The Good Road*, described by one skeptic as "a lively two-hour musical of propaganda for God," and the MRA's role as a "Religion to Change the World."[16] Carey McWilliams directly connected Ida Koverman with the MRA, noting she was at the local center of the nationwide network of "educators, feminists, dowagers, tennis players, admirals, generals, corporation lawyers, personnel managers, and reformed sinners," who supported Buchman and the MRA. The MRA's downtown headquarters welcomed "top movie figures" such as Joel McCrea and James Stewart, McWilliams wrote, and it was "the motion picture industry through the good offices of Mrs. Ida Koverman [who] . . . took the delegates on a tour of MGM studios." To another observer, Koverman, as "part of the inviting group," was "of the Public Relations for the Good Christ-like way."[17]

Ida Koverman was drawn to the MRA because of what Carey McWilliams called "the middle-class substitute for the camp meeting . . . the country-club anti-Communist international."[18] Even more appealing to her, however, was its God-centered principles that echoed those of her Christian Science faith—the belief in the power of the individual to heal one's body, and that change came through an individual's behavior and their relationship with God. The MRA's messianic vision resonated with her ideological sensibilities, and because she was a conservative Republican, the MRA also reflected her faith in individualism and self-reliance, limited government, and private charity rather than regulatory public legislation to heal and uplift social ailments.

The outward, grandiose techniques of the MRA appealed to Ida Koverman's sense of the dramatic and her passion for music and popular culture to elevate the collective spirit. She thrived in a world that perfected the fantastical alternate realities that appealed to the masses while it conveyed higher ideals. Moreover, she appreciated how Buchman understood the power of presentation. Ida Koverman was a fan of *The Pilgrimage Play*, a staple of the winter holiday season since its 1920 premiere at the open-air

Pilgrimage Theatre amphitheater, built especially to stage it after the Bowl declined to produce it.[19]

The Hollywood Bowl was one of Ida Koverman's favorite places that allowed her to indulge her passions for the performing arts and networking. It was a popular place to be and to be seen, and to enjoy a diversity of the world's greatest musicians, dancers, and performers.[20] Ida's patronage of the Bowl was well known, and her appointment to its board of trustees solidified her standing among the city's cultural brokers and institution builders. Mrs. Leiland Atherton Irish recommended Ida Koverman for a seat on the Los Angeles Art Association, an organization established in 1925. Also nominated at that time was County Supervisor John Anson Ford. Koverman and Mrs. Irish were also members of the board of the Santa Monica Civic Music Guild, where Mrs. Irish served as vice president and Ida Koverman, along with Mrs. Louis B. Mayer, were on the executive committee.[21] Ida Koverman and John Anson Ford would develop a friendship built around their mutual interests, which included their attraction to the MRA, classical music, and the promotion of historic legislation for public funding of the performing arts.

Once she joined the Bowl board, however, Ida Koverman's initiative for the Bowl to reconsider *The Pilgrimage Play* failed, and it remained across the street until its final performance in 1964. Supervisor John Anson Ford was a longtime supporter of the production, and after the venue was donated to the county in 1941, it was renamed the John Anson Ford Theater, which remains a vibrant arena to showcase a rich diversity of the multicultural performing arts of Los Angeles.[22]

George L. Eastman called upon Koverman when he was planning an MRA-sponsored Hiroshima Day memorial event on August 6, 1950, as part of its ongoing outreach in Asia to spread its message. Frank Buchman wrote to Koverman that this would "be an event that will need your careful attention," and he hoped she could get Mayer to participate as well, and Eastman would provide the details. Buchman reminded Koverman how well the MRA had been received throughout Europe and how "important events are being prepared for them in Washington," and that it was "amusing how this ideology of Moral Re-Armament is growing, and how effective it is in the life of nations." The memorial dinner at the MRA's downtown headquarters hosted two hundred guests, including Mayor Bowron.[23]

Later that year, Buchman boasted to Koverman about his work with United Airlines president William A. Patterson, which "they frankly say . . . averted a strike." He was holding an event to which Patterson and his family, staff, and pilots were going, and he hoped she would be able to come. "All this has made a profound impression" on the administrator of the Marshall Plan, who said the MRA was the ideological counterpart to the US reconstruction of war-torn Europe. Patterson and another business leader, Samuel Graham of Dixie Cup, Buchman said, "feel that this must get into the movies immediately," and he told Koverman that this was where she could "play an effective part." He closed affectionately with "loyal regards, believe me, yours very faithfully."[24]

Just as she had nurtured Louis B. Mayer's politically reciprocal relationship with Herbert Hoover, Koverman buttressed the friendship between Mayer and Frank Buchman and Buchman's fruitful entree into her social and professional networks whose interests often combined. Ida Koverman was a master facilitator, and while it appears that she merely served to promote the interests of these men, it turns out that once they were drawn into the gravity of her orbit, they could hardly discern the smoothness of the shift from when their interests were no longer their own.

CHAPTER 23

Music, Metaphysics, and Moral Custodian

As "the middleman between talent and the opportunity to showcase it,
. . . Ida was largely responsible for launching or nurturing the career of
MGM's contract mega-stars. A casual mention that Mayer should 'take
a look at' someone could make a career, and she was responsible for
some of MGM's biggest finds."[1]

THE OLDEST SINGLE-FAMILY HOME IN HOLLYWOOD HAD ORIGINALLY
belonged to Eugene Rafael Plummer on the estate that became Plummer
Park, and it housed the local bird-watchers' Audubon Society. Eventually, the residence was relocated to the site of the historic Leonis Adobe in
Calabasas on the eastern edge of the San Fernando Valley. The park was a
well-known community gathering place, sponsoring public performances,
sports, and celebrations of the city's diverse ethnic culture. During the Depression era, the park also housed the Meremblum Orchestra, founded in
1936, which soon continuously enrolled over a hundred young performers
who practiced and performed every Saturday. Many former Meremblum
musicians went on to professional careers playing in symphony orchestras throughout the country. Over time, famous guest conductors such as
Bruno Walter, Leopold Stokowski, José Iturbi, and George Szell took their
turn leading the young musicians, and famed violinist Jascha Heifetz was
a frequent visitor to the park well into the 1960s. Sitting along with Ida
Koverman were board members actress Beulah Bondi and MGM composer
Charles Previn. Ida Koverman found the youth symphony a source of
untapped talent for MGM and the broader film industry. Koverman was

recognized as a "leading sponsor" of the Meremblum Orchestra, applauded by syndicated society columnist Elsa Maxwell, who described Koverman as Louis B. Mayer's "alter ego," and one "who privately supports a fine student orchestra on her own, proving her more than an altruist."[2]

This particular role reflected the shared vision Koverman had with John Anson Ford to foster music appreciation and educational opportunities for children by learning to play instruments and perform with the orchestra. Just after Christmas 1944, Ford tried to enlist the help of Koverman's friend, ally, and Bowl board member Mrs. Leiland Atherton Irish, who had apparently failed to respond to Peter Meremblum's communication about promoting his group. Ford tried to prod Mrs. Irish's attention by telling her there were a "great number of influential people" who were eager to find a way to "better implement" the Meremblum program in order to establish a diversified musical institution. He nudged her with a handwritten note at the bottom of his formal letter: "I stand ready to call the group together when I hear from you."[3] It's unclear what her response was, but eventually Ida Koverman took up the cause.

The revitalization of the park became her primary goal in January 1946, when she began lobbying the board of supervisors to improve the quality and amount of space for the music program. As the Meremblum orchestra grew in size and popularity, the auditorium could not accommodate the number of folding chairs to seat the musicians and their instruments and music stands, nor could it fit their families who came to listen, and the increasing number of people who dropped in to hear them rehearse or perform. By then, there were 125 student and 90 senior orchestra members. Koverman argued that Plummer Park, "a greatly beloved spot," was desperately in need of improvements, evidenced by the many missed opportunities for "citizens who would like to enjoy the use of the Park" but could not because the demand "far exceeded the facilities."[4]

Appealing to the booster ethic of the city's elected officials, she noted that an enlarged auditorium "would be a credit to the County of Los Angeles." There was certainly enough unused land, and a larger auditorium could have multiple uses, such as for dances and classes. The design, she suggested, "could be arranged to shut off the stage in some way, when two separate halls were needed." Not surprisingly, Koverman's initiative was shepherded by John Anson Ford, and "the County moved to expand the facilities" with the construction of a larger auditorium, called Fiesta Hall, that had a seating capacity of five hundred. It was completed in 1950, and financing came through a community organization called "Friends of Plummer Park," which donated furnishings and interior appointments.[5]

Ida Koverman's interest in both the Meremblum Orchestra and the Hollywood Bowl came together when she and MGM music man Roger Edens organized a memorial concert for the acclaimed composer Jerome Kern in July 1946. The concert opened with the Meremblum Orchestra because Kern "always had a soft spot in his heart for this wonderful group." Composer Johnny Green conducted that night, and MGM's biggest stars performed, especially those featured in the recent MGM Kern tribute film *Till the Clouds Roll By*, such as Kathryn Grayson, Judy Garland, Frank Sinatra, Lena Horne, Gene Kelly, and Robert Walker, who had played Kern in the film.

The Kern gala was a huge success, drawing a filled-to-capacity crowd, but the night was not without controversy. Before the concert, it was rumored that Sinatra threatened to withdraw from the program when he learned that African American baritone William Gillespie was scheduled to open the show with "Old Man River" from *Showboat*, which Sinatra would sing again for the finale. The suspense lasted until the last moment because until he walked onto the stage while the orchestra played the introduction, no one was sure if he would show up.[6]

Perhaps it was a misguided publicity stunt, or it was a genuine misunderstanding. Whatever sparked the real or misrepresented incident, MGM felt it necessary for Sinatra to clarify the circumstances. A statement appeared in the *Afro-American* newspaper: "The Hollywood Bowl incident involving Mr. Gillespie and myself is one that I regret very much, and particularly the emphasis that has been placed upon it. The arranging of the Jerome Kern program that night was a matter in which I had no part. Upon my arrival, the program was shown to me and I objected to singing a song that was to be sung only 20 minutes earlier. At the time, I had no knowledge of who was to sing it ahead of me—I merely regarded it as poor showmanship. I suggested that the other singer be allowed to appear with another song. The fact that the other singer was William Gillespie, as I learned later, or that he was colored, certainly never entered into it."[7]

Another incident surrounding the Kern event further exposed tensions regarding America's mid-century racial divide. Soon after the concert started, word came that Lena Horne would not appear, but her decision was a conscious stance that reflected a problem bigger than just song choices. Koverman played a role in Lena Horne's path-breaking career as the first African American singer-actress to sign a long-term contract with any major Hollywood movie studio. But now, Horne was protesting MGM's deleting her scenes in films distributed in southern markets where they could offend white audiences. The immediate problem was the lineup of the Kern memorial, with Horne's songs scheduled throughout the program and not easily cut. Roger Edens and Judy Garland quickly went over Horne's songs, and when Judy appeared as the understudy, she performed them as if assigned to them all along.[8]

Throughout Horne's career, she aggressively countered racist policies and prejudices and fought MGM over her deleted scenes, whether it was studio policy or local distributors' decisions. Recognition of her efforts came in 1948, two years after the Kern memorial concert (not 1944 as cited in numerous accounts), when she received a Unity Award that honored "contributions to interracial and religious understanding." As a representative of MGM, Ida Koverman attended the ceremony held at the Second Baptist Auditorium, described as a night filled with the "glamorous . . . galaxy of Hollywood stars, producers and writers." Author J. E. Smyth somehow interprets Koverman's attendance at the Unity Awards as evidence that she not only did "not approve of the Hollywood witch-hunts," but also that "she continued to offer her tacit support to liberal 'message' films," such as those being honored that night for their promotion of civil rights and civil liberties: *Gentleman's Agreement, Crossfire*, and *Body and Soul*. Dory Schary produced *Crossfire* while he was at RKO, before he returned to MGM in 1948. *Gentleman's Agreement* was a Darryl Zanuck production at 20th Century Fox, and United Artists produced *Body and Soul*. To infer any opinion from Koverman's attendance that night completely ignores the fact that she was there in support of Lena Horne, who did not merely "attend with" Koverman but was being honored with a Unity Award in recognition of her success as MGM's first African American singer to break the color line in crossover parts that made her a movie star, and perhaps with the explicit encouragement by Ida Koverman.[9]

The successful collaboration of Ida Koverman and John Anson Ford wrought larger transformations to California's support of the performing arts. Some scholars have argued that the underlying motivation for the effort to expand public support for arts and recreation in Los Angeles was the threat to traditional, and white, genres from the rise of a flourishing multiethnic cultural diversity. The post-World War rise in juvenile delinquency was also a motivation, and often the two were conflated in efforts to promote or explain otherwise reasonable civic-minded legislation appearing to be infused with racism and fear. Whatever biases motivated the promoters of the public sponsorship of the performing arts, the steps taken by Ida Koverman, John Anson Ford, and their allies ultimately promoted multicultural artistic diversity and the preservation of creative traditions.

One statewide venture that Koverman, Ford, and other Southland notables promoted, which failed to materialize, was the construction of a state
centennial building. Nevertheless, John Anson Ford believed his friendship
with Ida Koverman had spawned an "awakening" of "the public to greater
support for cultural things." She was his "loyal friend," who "made possible
this new cultural era," fostering a "greatly intensified . . . relationship of
the Board of Supervisors to the field of music." Before their alliance, Ford
explained, "Supervisors had been appropriating only a few thousand annu-
ally, via a 'legal subterfuge,' namely through the Chamber of Commerce."
Ford and Koverman changed this in 1947 when they successfully lobbied to
secure a state law that "made financial contributions to non-profit musical
and dramatic enterprises a legitimate county expenditure."[10]

After California governor Earl Warren signed the arts bill into law, the
steady expansion of financial support ushered in a renaissance of public
cultural programs and institutions. Among the county's greatest benefi-
ciaries were those that Ida Koverman had served passionately, including
the Hollywood Bowl, *The Pilgrimage Play*, the Philharmonic Orchestra, and
eventually more than twenty neighborhood orchestras administered by
the Los Angeles County Music Commission. The new state law, however,
applied only to county expenditures, so Ida Koverman appeared before
the city council to urge the city's continued and expanded support for
the music in the parks program. She argued persuasively that "the music
program has done much to provide public entertainment and to attract
young people to beneficial music studies." Mayor Fletcher Bowron then
appointed Koverman to the Board of the Municipal Arts Commission after she had been serving as the chairman of the Citizens' Music Advisory
Committee, assisting the music bureau of the Municipal Art Department.
She served until April 23, 1951.[11]

The Opera Guild of Southern California held its fourth annual luncheon
at the Hotel Biltmore in November 1949, where it recognized Koverman
as one of its patrons. The Beverly Hills Hotel hosted another event after
guest conductor Serge Koussevitsky drew standing room only at the Hollywood Bowl, described by Hedda Hopper as "one of the pleasanter galas,"
who noted that she was accompanied by Ida Koverman and Governor
Earl Warren's daughter Virginia. Koverman had socialized with both of
Warren's daughters before, such as the time they were spotted "bustling
about" at a Jeanette MacDonald-Gene Raymond affair.[12]

The confluence of Ida Koverman's advocacy of talent and civic institutions was manifest in the early career path of Marni Nixon, who first
caught Koverman's eye as a violinist and then as a soprano with the

Meremblum Orchestra in Plummer Park. Koverman instantly knew that Nixon was a gifted musician, and she watched her "growth carefully over the next few years." In the meantime, Koverman became friends with Marni Nixon's mother, Mrs. Margaret McEathron Nixon.[13]

When Koverman learned of the financial burden that singing lessons presented for the Nixon family, Koverman arranged for Marni to be hired as a messenger girl on the MGM lot, and for free voice lessons by studio coaches. Marni understood from Koverman that she could be a viable alternative to Jane Powell if she "gave the studio any trouble." Powell behaved, and landing an MGM contract appeared more elusive. Eventually, however, Koverman led Nixon to a "new road," but not as "MGM's latest starlet as she had hoped." Instead, it was a path she described as one filled with ghosts.[14]

It started serendipitously when songwriter Bronislaw Kaper approached Nixon and jokingly asked, "Can you sing in Hindu?" [sic]. She said she could, but figured it out afterward, which led to her first off-screen part, dubbing the voice of Margaret O'Brien singing a Hindu lullaby in *The Secret Garden*. She appeared in unspoken bit parts in dozens of movies, and even drew on her skill as a violinist for *In the Good Old Summertime*, starring Judy Garland and Van Johnson. She dubbed many notable and some forgettable voices, including Ingrid Bergman's voice in *Joan of Arc*, Jeanne Crain's in *Cheaper by the Dozen*, sang the high notes for Marilyn Monroe's "Diamonds Are a Girl's Best Friend" in *Gentlemen Prefer Blonds*, and was Ida Lupino's voice in *Jennifer*.

In fact, Marni Nixon's voice would become one of the most recognizable in MGM's greatest musicals, such as for Deborah Kerr's Anna in the 1956 *The King and I*, Natalie Wood's Maria in 1964's *West Side Story*, and the lesser known part of Rita Moreno's voice in the arrangement of *Tonight*. She sang the high notes for Natalie Wood in *Gypsy* (1962), and she was the voice of Audrey Hepburn in 1964's *My Fair Lady*. By then, her behind-the-scenes participation was well-established, and she was no longer a publicity nightmare. She also appeared on-screen as Sister Sophia in the 1965 production of *The Sound of Music*. Baby boomers raised in households with a passion for movie musicals experienced the direct legacy of Ida Koverman as they watched these classics and listened to the timeless voice of Marni Nixon. After her formidable ghost-singing career, Nixon went on to an acclaimed career on the concert stage, on television, and as a recording artist. Nixon acknowledges that Koverman, whom she knew as the power behind the MGM throne, had played "an instrumental role" in the course of her life.[15]

When Ida Koverman told a radio audience in 1948 that "Religion is the most important thing in everyone's life," it was revealing and mysterious.[16] For the casual observer, it's easy to confuse Mary Baker Eddy's Christian Science with the Holmes's Religious Science, but it is less clear why adherents to either who circulated in Koverman's world failed to make the distinction between the two. Ida Koverman appeared to know the difference, and consistently described herself as a follower of Christian Science.

Variations of metaphysical, pseudoscientific religious theologies were widespread among Ida Koverman's network, and an extraordinary percentage of the people with whom she closely associated embraced one or the other. Ironically, Koverman and Mrs. Nixon might have bonded over religious faith, but Marni Nixon's assumption that her mother was a Christian Scientist raises the perpetual question of whether she was conflating it with Religious Science. Mrs. Nixon, according to her daughter, converted to Christian Science in 1925 after what she believed was a miraculous recovery from scarlet fever by her daughter Donyll. Mrs. Nixon's sister Nell, a devoted follower, influenced the process. What is strange, though, is that Mrs. Nixon was an author and an editor of the published works by Fenwicke L. Holmes. Fenwicke L. Holmes was not a Christian Scientist, but rather, he and his brother Ernest founded the Science of Mind, also known as Religious Science.[17]

Koverman's long time ally, IWC Commissioner Mabel Kinney, however, was an ally of Fenwicke Holmes, and she was a prominent evangelist of Religious Science, as she "worked quietly behind the scenes to connect celebrities and just plain folks with California's metaphysicians," by arranging "to have her favorite spiritual leaders receive official public proclamations, honors, and awards from lawmakers." A contemporary of hers recounted how "people trembled when they heard Mabel's name because she was powerful politically." She said Kinney was "very helpful in getting people like California Governor Goodwin Knight and others into our metaphysical events and things. She'd tell bigwigs in Holmes's church to do something and they did it because she was influential and she was helping them." Kinney served as president of the Women's Club Institute of Religious Sciences, and her 1969 funeral service, held in the Holmes Chapel, asked that in lieu of flowers, donations be made to Dial-A-Prayer at the Founders' Church of Religious Science on 6th Street.[18]

Jeannette MacDonald embraced Religious Science, acknowledged by her biographer as being "ripe for an alternative religion, having long ago stopped identifying as a Presbyterian." Her attraction "lay in its belief that one need not fear judgment in the afterlife, since God is love and the soul is 'forever and ever expanding.'" Presiding at her funeral was the controversial spiritual leader Dr. Gene Emmet Clark of the Church of Religious Science, Beverly Hills.[19]

Actor Robert Stack was one of Ida Koverman's favorites, whose mother was "a dedicated student" of Fenwicke Holmes, and his childhood was guided by Religious Science principles. Stack reasoned that actors, singers, artists, and performers of all kinds gravitated to the faith because the Science of Mind and performance were similar, in that "acting is a sense of a projection of the truth of living—it's allowing something to come alive purely out of mental states," making Religious Scinece "so popular with performers." He said, "It does the job without imposing mysteries, blinders, or dogma; it uses the intelligent you."[20]

Several other of Koverman's friends were associated with Religious Science, including Mary Pickford, Cecil B. DeMille, Robert Young, Robert Cummings, and Adela Rogers St. Johns; some even personally counseled by Ernest Holmes. Raised as a Religious Scientist, Esther Williams called upon her faith during a time of familial healing, and when she married her costar Fernando Lamas in a private ceremony at the Church of Religious Science in Beverly Hills in 1969. Lamas adopted it after rejecting his "Gothic Catholicism."[21]

Mickey Rooney's multiple memoirs are less clear about where he found God. When he married Baptist Ava Gardener, he was supposedly a Christian Scientist. Elsewhere, in the same work, Rooney indicates he was a follower of Religious Science, but in a later memoir, he credits the controversial talent agent Ruth Webb with his conversion to Christian Science. Yet in another book, it was one of his wives who introduced him to Religious Science.

Koverman's ally, former assistant US attorney general Mabel Walker Willebrandt, apparently converted to Christian Science after she adopted her daughter and felt "the need to attach herself to a church," just as her mother had done. Willebrandt's biographer suggests, however, that Willebrandt was less persuaded about the healing power of the faith, so both medical doctors and faith practitioners tended to her family. It's possible that Willebrandt was actually a temporary follower of Religious Science.[22]

Jean Harlow and her mother are consistently identified as Christian Scientists, as are Ginger Rogers and her mother, Lela. Bandleader Kay Kyser, actress Leatrice Joy Gilbert, and directors W. S. Van Dyke and King Vidor were as well, and before she converted to Judaism when she married Eddie Fisher, Elizabeth Taylor was a Christian Scientist. Joan Crawford underwent a religious conversion to Christian Science, about which she said she felt her religious "leanings helped me to gain and enjoy perspective."[23]

Composer Martin Broones and his wife Charlotte Greenwood were close friends of Koverman, and they were devout Christian Scientists. Broones wrote religious scores and lectured on Christian Science gospel. A print of a rare formal photograph of Koverman by photographer Clarence Sinclair Bull is inscribed by Koverman with her appreciation for the couple being "real people," and perhaps because of their shared spirituality.[24] The two women also shared athleticism, and so it couldn't just be a coincidence that, in 1953, the six-foot-tall, sixty-three-year-old Greenwood played a spirited senior swimmer as mother to Esther Williams in *Dangerous When Wet*.

It is certainly a reasonable assumption that Ida Koverman was Jewish, in part because of her last name, but members of Oscar Koverman's clan were a mix of Protestants and Catholics. It's also understandable to assume Koverman was Jewish because of her proximity to prominent Jews in the motion-picture industry. She was, in fact, a gentile amidst the legendary lineup of Jewish executives disproportionately represented within the industry, as well as actors who masked their ethnicities with stage names or conversions to traditional faiths and Christian Science. Louis B. Mayer biographer Neal Gabler has argued that for many Jews like Mayer, Christian Science provided "a convenient way-station from the faith of their fathers to complete assimilation in America," because "the beauty of Christian Science was that it made one less Jewish without demanding total surrender in return."[25] Koverman's Republican ally, attorney Mendel Silberg, however, lived the reverse. He had lived most of his life as a Christian Scientist until, perhaps under Mayer's influence, he more publicly joined his tribe when he rose to lead sectors of activist Jewish organizations during and after World War II. Even then, Silberg was a Jewish man in a profession filled with anti-Semites who kept the field of law tightly wrapped up for themselves.

Ida Koverman didn't need to worry about assimilation. She was part of the waves of midwestern Protestants who flocked to the Golden State from the boom of the 1880s to the mid-twentieth century. Her parents were married in the Methodist Episcopalian Church of Cincinnati, and they are buried in the Wesleyan Cemetery. As a single thirty-four-year-old, Koverman was a member of a Christ Episcopal Church committee set up to study ways to incorporate weekday religious courses into the curriculum of secular schools. Perhaps Koverman embraced her adopted faith after she arrived in California. Hollywood's movie colony and Southern

California in general were fertile ground for alternative religious and spiritual movements. By the 1920s, "mystics and magicians had become hot combinations" at Hollywood parties, and telepathists and mind readers replaced rumba experts and tennis instructors. One author noted how actors were drawn to psychics and metaphysicians advertising shortcuts to Louis B. Mayer's office in hopes of becoming the studio's next big star. Koverman's grandniece Mary recalled that when she was ailing, her aunt had a faith reading instead of calling a doctor. She also believed that Koverman "then started to groom George Murphy . . . who became a Christian Scientist too," surmising, "I guess you pretty much knew if you wanted to get any place that was the thing to do." It's not clear when Ida Koverman began to identify as a Christian Scientist, but her nephew Bruce was also an adherent. Hedda Hopper explained, "Ida was a Christian Scientist who, incredibly in the motion-picture business, clung to her job because, as she saw it, her special position of power gave her a phenomenal chance to do good." Koverman told her, "If you can't help somebody, what are you put here on earth for?"[26]

At the height of her influence inside of MGM, Ida Koverman's artistic sensibilities spread across the broader city landscape as she became a recognized cultural influencer and supporter of the city's musical arts. She sat on multiple committees and commissions alongside legendary benefactors and philanthropists, who curated the panoramic creative impulses of mid-century Los Angeles. Her position at MGM elevated her to positions traditionally allocated among the donors and financiers whose names emblazon edifices and monuments they fostered. For Koverman, appointments to prestigious committees enabled her to institutionalize her penchant for cross-fertilizing the musical and movie arts. It also legitimized her ability to circulate among the most famous and still-unknown artists, many of whom she aided in their successful transfer to the silver screen, and perhaps the direction of their spiritual journeys, however varied and unanticipated their paths.

Aside from her spirituality, the seventy-two-year-old Ida Koverman had strong feelings about sex—sex education, that is. When Dr. Alfred Kinsey published his decade-long research about American sexuality in 1948, it launched a firestorm about what appeared to be a vast disconnect between how the public perceived itself and how it behaved in the bedroom. It also fueled concerns about raising children in the postwar world, as part of a cluster of social insecurities that stemmed from a perceived breakdown of cultural standards, supported by statistics about rising rates of juvenile delinquency, divorce, the spread of venereal disease, and of course, the communist threat everywhere. The Cold War hysteria even politicized sex education, epitomized by California congressman Jack B. Tenney's state anti-communist committee, the Joint Fact-Finding Committee on Un-American Activities, which considered whether communists inspired a high-school sex-education program, inspiring the headline: "Tenney Fears Sex May Be Un-American."[27]

Everyone was talking about sex. Former Koverman ally, Hoover cabinet member, and president of Stanford University Raymond Lyman Wilbur was president of the American Social Hygiene Association, which studied sex education in light of "the problem of increasing social disease." Sexually transmitted diseases were associated with juvenile delinquency, and some blamed publishers for "books that deal so candidly and even enthusiastically with the easy ways of sex and crime," which were "bound to have a harmful effect on the fertile minds of youth." One local juvenile judge blamed young defendants' difficulties on exposure to indecent books. Others blamed the increase in radio broadcasts such as "Crime Doctor," and "Mr. District Attorney."[28]

Ida Koverman formally joined the debate about sex education in public schools on July 13, 1948, when she appeared on George V. Denny Jr.'s weekly *America's Town Meeting on the Air*, designed to fulfill the mandate of the federal government in their compact with commercial broadcasters to offer public-interest programming as a condition of receiving a license. Hollywood was blamed for a plethora of society's ills, so it's likely that Koverman's participation was designed to counter the perception that the industry corrupted the nation's youth. One newspaper described Ida Koverman as the "public relations director of MGM, where she is entrusted with the moral custody of children and young people of the lot," on top of which, as "a widow, Mrs. Koverman reared her sister's six children."[29] Ida Koverman was the picture-perfect matriarch to argue why it wasn't a good idea to teach sex education in public elementary schools. She had nurtured the careers of some of Hollywood's biggest stars, but she was hardly a widow, nor did she raise her nieces and nephews.

Moderator Denny welcomed his live and radio audience to Claremont's "fruitful valley," an appropriate place to discuss "the highly explosive subject" of sex education. He introduced Koverman as "the dynamic director of public relations of the biggest studio in Hollywood," who served on numerous boards and committees and who, as a "woman of resource and ability and great interest in public service," had a "particular interest in juvenile problems here and throughout the country."[30]

Joining Koverman to argue against the teaching of sex education in public elementary schools was the controversial Dr. J. Paul De River, who was described as the LAPD's sex psychiatrist (but more likely was trained as an ear, nose, and throat specialist) and who would raise eyebrows during his investigation of the still-unsolved grisly Black Dahlia murder. De River saw a correlation between the rise of public discourse about sex and the rise of juvenile delinquency. Speaking on behalf of teaching sex education in the classroom were Dr. Ralph O. Eckert, chief of the Bureau of Parent Education of the California Department of Education, and Mrs. Carmen Williams Boyle, a member of the governor's Crime Commission for Juvenile Justice.[31]

Following Eckert and Boyle, Koverman's prepared statement began with her agreement with the previous panelists on the "necessity for sex education" but differing on the ways to accomplish it and when such instruction should begin. Koverman believed that matters of sex should "await the period when [the child's] mind normally becomes interested in the subject," because it was a special period in a child's life when it didn't know its origin. To her, it was the difference between ignorance and innocence, and "the age of innocence is perhaps the most beautiful time in our lives." To a child, "everything is exciting and wonderful," and "neither the child nor its parents should be deprived of the happy innocence of those years." When the child's mind developed, however, the matter of sex "naturally becomes interesting," and the parents can then answer "very simply and adequately" any of the child's questions, but certainly not in "mixed groups" in school. In her idyllic world, premature discussion about sex would make everyone "self-conscious," and this could "destroy the normal relationship" between the parent and the child.[32]

The schools were already passing on the "essential knowledge of reading, writing, arithmetic, and so forth," and she felt "that in sending a child to school, you send him to be educated in things that you yourself perhaps can't educate him in as well, but I certainly do feel that sex education should be left to the family. After all, the fathers and mothers bring the children into the world and they certainly ought to have something to say and something to give them besides just clothing them. I feel very definitely that sex education should be taught in the home." If the parent lacked confidence or information, she argued there was ample information through qualified organizations, and books and pamphlets "in the minutest of detail," about the subject. And then, she said, "Religion is the most important thing in everyone's life," so, "if it has been deemed wise so far to leave the [religious] training to the parents and the home, it would seem equally wise to take the same attitudes towards sex education."

She shared a friend's experience with their eleven-year-old boy, who came home with questions about sex. The mother avoided the topic and handed him a magazine, after which the subject was dropped. The next day, the child returned home with his friends and asked to see the magazine. The mother pondered what questions might arise from their exploration, when suddenly, the boy turned to his friends and said, "There, see? These are the new planes I was telling you about." This underscored Koverman's point about not teaching a child to walk until he has made an effort to stand, or "teach a baby to eat meat before it has teeth." She explained "all nature grows gradually to fulfillment; first, the seed, then the plant, then the blossom, then back to the seed, but certainly not the blossom until the plant has grown strong enough to carry it."

Adding to this blend of romance and scientific homily was what she gleaned from her experience on the 1947 County Grand Jury, which drew from a broader context of societal fears about the changing nature of families, work, and women's roles in post-WWII America. Ida Koverman echoed FBI Director J. Edgar Hoover in his 1944 article that coined the phrase "adult delinquency," which would lead to the destruction of American individualism and free enterprise, and at its core, Director Hoover believed working mothers were to blame for the downfall of American civilization. She said she "found that practically every instance of juvenile delinquency which came before us was caused by broken homes. Children had been uprooted from their home surroundings. The grave trouble in all these cases was the lack of parental care and affection, in plain words, *adult delinquency*."[33]

Dr. De River chimed in that among the sex offenders he met, they had had sex education, but the wrong kind. Koverman more reasonably argued that she failed to see "where sex education in their early years would have been of any help in solving the cases of these children who appeared in court. The most frequently voiced complaint of parents seems to be their inability to instruct their children in sex. I heartily agree with Mrs. Boyle in regard to 'adult education' along these lines. Courses in this subject should not only be available but should be urged upon parents. Instructing your children in sex matters is your *bounden duty* and is a duty you dare not neglect."

The audience was eager to engage in a give-and-take, and one man asked Koverman, "Isn't it a proven fact that many divorces spring from lack of sex education of either one or both of the parties to the marriage?" to which she replied, "I think it's very true. I have no objection whatever to sex education. The only objection I have is the age." The man countered, "It seems to me that this education has to start pretty early on in order to accomplish its objective. Most of them are getting educated by the time they go to the marriage license bureau, but it doesn't seem to be early enough in practice as our divorce count would indicate." Koverman snapped back, "Would you advocate then training a child in sex education at the age of five or six or seven? Do you think that's necessary?" Not to let her have the last word, the gentleman quipped, "I believe that's about when it should start."[34]

Then, Koverman was asked what percentage of parents she believed had backgrounds that equipped them to adequately give their children sex education at home. She said it was a pretty hard question, but thought "any parent, father or mother, who is married and has children ought to know enough about sex to inform their children on any question they might ask." Dr. Eckert chimed in, "Well, if you had talked with as many parents as I have Mrs. Koverman, you wouldn't say that. . . . Even experts often don't know how to express or instruct even if they know the facts. . . . They're confused, anxious." De River came to Ida Koverman's defense and said that this was not his experience, and that women knew the facts.

The panelists gave closing statements. Koverman concluded with, "I personally do not feel that any arguments have been presented here tonight to change my position in the least. I still feel strongly that the responsibility is definitely that of the parents and if the parents fail, the entire system may eventually result in children being taken from their parents at a very early age and educated en bloc, which would be entirely deplorable." Dr. De River concluded with a passionate plea: "I call upon the parents to stop before it is too late in the name of God!"

CHAPTER 24

Propaganda and Pussy Willows

Hollywood observer Jimmie Fidler noted, "[Koverman] happens to
be one of the most powerful personages in the entire industry; when
she pulls the strings, world-famous stars dance like puppets."[1]

MOST OF IDA KOVERMAN'S CLOSEST ALLIES FORGED BONDS LONG AGO,
during a variety of Republican Party campaigns that extended during
her tenure at MGM. During the post-World War II years, divisions grew
within Koverman's inner circle, the MGM family, and throughout the
film industry that challenged the marriage between politics and pictures,
and raised doubts about their lasting compatibility. Soon after President
Harry Truman signed Executive Order 9835 requiring federal civil-service
employees to take a loyalty oath, Chairman J. Parnell Thomas of the
standing House Committee on Un-American Activities, more commonly
known as HUAC, held near-secret meetings at the Biltmore Hotel in Los
Angeles in May 1947. Thomas was looking for evidence that the Roosevelt (then Truman) administration and labor unions were forcing filmmakers to insert communist propaganda in Hollywood movies. Senator
Thomas, described as "a professional anti-Communist," and "a veritable
caricature of small-town prejudices and fear," "made witch-hunting the
perfect vehicle for him."[2]

Author J. E. Smyth asserts, "Koverman stayed out of the early stages of
the HUAC controversies," but, in fact, Koverman's network of influential
women were central to the historic events that shaped Cold War–era Hollywood. Her alliances and affiliations reflected her strong support of their

mission, and her close friends were rabidly vocal about their views and were members of aggressive anti-communist organizations. Ida Koverman's well-established reputation as a force of conservatism was reinforced when, in March 1948, her name was invoked during a congressional subcommittee hearing about aggressive anti-communist and anti-labor tactics, including those employed by MGM during the 1946 citywide studio strike. MGM had arranged through its chief of security, Whitey Hendry, to set up a special police force to break up picket lines outside several of the major studios, for which officers of ten local police stations were "handed extra dough by MGM" through Hendry and Virginia Nowak, a clerk of the Culver City police court. Submitted as evidence was an article from the *Hollywood Sun* that published the sworn statement of a participating officer outlining the studio's malfeasance, including the firing of an officer for arresting a truck driver after he barged through a picket line. The *Sun* surmised that such an infraction should have been called to the attention of "the new Los Angeles grand jury, except that it might embarrass the jury's new assistant forelady, Ida Koverman," described as "the persistent public relations counsel to M-G-M's L. B. Mayer."[3]

Koverman and Mayer's friend, Mabel Walker Willebrandt, advised women to report suspicious behavior of their friends and family, and to read *Counterattack*, a weekly publication that listed suspected individuals and events where communists would likely infiltrate across a broad spectrum of radio, television, law, civic and cultural clubs, and government agencies. Willebrandt even used redbaiting when she represented fathers in child-custody cases, when she raised questions about the character of the mother's supposed associations with communists.[4]

Koverman's friend, Lela Rogers, mother of Ginger, thought communists were lurking everywhere, and she confidently told the Parnell committee that her daughter "had bravely refused to speak a typical piece of Communist propaganda" in the Dalton Trumbo script *Tender Comrade*. Koverman told Hoover secretary Lawrence Richey that Robert Taylor was "one of our stars . . . a special protégé and pet of mine," who was the most "friendly" of witnesses to appear before the committee when he testified he felt coerced to appear in MGM's *Song of Russia* (1944).[5]

Koverman's brightest star-find was less accommodating to Thomas's interrogations. Judy Garland and other opponents of HUAC in the movie industry appeared on a half-hour radio broadcast, *Hollywood Fights Back*, critical of the investigation, sponsored by the newly formed Committee for the First Amendment, and allied with the American Civil Liberties Union. Garland told listeners, "Before every free conscience in America is subpoenaed, please speak up! Say your piece. Write your Congressman a letter! Airmail special! Let the Congress know what you think of its un-American Committee. Tell them how much you resent the way Mr. Thomas is kicking the living daylights out of the Bill of Rights!" She then told the press, "I've never been a member of any political organization but I've been following this investigation by Parnell Thomas' committee and I don't like it. We're show business, yes, but we're also American citizens. It's one thing if someone says we're not good actors. That hurts, but we can take it. It's something else again to say we're not good Americans. We resent that."[6]

Garland's public stand was a powerful testament that she was coming of age and establishing herself as an ideological opponent of her mentor Ida Koverman. The profound nature of this independence has escaped Garland's biographers, but it did not escape her contemporaries. The following April, the clash between Judy Garland and MGM was noted by the press, with the snippet, "If Judy Garland and MGM are feuding over Judy's political affiliations, it doesn't show in Metro's plans. She's booked for three films this year. The same rumors circulated about Katharine Hepburn, who immediately stepped into the best role she has had in years in *State of the Union*."[7]

Ida Koverman's alliances during the previous decades were now part of the biggest challenge to the marital compatibility between Hollywood and politics, as the ideological battles divided the Hollywood family. In October 1947, the public HUAC hearings continued in Washington, DC, where, among others, Walt Disney and Ronald Reagan testified about the threat of communists in the movie industry. Following the indictments of the Hollywood Ten, the industry's top executives, including Louis B. Mayer and MGM counsel Mendel Silberberg, who represented the Association of Motion Picture Producers, held a secret meeting at New York's Waldorf Astoria, where they enacted, as a cartel, a formalized blacklist. Previously, Silberberg helped MGM and other studios to respond to HUAC, and was considered "one of the prime movers in forestalling an official blacklist," instrumental in saving the jobs of targets of the American Legion's efforts to weed out commies wherever they were. Now, after growing fears of massive boycotts, the studio's eastern financiers caved in to the threats of the American Legion, the Catholic Church, and other organized, virulent anti-communist groups. The Waldorf Statement stated that anyone seeking employment who refused to sign an anti-communist loyalty oath would not be hired, and current employees who failed to sign would be fired.[8]

The irony is that soon after HUAC's senator J. Parnell Thomas won his seventh term, he was convicted of padding his payroll and billing the US Treasury for people who did not work in his congressional office. Just as the Hollywood Ten were held in contempt for taking the Fifth Amendment, Thomas refused to answer questions on the same grounds, but he was convicted and sentenced to eighteen months in the same federal prison that housed two of the Hollywood Ten he had convicted, Lester Cole and Ring Lardner Jr.[9]

In 1936, director Frank Capra recruited Mabel Walker Willebrandt to represent the newly formed Directors Guild of America (DGA). Following the 1947 Waldorf Conference, Willebrandt drafted the DGA loyalty oath, and the fight over it came to a head in a heated imbroglio in 1950 when Willebrandt proclaimed that communists had infiltrated ranks of the opposing Radio and Television Directors Guild, and were at the helm of the "very pinko law firm" representing Joseph Mankiewicz, who opposed the oath. Willebrandt's biographer generously suggests that Willebrandt was "torn between her detestation of a coercive government and her genuine concern at the threat of communism," but she "saw her first responsibility as protecting her client," the DGA.[10] In fact, Ida Koverman's closest friends, Hedda Hopper and Mabel Walker Willebrandt, had been using their professional platforms to aggressively warn Americans against the threat of communism.

The HUAC milieu of fear and party politics continued to preoccupy Ida Koverman. By the fall of 1947, Ida Koverman's behind-the-scenes politicking within the movie colony was working at full capacity in both public view and private arenas. Columnist Elsa Maxwell had previously observed that men and women of "different political beliefs and creeds" welcomed former Minnesota governor Harold Stassen in 1945. He made a "sincere speech" about the ramifications of the proposed United Nations, and Koverman believed he was a man of prestige, honor, and integrity. Roaming among the guests was "that grand gal Ida Koverman," who was making sure "everybody met everybody else." Everybody already knew each other, of course, but Maxwell recognized the unusual bipartisan nature of the affair, one that author J. E. Smyth suggests attested to Koverman's "ability to reach across party lines for the good of the industry's profile." Along with conservative and more moderate Republicans like Hedda Hopper, Robert and Betty Montgomery, Irene Dunne, and Governor Earl Warren's wife and daughters, it was one of many events also attended by liberals like Edward G. Robinson.[11]

Liberals were making their collective voices heard in the refounding of the Hollywood Democratic Committee (HDC), now revved up for the 1948 presidential election, with Judy Garland again appearing on a radio broadcast singing "Over the Rainbow" with lyrics supporting the committee. The star power of the HDC helped Democrats to reach smaller media markets where Republicans had controlling interests. They couldn't ignore Hollywood's movie stars, and inroads were made to promote voters to cross party lines and support Roosevelt.[12] The multilayered bond between Ida Koverman and Judy Garland was fraying at the ideological edges and soon, as the maturing movie star faced her most difficult challenges at the studio, Koverman's shoulder would be less able to minister to her former starlet. Their growing schism reflected the hardening lines between members of the MGM family, and Hollywood's intensifying polarized star system.

During the presidential primary season, notable for Stassen and Dewey's historic broadcast of a presidential candidate debate, Koverman saw Senator Stassen "making considerable progress," telling Lawrence Richey, "from where I sit it doesn't look too good" for her preferred candidate, Ohio senator Robert A. Taft. Between the two men, Stassen was the more liberal potential presidential contender, while conservatives supported Taft. Koverman defended her influence with Mayer as opposing forces sought his attention. MGM producer Edwin Knopf liked Stassen, and he wrote to him about a dinner Louis B. Mayer gave for Herbert Hoover, about whom he said, "As you no doubt have observed [he] has become a benign old man, not without humor and made what might be called a 'nice' impression on all those present." Knopf then approached Mayer about throwing a party for Stassen, but Mayer said he couldn't because his brother Jerry was very ill. Jerry Mayer was receiving treatment for cancer, which Knopf thought was an excuse because Jerry had improved. Knopf's suspicions of Mayer's reluctance was borne out when he learned from "Kay" Koverman that Mayer threw a dinner for Senator Taft, where Hoover whispered "Taft" into Mayer's ear.[13] Even so, seven days after Knopf's letter to Stassen, on September 27, 1947, at the age of fifty-six, Jerry Mayer fell into a coma and died after succumbing to smoke inhalation by a fire started by his fallen cigarette. A month later, Knopf threw a party for Stassen at his home in Santa Monica, attended by a broad roster of the movie industry.[14]

Koverman was a delegate to the upcoming Republican National Convention in Philadelphia. As usual, the group was divided. Mendel

Silberberg and Harold Lloyd pushed for Stassen, while her protégé George Murphy supported Governor Earl Warren. Murphy was a hit at the RNC, where he "caused one of the biggest splashes on opening day" when he led a parade shouting, "We want Warren, we want Warren!" after which Koverman's friend, actress Irene Dunne, seconded Warren's nomination. Dunne appeared self-conscious as she removed her glasses for the television cameras, "but finding she needed them to carry on, she put them back on and mumbled that the video audience would have to take her, glasses and all."[15]

Neither Taft nor Stassen could unite to defeat New York's Thomas Dewey's momentum, and when he won the nomination, he picked Earl Warren to join the ticket. During the campaign, Ida Koverman and actor George Murphy officially joined forces. They were credited with staging the Tom Dewey rally at the Hollywood Bowl, and Murphy was a featured speaker at a Dewey-Warren campaign kickoff luncheon held at the Palace Hotel in San Francisco, where Ida Koverman and Adela Rogers St. Johns also played a prominent part."[16] Dewey's pronouncements shifted leftward and upward until election night, when the race against incumbent Harry Truman was too close to call, and inspired the notorious publication of the *Chicago Daily Tribune* headline "DEWEY DEFEATS TRUMAN." Not only did Truman win the White House, Democrats won both houses of Congress.

Murphy became a successful actor at MGM, but he earned a reputation that forever grounded him merely as "a song and dance man," and partner to Shirley Temple or Fred Astaire. In fact, George Murphy was a widely popular movie star, albeit not of the A-list, and he became the face of MGM when it extended its reach into America's living rooms with the syndicated television series *MGM Parade*, promoting an upcoming movie or highlighting one of the studio's classics.

Sharing diverse interests, Ida Koverman and George Murphy became good friends. When Murphy signed with MGM in 1936, it was the "bastion of Hollywood Republicanism," according to Steve Ross, and this, Ross argues, helps to explain Murphy's political evolution. Ross says the "charming Irishman caught the eye of Mayer and Ida Koverman, who was the political tutor to the studio's young stars." Murphy embraced the mogul and the matron's "antipathy to Communism, taxes, and the New Deal," and he was drawn into conversations with prominent "conservatives such as Robert Taylor, Conrad Nagel, Jeanette MacDonald, and Robert Montgomery," not coincidentally, good friends of Ida Koverman. Murphy's leadership won him three terms as the Screen Actors Guild's first vice president and then its president in 1944. During his tenure, the

industry faced tumultuous battles over contests to win union representation contracts, such as for movie extras, now a legitimized segment of
studio production. More generally, the real or imagined threat of communist infiltration among the studio's rank and file and the focused and
industry-wide strikes and organizing efforts were often met with violent
opposition.[17]

In December 1946, Superior Court judge Georgia Bullock nominated Ida Koverman and her friends Grace Stoermer and George Murphy
for the 1947 Los Angeles grand jury, but Koverman was the only one
sworn to serve. Soon Murphy, Koverman, and their allies filed articles
of incorporation with the secretary of state in Sacramento establishing
the Hollywood Republican Committee (HRC) in 1947. Koverman and
Murphy were among the thirteen directors, along with Ginger Rogers,
Robert Montgomery, Adolphe Menjou, Walt Disney, Leo McCarey, Morrie
Ryskind, and others. The goal was to recruit 2,500 authorized members
out of a pool of applicants that had to be California residents and loyal
American citizens of good moral character who were interested in good
government and preservation of American institutions and ideals under
the constitution.[18]

Murphy told the press how "for too long a time a vociferous minority
has misled the public at large to believe that the majority of Hollywood
actors and actresses are either radicals, crackpots or at least New Deal
Democrats. We will vigorously seek membership in all ranks of the entertainment field and will present a solid front that will prove a vital factor
in returning the government to competent hands." Charter members
included Koverman's longtime friends and new allies: Bing Crosby, Fred
Astaire, Dennis Morgan, Joel McCrea, Randolph Scott, Dick Powell, Robert
Taylor, Barbara Stanwyck, Harold Peary, Mary Pickford, Penny Singleton,
Robert Sparks, Harriet and Ozzie Nelson, Jeanette MacDonald, Gene Raymond, Sam Wood, Edward Arnold, Walter Pidgeon and William Bendix."[19]

Murphy credits his conversion from a Democrat to a Republican as
growing out of a conversation with a Supreme Court justice, but at the
same time, he grew closer to Ida Koverman, who "nurtured, cajoled,
and . . . taught him all she knew." Even Hedda Hopper began to write
sympathetically about Murphy after he joined the GOP.[20] Koverman and
Murphy were a generation apart, but their friendship reflected similar
values stemming from their idealized familial reminiscences and a shared
passion for sports, swimming, and music. Murphy played a lot of baseball
before he came to Hollywood, so it is likely he appreciated how Koverman's father was a pioneering ball player. Murphy's father had been a

swimming coach at Yale University who successfully coached scores of Olympic competitors. Murphy had to have taken a keen interest in how Koverman promoted women's competitive swimming in Brooklyn and Los Angeles. Coincidentally, Murphy's grandfather had been a customs agent, the same career she was forced to leave so many years ago. Such similarities enhanced their political sympathy, which turned into a powerful force that shaped California and American political history in the decades beyond Koverman's long-lived incarnations.

During the 1948 RNC, after Murphy established his political credentials and personal charisma, Will Hays, the former party chair, postmaster general, and the then-president of the MPPDA, broached the subject of Murphy's taking the leap into electoral politics. When Koverman heard about Hays's suggestion, "she nearly flipped; she was so pleased," concurring wholeheartedly with Hays, adding, "You know George, you do have a flair for politics."[21]

Larry Parks was married to actress Betty Garrett, who thought Ida Koverman was "a marvelous little old lady," and credits her with giving her a career boost at MGM after the studio had struggled to find a place for her. The turning point came during the annual bash for Louis B. Mayer's birthday. Koverman would "always put together a huge party in the commissary that everyone on the lot was commanded to attend," and this time, Koverman decided to showcase the newer, younger contract players rather than the more familiar box-office stars. Koverman asked Garrett to perform, so she worked up a few numbers with her accompanist, but on the day of the celebration, she realized that the hires were children, except for her. Garrett's instinctive comedic skills kicked in to the delight of everyone, and the studio finally found her a niche. The next day she was "called into four or five producer's offices and walked around the lot with at least that many scripts under my arm."[22]

Prior to Mayer's July 1948 celebration, Betty and her husband had been visited by a man who mysteriously showed up at their Nichols Canyon home "with an ominous piece of paper" that turned out to be a subpoena from HUAC. Luckily, the Los Angeles hearings were postponed, but they soon resumed in Washington. In the meantime, both of their careers appeared unaffected by the witch hunt, and while at the studio, the two actors performed with their colleagues, whose politics they found repelling. One of Garrett's costars was George Murphy, who was the darling of the aggressive anti-communist Motion Picture Alliance and "a friendly witness" for HUAC, testifying that he always scrutinized his scripts for

"Communistic content." Garrett hated Murphy's politics, but she thought he was "always the perfect gentleman and treated" her with "kindness and affection." During the 1948 filming of *The Big City*, Murphy helped Garrett deliver a tearful monologue that required a close-up of her. Uncharacteristic of big talent, or so she believed, Murphy stood outside of the frame but where she could see him and to help her, he cried along with her as she said her lines.[23]

That same year, Betty Garrett was one of the MGM stars that attended the launching of KMGM, the studio's West Coast FM version of its New York radio station. Beneath the giant searchlights in the parking lot of "The World's Biggest Drugstore," the Rexall Building on Beverly and La Cienaga Boulevards, a cavalcade of MGM stars gathered for the inaugural broadcast. After Mayor Fletcher Bowron welcomed the new station, he chatted with Ida Koverman amidst the cacophony of the ceremony. Dinah Shore, Hoagy Carmichael, Johnny Mercer, Mel Tormé, and other crooners sang, and the lineup included many of Koverman's favorites, including Kathryn Grayson, Walter Pidgeon, Esther Williams, and Margaret O'Brien, and Lassie entertained a hundred orphans who were bussed in for the occasion. After five years of a variety-musical format of classical and contemporary music from 3:00 to 10:00 pm, KMGM went dark, and the station was reestablished by the Beverly Hills record "and Hi-Fi" store owners Arthur and Jean Crawford as KCBH in 1954.[24]

Over the next few years, the HUAC net closed in on actor Larry Parks, now summoned to appear on March 21, 1951. During his public testimony, Parks admitted that as a young man of twenty-five, in 1941, he had joined the Communist Party because it was the "most liberal" of the political parties, but four years later he lost interest and left its ranks. He refused to identify anyone he believed to have similarly experimented because it was "not the American way . . . to force a man to do this is not American justice." HUAC adjourned to executive session, where rumors surfaced that Parks did provide names. Whether or not he did, the career of the Oscar-nominated actor was over, and it took a toll on his wife, Betty Garrett, and forever altered her view of Ida Koverman. Garrett attended a charity committee meeting held at Pickfair, where everyone was asked how they wanted their placecards to read, with either their professional or married name. When it was her turn, she said, "Mrs. Larry Parks," which prodded Ida Koverman to take her aside to say, "You little idiot." She didn't understand what Koverman meant until later that day, when, Garrett recalled "this poor lady" called and "kept saying 'I am really sorry,

I don't want to do this, but they told me I had to make the phone call,'"
because one of women had complained that they didn't want "Mrs. Larry
Parks at that luncheon."[25]

Ida Koverman's life wasn't only about politics, parties, and pictures—it
was also about pussy willows. Koverman's entrepreneurial instinct and
creative aesthetic collaborated soon after she and Hedda Hopper attended
the Republican National Convention, when Boston's premiere horticul-
turalist, L Sherman Adams, gave Koverman some lovely orchids. Two
years later, Koverman invested in a flower shop from proprietor Doris
Jay in the iconic Farmers Market complex. Koverman began importing
orchids from L. Sherman Adams, who had developed a special distribution process. With her endless round of parties and luncheons and gala
affairs, with their standard and exotic floral arrangements, it made sense
to seek a creative outlet and a cost-cutting avenue for those personal and
professional affairs. Hopper promoted her friend's new venture, telling her
readers how "you won't have to send flowers to Ida Koverman. . . . She's
opening her own 'Flower Mart' at the Farmers Market." Koverman didn't
manage the day-to-day of the Flower Mart. Former vaudevillian Eunice
Burnham, whose stage partner had been Koverman's friend Charlotte
Greenwood, would run the shop.[26]

Local columnist Fred Beck offered details about the unique offerings
of Koverman's store, writing, "it's Puss-ee Will-o Time in Cali-forn-yah!"
and "now one of the flower shops out here is proprietored [sic] by Ida
Koverman and besides plain old alley pussy willows—Ida's shop is showing
some very unusual ones which, instead of being straight stemmed are—
well—they're shaped like a Question Mark. If you are one who likes to
make floral arrangements—by all means buy these curvy, swervy, pussy
willows. They lend themselves beautifully to erotic, exotic, neurotic floral
arrangements."[27]

CHAPTER 25

Wounded Women, Women Warriors

THE YEAR 1949 STARTED WITH IDA KOVERMAN'S USUAL NETWORKING, social engagements, and correspondence. Herbert Hoover thanked her for her cheerful Christmas greeting, which came during what he called an "otherwise somewhat dreary scene." It was a cold, devastating winter everywhere, but Koverman had cause for joy as she congratulated Mayor Fletcher Bowron for announcing he was seeking re-election. "I deeply appreciate the great service and sacrifice," she wrote, and urged him to "please call on me for any service" she could "render in the campaign." Bowron warmly responded just after Los Angeles recovered from a freak-ish, massive three-day snowstorm, affectionately noting how "it has been good to have you as a member of the official family," which "merely supplements what I have told you personally. I appreciate your friendship, help and advice very much."[1]

After the salutations, Louella Parsons reported the shocking news that Ida Koverman was gravely ill in a Burbank hospital. The seventy-three-year-old Koverman was still too ill to attend a gathering for Maine's US senator Margaret Chase Smith hosted by Adela Rogers St. Johns. Two weeks later, however, Hedda Hopper happily told her readers Koverman had "completely recovered," and bought a house in the charming Whitley Heights neighborhood in the Hollywood Hills. She was glad her friend was "domiciled in her own nest again," but it's unlikely Koverman actually owned the property or any other.[2]

Koverman had lived at 2037 Whitley Avenue in 1936, but Hopper was referring to 6691 Whitley Terrace. Oddly enough, supervisor John Anson Ford listed yet another Koverman address in 1949 as 6697 Whitley

Terrace, the home of her frequent escort, director Robert Vignola. It appears that one of the perks of her MGM job was free housing or, at the very least, the ability to lease homes in neighborhoods well above her pay grade. California's average rent in 1940 was twenty-seven dollars, a small percentage of her monthly income, but in the upscale neighborhoods where she lived, they were obviously much higher, and often they were owned by and then rented to industry insiders. Pinning down her residences remains a challenge, such as in March 1949, when she was also supposedly residing on Sycamore Avenue in the adjacent Hollywood Heights neighborhood. Wherever she received her mail, in March 1949, she was invited to attend the MRA's annual World Conference being held in Caux, Switzerland, the MRA Mecca. Adela Rogers St. Johns wanted to tag along, but Koverman did not attend.[3]

Koverman returned to MGM soon after her illness, in the early months of 1949, where she found the atmosphere heavy with tension, and Mayer's vacillating moods ranging from indifference to depression. He was feeling the weight about the diminishing returns felt throughout the movie industry, but this was compounded by his personal conflict with producer Dore Schary. Mayer had asked Schary to return to MGM the previous year, but Schary only agreed if he maintained creative independence. It turned out to be a devil's bargain, made with built-in ambiguities, and so effort to compartmentalize their differences, management styles, and artistic visions ultimately clashed. Mayer had cultivated a studio culture now on its wane, while Schary represented a new breed of moviemakers, and many thought he was in the genius mold of the late Irving Thalberg. Ultimately, however, his presence at the studio quickly alienated some, and his liberal politics offended many.[4]

When the exigencies of immediate crises abated, in May 1949, Hollywood Assemblyman Kent Redwine and Ida Koverman worked together again in Sacramento, this time on the "attaches ball" [sic] for office staff and "desk people," paid for by lobbyists and called by one cynic "the Big Chisel." Koverman assisted Redwine in carrying "the load for the entertainment," because "everybody wanted to see the stars."[5]

Koverman's jaunts to Sacramento sustained her reputation among professional women throughout the state, and, to some, she served as a role model for female aspirants seeking business careers in the movie industry. When Woodbury College awarded Ida Koverman an honorary master's degree in August 1949 in recognition of her civic and cultural achievements, the honor reflected the school's evolution from its earliest days in 1933, making it the West's oldest private co-educational business school. It soon opened a Hollywood branch to expand their motion-picture training department, where students could earn a degree as either executive-studio secretarial or executive-studio accounting personnel. Koverman was called upon to lecture about careers outside of the movie industry, such as when she spoke on "Vocations and Avocations," at the Hollywood branch of the organization of Business and Professional Women.[6]

Koverman's friend Mrs. Gertrude Rigdon, who was more obscure than the 1934 description of her as a "well-known film executive and scenarist," was, in fact, instrumental in launching the Woodbury program. She was a writer for RKO Radio-Pathe Studios, and she received a copyright in 1932 for a story that turned into 20th Century Fox's screenplay *Hold Me Tight*. Gertrude Rigdon and Ida Koverman led diverse and intersecting lives, and their mutual interests helped them to build a pipeline of support staff for the motion-picture industry, while lobbying legislators and entertaining them at the same time.[7]

When California governor Earl Warren ran for an unprecedented third term, Ida Koverman joined the bipartisan Women's Advisory Committee of the Women for Warren campaign in September 1950. Joining her were her longtime pals Mabel Kinney and Grace Stoermer. While Koverman and her friends supported the moderate Warren, they broke with his dislike of Richard Nixon, when they aggressively campaigned for Nixon in his controversial Senate race against the former opera star Helen Gahagan Douglas, a former Democratic congresswoman and the current wife of actor Melvyn Douglas.[8]

Nixon's 1950 senate race did encourage women to engage in a cross-party alliance, including Koverman's friend, Democratic national committeewoman Mrs. Harry Goetz, but it was to oppose Douglas and to support Nixon. Koverman and her friends Mabel Kinney and Hedda Hopper joined the new bipartisan group, "Women for Nixon," that sought to appeal to both Democrats and Republicans to support Nixon, who could best defend against communism and promote California's interests in Washington, DC. After Nixon won the primary, Koverman prepared for a pro-Nixon television special with her allies, screenwriter Frances Marion, Esther Williams, and Buffy Chandler, the wife of the *Los Angeles Times* publisher. Hedda Hopper told her readers that even "Little June" Allyson, who was expecting a baby in December, was working very hard for Nixon. Hopper said, "Now, if we get Lana Turner, we'll have our top glamour girls," and she reminded everyone not to forget Hattie McDaniel, the Oscar-winning African American actress from *Gone with the Wind* actress, who was also on Nixon's TV show.[9]

A longtime Koverman friend, actress Irene Dunne was a stalwart conservative Republican and Nixon supporter, but she needed convincing to appear on the KTTV telecast. Koverman and Hopper prodded her, and she amply rose to the occasion by urging Democrats to support the Republican candidate because "America is faced with so critical a situation that partisanship must be forgotten by those who would preserve our way of life." Dunne advised listeners that it was more important to judge an elected official for their record, and "when a woman does not measure up, as in Douglas's case, they should vote for a man as qualified as Nixon," especially because he was the best candidate informed about "the international Communist conspiracy."[10]

The 1950 Senate race was historic on numerous counts, including it being the first employment of the "dirty tricks" now associated with "Tricky Dick" Nixon's later campaigns. It served as an inspiration for Ronald Reagan's quiet conversion from the Democratic to the Republican Party. Publicly Reagan supported Douglas, but after hearing actress ZaSu Pitts's fiery anti-Douglas speech, calling her a "pink lady" who would allow communism to spread, Reagan started to quietly raise money for Nixon. His new wife, the conservative Nancy Davis, encouraged this red shift, and she supported his eventual move into the electoral arena. The "pink lady" comment was first used by Douglas's Democratic primary opponent, newspaperman Manchester Boddy, who charged that Douglas was pink right down to her underwear, but it was popularized by Nixon in the general campaign, where he won a resounding victory over the former opera star.

Author J. E. Smyth argues that because "outside of the studio," Koverman had "mixed" with Democratic and Republican women alike, in 1950 "Koverman alienated many of her Democratic female colleagues when she took part in Richard Nixon's divisive senatorial campaign."[11] By then, everyone knew Ida Koverman was an aggressive conservative Republican, so her support of Nixon hardly offended anyone. The assertion that Ida Koverman "did much to break the strong, cross-party alliance that had linked Hollywood's working women since the 1920s" not only misrepresents Koverman, but it also misstates history.

Smyth argues that Koverman's support of Richard Nixon meant that "as one of California's leading Republican organizers," she "could not have abstained from the campaign without raising eyebrows." There is no indication that Koverman had ever considered supporting anyone other than Nixon. While there is no direct evidence, as Smyth asserts, that Koverman was an advocate for equal rights, Koverman did support candidates regardless of their sex if they allied with her worldview. But it is a stretch for Smyth to paradoxically conclude that because Koverman failed to support Douglas, who had "fought for many women's issues," Koverman chose "political party over other women," and that when Koverman urged other Hollywood women to join the KTTV program, she was destroying some kind of imaginary, decades-long, cross-party alliance.[12]

Throughout the 1920s, Ida Koverman was entrenched in Los Angeles party politics, and by the end of the decade she had successfully cultivated ties within the Hollywood community. She was never a part of a cross-party female-centered alliance, articulated in terms of "working women," except for the value that "womaness" had played within the larger Republican Party recruitment strategy to promote Herbert Hoover's presidential ambitions. Furthermore, Helen Gahagan Douglas had not even inspired a broad base of female support within her own party. Helen Gahagan Douglas was an icon for liberal Democrats, who indeed had made steady gains in California throughout the Roosevelt and Truman years, but she was not a unifying force, and none of Ida Koverman's close friends were going to vote for Douglas when they had a local Cold Warrior in Richard Nixon. Whatever allegiance women had to one another inside the movie industry was never perceived as having anything to do with crossing party lines, and in fact, in Ida Koverman's circle of on-screen and upper-level creative talent, their partisan lines had been clearly defined for decades, and except for extraordinary industry affairs, were adhered to in their day-to-day social gatherings.

Until the New Deal era of the 1930s, California Democrats were a minority party, so Koverman's toughest political battles were waged in the primaries between Republican Party factions. Golden State governors were all Republicans except for Culbert Olson's short reign before the thrice-elected Republican Earl Warren, who did have bipartisan support but refused to endorse Nixon in 1950. Ida Koverman and her partisan girlfriends like Hedda Hopper did not seek to overcome the ideological divide in order to promote female candidates, nor did she publicly use her political stature to advocate on behalf of "working women" as a separate group. Hopper further illustrates the point when she "smelled dirty politics" while speculating about the dirty deals made to thwart Nixon's nomination, because "our studios who prefer the shade of red don't want him as senator."[13]

In 1940, Ida Koverman and friends of both sexes vocally supported presidential candidate Wendell Wilkie, in public opposition to Roosevelt supporters. Two camps emerged, and among those for Wilkie were

Koverman and her friends Irene Dunne, Susanna Foster, Irene Hervey, Hattie McDaniel, Una Merkle, ZaSu Pitts, Adela Rogers St. Johns, Ruth Waterbury, and Hedda Hopper, most of whom joined Koverman on the Nixon bandwagon a decade later. The 1950 Douglas-Nixon contest signaled nothing new about Koverman potentially alienating a supposedly allied womanhood in Hollywood. In fact, it reinforced their long-standing, deep divide.[14]

In spite of Hollywood's unified support of the troops at the Hollywood Canteen or on military bases, Koverman and other conservative women aggressively promoted candidates who reflected their worldview, and their fervor and aggressive tactics only intensified during the postwar era. Documenting decades of Koverman's parties and public events indicates that women who were polarized at the polls rarely socialized outside of apolitical civic or cultural activities.

While Koverman might have encouraged women's ambitions, she equally fostered men's careers because she appreciated talent where she found it. Ida and her friends, particularly Mabel Kinney, were members of the state association of Business and Professional Women that viewed women as individuals who should be unfettered in the market place and be free from labor-union organization and intrusive legislation aimed at protecting their separate interests. At that time, the California BPW also did not adhere to the notion that women should vote for a female candidate just because of her sex and regardless of her party affiliation.[15]

Nevertheless, Ida Koverman and Helen Gahagan Douglas shared a passion for opera, and that alone should have brought them together as friends, across party lines. Douglas had been a successful opera singer before moving to Hollywood and her election to Congress in 1944. Like most of Ida Koverman's friends, Douglas was a dynamic, charismatic figure, but Douglas eschewed the celebrity culture in which Koverman thrived, and she was uncomfortable with the extracurricular activities of the movie colony in the way Ida Koverman and her friends had long circulated and politicked.

The two women also shared notoriety as interlopers. Her prominence in the Democratic Party, however, did not come from her rising up through the ranks or the grassroots, and as a Northern Californian she was not attached to the local party apparatus. In 1923, when Koverman was on the shortlist for the post of Republican national committeewoman, progressive Republican Katherine Edson vociferously opposed her. Douglas's appointment as Democratic national committeewoman in 1940 inspired similar resentment from seasoned conservative Democratic women who believed she was an outsider who had usurped the spotlight from more deserving partisans who had earned the coveted post.

The irony is that Ida Koverman did support a woman running for elective office in the 1950 primary season, but she was running in Connecticut. Vivien Kellems had made a fortune as a cable grip manufacturer and then used her wealth to spread her hardliner opposition to federal income taxes and President Harry Truman. She first ran for a congressional seat in 1942 and virulently opposed Clare Boothe Luce, arguing that since Luce was a nonresident, she would have a hard time running a campaign from her ivory tower at New York's Waldorf Astoria. She claimed a Luce victory would help those who sought to "nullify our Constitution and substitute an evil internationalism for our true democracy."[16]

Kellems attracted national attention, including that of Hedda Hopper, who hosted a gathering for her in Los Angeles where she struck up a friendship with Koverman. Koverman was both impressed and overwhelmed with Kellems, writing to her, "You were wonderful the other night but you gave us so much our poor little heads couldn't hold it all. The girls (me too) would be most grateful if you'd jot down in sort of memo form and briefly, some of the facts and figures you gave us so that we can use them. They're much excited and eager to get going—think your trip will be most productive. Love, Ida."[17]

Hopper was more pessimistic, telling Kellems, "The results from the dinner you spark-plugged at my house have been practically nil," and she blamed Ida Koverman, who was "busy on her own plans." Actress ZaSu Pitts also attended the dinner, and she and the others were "very anxious to get to work," but they hardly knew what steps to take next. Hopper cryptically added, "ZaSu has some friends who are very much opposed to Miss Koverman," and while Kellems's visit "gave us all a terrific shot in the arm. . . . You know how it is. . . . Ladies plan and unless there's someone there holding the whip over them, they forget." Hopper again put the onus on Koverman for the failure to organize the group on Kellems's behalf. "The meeting which you started in my house hasn't developed many workers," she said, and "while Ida has said several times we must get together, I didn't feel there was any heart behind it." She repeated the slight to Koverman by adding, "last Saturday, I had ZaSu, Mrs. Harry Goetz and yours and ZaSu's friend, the one opposed to Miss K."[18] Hopper's letters belie her public affection for Koverman, but they also suggest the obvious, that Koverman was the one who held the whip while Hopper was a bullhorn provocateur, ill-equipped in the practical political arts.

Koverman did actively facilitate Kellems's introduction to her other friend, Adela Rogers St. Johns, when she was in New York. Koverman also suggested Kellems call on Mrs. John A. (Ella) Brown, a mutual friend of hers who was a friend and neighbor at the Waldorf Astoria to Herbert Hoover. Koverman reminded Kellems that she had mentioned Mrs. Brown before, saying, "You may recall I told you she is a well-to-do widow (Republican) with nothing to do, and I think she might be very helpful in your program."[19]

Kellems told Koverman she was going to invite Mrs. Brown to the April 11 meeting of the Minute Women, a new group she and sculptor Mrs. Suzanne Silver-Cruys Stevenson would formally announce, and where she also hoped to win endorsement as a candidate for the US Senate. The Minute Women was one of scores of radicalized, ultraconservative Cold War–era groups sounding the alarm about the excesses of the federal government and communist infiltration throughout American society. Kellems wrote Koverman, "If they turn me down, I shall fall flat on my face."[20]

Six hundred women attended the Minute Women rally and elected Mrs. Stevenson its national chairman, who correctly anticipated "the spread of chapters throughout the country." Two years later, there were fifty thousand members across forty-seven states, with Southern California claiming some of the largest contingents. Because of the group's secretive nature, the exact number and membership is unknown. Though the group didn't endorse Kellems, one woman suggested she leave the group if she became a political candidate. Koverman wrote she was "glad you didn't have to fall flat on your face. I know you will win," and signaling their accelerated friendship, she closed with, "affectionately, Ida Koverman." Kellems thanked Koverman, writing, "It looks good, but I am keeping my fingers crossed," and also signed off, "affectionately." By early May, Kellems was campaigning, making two or three speeches a day.[21]

Thus, Ida Koverman's interest in politics, aside from her earlier mission to elect Herbert Hoover, was ideological and not gender-based. She certainly encouraged women to run for office, as she had with Hedda Hopper and Vivien Kellems, if they allied with her policy views. She also had another unusual connection to Connecticut and the Minute Women. Mrs. Hester McCullough of Greenwich, Connecticut, was married to John T. McCullough, a photo editor for *Time* magazine. Described as a "heroine of the political right," Hester McCullough, head of the Minute Women's Committee against Subversive Activities, gained notoriety when she accused two performing artists of communist sympathies. When they sued

McCullough for libel, their lawsuit made national headlines as a conservative cause célèbre. McCullough had read the rabid anti-communist publication *Counterattack,* and on her husband's advice, she protested the upcoming appearance of Larry Adler and dancer Paul Draper. During the trial, Mrs. McCullough testified, "If a real American wants to stand up for his country and keep people who are trying to betray it out of his town he gets sued. Communists seem to have the freedom of speech in this country."[22]

Prior to the trial, Mrs. McCullough visited Los Angeles in March 1950 seeking evidence, and likely financial assistance, for her defense, including a dinner at Romanoff's hosted by Hedda Hopper. Hopper later reported that John McCullough surprised her with news that Ida Koverman was his godmother. Other than Cincinnati origins, there is little public information to speculate about the web of relationships that led to his becoming Koverman's godson, and if so, how well he even knew her. Regardless, two months later, the case ended with a hung jury.

The blossoming friendship between Koverman and the controversial Vivien Kellems reinforces Koverman's prioritization of political ideology over identification with political womanhood, and it places her squarely within the mushrooming right-wing groups sprouting up during the early Cold War years. It also exemplifies how Koverman continued to maneuver as a political operative as she built networks between women with money and motivated women.

Nevertheless, whoever Koverman supported and whatever her ideological persuasion, these factors didn't preclude Ida Koverman from worrying about the studio's box-office returns, or worrying about Judy Garland, who had become increasingly unstable. In spite of their political differences, which had likely contributed to their growing alienation, the tension surrounding Garland's ongoing personal struggles were taking their toll on Ida. Just as a mother internalizes their child's turmoil, Judy's kinship with Koverman was the closest relationship Ida came to experiencing motherhood. Judy's career demonstrated Ida's brilliance as a talent scout and her value to the studio, but her personal troubles might have suggested to Koverman that her maternal instincts had failed miserably.

Outside of politics, music and motion pictures weren't Koverman's only passions. Her appointment to the city's Municipal Art Commission offered her another opportunity for her to exercise her artistic sensibilities and civic pride, by launching public exhibitions of eclectic master art works donated from the private collections of Hollywood celebrities and local luminaries, combined with lectures, art demonstrations, and a newsletter.[23]

CHAPTER 26

The Mogul and the Matron

"A tall, stately woman with a somewhat disconcerting resemblance to her employer, she served Mayer for more than two decades. . . . She lived modestly, . . . but this austerity did not reflect her importance at the studio."[1]

ON JUNE 15, 1945, IDA KOVERMAN AND LOUIS B. MAYER ATTENDED THE intimate wedding of Judy Garland and director Vincente Minnelli at Judy's mother's home. Everyone was anticipating that Minnelli would stabilize his new bride's recent erratic behavior, along with "the intervention" of the "strong arms" of Ida Koverman, so that Judy could look to a brighter future at MGM. Four days later, Ida Koverman went out with her friend, Ruth Waterbury, film critic, writer, editor for *Photoplay* and *Silver Screen*, and five-time president of the Hollywood Women's Press Club. They were passing out free tickets for a performance by the Brentwood Service Players at the nearby Westwood campus of the Veterans Administration. It wasn't a particularly warm day, but Koverman might have failed to realize her stamina remained precarious after her recent illness, and without warning, she "suffered a complete collapse." In spite of the initially alarming news, Waterbury simply sent her friend home rather than feeling the need to call an ambulance.[2] Koverman quickly resumed her social life, such as attending the usual variety of engagements, including hosting a dinner party before the opera *Faust* at the Hollywood Bowl. Gershwin Night at the Bowl earned Koverman a bit copy when she came to the aid of comedian Red Skelton. He was told to stop taking photographs because he wasn't a union member, on top of not having a ticket for the show.

Ida Koverman intervened, and soon Skelton continued snapping away, supposedly for a coffee-table book showcasing his skills.[3]

Unfortunately, the peaceful interlude around Judy Garland's marriage to Minnelli was short-lived. After numerous personnel changes, she was dropped from the production of *Annie Get Your Gun*. Her exhaustion was so severe that she was hospitalized at Boston's Bent Hospital, where, years later, she would coincidentally be tended to by one of Oscar Koverman's descendants. Taking Garland's place was Paramount's loaned-out Betty Hutton, whose performance established her legacy, in spite of a relatively short film career. Judy's problems added to the tension between Mayer and Dore Schary, and East Coast executives; Mayer was sympathetic to his troubled star, Schary was indifferent, and New York's Nicholas Schenck wanted to dump her altogether.[4]

Koverman's dual role at MGM was to serve the interests of the studio and her immediate master, Louis B. Mayer. The usually blurred lines were never more evident than during the filming of *The Pirate* (1948), costarring Judy Garland and Gene Kelly. When Koverman viewed the day's rushes, she became so alarmed she ran to the screening room where Mayer was watching other footage. She urged Mayer to see what she found so objectionable. When he hesitated, she looked around the dark room, and when she saw other executives nearby, she lowered her voice and said, "Look . . . what I saw on that screen will make your skin crawl." After viewing the day's filming, he knew he had to act quickly because they were going to shoot more of the same the next day. Koverman said, "If the press gets hold of this, the whole studio's going to be in trouble."[5]

Koverman had helped Judy through studio conflicts for years, but now the exaggerated comic sensuality of her character, Manuela Alva, caused another kind of agitation on the set. Gene Kelly's Serafin was equally provocative with his black tights that sensually accentuated his muscles in a way his usual wholesome and unflattering slacks had always avoided. The whole production was a delightful, campy satire of movie operettas, but Garland's over-the-top caricature required her to be in a constant state of unabashed, hysterical arousal. The most starkly sexual sequence, however, didn't survive Koverman and Mayer's censorship. The scene that caused Koverman's palpitations was a tribal dance where the two stars crossed the line between comedic romance and undulating body contact. When Mayer recovered from near apoplectic shock, he told Koverman to find every inch of the footage and burn it.[6]

There was more to Garland's travails during production of *The Pirate*. Marni Nixon even observed Garland's outbursts, and when Hedda Hopper visited Garland in her dressing room, she found her "shaking like an aspen leaf," complaining that everyone who once loved her had now turned against her. She railed against her mother, whom she believed was tapping her telephone, and then she repudiated Koverman, the next highest on her "hate list." A little while later, Hopper saw Garland assisted into a limousine, still wearing her costume and make-up. [7]

There were suspensions, replacements, recuperations, and rapprochements, but Judy's lows grew darker, and her actions grew more self-destructive. Some of the people closest to her were caught up in the melodrama of her paranoia, such as Kathryn Grayson, whom Judy would call in the middle of the night and beg to come over. Sometimes Grayson went, but after a while, Koverman or Benny Thau would call to tell her not to go and advise her to take care of her own health, so she could show up to work at 7:00 a.m.[8]

After her suspension, Judy's despair was palpable throughout the first summer day, June 21, 1950, while her agent, Carleton Alsop, negotiated with the studio. Suddenly, without warning, Judy jumped up and ran into the bathroom. Less than two weeks into her twenty-ninth year, Garland was physically and mentally exhausted, and in one of several bouts of utter hopelessness, she slammed a water glass against the floor, picked up a shard and ran the sharp edge along her throat. After hearing the sound of crashing glass, someone threw a chair to knock the door down. Minnelli grabbed her and wrenched the glass out of her hand just as she was about to slash herself again. He held her while she wept and someone called the doctor.[9]

The wound was superficial and no stitches were necessary, but the one Minnelli stopped could have mortally wounded her. Whitey Hendry and a dozen studio police guarded the Minnelli-Garland home as the press and some fans began to assemble around the property. Ida Koverman and Katharine Hepburn, alerted by the studio, were among the few allowed in the house. Koverman stayed an hour, and when she emerged, she walked toward her chauffeur-driven car as the press hounded her for a statement. All she quipped was, "You have your job to do, and I have mine." The doctor said Garland's injury was inflicted "during a moment of vexation," but the studio said, "It was an impulsive, hysterical act." Mayer privately lamented to Koverman, "We should have given her more time off. We should have put her in fewer pictures." Garland's throat healed, and by June 29 her manager told reporters she was embarrassed about it all but was happy to see so many people expressing their sympathy with her.

The highly publicized battle between the studio and Judy finally ended on September 26, with Garland released from her contract.[10]

Conflicting emotions must have gnawed at Koverman, and as a devout Christian Scientist, she realized how the power of the mind over the body could not only heal, but could also harm. She might have pondered this and her feelings about her falling star after the massive, debilitating stroke that paralyzed her soon after Garland's break with MGM. After the initial emergency, Ida Koverman was moved to long-term convalescence at the Monte Sano osteopathic hospital in Glendale, but the initial prognosis was dire, with the unlikely chance she would ever make a full recovery, or ever walk again.

The timing of her stroke would ultimately impact her own life and bigger historical events beyond her control. Early on, however, on October 16, 1950, the *Christian Science Monitor* published a profile of her that remains a singular portrait of Koverman's day-to-day life at MGM, illustrating how she blended her management of the studio with political minutiae and maintained her network of professionals, partisans, and the press. She told columnist Harriet Blackburn that she was "mixed up in many outside things and Mr. Mayer is glad to have it that way."[11]

One minute she handled a call from the publicity director for Senator Robert Taft of Ohio, and the next call was from her old friend, MGM singing star Jeanette MacDonald, who wanted to set up a dinner date. She talked to William Meiklejohn, talent scout at Paramount, who wanted her to send an MGM representative to the upcoming charity tea for the Community Chest. She talked to someone about a young man going into the Navy, who needed a letter of recommendation for a plum commission. She was serving again as a board member of the Hollywood Republican Committee, so after *Los Angeles Times* political columnist Kyle D. Palmer called her about it, she told the *CSM* reporter, "I'm doing a job that interests him now, helping with the Women-for-Nixon committees." Koverman then took care of getting Ethel Barrymore a parking pass at the Hollywood Bowl, and then she took the opportunity to promote the future Mrs. Ronald Reagan, actress Nancy Davis, whose small emergency was to expedite the installation of a private telephone line. Koverman described Davis as "our young star in *The Next Voice You Hear,*" who played "a good part very well and the picture is beginning to show excellent box office returns in New York." Although the movie ended up losing money, Koverman liked how the film "has more spiritual content than any picture we've had for some time, and is leading the way for others like it." The accompanying photograph shows Koverman with Jeannette MacDonald and José Iturbi looking over costume sketches: "Ida Koverman's versatility at MGM makes her ideas much sought after in the studio."[12]

Koverman was most proud of her supervision over the design of Mayer's executive suite. As the mogul's gatekeeper, she described his inner sanctum in a way that counters prevailing notions derived from black-and-white photographs and persistent descriptions that it was designed by MGM set designer Cedric Gibbons and was unusual for its variations on the shade of white that reminded visitors of a hospital room. This more accurately describes the interior of Mayer's home in Santa Monica. Koverman's analysis is supported by the reporter's firsthand viewing during her tour, first through a "quiet corridor . . . to large double doors . . . [that] flung open," to reveal "as mellow a business office as I have ever seen." By late 1950, the interior office was a palate of "dusty rose," with a "rich, warm carpeted floor," and only as the color moved up the walls did the "shading [turn] into gentle cream" color. A big, friendly desk faced the entrance, with pleasant lighting overhead. Koverman explained the psychology of her choices: "If you were angry or disturbed, when you entered this room, you couldn't feel that way very long, could you?" There was a big "hospitable fireplace . . . to grace the left wall," about which she had to "do a lot of persuading to convince the architect." There were a "series of short tables put together" that Mr. Mayer found "convenient for the various social affairs we have to honor some of our people."[13]

In spite of the publicity, Ida Koverman struggled to overcome her debilitating condition and growing despair. Louis B. Mayer felt the brunt of her absence as his relationship with Dore Schary deteriorated. The chronic scuffles were more frequent and by November, the two men were hardly speaking, communicating through memos and intermediaries. In spite of Schary's success reversing the studio's finances and gaining critical recognition, Koverman wasn't there to absorb the shockwaves that signaled the pending implosion. Chronicles that detail Mayer's travails fail to note the downward spiral accelerated during Koverman's prolonged absence.

Louis B. Mayer wrote to Herbert Hoover about Koverman's predicament, and Hoover wrote to her, exuding the familiarity that came with their decades of friendship: "Mr. Mayer tells me you are laid up. That is improper even if you and I are getting older and older. We have marched together now for nearly thirty years and I don't want my old companions-in-battle to show signs that we are old. There is still fight in both of us and with sufficient . . . new drug inventions, we ought to be able to keep going for some time yet. Anyway, I just wanted to send you my affections and my hopes that you will be out quickly. Faithfully, yours."[14]

Ida Koverman needed all the pep talks she could get; facing what at first to her seemed a catastrophic future of physical limits and financial duress. Hedda Hopper and Mabel Walker Willebrandt saw their friend's despair and near hopelessness. When Koverman's friend and secretary Evelyn Jaeger responded to Hoover's letter, she couldn't hide the severity of Koverman's condition. She said Ida was pleased to get his message, but "she said to tell you that she's still got the spirit, but at the moment is not able to move very much." Jaeger wrote that her doctor "assures her that while it will take some time, she will be 'ok' again," but for a while, no one was convinced this was so. Nevertheless, Jaeger was optimistic: "We are all greatly encouraged by the sustained improvement in her condition, and it may be that she will be able to return home in another several weeks." It ended up taking another two months, but Jaeger added, "Meanwhile, her interest in the current political situation is unabated." Koverman thought Hoover's recent speech "was the sort of statement that the leaders of our country should have made but which, unfortunately, they seem incapable of matching in the realm of statesmanship. It is to be hoped and prayed that your direction will be followed."[15]

Two months later, Koverman wired Hoover after his "wonderful speech" that she hoped "everyone in the world could hear." He found it "heartening and encouraging" to get such messages from old friends, and he hoped she would use her voice of influence on behalf of this shared point of view. He closed with, "I hope you will have a happier New Year than the last, for that will mean the world has become better!"[16]

As Koverman's body seemed to be improving, Garland's psychological state deteriorated, as did her marriage to Minnelli. Just two days before their final divorce decree, Hedda Hopper joyfully informed her readers on December 21, 1950, that Ida Koverman was out of the hospital and back at home. No one was counting Koverman out, even though she was still unable to assist in the holiday preparations at the Ambassador Hotel, her name remained on the committee and guest lists. She was unable to attend meetings of the Municipal Arts Commission, so when members sent Mayor Bowron get-well wishes after his emergency gall-bladder surgery, her name was included in absentia.[17]

The weeks dragged on, and Koverman's usual optimism began to fade. "After twenty-two years of hard work," Hopper wrote, Ida Koverman feared she would never walk again, and she loathed contemplating that she might "become a liability rather than an asset." Up to now, Hedda just assumed MGM provided "handsomely" for her friend, but she became alarmed by rumors that Ida's bills were piling up. She broached the subject with Koverman, who confessed, "I should have quit years back . . . but I couldn't. I should have provided for myself when I was younger. Then it was too late."[18]

Ida was obviously embarrassed, and as tears filled her eyes, She told Hedda that Mayer wouldn't put her on the studio pension plan. Infuriated, Hopper recruited Louella Parsons and Mabel Walker Willebrandt to force Mayer to help his right-hand woman. Mayer asked Howard Strickling to float the idea of Koverman going to the Motion Picture Country House in Woodland Hills. Hopper rejected the idea on Koverman's behalf, yelling into the phone to Strickling, "You let him do that, and he will be the sorriest man ever born!"[19]

On one of her earlier visits to the studio, Mabel Walker Willebrandt saw one example of Mayer's momentary but explosive treatment of Koverman, when he was berating Koverman and threatening to dismiss her. He muttered to Willebrandt, "Kay Koverman talks too much. . . . I've got to get rid of her. People don't want me to, but I will." Willebrandt knew Koverman's value to the studio, so she used her own influence to corner Mayer into helping their mutual friend. Willebrandt had begun working on a strategy to oppose a pending federal tax law that would deny casual horse breeders like Mayer from claiming depreciation on their stable losses unless the stables were shown to be a primary source of income. Willebrandt told Mayer, "I need your cooperation and Kay's too. . . . and I will tell you right now that unless I can have her help with you and unless you keep her on the payroll, we won't possibly win," because Ida's years of lobbying on behalf of MGM interests would be crucial for success. To ensure Mayer would retain Koverman, Willebrandt offered to waive her yearly retainer of $75,000, so "it was no small gesture for the money-conscious Willebrandt." Hopper said Willebrandt "stopped him in his tracks," and he "wriggled like a struck fish trying to get off the hook, but Mabel wouldn't let him free." When the tax bill died by one vote in a conference committee, Mayer thanked Willebrandt, but "made it clear that he couldn't really give her any credit," because he thought the magic name of Mayer "worked the trick in Washington."[20]

Koverman's friends could not keep her from sinking into despair. She prepared to sell her beloved Steinway piano, but just as the moving men began to roll it out the door, Hedda drove up. She ran to them, yelling, "Oh, no, you don't! Put that back in the house!" They did, and then she called MGM's New York office from Koverman's bedside. The next day, a bouquet of red roses arrived with a card signed by Louis Lurie, the San Francisco financier Hopper nicknamed "the Midas of the American theater scene" because he financed so much of it, and since he owned so much real estate there, he was also known as "Mr. San Francisco." The incident helped to rally Koverman to fight, and as Hopper recounted, she didn't stop until, against all odds, she was able to walk again. Hedda Hopper told readers that as a Christian Scientist, Koverman gave "credit for her recovery to the highest power, which transcends all medicine."[21]

The night before Christmas 1950, Hedda visited Koverman to give her a present. She saw a huge silver bowl overflowing with five dozen American Beauty roses sent by Mayer's friend, Kaufman T. Keller, president of Chrysler Motors Corporation. Hedda asked Ida what Mayer sent, and she directed, "If you go into the living room and take the cover off the cardboard shoe box, you'll find his present." She opened the box only to find it filled with a batch of homemade cookies. Furious, she called Louis Lurie again, who after a long silence said, "I can't believe it, Hedda." The next day, Koverman called Hopper to tell her she had just received a check by special delivery from Lurie.[22]

Frank Buchman was oblivious to the turmoil going on at MGM and Koverman's illness. He was frustrated that he failed to reach Koverman in time to pass on his invitation to Louis B. Mayer to the MRA's National Assembly while Mayer was on the East Coast. He wrote directly to Mayer about "what a priceless afternoon" he had aboard the Saturnia watching the MGM movie *Challenge to Lassie*. He wondered, "How many people take the trouble to write L. B. Mayer . . . and tell him about all the good he spreads throughout the world." Never missing an opportunity to charm the mogul, Buchman said, "God bless the merry gentleman who makes a film like that possible." He sent regards to Koverman and Howard Strickling, whom he was looking forward to seeing during his visit in early January.[23]

Koverman kept in touch with Frank Buchman through mutual friends and their own intermittent communication. He was planning a trip to Los Angeles, and in anticipation of it, Buchman sent her New Year's salutations, which offered another opportunity to cultivate Mayer through his friendship with her. Buchman was effervescent about their upcoming reunion, writing, "It is jolly to think that we are so near together again," and he invited her to lunch at "the Club," MRA's downtown headquarters. He enticed her with, "I have with me an interesting group of people and shoals of news," and how "there was going to be 'a thrilling meeting,'" and he hoped she would be able to "manage that." Buchman told her about the MRA's "interesting show . . . appearing in New York next week called *Jotham Valley*," with songs written by Cecil Broadhurst, who starred in its brief 1951 Broadway run. Buchman's letter closed with "feel free to bring any friends on Sunday." One devotee of the MRA explained how the play "has encountered the opposition of the Communists and the homosexuals in the theater, the former because they do not want men to think that the nature of man can be elevated by his own will, and the homosexuals because they excuse their indecencies on the ground they cannot help themselves. They say they are not evil but just that way because they are just that way."[24]

Until Evelyn Jaeger wrote to Buchman in February 1951, he had no idea about Koverman's incapacitation. Jaeger told him that "Mrs. Koverman has been home several months now and is gaining in health," and that she regretted missing them all in Washington. Jaeger passed on Koverman's "warmest personal regards and all good wishes." Buchman responded that he was "delighted to be in touch" with Koverman again, and that her friendship "means much to me and I value it." Their reunion never happened because Koverman was still too ill to attend the dinner Louis B. Mayer hosted for Buchman. Whether he visited with her or not, he later told her the affair was attended by "some of our old friends like Howard Strickling." [25]

Buchman invited Koverman to a dinner, noting that he was "sorry you are not a man, but you do ten men's work!" He invited her to the MRA's downtown club where he hoped to give her the details about who attended the MRA production at Beverly Hills High School, a venue Koverman had suggested back in July. Actors Joel and Frances McCrea attended, as did Mr. and Mrs. Leo McCarey, bandleader Kay Kyser, Ronald Reagan, and Jimmy Stewart, who said more movie people should see it for moral uplift and to learn how to put on a good play and hear superior music. Fox West Coast movie executive Charles Skouras saw the show; Buchman said he "seemed captured every minute." By then, Skouras was the highest paid executive in America, and apparently he was so enthusiastic about the performance that he asked Buchman "why in the world we hadn't put our publicity into his hands when we arrived." Not only had Skouras given up attending the premiere of *Show Boat* in favor of *Jotham Valley*, he also hosted a pre-show dinner at the Ambassador Hotel. Buchman was like a star-struck teenager as he recounted to Koverman that Gene Raymond, Jeannette MacDonald's husband, was there, and reminded her he first met him at a luncheon at MGM she "so gaily launched twelve years ago."[26]

A month later, Buchman wrote that he was delighted to be seeing Koverman that evening, along with Howard Strickling, who he had admired for a long time. The following day, however, he was disappointed that she failed to show up. He lamented, "Dear Ida, . . . alas, I sat waiting for person after person entering the theatre and finally at the last moment someone came up with three hundred people waiting to get in who couldn't get in. So, I said, 'where is Ida?'" It was only then he was told, and he admonished the "naughty children" who failed to tell him that she had phoned in her regrets earlier in the day. Buchman concluded, "Well, I know it was some good excuse you had," and moved on to the subject of having Hedda Hopper come on Saturday night, but, for some reason, that seemed a complicated matter. He asked, "Is that wholly impossible? I will let you decide if this is the moment. But the thought just occurred to me that it might be all right to invite her and for you to do it. I am leaving this for you this morning. Always faithfully."[27]

The following year, Jack Currie and Bennet Hall telegrammed Ida Koverman at MGM: "Moral Rearmament and tourists anxious to have film *This Time for Keeps* shown here. Important film for the welfare and business on the island. Full credit to Metro Goldwyn [sic]. Wire Collect. Film made on Mackinac Island. Will appreciate arrangements made through local theatre Orpheum who book out of Detroit office." She quickly wired back that the booking manager would arrange the film for them, and added, "Hope to see you sometime around middle of July," and added an FYI note at the bottom to Frank Buchman ending with "See you soon. Love, Ida."[28]

In spite of her forced absence from the studio and her usual local outings, Koverman could take solace that no one was forgetting about her. On December 31, 1950, the *Los Angeles Times* named Ida Koverman as one of its first Women of the Year Silver Cup recipients honoring women of achievement and leadership in Southern California. Except for the wife of the actor Spencer Tracy, none of the other ten women were obvious associates of Ida Koverman. Her tribute was inspired by her being "most responsible for much that makes for good taste and beauty in screen music; as one who helped many little stars become big stars and to stick with their careers when things got rough; who has also urged so many women to join and work for the Republican Party," and for providing "the firm touch of a woman," in many philanthropic organizations and civic groups, who knew what needed to get done.[29] First started by Dorothy

"Buffy" Chandler, the Silver Cup Award continued until 1977, with almost three hundred women honored in the fields of science, religion, the arts, education and government, community service, entertainment, sports, business, and industry. Ida Koverman's record of achievement crossed many of these categories, and she certainly epitomized the criteria used to select recipients: recognizing "women of concept and vision, who by outstanding achievement to their fields of endeavor, have created and produced improvements affecting all our lives."

Evelyn Jaeger sent Herbert Hoover a copy of the *Times* tribute, to which he replied that it was "indeed a pleasure to read of Mrs. Koverman's good news. She is a great lady." Others thought so too. In January 1951, the California Assembly passed a concurrent resolution "extending wishes for speedy recovery of Ida R. Koverman." They resolved that because she had "displayed a keen intelligent interest in the legislative process and in the Legislature," and because she was held in great esteem and respect by every member of the Legislature," both chambers agreed to "extend to Ida R. Koverman, expressions of warm regard and sincere good wishes for her most rapid recovery."[30]

When she was feeling better, she assisted the plans to establish the John Tracy Clinic for deaf children, named after Spencer Tracy's afflicted son. Esther Williams chaired the motion-picture benefit committee along with actresses Maureen O'Hara, Cyd Charisse, Janet Leigh, and Vera-Ellen. Mrs. Tracy believed that Louis B. Mayer was preoccupied, and after he apparently showed little interest in the charity event, she suspected Mayer just needed a little coaxing, and Koverman came up with an angle, knowing "Mayer could be difficult." Whatever their strategy, it was successful, because Mayer ended up hosting an organizing conference. Mrs. Tracy recalled how MGM furnished the orchestra and advertising, sold extra tickets, and promised use of their carpet, which was cleaned and freshly died a deep crisp red. MGM's stars showed up, and so did Louis B. Mayer. The movie originally selected was *Cass Timberline*, set to premier in April 1951 at the Egyptian Theatre, donated by owner Charles Skouras, but the movie that actually premiered was Spencer Tracy's *Father's Little Dividend*. Ida Koverman's political protégé George Murphy served as the master of ceremonies, who introduced Spencer Tracy, and he then introduced his wife.[31]

When Koverman finally ventured on to the studio lot, Hedda Hopper reported what "a grand day" it was to see the chauffer drive her around from set to set to greet her friends. She made a few entrances, walking slowly with a cane, but she was welcomed with cheers and an outpouring of affection. Stunned at the reception, Koverman said, "I never knew before how many friends I had. But I sure found out." Hopper was optimistic Koverman would soon return to work and "occupy her own desk again."[32] She was right.

On Monday, May 14, 1951, Ida proudly sat down at her desk surrounded by the walls filled with autographed photographs. The moment of victory, however, was quickly tempered by the simmering fued between Louis B. Mayer and Dore Schary. Two weeks later, on Wednesday, May 30, *Variety* published the stunning news that Louis B. Mayer was retiring from MGM. *Variety* reported that larger forces were conspiring against the movie industry, and this was true, but at MGM they exacerbated the tensions derived from the creative differences and uncompromising personalities of Mayer and Schary. From New York, Nicholas Schenck saw the bigger picture, and perhaps the future, and he decided that MGM's future looked brighter with Dore Schary at the helm. He made his decision after a series of missteps and maneuvers during the erratic negotiations with Mayer that, to some, seemed designed by Schenck to force Mayer's resignation, effective August 31, 1951.[33]

That the downturn between Mayer and Schary came during Ida Koverman's temporary exile appears to be more than coincidence. It's entirely possible that had she been working close by at her desk, the Mayer-Schary fiasco might have been averted. She had incontrovertibly served as his arbiter and referee in countless encounters, and Mayer needed her more than ever during the winter and spring of 1950–51. She had deflected potential conflicts, massaged his ego, and dampened his explosive ire. Before her absence, she had helped to alleviate Mayer's discomfort with Schary, such as when the two of them met in his office and Mayer silently buzzed her to come in with refreshments to cut the tension he felt in Schary's presence.[34]

Mayer's manic behavior is a standard in biographical accounts, but the increasing intensity of his irritability during the months before the announcement of his departure and in its immediate aftermath underscore Koverman's importance in preserving the tenuous peace. Author Bosley Crowther suggests insiders believed if either man had been willing to compromise, the whole debacle could have been avoided. If Mayer allowed Schary the creative freedom he had expected when he returned to the studio, he could have kept Schenck out of their squabbles. Mayer could have remained the studio figurehead if Schary had only strategically demonstrated a little deference to Mayer. What's more, Mayer could have provided Schary his own buffer to Schenck's heavy-handed oversight.[35]

By the time Koverman returned from her long absence, which lasted throughout the fall of 1950 until May 1951, the men's relationship was irretrievably damaged. This singular factor stands out even with all other contributing causes for MGM's worries, and it is invariably ignored in detailed chronicles of Mayer's fall from grace. In absentia, Ida Koverman was unable to navigate what was, from the start, the uneasy alliance between Mayer and Schary. Similar to Ralph Arnold's departure from the Republican County Committee weeks before the 1928 presidential election, Ida Koverman now "lived to see King Louis deposed from his throne," but Hedda Hopper insisted it "couldn't have given her any joy, because she wasn't that kind of woman."[36]

The context for Hopper's opinion went as far back as the aftermath of Herbert Hoover's 1928 presidential victory, when Mayer was disappointed that he didn't receive a high-level appointment, and he "pinned the blame on Ida." It is unlikely Mayer ever seriously entertained taking a post that would interfere with his movie empire in Los Angeles, but Hopper thought Mayer's attitude toward Koverman suddenly changed so that "she could do nothing right for him," and he "fumed" whenever he had to walk passed her desk, which he had to do whenever he left his office. Later, Hopper believed that because Mayer was keenly aware of how Koverman "was running the show now instead of him," he thought "she was usurping power that was his," for which "he turned on her like a tiger." To Hopper, "that was Mayer's way," but Koverman "had too many friends for him to reach her at that time."[37] Mayer's failure to recognize Koverman's financial distress during her convalescence reinforced Hopper's disdain for Mayer. Mayer might have failed to realize the dire circumstances of Koverman's situation, but it was because of her relationship and proximity to him that she lived a lifestyle and enjoyed the power and the perks of her office financed by MGM.

Biographer Charles Higham ponders what he saw as an inexplicable choice by Ida Koverman to stay at MGM after Mayer left, and he wonders if this reflected a rift between the mogul and his matron.[38] In spite of momentary explosions, Louis B. Mayer relied upon Koverman in innumerable ways, unlike any other relationship he had, both in its depth and in its duration. Their relationship was forged by his esteem for her skill and taste, and his keen awareness of their mutual ambitions and passions. Theirs was a rare collaboration across time and dimensions of culture and politics, and it withstood Mayer's volatile highs and lows at the studio and in politics. Nevertheless, as the golden era of the studio system was facing its imminent demise, their relationship changed too,

and while it was time for Mayer to leave, the studio still served Ida Koverman's need beyond that of its first master. It was her lifeline, financially
and viscerally. She might have loved her job, but she stayed because she
needed the money, and she couldn't give up a steady salary for whatever
new venture Mayer might undertake.

Hopper said she had to implore Dore Schary to keep Koverman on
salary, and it is possible he needed some convincing, but Hopper's vitriol
toward alleged communist sympathizers included liberal Democrats like
Schary.[39] Koverman's hardcore politicking was part of her living legacy,
and she and Schary were hardly strangers, so there was likely a well-
established implicit understanding between them. What's more, he must
have realized, with or without Hopper's coaxing, that Koverman was
an invaluable asset to have sitting just outside his new executive suite.
Regardless, in explaining why she stayed as long as she did, Koverman
said, "I wouldn't have to do it . . . if I'd provided for myself when I was
younger."[40]

Ida Koverman stayed in touch with Louis B. Mayer, and his post-MGM
activities were well publicized. Along with his ongoing battles with Loew's
and investment in Cinerama, he built a new home with his new wife,
Lorena. Dore Schary was much celebrated while at MGM, including by
Mayer's friend, financier Louis Lurie, who threw a party to honor Schary's
now-classic *The Blackboard Jungle*. When Mayer's former secretary Florence
Browning visited the studio, Koverman told her that Mayer was "pouting
out there in Bel-Air."[41] Regardless, Schary was a well-known Democratic
Party activist, and this came to matter in the course of his own piloting
of the MGM ship. Joseph Vogel replaced Nicholas Schenck at Loew's,
and he too had little affinity with Schary. When Schary supported liberal
Democrat Adlai Stevenson in 1952, Vogel and Loew's Republican board
members were incensed. When Vogel eventually fired Schary in 1956, it
was, in part, because of the many political enemies he made throughout
the enterprise.

CHAPTER 27

Outstanding Woman of the State

"She brought a dignity and class to the studio and, with her
gray hair, glasses, and matronly appearance, was treated like
the 'Queen Mother.'"[1]

THE NEW DECADE FOUND IDA KOVERMAN CONTINUING AS A FORMIDABLE
presence circulating within the city's iconic institutions where culture
and politics thrived. After her lengthy recovery and return to work, she
resumed her service on the board of the Hollywood Bowl and its opera
subcommittee when chairman Marco Wolff replaced actor Harold Lloyd.
Sitting with her were friends and familiar faces such as opera singer Lawrence Tibbett, music arranger Johnny Green, developer C. E. Toberman,
early Bowl promoter Dr. T. Perceval Gerson, Mrs. Joseph L. Levy, and
Vladimir Rosing. In January, she gave a speech at the Ambassador Hotel for the Los Angeles Advertising Women's group on the subject of
women in business, where MGM costume designer Helen Rose was also
a featured guest. In May, the Phi Beta Fraternity, a women's professional
organization dedicated to the promotion of music and speech, honored
Ida Koverman, listed as "a patroness," along with actresses Ruth Hussey
and Elizabeth Taylor.[2]

1952 was also a presidential election year, so Koverman's political
antenna was fully extended, but she was pessimistic about the upcoming Republican National Convention in Chicago because she feared the
national committee would fail to seat members who "know something
about politics." She lamented to Herbert Hoover, "I have never seen such
kindergarten efforts, so our little group is carrying on independently, and

doing the best we can." She was discouraged about the "state this country is in" and "how Republicans, as usual, are doing everything they can to defeat themselves. . . . Let's hope that we can block it."[3]

In anticipation of her trip to Chicago, Frank Buchman invited her to MRA headquarters on Michigan's Mackinac Island. She enthusiastically RSVPed: "It sounds most inviting and I probably will be there with bells on." She looked forward to seeing their mutual friends, who Buchman thought were just the right ones for a quiet restful vacation. Marian and H. Kenaston Twitchell took her on a trip along Lake Michigan, and then a short boat ride to the island where he guaranteed comfortable quarters would wait. H. Kenaston Twitchell was a longtime official in the MRA who would later author *Regeneration of the Ruhr* (1981), about the communist threat in Europe. Twitchell and his wife and children were devout followers of Buchman, and Mrs. Twitchell advocated Buchman's notions about marriage and gender roles, arguing that the MRA has "given a pattern to us women, and restored to America the real dignity and grace of service." She saw a wife's job as not just a supportive one to her husband, but even a subordinate one in order to "create a framework of living that makes statesmen, a sound family life that creates inner strength, trust, peace, backing, and fun." She said she had been a nagging wife, but their family life changed for the better once she started to defer to her husband, preaching, "It was absolutely black one moment and change the next. . . . It was a glorious experience."[4] While Koverman was an independent, professional woman, her success and her power, in part, came from her official capacity as a support to influential men.

When Koverman supported a candidate or a cause, her name still carried weight and the press took notice, such as when she supported moderate Republican Mildred Younger's run for a state senate seat. Younger gained national visibility after Earl Warren asked her to give the seconding speech to the motion of his presidential nomination at the convention. Mildred Younger was the wife of Evelle Younger, who went on to become California's attorney general. Koverman cochaired a luncheon for Younger at the Biltmore Hotel. Koverman's friend, writer Adela Rogers St. Johns, introduced Mrs. Younger, declaring, "There should be more women in public office." St. John said because women held "positions of distinction in numerous fields—except politics," it was time for them to get involved in the electoral arena.[5] Younger won the Republican primary, but she narrowly lost the general election to Democrat Richard Richards. She went on to host a local radio show aimed at women until a car accident damaged her vocal chords.

General Dwight D. Eisenhower's "I like Ike" campaign appealed to Koverman and a broad spectrum of Republican women. So did his popular vice presidential candidate Richard Nixon. The election attracted new battalions of Cold Warriors who marched alongside Koverman's standard-bearers Hedda Hopper, Grace Stoermer, and Irene Dunne, who now sponsored a motorcade protesting President Harry Truman and "reds in government." Hedda Hopper's political cachet was rising, aided by her direction of the "Nixon's Women's Brigade for Ike" and bringing "filmsters to rallies in western Los Angeles." A dozen vehicles headed out from the Farmers Market, timed to coincide with a KCSB broadcast, "Coffee Hour with Eisenhower." Incendiary costumes and placards drew gasps of disdain and delight along the route, such as the person dressed in Russian costume standing up in a convertible with the sign, "we Red Russians never had it so good." Carpetbags labeled "military information" and "atomic secrets" swung from women's arms, and some wore barrels labeled "American taxpayers" as they threw wads of fake money out of a box tagged "taxpayers' money." Hedda Hopper "got this thing rolling," Koverman told Hoover, and because it was "quite successful," she thought it "really should be copied all over the country." She was going to send Hoover a list of all of the signs and placards, hoping he would approve of them, including "the give-away money" she described as "my pet idea."[6]

Hedda Hopper was incorporating her aggressive partisanship in her columns and public appearances while Koverman remained behind the scenes as the consummate campaigner. She confided to Herbert Hoover that it was his coaxing that reinvigorated her "present efforts," because he urged her not to give up the good fight while she was recuperating from her stroke. "If you remember," she said, "you wrote me a very lovely little note when I was so ill in the hospital and told me that I had to get well because we still had some fights to get settled." Hopper had traveled to New York, after which Koverman told Hoover she "came back singing [his] praises to such an extent that I find that I really have a rival." Hopper was "a great gal," she said, who was now "another loyal friend to your legions."[7]

After the Eisenhower-Nixon victory, Ida Koverman was honored by the Motion Picture Council, a group with a mission to provide film critiques to the public to ensure they embodied "respectable" themes and subject matter. Back in 1948, she was an honored guest, but now the Council awarded Koverman a special citation for "her untiring efforts and spirit of loyalty to the great American principles, and her helpful cooperation with the Southern California Motion Picture Council, both as an individual and a member of the motion picture industry." During its then twenty-one-year history, Koverman was only the third recipient, along with Hollywood giants and renowned conservatives Cecil B. DeMille and Walt Disney.[8]

Resuming her star searching, Koverman "discovered" sixteen-year-old Christine Wallas, who she saw as a potential replacement for Kathryn Grayson (who was departing MGM), and whose voice Koverman compared to opera diva Marian Anderson. Unfortunately, after Ida got MGM to put her under contract, the studio failed to find a place for Wallas's awkward teenage image and dropped her after a year.[9]

When Mayer left the studio, he suggested Esther Williams leave with him, but she knew it was more important to remain where the swimming pool and movie sets were already in place to showcase her unique talent. After having developed a cozy rapport with Louis B. Mayer, she had little affection for his successor Dore Schary. Williams's most memorable film is the extravaganza *Million Dollar Mermaid* (1952), which has come to epitomize the excesses of Busby Berkeley's hyperstylized, yet technologically astounding, productions, but with an aquatic twist. The production was based on the life of famed Australian swimmer Annette Kellerman, who revolutionized modern women's bathing apparel and appeared as herself in numerous films. The confluence of the motion picture with a famous swimming legacy couldn't have been lost on Ida Koverman, and to Williams's pleasant surprise, swimming was central to the plot, unlike her other films where it was peripheral to the storyline. Williams's relationship with Schary never improved, and after one more picture, *Jupiter's Darling* (1955), she parted ways with MGM. There was a complication surrounding her signing contract that came up again when she left the studio in 1956, causing her to reflect on what Koverman had previously told her, that the real reason she was brought to the studio back in 1941 was "to sleep with [Sam] Katz."[10]

This singular anecdote fails to prove any notion that Koverman purposefully enabled sexual exploitation or the purported sexual escapades of those in and out of power all around her. She did go to great lengths to bolster MGM's contract players and sometimes their parents and siblings. Judy's mother had been living in Dallas with her other daughter, Virginia, until Judy's suicide attempt in June 1950. She stayed in Los Angeles and resumed her friendship with Ida Koverman. In July 1951, the two women were spotted dining together at the Hollywood Bowl's patio restaurant. Judy had cut off all ties to her mother and Ida Koverman after her split with MGM. The following year, when Ida learned Ethel was struggling financially, she told her, "Now, listen, this is just ridiculous. You've spent a fortune on Judy. She owes you something." Ethel took Ida's advice, but to no avail. She tried to see her daughter in April 1952 when she appeared with the Los Angeles Philharmonic. Ethel went backstage but Judy refused to see her, sending out her then husband, Sid Luft, to talk to her instead."[11]

Previously, Koverman helped Garland's sister Virginia get a job at MGM, and now she assisted Ethel getting hired at the Douglas Aircraft plant in Santa Monica. She earned $60 per week as a clerk, assigned to copy-read purchase orders. After six months, one day in January 1953, Ethel failed to show up for her shift. Four hours later, her body was found lying between two parked cars in the parking lot. She was fifty-six years old, but the coroner said she died of natural causes. Longtime family friend Harry Rabwin was surprised at the news, and noted that Ethel had been in good health and had indicated she had no plans of slowing down.[12]

Mayor Bowron appointed Ida in February 1953 as one of the forty-seven members of the Holland Flood Disaster Committee to direct relief after one of the worst floods in its history. The following month, Herbert Hoover's secretary Bernice Miller wrote to Ida about Hoover's upcoming speech at Case Institute of Technology in Cleveland on April 11 on the topic of a "dangerous development which is undermining one of the pillars of our freedom," entitled the "Socialization of Electric Power." Miller told Koverman, "I am depending on the help you have always given on these occasions which has important results," and that "it would be helpful to have as wide as possible newspaper publicity about the date" of the radio broadcast "in your local press." Ida wrote back on April 2 that the broadcast would emanate from Los Angeles over station KNX. She said she was following up with Miller's suggestion about publicity and she was "getting in touch with as many of our friends as possible." In May, Ida Koverman and movie-studio executives and actors came out in support of Mayor Fletcher Bowron's re-election. Bowron appealed to liberals and conservatives, so joining Koverman were Dore Schary, Ronald Reagan, and Leonard Spigelgass.[13]

In February 1953, Peter Meremblum asked John Anson Ford if his orchestra could play at the Hollywood Bowl in the summer. That same month, the county recognized the efforts of supervisor John Anson Ford, Mrs. Leiland Atherton Irish, and Ida R. Koverman with the headline, "Leaders Get Invitations to Anti-Red Play" and a performance of Bowl board member Vladimir Rosing's *The Lash Changes Hands* at Plummer Park's Fiesta Hall.[14]

Later that year, Koverman's friend screenwriter Frances Marion hosted a wedding at her home where Koverman, Hedda Hopper, and ZaSu Pitts made up the small guest list. The bride was actress Madge Meredith, whose conviction in a bizarre kidnapping case was overturned in part due to a letter-writing campaign launched by ZaSu Pitts and Hedda Hopper. Governor Earl Warren commuted Merdith's sentence, and after her release on July 14, 1951, Ida Koverman attended her nuptials, enabled by an unusual case of how she and her allies made good use of their political connections. [15]

Ida Koverman's public voice was not as loud, nor was she as visible as she had been in previous decades. But her name still carried gravitas, and still found among the list of names of the city's notables endorsing political candidates or causes, and the press still followed her social activities, such as when she attended a showing of Ross Shattuck's paintings at the International Galleries. The San Francisco Advertising Club honored her as "the outstanding woman of the state" at a luncheon organized by Hulda McGinn, who invited Herbert Hoover to send a telegram, letter, or tape-recorded message to be read at the event. She hoped to have a few films "made in Hollywood of some of the great people in whose lives she has so beautifully played a role," she told Hoover, and "how greatly she honors and loves you." She said, "Ida always does such kind things for others but so rarely gives us a chance" to do the same for her.[16]

When Hoover wrote a letter for Mrs. McGinn to read, she was giddy with excitement that Hoover even responded. Such a letter would be "deeply appreciated," she wrote, and he could imagine how happy it would make Ida to hear it. "It would mean more than anything I can think of. Ida Koverman has done so much." She closed with, "If you only were President again!" Hoover's affection for Ida Koverman was explicit. It read: "I have known Ida Koverman more years than she will admit. In every one of those years, she has done a multitude of good deeds. Between good deeds, she has been loyal to her friends and the things she believed in. And she had only good friends and believed in only good things. In general she is a grand girl."[17]

Mrs. McGinn was the public relations director of the California Theatres Association and Affiliated Industries, which involved addressing social and civic problems affecting motion-picture theatres and serving as a "legislative observer" of these matters. McGinn was described as "one of the most familiar legislative advocates on the capitol scene," and she was a former president of the San Mateo County Republican Women's Club.

Koverman and McGinn's friendship grew out of their mutual political interests and lobbying efforts.[18]

As a member of the board of directors of the Guild Opera Compny, Koverman, with Mrs. Irish, headed the receiving line at the premier performance of "Los Angeles' own ballet," which gave an "invitation performance" in November 1953. The following month, Koverman and Mrs. Irish assisted with the Los Angeles Chamber of Commerce Christmas luncheon, where Mrs. Max Frank Deutz was installed as the new president of the Women's Division, a post Ida Koverman had held many years before.[19]

The tone of Koverman's relationship with Mrs. Irish was evident in Koverman's letter of introduction to Herbert Hoover, when she described her as a "very dear friend . . . whom we call Miss Los Angeles." Mrs. Irish was traveling to Havana, Cuba, through New York, so Koverman hoped to set up a meeting "between her dear friends" at the Waldorf Astoria. Koverman explained Mrs. Irish was "a very prominent woman," and she was "undoubtedly" sure that Hoover already knew about how she had "been a supporter and admirer of the Chief for the last 30 years and is extremely active and influential in all civic and cultural matters." What's more, Koverman stressed, Mrs. Irish "doesn't want anything nor does she have any ax to grind—she is just a good, active Republican admirer of the Chief."[20] Such candor was part of Koverman's success in building networks of powerful people to promote candidates and causes.

CHAPTER 28

Exit Stage Right

Award-winning screenwriter Virginia Kellogg described how as Ida died in her arms whispering "this isn't the end," Kellogg comforted her, saying, "No, this isn't the end, because there is no end for Ida Koverman."[1]

WHEN SHE WASN'T OUT AND ABOUT, IDA KOVERMAN'S EVENINGS WERE spent in her apartment on Laurel Avenue, nestled between the famous Sunset Strip and Fountain Avenue in West Hollywood. Whether she was alone embroidering petit point purses that she gifted to friends, her life was still filled with music when she sat at her beloved grand Steinway piano or played selections from her sizable record collection. September 1954 was a particularly busy month, which included one of the more creative birthday parties she had attended over the years. It was held at the former estate of writer Frances Marion, the 120-acre Enchanted Hill manor atop Benedict Canyon Boulevard hosted by aviation engineer inventor Paul Kollsman. Among the versatile guests were Indian filmmaker Mohan Bhavanani, his wife Enakshi, and his son Ashok, a Princeton architectural student. Other guests were Robert Balzer, seminal wine journalist and connoisseur to the stars, and world-renowned Lithuanian-born sculptor Boris Lovet-Lorski. After the candlelight dinner, the Lester Horton modern dance group performed with the lights of the city as a sparkling backdrop.[2]

During the final years of her life, Koverman's beloved Republican Party was even more splintered from its perennial divide between progressives and conservatives. Southern California found many of her fellow partisans

wading in the radicalized waters of extremist ideologues gaining traction
in mainstream California politics. During and after the Second World War,
midwestern migrants to Southern California brought their indigenous conservatism with them, and it spawned pockets of more dramatic shifts to the
right. During the gubernatorial campaign of 1954, California Republicans
were again fighting for the soul of their party. It would be Koverman's last
battle, and she retained her visibility throughout the season.

Koverman and her friends Hedda Hopper, Mrs. Irish, Grace Stoermer,
Virginia Kellogg, and Evelyn Jaeger were members of the women's executive committee for Goodwin "Goodie" Knight, who, as lieutenant
governor, assumed office when Governor Earl Warren was appointed to
the Supreme Court the year before. Knight was a moderate who had bipartisan appeal like his predecessor. Conservatives were concerned about
his views on organized labor, so Koverman and her clique arranged a tea
for Knight to clarify his stand on the controversial anti-union "right to
work" state laws gaining steam throughout the country. Grace Stoermer
introduced Knight with the caution that "all eyes are on the State," to
see if Knight could keep Warren's coalition of liberal and moderate supporters. Goodie Knight recognized "the so-called right to work" measures
had been "a tremendous burden to every Republican running for office."
Harkening back to the Charles Moore campaign, Knight had reassured
conservatives that he was running as a representative of all Republicans,
and his message resonated with voters, who elected him to maintain a
moderate course for the state.[3]

A month later, US senator William Knowland raised the alarm about
the extremists trying to seize control of the party. Knowland was a tower-
ing figure in American conservatism, determined to rid the government
of communists, perverts, New Dealers, and labor unions.[4] Known as "the
Senator from Formosa" because of his "love affair" with Chiang Kai-shek,
Knowland worked with the Asia First lobby designed to redirect US foreign
policy priorities from Western Europe to East Asia. During one of Knowl-
and's local events, Ida Koverman sat prominently at the head table during
his incendiary speech, sponsored by the Federation of Republican Women.

Senator Knowland told his audience that if their party lost the November election, the country would come under the command of labor leaders
like Walter Reuther and liberals like Hubert Humphrey, who would usher
in "a super-duper New Deal" that would make Harry Truman look like a
moderate. To Knowland, "Our free enterprise system of government will
be beyond rescue," because "the nation cannot stand another 30 years of
similar trends toward nationalization and Socialism." Such hyperbole had

always been fodder to this group, but the audience of five hundred went wild at the mere mention of Joseph McCarthy, interrupting his speech with applause and cheers that clearly signaled their "continuing approval of Senator McCarthy."[5] Whether Koverman joined the demonstration or not is unclear, but even Knowland had criticized McCarthy's bizarre accusations of disloyalty targeting America's esteemed leaders, which eventually led to a Senate resolution of condemnation against McCarthy, the third such rebuke in its history.

Soon after the election, Ida Koverman resumed her pastime of keeping her eye out for new talent. In mid-November, she arranged a screen test for ex-football player Peter Palmer, who was studying with Nelson Eddy's vocal coach. Palmer went on to a long singing and acting career, most notably as the lead in both the successful Broadway production and Paramount movie *Li'l Abner*. Her attention then turned to a more somber task when the legendary actor Lionel Barrymore died on November 15, and she almost single-handedly arranged the memorial service. Three days later, her presence at the funeral was noted by the press for her being one of the studio veterans with whom Barrymore had worked for decades and as one of the sincere mourners who really knew him. Neither Louis B. Mayer nor Dore Schary attended; Mayer was visiting a doctor up north, and Schary was ill.[6]

The effort on behalf of Barrymore took its toll on Koverman. A couple of days after, she wasn't feeling very well, and her friends, the writer Virginia Kellogg, described as Koverman's protégé, and Betty Rothschild, spent the night with Koverman when her housekeeper could not be there. They said goodnight, perhaps anticipating a pleasant breakfast together the next morning, but instead, that night into the early morning of November 24 turned into a deathwatch. Just before 3:00 a.m., the two sentries were startled by the sound of their friend gasping for air. Virginia Kellogg cradled Koverman in her arms as she mumbled, "This isn't the end." Kellogg whispered, "No, this isn't the end, because there is no end for Ida Koverman." Now "past pain," Kellogg believed Koverman saw death as a mere transition and as an opportunity to reincarnate in a new place, perhaps not unlike what she had done throughout the life she lived this time around. Kellogg also thought Koverman "hastened her own death" by staying up "late into the night for stars to honor" Lionel Barrymore just days before.[7]

Ida Koverman's funeral was held at the Pierce Brothers Chapel on Maple Drive in Beverly Hills.[8] The crowd overflowed into the street after the one hundred and fifty seats quickly filled with an equal number sitting or standing in an adjoining room, in the aisles, on the steps, or wherever they could find a spot to listen to the service, conducted by the first reader of the First Church of Christ Scientist.

This time, Dore Schary showed up. His presence and the catalog of political and Hollywood figures inspired Kellogg to write that Ida Koverman's memorial service was "the most moving in Hollywood history." Kellogg's affection for Ida Koverman can excuse her hyperbole, but she wasn't alone in her observation that "no other figure in the film industry has inspired such voluntary tribute from every section of the country." What's more, Kellogg's larger point was that no one was called or invited to attend the service—people just showed up once they learned of the death days before. Out of the scores of the "unsummoned" were Grace Stoermer and Mrs. Irish, both of whom Ida had spent much of her public life during the last year.[9]

Mourners filed passed the open casket, where they saw Ida Koverman lying with her hands molded around a single long-stemmed red rose given by Patrick Gleason, described as Ida's favorite Godchild, an adopted son she had helped find for a couple she had known. The card simply read, "Hello, Ida."[10] The musician's union volunteered their services, a poignant gesture reflecting their mutual admiration. In lieu of flowers, Koverman asked donations be made to the Motion Picture Country House. Regardless, two hundred floral arrangements filled the church.

During Koverman's pre-MGM years, she had honed her hardcore, scorched-earth politicking that discouraged handshaking across partisan isles. Evidence of her subsequent success at building cross-party alliances was summed up by one mourner, writer Leonard Spigelgass (and future producer of the television series *MGM Parade* hosted by George Murphy), who said he "had never seen so many Democratic mourners at a Republican leader's last rites."[11] Many of the "elder statesmen . . . had never attended a motion picture memorial before." Longtime partisan attorney Joseph Scott was there, as was Sheriff Eugene Biscailuz. Mayor Fletcher Bowron attended, and Governor Knight sent a telegram read aloud: "You and I and all of us have lost a dear friend in the passing of Ida Koverman. She loved and served California and her memory will be with the people of her beloved state always." Supreme Court Chief Justice Earl Warren and FBI Chief J. Edgar Hoover wired condolences.[12]

George Murphy gave the plenary eulogy about his friend and mentor, "Mrs. Hollywood." He proudly considered himself "one of Ida's boys," and told mourners how some of Hollywood's biggest stars would "never have had their chance had it not been for the perception and appreciation of Ida," and "others who had their chance . . . would have frittered away their success except for Mrs. Koverman's watchfulness." She nurtured her flock from their first auditions through their difficult transition to stars of the silver screen.[13]

MGM "fixer" Eddie J. Mannix reflected how Koverman's "sage advice" had long been treasured by scores of industry personnel because she was "counselor and confidante to more young stars than any other individual in Hollywood." She was more than just the official head of public relations. Dore Schary spoke eloquently as he summarized how "Ida Koverman was one of America's great women. She will be greatly missed, not only by her many friends at Metro-Goldwyn-Mayer and in the motion picture world, but by our country, state and community. To the very last moment of her rich and full life, her boundless energy and enthusiasm kept her busy with good causes."[14]

The service provides evidence of the high esteem Koverman had inspired in both depth and diversity. A network of agents, lobbyists, and public-relations personnel for the movie industry were represented by William Morris agents Abe Lastfogel, Art Ruth, and former agent and Hollywood Bowl director Wynn Rocamora. Wendell M. "Doc" Bishop, a Fox Studio public-relations executive was there, and he recalled how Koverman had "made friends, made people, made families." The day before she died, Doc had confirmed their trip to Sacramento for the opening session of the legislature. Her last words to him were, "Don't cancel me out," and he didn't. He said, "her reservations still stands." Hulda McGinn delivered a message from legislators in Sacramento. She said elected officials had repeatedly asked Koverman to run for office because "she was the only woman who ever had Sacramento's unanimous endorsement, but she preferred to stay behind the scenes."[15]

Virginia Kellogg wrote that "there were never so many multi-colored mourners at another film funeral. Negros [sic], Chinese, every creed and color," sat in the pews because Ida Koverman "knew no color line." "Another unique tribute," Kellogg noted, was the attendance by "the hard-hitting ladies of the press," like Hedda Hopper and Florabel Muir, who were there, "not covering the story but weeping openly for a friend."[16]

Filing past the open casket were several MGM executives, including Benny Thau, Howard Strickling, Kenneth MacKenna, director Robert Z. Leonard, longtime publicist Frank Whitbeck, Barrett Kiesling, and casting director Billy Grady. Larry Parks, Tom Keene, James Stewart, Barbara

Stanwyck, Buster Keaton, Fernando Lamas, Kathryn Grayson, Arthur Freed, Sam Zimbalist, Carey Wilson, Pandro Berman, Edward G. Robinson, Mrs. Irish, and Mildred Younger were all there.[17]

Louis B. Mayer was the last to view Koverman's body and then he sat in the front row next to his longtime friend and financier Louis Lurie. A reporter approached them and asked if Mayer was the one who accounted for Ida Koverman's achievements after bringing her into the film industry as his executive secretary. Lurie jumped to answer, "The reverse is true; Mrs. Koverman accounted for Mr. Mayer's achievements." Three years later, Louis Lurie told Hedda Hopper during his party for actor Mike Todd that he was donating $10,000 in Ida Koverman's name to her favorite charity.[18]

Koverman's secretary, Evelyn Jaeger, telegrammed details about the funeral to Herbert Hoover's secretary, Bernice Miller. Hoover was traveling in Europe and had not heard about Ida's death until he received Hedda Hopper's letter a few days later. She told Hoover, "You would be very embarrassed, I am certain, if I told you all the wonderful things Ida has told me about you. There is no other man she respected and honored so much." He wrote back to Hopper, "She was one of my most staunch friends and it is difficult to think she has gone."[19]

Ida Koverman and Hedda Hopper shared many mutual friends. Upon learning of Ida's death, L. Sherman Adams, the orchid master, wrote to Hedda that he was very sorry to hear and, of course, sent flowers. Noted San Francisco attorney Jake W. Ehrlich, the inspiration for the character Perry Mason and close friend of Louis Lurie, wrote to Hopper, "Just a note to say you and I have lost a great friend in the passing of Ida Koverman." Publicist Harry Brand, husband of the renowned women's prison reformer Sybil, told Hopper her tribute to Koverman was beautiful, and he knew how much she meant to her and her many friends, adding, "We all found consolation in the kind things you said about her."[20]

Even after her death, Koverman's name remained listed among local liberal and conservative leaders associated with a December 10 event by the Los Angeles Urban League Ball, along with Hedda Hopper, Mrs. Loren Miller, Hon. Augustus F. Hawkins, Hon. James Roosevelt, Mr. and Mrs. Samuel Goldwyn, Dory Schary, and Mayor Fletcher Bowron on the exclusive guest list. This city's movie studios, radio, and television networks were joining the effort.[21]

Memorials read into the public record are common ways elected officials can honor or curry favor with their constituents. They are often token biographical snippets, and rarely emotional expressions of deep remorse. During the session following her death, however, the California legislature passed a concurrent resolution "relative to the memory of Ida R. Koverman." For Ida Koverman, the historical record conveyed a more profound acknowledgment that her sudden passing "constituted a serious loss to the people of the State of California in general and in particular to all persons in connection with or interested in the motion picture industry." Aside from her "distinguished career" in the entertainment industry, she was "keenly interested in public affairs," and was an advisor to governors and presidents, who had "familiarity with the functions of government and her constructive efforts in this field." While working for MGM, she was an "active participant in numerous social, industrial, civic and philanthropic organizations of state-wide and national importance." She was also "recognized generally as a person of unusual taste and discrimination in all matters pertaining to the stage." Regarding legislation, elected officials were "referred" to her "for information and suggestions" relating to the entertainment industry and "other fields of endeavor with which she was intimately conversant." They were particularly grateful to her "for her kindness" in arranging appearances by "the most prominent and successful entertainers," which "on many occasions" relieved "the tension and strife of legislative life." Ida Koverman "by her understanding, her high order of intelligence and unusual aptitude in character analysis together with her wisdom and kindly disposition caused her to be regarded as a mother to numerous active participants in the world of stage and screen." The members of the California legislature "feel that her demise should be marked by more than passing interest in that her career and her fine human characteristics should be called to the attention of the young people in the State in order that they might be inspired to emulate her fine example," and, therefore, be it "resolved by the Senate of the State of California, the Assembly thereof concurring, That the Legislature deplores the passing of this fine, warm-hearted example of womanhood and desires by this resolution to pay tribute to her memory," and the days' adjournment on January 20, 1955, was made in honor of Ida R. Koverman.[22]

Julia Wark was the sole executor of Ida Koverman's estate, described as her manager, and to whom she bequeathed $500 along with her "eternal gratitude for her care and interest in my welfare." Bruce Hawkins, the son of her niece Katherine Hawkins, received one thousand dollars, and to his wife, Joanette, Koverman gave her prized Steinway piano and record collection. Ida R. Koverman died in her rented apartment on Laurel Avenue in West Hollywood, a former family mansion long converted into an income property, and decades later awarded historic status. Contrary to a December 1945 news item, Ida Koverman did not have an estate of hundreds of thousands of dollars.[23] She held no property and her entire estate, including furniture, art, jewelry, and insurance policies was, after expenses, valued at $16,600, a paltry sum for a woman without dependents and of her longstanding professional stature. She lived much of her life in the public's eye; almost everything she did from 1929 on was a subject of public consumption, but no one knew about her struggles, so as she had lived among the rich and famous, it was just assumed a substantial inheritance awaited her near and extended heirs.

Koverman left her "esteemed friend" Virginia Kellogg her books, sapphire and diamond ring, and "her free selection of as many as she likes of my paintings." Virginia Kellogg was a Koverman protégé and a two-time Oscar-nominated screenwriter for *White Heat* in 1949, and a year later, for *Caged*. She had an autographed photograph from Ida that read, "I would rather have the small worries of too little, than the empty satisfaction of too much." She left her 1953 Dodge to her "loyal and dear friend" and secretary, Mary Evelyn Jaeger, valued at fifteen hundred dollars, which Hopper suggests Louis B. Mayer gave her in a rare burst of generosity.[24] She also left Jaeger her paintings by the versatile artist Angna Enters, among whose talents were mime, photography, dance, and writing, and who is credited with writing stories for two MGM's films, *Lost Angel* (1944) and *Tenth Avenue Angel* (1948), which starred George Murphy, Angela Lansbury, and Margaret O'Brien. Soon after Ida had recovered from her stroke, Hedda Hopper reported "our beloved Ida Koverman" was in the "star-studded house watching" a "rare adult performance" by Angna Enters. Greer Garson and Agnes Moorehead were there, as was Charlie Chaplin Jr., who Hopper said was there "learning pantomime from an expert" because "Angna does more with pantomime than most actors do with a script."[25]

Jack Norris, son of Koverman's "beloved niece" Laura Norris, was gifted "the entire balance of my estate, both real and personal, after payment of all my debts." Curiously, Charles Higham notes that when Ida Koverman died, she had not bequeathed even the smallest of mementos to Mayer. When Ida Koverman finally decided it was time to make out her will in 1953, she and Mayer were still communicating, but their day-to-day intimacy had ended. [26]

After the 1954 *Cincinnati Enquirer* notice of Ida Koverman's death, Jessie Price Koverman clarified that Ida Koverman was not a widow when Oscar died, but was in fact the "Divorced Spouse." It took another two decades for Jessie Koverman to correct the public record, and it is the only morsel of information about what happened to Ida and Oscar Koverman after 1910. Jessie Koverman stayed in Cincinnati after her husband's death, living near her in-laws, Harry and his wife, and Charles Koverman, assistant pastor at St. Paul's (Roman Catholic) Church. She traveled around the country, including attending the Girl Scouts' thirtieth anniversary celebration. Oscar did not accompany his first wife to California, but Jessie's account fails to reveal why they married and why they remained married long after she left Ohio. Nevertheless, Jessie Koverman, the other widow, outlived Oscar and Ida, until April 30, 1963.[27]

One author has suggested that the deaths of Cecil B. DeMille (1959), Louis B. Mayer (1957), and other rabid anti-communists, coincided with the end of the Red Scare in Hollywood.[28] Ida Koverman's death in 1954 more accurately frames the end of that era, when the star system lost its gravitational pull. Koverman was a magnetic, centrifugal force; a powerful dark energy that charged the MGM star machine. However, the longer view of her life is one that exemplified the strong, professional, and politicized "new woman," who became a civic-minded, middle-class matron. In her third incarnation, she nurtured some of the biggest movie stars to international acclaim as she lived a life of childless motherhood and husbandless widowhood; she was the Lioness of Hollywood.

CHAPTER 29

Epilogue

Guiding Light Legacy

Hopper said of her best friend Ida that she was a "star maker, political advisor, civic and cultural leader," and a "guiding light," and "we shall never see her likes again."[1]

IDA KOVERMAN LIVED A LONG LIFE, EVEN THOUGH THE DISTINCT PHASES of it makes it seem like she had more than one. She was born in the year of the Compromise of 1876, when the North gave up reconstructing the South, followed by the Gilded Age, which brought exponential industrial growth accompanied by violent class warfare and methodical extermination of native tribes. As Koverman grew to maturity, agrarian populists and urban progressives challenged the inequality wrought from the excesses of unfettered capitalism, and by the century's end, the frontier had expanded beyond its landed borders, inspiring many to believe America's new empire confirmed its exceptional destiny. Like millions of other skilled, white-collar women, Koverman lived an urban lifestyle, and she enjoyed the freedom and new entertainment that came with the modernization of metropolitan culture. After overcoming the pitfalls that sometimes came with single life in the city, she moved to Southern California, where her cosmopolitan existence flourished after the Great War, spending the "roaring twenties" building a female-centered partisan network that refashioned the state and national politics that put Herbert Hoover in the White House.

Hoover's victory signaled that Ida Koverman, the kingmaker, was also the premiere matchmaker to the marriage between Hollywood and politics. She segued this role to MGM, where she became a movie-star maker while finding new ways to blend politics and pictures, including her sponsorship of gossiper Hedda Hopper and actor turned political activist George Murphy. Ida Koverman's life fits neatly into the history of Hollywood, but also within the scholarship about the origins of mid-century conservatism, expanded by research into women's political conservatism. Michelle Nickerson, for example, noted that when Arizona's US senator Barry Goldwater ran for president in 1964, his public relations men "galvanized female volunteers" in ways that Herbert Hoover and Dwight D. Eisenhower had not because Goldwater's campaign exploited the "well-established grassroots political edifice" that women had created.[2] Ida Koverman's experience suggests that the foundation of this edifice came much earlier as Herbert Hoover's supporters constructed a political machine of women warriors, and Koverman played a central role in this previously unexplored and decidedly self-conscious ideological "conservative" political movement of the pre–New Deal years.

Historian Lary May has suggested one legacy of the Red Scare was that it was a struggle within "the film capital that revolved around control of the symbols and values carried by the mass media and popular culture," with Hollywood "at the center of a struggle to determine political ideology and culture in post-war America." Even in death, Koverman's life underscores this view. In 1956, HUAC investigated blacklisting in the entertainment industry. American Legion High Commander James F. O'Neil submitted a copy of a 1953 article by J. B. Matthews entitled "Did the Movies Really Clean House?" Matthews concluded that Hollywood did *not* clean its own house, and instead he argued that communists had "performed a remarkable historical service, quite by inadvertence to be sure, in listing the names of Hollywood notables who were not 'in there pitching for the common man.'" Among them were Ida Koverman and other well-known outspoken anti-communists Ginger Rogers, Robert Montgomery, Adolphe Menjou, George Murphy, and Walt Disney.[3]

There is no clearer direct link between Hollywood and the conservative wing of the mid-twentieth century Republican Party than the relationship between Ida R. Koverman, MGM, and George Murphy, whose election to the US Senate in 1964, many believe, paved the way for the ascendancy of fellow thespian Ronald Reagan. Two months after Koverman's death, MGM fixer Eddie Mannix appointed George Murphy to take over her post at the helm of MGM's public relations office. The job included taking over

"Koverman's work in keeping in touch with the political scene." He was well prepared. His earlier leadership role with the Screen Actors Guild and the Republican National Committee served him well in his new job, which would include keeping tabs on state and federal legislation of interest to the industry, and MGM in particular. Like Ida Koverman, Murphy would also scout for talent.[4]

George Murphy's 1964 US Senate victory was a rare Republican triumph in a Democratic year. Like Reagan later, even some Democrats "warmed to his glib charm," and his campaign appreciated how, he said, the "ladies campaigned for him 'all over . . . like a pack of muskrats.'" Murphy attracted votes from opponents of the controversial proposed civil rights legislation, the California Rumford Fair Housing Act, and as the victor, Senator Murphy opposed President Lyndon Johnson's efforts on the national level to outlaw discrimination in the sale or rental of private property. Murphy also opposed federal aid to education, Medicare, the war on poverty, and foreign aid. His brief consideration as a 1968 vice presidential contender ended when throat cancer began to muffle his voice, and then a scandal about being on the payroll of Technicolor throughout his Senate tenure. After losing to Democrat John Tunney in 1970, George Murphy joined the public-relations chorus promoting Chang Kai-shek and the Taiwanese government.[5]

To Koverman's grandniece, Mary, her great-aunt Ida was a loving, caring, and generous person, but at some point in Mary's life, she came to frankly understand that her great-aunt was just like everyone else in the star machine. While she genuinely appreciated, nurtured, and showcased the talent at MGM, her aunt was part of what was just a moneymaking machine.[6]

Even so, for Ida Koverman, it was much more than that, for she had mentored a president, a syndicated newspaper columnist, actors, musicians, and with mogul Louis B. Mayer she had forged a unique bond in its duration and character. When Koverman first arrived at MGM in 1929, writer Frances Marion said she believed Koverman had come highly recommended by Herbert Hoover, and, as such, was a political power at the studio who was able to guide the destinies of actors who needed favors and advice. Mayer was a good listener, but he rarely listened to anyone as carefully as he did to Ida Koverman. He depended on her, and she firmly guided him. The MRA's Frank Buchman wrote to "dear Louis B. Mayer" four months before Mayer's death in 1957, recalling "the constant care you and our devoted friend, Ida Koverman, have always given our distinguished guests in Hollywood."[7]

While Louis B. Mayer's legacy remains unrivaled in Hollywood history, Ida Koverman's now comes into focus in her own right as an unparalleled kingmaker, star maker, and cultural influencer. She successfully reincarnated herself as she merged the worlds of politics and pictures, and she reshaped the contours of both. Her legacy is no longer one of an imagined narrative, nor does she remain an invisible force circulating within the MGM galaxy like the gravitational pull of a black hole, discernable only through its impact on everything around it. Now, alongside these other heavenly bodies in MGM's universe, Ida Koverman's life and legacy glows brightly for today's stargazers and for those still light years away.

NOTES

PREFACE: "SHE DAMN NEAR RAN THE STUDIO!"

1. Alma Whitaker, "Women Lose Ground to Men in Film Work," *Los Angeles Times*, July 14, 1935, p. 1.

2. Jean Wood Fuller, *Organizing Women, Careers in Volunteer Politics and Government Administration*, pp. 29–30.

3. Scott Eyman, *Lion of Hollywood*, p. 137.

4. Mary C. Brennan, *Wives, Mothers, and the Red Menace: Conservative Women and the Crusade Against Communism;* Kathryn Cramer Brownell, *Showbiz Politics, Hollywood in American Political Life;* Ronald Brownstein, *The Power and the Glitter: The Hollywood-Washington Connection;* Donald T. Critchlow, *When Hollywood Was Right: How Movie Stars, Studio Moguls, and Big Business Remade American Politics;* Matthew Dallek, *The Right Moment: Ronald Reagan's First Victory and the Decisive Turning Point in American Politics;* Michelle Nickerson, *Mothers of Conservatism: Women and the Postwar Right;* Kathryn S. Olmsted, *Right Out of California: The 1930s and the Big Business Roots of Modern Conservatism;* Steven J. Ross, *Hollywood Left and Right: How Movie Stars Shaped American Politics;* Catherine E. Rymph, *Republican Women: Feminism and Conservatism from Suffrage through the Rise of the New Right;* Kurt Schuppara, *Triumph of the Right: The Rise of the California Conservative Movement, 1945–1966.*

5. Bosley Crowther, *Hollywood Rajah*, p. 127. Greg Mitchell, *Campaign of the Century*, p. 29, 304.

6. Neal Gabler, *An Empire of Their Own*, p. 115. *Popcorn Venus* (1973) pointed out that Mayer "occasionally recognized and employed female talent [behind the scenes]," and "Ida Koverman was his most influential administrative assistant." Samuel Marx's *Mayer and Thalberg: The Make-Believe Saints* covered similar territory in 1975, while *The MGM Girls: Behind the Velvet Curtain* (1983) suggests Koverman repeatedly intervened in studio politics and policy to solve one crisis after another. Scott Eyman, *Lion of Hollywood*, p.137. Charles Higham, *Merchant of Dreams: Louis B. Mayer, MGM and the Secret Hollywood*, p. 139, 153.

7. J. E. Smyth, *Nobody's Girl Friday*, p. 89.

8. Snippet from draft of article, "Laying Foundation Stones," by Ralph Arnold, for *Historical Society of Southern California Quarterly*, I, II, III, 1955 (hereafter Arnold draft).

9. The title of this book is derived from several quotes made by Robert Vogel, who had variously described Koverman as running "the whole damn thing," and, "yes. Ida Koverman. Damn near ran the studio," and "she, as I say, jolly well ran the studio." An

Oral History with Robert M. W. Vogel by Barbara Hall, 1991 Academy Foundation. Oral History Program Margaret Herrick Library, AMPAS, p. 101.

CHAPTER 1: SECRET MEETING, PART I: WANTED WOMAN

1. *Cincinnati Enquirer*, December 3, 1909, p. 14; *Ogden Standard*, December 7, 1909, p. 7.

2. City Directory; Listed in *Williams' Covington and Newport Directory* in 1894 and 1895; *Northern Kentucky Photographers' Index*. Jeffrey Weidman, *Artists in Ohio, 1787–1900: A Biographical Dictionary*, p. 118.

3. Peter Morris, et al., *Base Ball Pioneers, 1850–1870: The Clubs and Players Who Spread the Sport*, p. 139. The 1880 US Census has the family living in Cincinnati's Third Ward. Patrick Mondout, "Baseball in Cincinnati: A History," *Baseball Chronology: The Game since 1845*, June 1, 2008.

4. Selfcraft.net; p. A4; *Decatur Weekly Republican*, June 16, 1881.

5. One source suggests John Brockway and his family lived in Cincinnati's West End, known as Millionaire's Row in the late 1800s. *Research Hints, Helps and Links: Photographic Artists and Studios in Cincinnati* website; D. J. Kenny, *Illustrated Cincinnati: A Pictorial Hand-Book of the Queen City*, 1875. Over-the-Rhine blog, otrmatters.com/history.

6. *Studio Club News*, November 14, 1938, pp. 1–3. Thanks to Ned Comstock of the Cinema-Television Library, USC (hereafter *SCN*). Author's interview with Mary Troffer. Catherine later married a local boy, Francis (Frank) Hawkins. Their daughter, Mary Louise Hawkins (Troffer), provides the only firsthand familial recollections about Ida Ranous Brockway Koverman. Mary's siblings were Edward, Robert, Kathryn, Bruce, and Irma and Verna (twins).

7. Mary Brockway (Moore). Email correspondence from Eileen J. Coppola to author, 2003.

8. Ohio City Directory (Jeweler). *Bearings: The Cycling Authority of America*, vol. 5, no. 21; June 21, 1892; *SCN*.

9. *Cincinnati Enquirer*, April 22, 1898, p. 7. Unknown newspaper, April 1, 1884; *Musical Courier*, January 1902, vol. 44, p. 15, 44. Numerous newspapers, January 28, 1901; *Salt Lake Herald-Republican*, December 7, 1909, p. 1.

CHAPTER 2: "THE OTHER WOMAN"

1. *Cincinnati Enquirer*, December 2, 1909. Newspapers throughout the country published the two-year serial coverage of the Big Four scandal, either through verbatim syndication or variations thereof, such as "New Angles in Warriner Case . . . Ida Brockway Disappears and Loses Her Job" in the *Akron Beacon Journal*, December 3, 1909, p. 1.

2. Ancestry.com.

3. *Cincinnati Enquirer*, December 2, 1909.

4. Her father was Martin Funk Timmonds. *New York Times*, December 27, 1909.

5. Ancestry.com.

6. *Cincinnati Enquirer*, December 2, 1909; *New York Times*, November 30, 1909.

7. *Portsmouth Daily Times*, November 10, 1909.

8. *Daily Saratogan*, February 4, 1910.

9. *New York Times*, November 2, 3, 4, 6, 8, 10, and 11, 1909; February 4, 1910. *History of Cincinnati and Hamilton County Ohio*, p. 787; *Cincinnati Chamber of Commerce Annual Report*, vol. 55.

10. *Morning Oregonian*, February 2, 1910.

11. *New York Times*, November 4, 1909; *Cincinnati Enquirer*, December 2, 1909.

12. *San Francisco Call*, November 12, 1909, p.1.

13. *New York Times*, November 10, 1909.

14. *New York Times*, November 11, 1909; *Portsmouth Daily Times* November 10, 1909; *Carroll Herald* (Iowa), November 17, 1909.

15. *Coshocton Daily Times* (Ohio), November 15, 1909, p. 7; *New York Sun*, December 2, 1909; *Cincinnati Enquirer*, December 3, 1909; *Yakima Herald*, December 8, 1909.

16. *New York Times*, November 28, 1909; *Nebraska Journal*, December 4, 1909; *Duluth Evening Herald* and *Arizona Republican*, December 7, 1909.

17. *Cincinnati Enquirer*, December 2, 3, 1909; *Nebraska Journal*, December 4, 1909.

18. *Duluth Evening Herald and Coshocton Daily Times* (Ohio), December 7, 1909, p. 5.

19. *Duluth Evening Herald*, December 10, 1909, p. 1; *Anaconda Standard*, November 11, 1909.

20. Smith was a candle and fertilizer manufacturer, who two decades earlier was Cincinnati's "popular" Republican and "energetic" reform-minded mayor. Darcy Richardson, *Others: Third Parties During the Populist Period, Vol II*, p. 19, iUniverse; *Nebraska Journal*, December 4, 1909.

21. *New York Times*, November 16, 18, 1909; December 22, 1909.

22. *New York Times*, November 18, 1909. Initially, Mrs. Ford was going to be tried on three counts: blackmailing Charles Warriner, receiving stolen money (from Warriner), and, sending threatening letters through the US mail. Two counts were dropped after her first trial date was postponed, but she had a jury trial on the sole count of blackmail. *Cincinnati Enquirer*, December 11, 1909, p. 18; *New York Times*, June 10, 1910.

23. *New York Times*, December 4, 1909.

24. *Washington Herald*, December 4, 1910.

25. *Portsmouth Daily Times*, December 1, 1909, p. 1.

26. *New York Times*, November 22, 1909; December 27, 1909 January 31, 1910; *Cincinnati Enquirer*, January 28, 1910.

27. *Cincinnati Enquirer*, January 28, 1910.

28. *Los Angeles Herald*, February 5, 1910; *Daily Saratogan*, February 4, 1910; *New York Times*, November 11, 1909; *Anaconda Standard*, November 11, 1909. "Woman Will Tell Blackmail Story: Mrs. Stewart [Ford] Declares She Knows All About Huge Defalcation by Railroad Treasurer and Will Relate Sensational Facts in Court—Never Received a Cent from Warriner."

29. *Portsmouth Daily Times*, December 1, 1909.

30. *New York Times*, February 4, 1910.

31. *Los Angeles Herald*, February 5, 1910; *Cincinnati Enquirer*, February 5, 1910.

32. *New York Times*, June 10, 1910.

33. *New York Times*, June 15, 18, 1911; *Lebanon Daily News*, June 16, 1911; *Duluth Herald*, June 15, 1911.

34. *New York Times*, September 10, 1910; *Charlotte News*, June 16, 1911; *New York Times*, June 18, 1911. Edgar Cooke filed three lawsuits, including one against the Big Four and its general counsel and another against prosecutor Hunt. just days after the thirty-three year-old Henry Thomas Hunt was elected as the new "Boy Mayor" of Cincinnati, Cooke sued Hunt for providing false information, claiming damages for $100,000 for the libelous

and malicious prosecution against him that grew out of the Warriner case. *Cincinnati Enquirer*, January 24, 1912, p. 8.

35. *New York Times*, November 10, 1909; February 4, 1910; *Carroll Herald* (Iowa), November 17, 1909. Apparently, such plans had already been in the works, but Ida R. Brockway's exposure of the Warriner crimes expedited the pace of historical change. *Chateaugay Record* (New York), October–December 1913.

CHAPTER 3: MERMAIDS AND MATRIMONY

1. "As You Like It," *Evening Independent*, (Massillon, Ohio) December 2, 1910, p. 3.

2. *Indianapolis Star*, December 2, 1910, p. 10. *Cincinnati Enquirer*, December 2, 1910, p. 11.

3. Relative Eileen Coppola explained because both of Ida Brockway's parents had died, they wed in the company of her cousins Harry and Mary Brockway in Indiana. Author email with Eileen Coppola, May 2003. Ida Koverman was first cousin by marriage to Howard O. Koverman, father of Bud, who said Ida and Oscar might have known each other casually for a while. Bud had a notion that Ida was involved in some way with a bank scandal in Northern Kentucky, which inspired her marriage, and to get out of town to establish a new identity. Author email from Howard C. "Bud" Koverman, May 5, 2003.

4. Ida Brockway was a stenographer in Norwood, Columbia, but the Norwood directory has her living in a room at 5108 Carthage Avenue, *Norwood*, p. 227. Living at the same address as Oscar Koverman were H. N. Koverman, manager, real estate department, Bush Parker's; Kate Koverman, widow of Henry; and Mamie L. Koverman. *Ohio and Florida, City Directories, 1902–1960, Ohio, Hamilton, 1909–1910*. One family chronology indicates Oscar had five siblings, while the 1900 census listed only four, with one sister, Geneva, born in November 1878, only two months after Oscar. "Descendants of Herman Henry (Oevermann) Koverman; Family Tree Master Online; *Twelfth Census of the United States*; Sch. no. 1, Population Columbia Township, Norwood, Ohio, East Precinct, p. B.

5. List or Manifest of Alien Passengers for the United States. Noted as a citizen of the United States. *The New York Times*, August 27, 1911; *Brooklyn Daily Eagle*, March 27, 1913, p. 8. Oscar is listed as living with his widowed mother Katherine, and one sister, Marie L., in the *Williams' Norwood Directory for 1911–12*, p. 12. US World War I Draft Card, 1917–1918. Ancestry.com.

6. *Cumulative Daily Digest of Corporation News*, 1914:2, p. 357; from *Journal of Commerce*, August 25, 1914, p. 2. University of Illinois at Urbana-Champaign/Hathi Trust Digital Library.

7. *U. S. City Directories, 1821–1989, New York*. In 1915, Ida is listed only as a cashier and no mention of her place of employment. *Brooklyn Daily Eagle* identifies her as Jessie F. Turner of New York, found in *Brooklyn Life from Brooklyn*, New York, April 16, 1916 and New York State Census, 1915. Application for marriage license, a pre-marital certificate no. 16,831 is for Charles W. Brockway and Jessie A. Turner, both living in Summit County, Ohio. Jessie was born in Clarksburg, West Virginia, and her father was John R. Turner.

8. *Brooklyn Life from Brooklyn, New York*, August 5, 1916, p. 16; September 2, 1916, p. 18.

9. David E. Barney, *American Genesis: The Archeology of Women's Swimming at the 1920 Olympic Games*, p. 211; 219. Linda J. Borish, "Women, Sport and American Jewish Identity in the Late Nineteenth and Early Twentieth Centuries," in Timothy Chandler and Tara Magdalinski, *With God on Their Side: Sport in the Service of Religion*, p.85.

10. *Albuquerque Journal*, March 16, 1931, p. 2. Founding date: October 20, 1917. Harold A. Lerch and Paula D. Welch, *The Women's Swimming Association: The Golden Years, 1920–1940*, p. 91. "Star Mermaids of City Form a New League," *New York Tribune*, January 10, 1918, p. 15. *New York Times*, October 21, 1917, p. 122.

11. The *New York Tribune* announced the upcoming January 19, 1918 meet on January 10, 1918, p. 15. Borish, "Women, Sport and American Jewish Identity," pp.100; 102.

12. *The Brooklyn Daily Eagle*, December 18, 1918, p. 2 and April 5, 1919, p. 7. Borish, "Women, sport and American Jewish identity," p.85.

13. The physics of the American stroke enhanced a swimmer's ability to "skim over the water," an important factor for endurance by providing more power with less effort. David A. Barney, *American Genesis*, pp. 211–12. "Mermaids in Dead Heat," August 29, 1919, p. 13; *Brooklyn Life*, May 29, 1920, p. 5; *Brooklyn Daily Eagle*, July 18, 1920, p. 5 and February 5, 1924, p. 24. "Misses Boyle and Bleibtrey Set New Figure for 300-Yard Swim," *Brooklyn Life*, July 31, 1920, p. 11. See *Report of the United States Olympic Committee by U.S. Olympic Committee regarding Seventh Olympiad*, p. 365. Another long-term resident of the Hotel Shelburne was champion swimmer, Charlotte Boyle. *Albuquerque Journal*, March 16, 1931, p. 2. See also WSA Archives, The Henning Library, International Swimming Hall of Fame, Fort Lauderdale, Florida; scrapbooks, 1915–1917.

14. In a 2006 retrospective, Jerry Person described Ida Koverman as "America's foremost swimmer." Jerry Person: *Water Carnival of 1922.* October 5, 2006, A Look Back website. *Santa Ana Register* August 2, 1921, p. 6. *Los Angeles Times*, January 25, 1922, p. III3; "Mercury Swimfest," *Los Angeles Times*, March 1, 1922, p. III1; *Los Angeles Times*, April 6, 1922, p. III3; *Los Angeles Times*, July 4, 1922, p. III5; *Los Angeles Times*, May 23, 1922, p. III1.

15. One WSA competitor was sixteen-years-old Gertrude Ederle, who won twenty nine-world records between 1921 and 1925. Ederle's challenge to be the first woman to swim across the English Channel was partly financed by the WSA. After failing her first attempt, she was successful in 1926. Larch and Welch, *The Women's Swimming Association*, pp. 93–94.

16. *U. S. City Directory, Los Angeles*, 1920. California Voter Registration, 1900–1968; San Francisco County, 1920, Roll 25. US Census, 1920.

17. *Sacramento Union*, October 19, 1913, p. 1.

CHAPTER 4: CATHEDRAL OF COMMERCE

1. *Milwaukee Journal*, February 20, 1936, p. 8. *Studio Club News*, November 14, 1938, pp. 1–3. J. E. Smyth repeats the claim in her 2018 *Nobody's Girl Friday: The Women Who Ran Hollywood*, p.76. Notary post expires, March 30, 1918, *Benders' Lawyers' Diary and Directory*, p. 1220 Christopher Finch and Linda Rosenkrantz, *Gone Hollywood: The Movie Colony in the Golden Age*, Doubleday, 1979, pp. 253–54.

2. A. P. Cartwright, *Gold Fields Paved the Way*, p. 113, 126.

3. A. P. Cartwright, *Gold Fields Paved the Way*, p. 183.

4. A. P. Cartwright, *Gold Fields Paved the Way* p. 113. Robert Freeman Smith, "Wilson's Pursuit of Order," in Thomas G. Paterson *ed., Major Problems in American Foreign Policy*, vol. 1, pp. 513–30.

5. *Investigation of Mexican Affairs: Preliminary Report*, vol. 2, part 1, p. 299. Ramon Eduardo Ruiz "Mexico at the Whim of Washington," in *Major Problems in American Foreign Policy*, vol. 1, pp. 530–41.

6. The 1900 US Census lists Phoebe May Fisher as a widow.

7. *Mines Register: Successor to the Mines Handbook and the Copper Handbook*, 1905, p. 88; *Chemical & Metallurgical Engineering*, vol. 19, p. 428. Keene also served as director of another GFADC subsidiary, the South American Gold and Platinum Co., *Engineering and Mining Journal*, vol. 108, no. 1, July 19, 1919, p. 115; *City Directory of Los Angeles, 1920*; *Engineering and Mining Journal*, vol. 109, no. 1, April 3, 1920, p. 82. Two years later, the forty-four-year-old McDougall died of a lung infection after an emergency appendectomy, and Keene committed suicide by carbon monoxide poisoning in September, 1940. *Chicago Tribune*, September 27, 1940, p. 16.

8. The donation entry listed it as coming from A. E. W. through Amor F. Keene in Ralph Arnold, "Laying Foundation Stones, I," *HSSCQ*, p. 111; Gary Dean Best, *The Politics of American Individualism: Herbert Hoover in Transition, 1918–1921*, pp. 55; 70–71.

9. Ralph Arnold, "Laying Foundation Stones, I," *HSSCQ*, pp. 99–124; Ida Koverman to Ralph Arnold, October 8, 1920. RAP.

10. Ida Koverman to Ralph Arnold, June 20, 1922; October 8, 1920. RAP.

11. Joan Hoff Wilson, *Herbert Hoover: Forgotten Progressive*, pp. 7–17; 76.

12. *Glendale City Directory, 1911–1912*, p. 59; *1915–1916*, p. 71, *1923*, p. 255; *Los Angeles City Directory, 1918. U.S. City Directories, 1821–1989, Los Angeles*, 1936.

13. US census 1940 lists a sixty-six-year-old, Ohio born May B. as wife of sixty-one-year-old John J. Boyer. Mary Louise remembers visiting her grandmother in Culver City during the early 1930s.

CHAPTER 5: "NOW IS THE TIME FOR ALL GOOD WOMEN TO COME TO THE AID OF THEIR PARTY": POLITICAL OPERATIVE

1. Ralph Arnold, "Laying Foundation Stones, Pt. I," *HSSCQ*, p. 119.

2. Ida Koverman to Ralph Arnold, April 14, 1920. RAP.

3. Ida Koverman to Ralph Arnold, November 5, 1920. RAP.

4. Fred W. Upham to Joe Crail, May 5, 1920. RAP.

5. One report says that Johnson lost Los Angeles by only 511 votes. Richard Coke Lower, *A Bloc of One: The Political Career of Hiram H. Johnson*, p. 379, fn.101.

6. Royce D. Delmatier, Clarence F. McIntosh, Earl Waters, eds. *The Rumble of California Politics*, p. 214.

7. "Hoover National Republican Club," *Who's Who in the States*, June 1, 1920. Ida Koverman to Ralph Arnold, November 5, 1920, p. 4. RAP. Years later, Ralph Palmer Merritt's credibility was called into question when he wrote a controversial recollection about his supposed intimate role in the events surrounding the last days of President Harding's life in San Francisco. For discussion on Merritt, see Kathryn Olmsted, *Right Out of California*, p. 42.

8. Ida Koverman to Ralph Arnold, November 5, 1920. RAP; Archive of Material Related to Hoover's Attempted Purchase of Land in the Southern San Joaquin Valley of California, September 1933.

9. Ralph Arnold, "Laying Foundation Stones, I," *HSSCQ*, p. 120. Marguerite J. Fisher, and Betty Whitehead, "Women and National Party Organization," *American Political Science Review* 38, October 1944, p. 896.

10. Ralph Arnold, "Laying Foundation Stones, I," *HSSCQ*, p. 122.

11. Ralph Arnold to Edgar Ricard, October 27, 1921. RAP. Along with Mrs. Oliver P. Clark, former US senator Frank Flint, and well-known progressives. Myra Nye, "Women's Work, Women's Clubs," 1920 folder. CBP.

12. As a result, California remains among the states with the highest minimum-wage, exceeding federal levels first established during the New Deal. See Jacqueline R. Braitman, *Katherine Philips Edson: A Progressive-Feminist in California's Era of Reform*, PhD dissertation, UCLA 1988.

13. Ida Koverman to Ralph Arnold, October 6, 1920. RAP. *Los Angeles Times*, October 5, 1920, found in Richard Dale Batman, *The Road to the Presidency: Hoover, Johnson, and the California Republican Party, 1920–1924*, p. 165, PhD dissertation, USC 1965.

14. Ida Koverman to Ralph Arnold, October 12, 1920. RAP.

15. Ida Koverman to Ralph Arnold, October 12, 1920. RAP.

16. Ida Koverman to Ralph Arnold, November 5, 1920; Ida Koverman to Ralph Arnold, October 12, 1920. RAP.

17. Ida Koverman to Ralph Arnold, November 5, and Ralph Arnold to Ida Koverman, November 12, 1920; Ida Koverman to Ralph Arnold, October 12, 1920. RAP.

18. Ida Koverman to Ralph Arnold, October 12, and November 5, 1920, RAP.

19. Ida Koverman to Ralph Arnold, November 5, 1920. RAP.

20. She warned Arnold that there "were rumors, many of them from people who are in a position to be well posted, that Johnson will double cross Harding and as a matter of fact some go so far as to say that he has sold out to the other side." She said "many of Mr. Hoover's supporters were clamoring for him to get into some sort of race here—he wanted me to get that word to you and to tell you that they would all rally to Mr. Hoover just the moment he would permit them to do so. Johnson's speeches for Harding here are doing great harm—his anti-League talk is killing many votes and unless something drastic is done, I fear the state may go Democratic—many whom I would have banked upon, tell me that they intend to vote for Cox. Men with whom I've talked all seem to think that our Chief can do more to swing the state in line than any one else. The people do want a League of some sort and Johnson and Borah are both creating an idea that the Republican Party will 'scrap' the League and it is doing great harm. Mr. Hoover's assurances will do much to undo the harm that is being done." Ida Koverman to Ralph Arnold, October 12, 1920. RAP.

21. Ida Koverman to Ralph Arnold, October 12, 1920; Ralph Arnold to Mrs. Koverman, October 26, 1920. Ralph Arnold to Ida Koverman November 12, 1920. RAP.

22. Ida Koverman to Ralph Arnold, October 12, 1920. Ida Koverman to Ralph Arnold, November 5 and 12, 1920. RAP.

23. Ralph Arnold telegram to I. R. Koverman, October 22, 1920. On October 25, 1920 she wired Arnold about a meeting where "a few loyal ones" were called upon to approach Chandler of the *Los Angeles Times* and that the "candidate election here practically impossible unless Chief [Hoover] can help. She presumed Hoover's attention was "vitally necessary," such as a "one public speech California for local candidate." Four days later, however, she informed Arnold that Chandler had failed, and the candidate will see Hoover in Palo Alto to come to some understanding whereby Hoover's desired endorsement can be telegraphed widespread Monday papers. Chandler thought the candidate believed "our old opponent" supported him, but "which we all believe is false. Have done best I could and believe desired result will obtained [Ida] Koverman." Ida Koverman to Ralph Arnold, October 25, 1920. Ida Koverman to Ralph Arnold, November 5, 1920. RAP.

24. Ida Koverman to Ralph Arnold, October 6, 1920; Ida Koverman to Ralph Arnold, October 12, and October 26, 1920. Ralph Arnold to Ida Koverman November 12, 1920.

25. Ida Koverman to Ralph Arnold, November 5, 1920. Ralph Arnold to Ida Koverman November 5 and 12, 1920. RAP.

26. Over a twenty-four hour period, Koverman and Arnold exchanged intense correspondence indicating that organizations on Hoover's behalf were being directed from quarters all over the country, perhaps threatening to swallow up Koverman's services in Southern California. In the meantime, she coordinated a new channel through Judge H. M. Wells whom she asked Arnold to "wire motive back of this utilization most unusual and powerful organization for Chief through enlistment extraordinary active influential valuable California membership otherwise inaccessible. Also has other advantages cannot state here am working on plan of Chief fighting old opponent for his present position two years hence and believe this opportunity should be seized immediately." Ida Koverman to Ralph Arnold, December 6, 1920; Ida Koverman to Ralph Arnold, December 7, 1920. Joan Hoff Wilson, *Herbert Hoover: Forgotten Progressive*, pp. 73–79. Richard Batman, *Road to the Presidency*, p. 172. Ida Koverman to Ralph Arnold, November 5, 1920, p. 3. RAP.

27. Richard Batman, *Road to the Presidency*, pp. 303–4.

CHAPTER 6: A WOMAN OF NO DISTINCTION

1. Louis S. Lyons, *Who's Who Among the Women of California, vol. I*, p. 318. *Van Nuys News*, June 20, 1922, p. 1.

2. Ida Koverman to Ralph Arnold, June 20, 1922. RAP.

3. Ralph Arnold to Parley M. Johnson, December 7, 1922. RAP.

4. Ralph Arnold, "Laying Foundation Stones, I," *HSSCQ*, p. 246. Richard Batman, *Road to the Presidency*, pp. 216–17.

5. Ralph Arnold to Hon. Herbert Hoover, August 4, 1922. RAP. Ralph Arnold, "Laying Foundation Stones, II," *HSSCQ*, pp. 245–6; Richard Batman, *Road to the Presidency*, pp. 209; 212; 225. *Los Angeles Times*, July 16, 1922. Hiram Johnson won 313, 539 or 56.71 percent of the vote compared to Moore's 239, 320 votes or 43.29 percent.

6. Richard Coke Lower, *A Bloc of One: The Political Career of Hiram H. Johnson*, p. 392, fn. 44. Ralph Arnold to Herbert Hoover, November 10, 1922. RAP.

7. She spoke about bills before the California legislature worthy of support by the Women's Legislative Council, including a community property bill that would "give a fair recognition of the right testamentary power in the wife as regards community property," and another to provide State aid to children up to sixteen years old whose parents are too poor to send them to school. The other was a revolutionary bill that would provide "that violation of the chastity of a boy shall receive the same penalty as a similar offense against a girl." While the club took no action, its members were generally favorable. Myra Nye, *Los Angeles Times*, January 12, 1921, p. I16. Nell Ray Clarke, "The First Lady of the Land," *The Woman Citizen*, vol. 4, no. 19; February 10, 1923, p. 11. Special Collections, University of California, Santa Cruz.

8. Richard Batman, *Road to the Presidency*, p. 216. Ralph Arnold to Herbert Hoover, August 4, 1922. RAP.

9. Herbert Hoover to Ralph Arnold, September 23, 1921. RAP.

10. Ralph Arnold telegram to Herbert Hoover, November 2, 1921; N. L. Porlet to Herbert Hoover, November 1, 1921. RAP.

11. Herbert Hoover to Ralph Arnold, November 14, 1921 and November 2, 1921. RAP.

12. Ralph Arnold, "Laying Foundation Stones, II," *HSSCQ*, p. 254. Ralph Arnold telegram to Herbert Hoover, November 22, 1921. RAP.

13. Anna L. Harvey, *Votes Without Leverage, Women in American Electoral Politics, 1920–1970*, p. 181. *Washington Post*, December 16, 1923, p. 14. CBP.

14. Earl C. Behrens, *San Francisco Chronicle*, July 8, 1923, p. 4. Ironically, the column to the left reported the upcoming celebration of the seventy-fifth anniversary of the 1848 Seneca Falls Convention. Incumbent governors who are titular heads of their parties select their state's national committee members.

15. Katherine Philips Edson to Mrs. Harriet Taylor Upton July 3, 1923; Katherine Philips Edson papers; Special Collections UCLA (hereafter KPE to Upton). Fisher and Whitehead, "Women in National Party Organization," *American Political Science Review* 38 (October 1944), p. 903.

16. Upton letter KPE. Fisher and Whitehead, "Women in National Party Organization," p. 899. Observers of the post-suffrage years suggested that after a couple of election cycles, any woman selected for a party office was likely deemed as being manageable by their male colleagues, thereby getting two national committee posts for the price of one. KPE to Upton.

17. Ida Koverman to W. C. Mullendore, June 26, 1923. Two weeks later, she was told her request would be forwarded on to RNC headquarters. Christian A. Herter to Ida Koverman, July 11, 1923. HHPL.

18. Numerous letters from Ralph Arnold, June 27, 1923. California Governor Friend W. Richardson, state senators F. A. Arbuckle, F. J. Powers, state treasurer Charles G. Johnson, and agriculturalist Charles C. Teague were among those contacted. Teague's support was unlikely. He had been a strong Hoover supporter, but he liked Johnson's stand on the protective tariff. He had also been a frequent ally of Katherine Edson. Ray Lyman Wilbur to Ralph Arnold, July 6, 1923. RAP.

19. KPE to Upton.

CHAPTER 7: HARDING'S DEMISE, COOLIDGE'S RISE: IDA KOVERMAN AND WOMEN IN THE GOP

1. Ralph Arnold to C. A. Welch, August 9, 1923; Harry Chandler to Ralph Arnold, August 20, 1923. RAP.

2. July 31, 1925. Listed on the American Peace Award stationery of the Los Angeles World Court Committee, announcing the August 20, 1925, meeting at the Los Angeles City Club, which included progressive and conservative Republicans Mrs. I. R. Koverman and Louis B. Mayer, with Koverman's signature among those at the bottom. RAP.

3. William M. Garland to Ralph Arnold and Ida Koverman, February 2, 1924. RAP.

4. E. P. Clark to Ralph Arnold, February 5, 1924. For now, Ralph Arnold read between the lines and decided that the whole mess forced him to resign from the executive "committee of five," of the statewide Coolidge League. RAP.

5. Mark Requa to Ralph Arnold, April 10, 1924; H. A. Lyddame to Ralph Arnold, September 16, 1924. RAP.

6. Ralph Arnold recognized Helen Matthewson Laughlin as a woman distinction, whose participation in the upcoming national convention was crucial if the party was to have "a mighty slim chance of ever maintaining a high standard," and to create a balanced delegation. Arnold also realized that women like Laughlin "should be placed in the forefront of our fighting ranks." Since Laughlin was also a member of the University of California's Board of Regents, Arnold urged Regent William Crocker to counter opposition to Laughlin's selection as a delegate. He was aware of Ida Koverman's status as an independent woman, so Arnold wanted Crocker to know that Mrs. Laughlin's position with the university was her only source of livelihood, and he hoped his advocacy wouldn't jeopardize her standing in any way. C. C. Teague to Ralph Arnold, May 30, 1924; Ralph Arnold to C.C. Teague, May 29, 1924. RAP.

7. Charles A. Johnson to Ralph Arnold, April 1, 1924. RAP. Richard Dale Batman, *The Road to the Presidency: Hoover, Johnson, and the California Republican Party, 1920–1924,* pp. 276; 277–8.

8. Katherine Philips Edson regarding Johnson for President Club signed form letter, To the Republican Women in California, April 28, 1924. KPE. Batman, *The Road to the Presidency,* p. 278. Herbert Hoover to Ralph Arnold, May 7, 1924. Marshal Hale to Ralph Arnold, May 16, 1924. Ralph Arnold to F. W. Steerns, May 9, 1924; Ralph Arnold to Charles H. Toll, May 10, 1924; Ralph Arnold to Hon. C. Bascom Slemp, May 8, 1924. RAP.

9. Ralph Arnold to Hon. C. Bascom Slemp, May 7, 1924; Ralph Arnold to Miss Concha V. Savage, May 19, 1924. Willis A. Baum to Ralph Arnold, May 16, 1924. RAP.

10. "Convention Special Off Next Week," *Los Angeles Times,* May 28, 1924, p. A6. Ida Koverman telegram to Ralph Arnold, May 30, 1924. The RNC was held in on June 10–12 in Cleveland, Ohio. Ida Koverman "Kay" to Ralph Arnold, June 10, 1924. Charles A. Johnson to Ralph Arnold, January 28, 1924. Marshal Hale to Ralph Arnold, May 16, 1924. Some observers saw the potential of a major controversy because *Los Angeles Times* publisher Harry Chandler and other reactionary interests were less interested in promoting Coolidge's candidacy than in having allies to help defeat proponents of the public ownership of the city's utilities. Unk. "EO/H" author to Willis J. Abbott, *Christian Science Monitor,* May 7, 1924. RAP.

11. Michael P. Rogin and John L. Shover, *Political Change in California,* p. 68. *Pittsburgh Post-Gazette,* June 12, 1924, p. 11.

12. Silberberg also sat on a special policy-making committee with Charles Teague and Senator Frank Flint. Charles A. Johnson to Ralph Arnold, June 30, 1924. RAP.

13. H. P. Stokes to Lawrence Richey, October 1, 1924. HHPL.

14. Glen Jeansonne, *The Life of Herbert Hoover: Fighting Quaker 1928–1933,* p. 56. W. C. Mullendore to Ralph Arnold, January 13, 1923. RAP.

15. Unknown, to President, White House, Washington, DC, c/o Mr. C. Bascom Slemp, Secretary to President, August 12, 1924. RAP.

16. Ralph Arnold to Ed. T. Clark, November 14, 1924; Ralph Arnold to Herbert Hoover, December 5, 1924; Ralph Arnold to Ed. T. Clark, December 5, 1924. RAP.

CHAPTER 8: "A PECULIAR BUSINESS"

1. Kerry Segrave, *Extras of Early Hollywood: A History of the Crowd, 1913–1945,* p.163. See also Anthony Slide's *Hollywood Unknowns: A History of Extras, Bit Players, and Stand-Ins.* Jackson: University Press of Mississippi, 2012.

2. Industrial Welfare Commission Minutes, November 18, 1925; Kerry Segrave, *Extras of Early Hollywood,* p. 19.

3. IWC minutes, November 18, 1925.

4. IWC minutes, November 18, 1925.

5. IWC minutes, November 18, 1925; Wage Board meeting, pp. 30–31.

6. Fred Beetson to All Members, June 13, 1925, MPPDA Digital Archive 1922–1939.

7. IWC minutes, November 18, 1925, pp. 42–43; November 24, 1925; Beetson, MPPDA.

8. IWC minutes; Wage Board meeting, November 24, 1925, pp. 2, 4–7.

9. IWC minutes, November 24, 1925, pp. 39, 42–3. With the advent of sound, the number of extras declined. For 1928, just over 276,000 were processed. Kerry Segrave, *Extras of Early Hollywood,* pp. 142–3.

10. Articles of Incorporation, MPPDA Digital Archive, 1922–1939.

11. Anthony Slide, *Hollywood Unknowns*, p. 65; Kerry Segrave, *Extras of Early Hollywood*, p. 139.

12. IWC minutes, November 24, 1925, pp. 7–9, 11–12, 19.

13. IWC minutes, November 24, 1925, p. 21.

14. IWC minutes, January 24, 1925, pp. 27, 47. The hearing continued with a discussion about transportation and the problem of getting extras home late at night, and the subject of comfort and hygiene regarding toilet facilities for filming away from the studio out on locations. This was a concern for a big star like Anita Stewart who had approached Katherine Edson about it. Fred Beetson piped up that only the highest type of facilities would be furnished. Extras also complained about wearing unclean clothing and bathing suits, so it was suggested that the studios follow the most basic requirements set by public swimming pools for common care and cleanliness.

15. Kerry Segrave, *Extras of Early Hollywood*, p. 21

CHAPTER 9: FEDERATION, FINANCES, AND FRIED CHICKEN

1. Estelle B. Omdalen to Ralph Arnold, June 15, 1925. Draft of Ralph Arnold's "Laying Foundation Stones, Part III: Women in Politics," 73a, p. 76, RAP (hereafter Arnold draft).

2. National Republican Information Bureau of the Republican Women's Federation of California (RWFC), 1924. The document outlines the establishment of the RWFC but focuses on the evolution of the Northern California network. Arnold draft, p. 75. RAP.

3. Ida Koverman to Ralph Arnold, April 9, 1925; Memo from Ida Koverman to Ralph Arnold, April 30, 1925. RAP.

4. *Los Angeles Times*, October 21, 1924, p. 3. Nellie's brothers were John J. and Arthur H. Kelley.

5. Arnold draft, p. 78. RAP.

6. Ida Koverman to Ralph Arnold, April 30, 1925. RAP. *Van Nuys News*, May 22, 1925, p. 6.

7. Ralph Arnold to Mrs. Herbert Hoover, May 16 and 25, 1925. RAP.

8. "Republican Women of State in Convention," *Los Angeles Times*, June 21, 1925.

9. Belle Lloyd to Ralph Arnold, July 23, 1925. RAP.

10. June 21, 1925 reporting designates Mrs. Clark. Ralph Arnold's recollection says Mrs. Florence Collins Porter presided. Ida Koverman to H. C. Hoover, June 11, 1925. HHPL. "Republican Women of State in Convention," *Los Angeles Times*, June 21, 1925.

11. Arnold draft, p. 79. "Republican Women of State in Convention," *Los Angeles Times*, June 21, 1925. Ralph Arnold to Harry Blair, date unk. RAP.

12. *Los Angeles Times*, October 23, 1925, p. 22. Innovative Interfaces; University Libraries, 2004. UCB-Music Poop 1925-K; OCLC#: 44920825. He became a Republican Party activist in Maryland and in May of 1928, he ran as a delegate supporting Frank O. Lowden over "Democrat" Herbert Hoover for the presidential primary May 5, 1928, *The News from Frederick, Maryland*, p. 9. There is a reference made by Hoover's secretary, Lawrence Richey, about a letter Sharpe had written to Koverman in 1927, but the letter failed to survive the "Koverman as subject" in the Hoover archives. Mr. Richey to Mr. MacCraken, July 13, 1927. HHPL. Ed Sharpe was a long-time employee of the Southern Pacific railroad, in charge of "development and colonization," who subsequently moved east to promote the burgeoning aeronautics industry with the Aviation Corporation. *San Bernardino County Sun*, November 5, 1925, p.1 and February 24, 1928, p. 8. Lucas went on to handle notable

cases, including the investigation into the alleged kidnapping of Aimee Semple McPherson, the controversial evangelist whose gatherings the Angeles Temple attracted a generation of devoted followers. *Heraldsburg Tribune*, July 2, 1926, p. 1.

13. Owned at that time by *Los Angeles Times* publisher Harry Chandler. Chandler unabashedly promoted his conservative views through the new medium of the airwaves in the guise of broadcasting community events, and as such, Ida Koverman's presentation fulfilled this mission par excellence. Leonard Pitt and Dale Pitt, *Los Angeles A to Z*, p. 415. Text of radio station KHJ and *Los Angeles Times* copy addressed to "Friends of Radio Land and of the Republican Women's Federation of California," October 23, 1925. RAP. *Los Angeles Times*, October 21, 1926, p. A5 reports that Ida Koverman was among the speakers.

14. *Los Angeles Times*, November 1, 1925, p. 19.

15. Ralph Arnold to Herbert Hoover, October 21, 1925. RAP.

16. Ralph Arnold to Herbert Hoover, October 21, 1925. RAP.

17. Ralph Arnold to P. E. McDonnell, May 25, 1925. RAP.

18. Ida Koverman to Ralph Arnold, December 2, 1925. RAP. Some could argue that to the extent that women were organized, primarily with the backing of big business interests, they were basically pawns of the real power brokers who controlled American politics and government through careful nurturing of the Hoover persona, with espousals of a humanitarian and philosophical ideological framework that shrouded the real motives of his worldwide business-industrial network. Motion-picture studios had a lot to gain from Secretary of Commerce Hoover's support. Radio, distribution, labor, taxes, antitrust, and Ralph Arnold's interest in the development of an oil depletion allowance were all a part of the policy potential. Such conspiratorial thinking explained the rise of Herbert Hoover and his Southern California connection to the Julian Petroleum stock scandal.

19. *Los Angeles Times*, August 2, 1925, p. 25.

CHAPTER 10: PETROLEUM AND PARTISANS

1. Alma Whitaker, *Los Angeles Times*, December 5, 1926. Undated copy in CBP.

2. The October 30 luncheon welcomed the public to meet Secretary Hoover. *San Bernardino County Sun*, October 24, p. 7, and 30, 1926, p. 1. As Mrs. Winn's stature rose within the women's club and partisan network, she and Ida Koverman frequently appeared together or were on the lists of attendees or as special guests in events throughout the Southland. *San Bernardino County Sun*, October 30, p. 12, and October 31, 1926, p. 22.

3. *San Bernardino County Sun*, October 31, 1926, p. 22. Misspelled as Ida "Coverman" in a letter from Mabel Walker Willebrandt to Dearest Winnie, September 13, 1926. MWWLOC.

4. The Federation also supported the Swing-Johnson bill, which dealt with the Colorado River project's reservoir and Boulder Dam, and "unequivocally" supported "that great Republican principle of protective tariff." *San Bernardino County Sun*, October 31, 1926, p. 22.

5. Ida Koverman to Herbert Hoover February 7, 1925 referenced in February 16, 1925 letter from Ralph Arnold to Mr. L. R. Richey, "Matters to be taken up with Mr. Hoover." RAP. Various sources including USC yearbook, professional indexes, and newspapers.

6. Ralph Arnold to Mr. Fayette B. Dow, Washington, DC, date unknown. Ralph Arnold, "Laying Foundation Stones, III," p. 308. Ralph Arnold to President Coolidge via *Los Angeles Times* wire, June 12, 1925. RAP.

7. Ralph Arnold to Herbert Hoover, April 30, 1926. RAP.

8. Ralph Arnold to Herbert Hoover, April 30, 1926. RAP. Jules Tygiel, *The Great Los Angeles Swindle: Oil, Stocks, and Scandal During the Roaring Twenties*, p. 167.

9. John Buntin, *L. A. Noir*, p. 30; John F. Booth to Ralph Arnold, June 1, 1926. RAP.

10. James W. Everington to Ralph Arnold, February 4, 1926. RAP.

11. Ida Koverman to Ralph Arnold, December 2, 1925. Ralph Arnold to Lawrence Richey, November 18, 1925. RAP.

12. Lorin L. Baker, *That Imperiled Freedom*, p. 71. Before becoming President Coolidge's first Cabinet appointment, Wilbur was an attorney, a Superior Court judge, and Chief Justice of the California Supreme Court. Ralph Arnold to Louis B. Mayer, September 1, 1926. Christopher Finch and Linda Rosenkrantz, *Gone Hollywood: The Movie Colony in the Golden Age*, p. 253. Charles A. Javry/Davry to Louis B. Mayer, chair of Finance Committee, Republican County Central Committee October 3, 1926. RAP.

13. Scott Eyman, *Lion of Hollywood: The Life and Legend of Louis B. Mayer*, p. 141.

14. J. Edgar Hoover to Ralph Arnold, June 2, 1926. RAP. *Los Angeles Times*, September 2, 1925, p. A2.

15. Charles Higham, *Merchant of Dreams: Louis B. Mayer, MGM and the Secret Hollywood*, p. 122; Jules Tygiel, *Great Los Angeles Swindle*, pp. 180–85; 202.

16. Jules Tygiel, *Great Los Angeles Swindle*, pp. 7; 180; 301–2. *Los Angeles Evening Herald*, July 11, 1930, p. 1.

17. Scott Eyman, *Lion of Hollywood*, p. 136; Jules Tygiel, *Great Los Angeles Swindle*, p. 180; Charles Higham, *Merchant of Dreams*, p. 121.

18. Ralph Arnold to Ida R. Koverman, July 13, 1927. RAP. The Montana company was having trouble of it's own though, enough that Arnold tried to reassure local residents the company was doing well. *Billings Gazette*, July 23, 1927, p. 5.; *Independent Record*, Helena, Montana, August 11, 1927, p. 6.; *Havre Daily News*, January 10, 1928, p. 1.

19. " . . . which we are trying to work out and cannot tolerate the WJJD program. We want a new affiliation combining WQK and WMBB with WEBH. Our present main hookup on the same wavelength three hundred sixty five point six. Chief vitally interested in this matter and I want the people in Washington to know his interest. What we want is thr [sic] removal of WJJD from the three hundred sixty five point six wage length and WOK and WBBM brought up to that wave length with WEBH. This is the only real radio hookup Chief has and we are certainly entitled to have one good clear channel, which they have given to the *Chicago Tribune Daily News and Journal*. Our chief competitor is the oldest station in Chicago and probably the best." Louis B. Mayer telegram from Culver City to Ida Koverman in Washington, DC, December 2, 1927. RAP.

20. Eyman, *Lion of Hollywood*, p. 140.

21. Citing an account he wrote for October 7, 1928. Ralph Arnold, "Laying Foundation Stones, III," p. 315. July 10, 1931, Progressive Finance Corp. v. Vining, 115 Cal. App. 423 (1931). Her firm was Willebrandt Horowitz.

22. Lawrence Richey to Ralph Arnold, September 4, 1931. RAP.

23. Scott Eyman, *Lion of Hollywood*, p. 135–6

CHAPTER 11: KINGMAKER, 1928

1. Ronald Brownstein, *The Power and the Glitter: The Washington-Hollywood Connection*, p. 19.

2. The newsletter was the brainchild of its editor Mrs. Florence Collins Porter, who had been a journalist with the *Los Angeles Herald* and *California Outlook*. Issue referenced as December 17, 1927, in *Modesto News-Herald*, January 10, 1928, p. 12. Also mentioned were Mrs. Charles Van de Water and Nellie Kelley. "Official Organ Launched," February

19, 1928, *Los Angeles Times*. See Ralph Arnold, "Laying Foundation Stones, Pt. III," p. 303. *California Elephant*, April 1928, p. 5. CBP.

3. The *California Elephant* detailed the activities in, "People One Meets at Headquarters," noting the "large number of trained workers" who bustled about setting up and attending luncheons and committee meetings. *California Elephant*, April 1928, p. 5. CBP.

4. Ida Koverman to Ralph Arnold, February 25, 1928. RAP.

5. Kyle D. Palmer, *Los Angeles Times*, April 8, 1928, p. B4. Mayer's speech was on April 26, 1928. Ray Lyman Wilbur, *Memoirs*, p. 388.

6. *Official Report of the Nineteenth Republican National Convention*, p. 70. *Los Angeles Times*, June 17, 1928, p.3; Dorothy M. Brown, *Mabel Walker Willebrandt*, p. 230.

7. *Los Angeles Times*, June 17, 1928, p.3. Ida Koverman to Mrs. Robert (Clara) Burdette, May 8, 1928. CBP.

8. *Los Angeles Times*, June 4, 1928, p. A2.

9. *Los Angeles Times*, June 10, 1928, p. A2. Welland R. Gordon, "Californians Paint Town, Kansas City, But poppy and orange hues supplant traditional color when native sons hit Kansas City," paper unk. June 10.

10. *Los Angeles Times*, June 7, 1928, p.2; June 10, 1928, p. 2; June 12, 1928, p. A4. The other women alternates were Effie Easton (San Francisco); Edith Weir Van de Water (Long Beach); Sarah E. Kellogg (Van Nuys); Desire Fricot (Angels Camp); Gussie Stewart (Auburn); Mrs. E. N. Brown (San Francisco); and Mrs. Howard C. Dunham (San Diego). The men were Buron Fitts, Frank F. Flint, and John R. Quinn from Los Angeles; and Mark L. Requa, Marshal Hale, James Rolph Jr., and Will J. French from San Francisco. Welland R. Gordon, "Californians Paint Town," *ORNRNC*, p. 51.

11. *Los Angeles Times*, June 13, 1928; *ORNRNC*, p. 177; 185.

12. Ralph Arnold, "Laying Foundation Stones, III," pp. 313–14. The newly elected members of the national committee included William H. Crocker and Mrs. O. P. Clark, who also made it on to the executive committee. C. C. Young was selected to the committee designated to notify Hoover of his candidacy, and Willebrandt similarly for Curtis. *ORNRNC*, pp. 254–55. California's delegation was represented on various committees, including C. C. Teague on the Committee on Resolutions and Buron Fitts on the Committee of Vice Presidents of the Convention.

13. Ralph Arnold to Herbert Hoover, July 10, 1928. RAP; Ida Koverman to George Akerson, July 16, 1928. HHPL.

14. *St. Louis Post-Dispatch*, July 10, 1928, p. 2.

15. Ida Koverman to Ralph Arnold, July 18, 1928. RAP. Citation includes previous paragraph.

16. Henry M. Robinson to Ralph Arnold, August 19, 1928; Ralph Arnold to Arthur S. Crites, September 4, 1928. RAP.

17. Ida Koverman to Herbert Hoover, August 2, 1928; Ida Koverman to Herbert Hoover c/o Miss Shankey, August 11, 1928. Ida Koverman to Hon. Herbert Hoover, August 11, 1928. HHPL. *Los Angeles Examiner*, August 6, 1928.

18. William G. Bonelli to Herbert Hoover, August 10, 1928; Ida Koverman to George Akerson, August 14, 1928. HHPL. Ida Koverman to George Akerson, August 13, 1928; George Akerson to Ida Koverman, August 14, 1928; Ida Koverman to George Akerson, August 15, 1928. Hoover's party included Mr. and Mrs. Hoover, Allan Hoover, William J. Donovan, George Barr Baker, and Mark Requa. RAP.

19. "Women to Aid Hoover Fight," *Los Angeles Times*, September 9, 1928, p. C25. Ralph Arnold, "Laying Foundation Stones, III," pp. 313–14.

20. "The Watchman," *Los Angeles Times*, p. A1; *Los Angeles Examiner*, September 12, 1928.

21. *Los Angeles Examiner*, September 12, 1928. Ida Koverman offered her perspective to Arnold about the meeting, noting that Pasadena's William H. Archdeacon and his cohorts in the Ninth District were aided and abetted by Ed Dickson, who tried to defeat her for secretary. Archdeacon had served as president of the Pasadena chamber of commerce, was a member of the Republican County Committee, and was chair of the City Protective Association.

22. Arnold's handwritten attribution would not make it into the final version of his account detailing the Hoover movement. It remains hidden as a scrap embedded within his drafts of the article in the Ralph Arnold Papers at the Huntington Library.

23. Ida Koverman to Ralph Arnold, September 11, 1928.

24. Harriet B. Blackburn, "Ida Koverman Makes Name in Hollywood's Movies, Though Not on Screen," *Christian Science Monitor*, October 12, 1950, p. 12.

25. Various entries related to Ralph Arnold and Ida Koverman in RAP. Ida Koverman to Lawrence Richey, September 27, 1928; Lawrence Richey to Ida Koverman, October 2, 1928. HHPL.

26. Display ad, *Los Angeles Times*, October 19, 1928, p. 3; *Los Angeles Times* October 11, 1928, p. 10; Ida Koverman to Mark Requa, October 12, 1928. RAP. *Los Angeles Times*, October 28, 1928, p. C8. *Los Angeles Times*, October 28, 1928, p. 44.

27. Famous tenor Joseph Diskay was the performer. *Los Angeles Times*, October 22, 1928, p. 5. Lawrence Richey to Mr. George B. Bush, December 3, 1928. HHPL.

28. Lawrence Richey to Ida Koverman, November 17, 1928. Koverman as Executive Secretary Republican State Committee, Alexandria Hotel. George B. Bush to Lawrence Richey, November 27, 1928; Lawrence Richey to Mr. George B. Bush, December 3, 1928. HHPL.

29. Ralph Arnold, "Laying Foundation Stones, III," p. 313; 318, and scrap of paper cut from final draft in Arnold papers.

CHAPTER 12: MATCHMAKER: POLITICS AND PICTURES

1. Neal Gabler, *An Empire of Their Own: How the Jews Invented Hollywood*, p. 115.

2. Myra Nye, "Home, Club and Civic Interests of Women; Women Rally at Celebration; Join with Men in Banquet Following Election; Flattering Encomiums Made by Male Cohorts," *Los Angeles Times*, November 25, 1928, p. C20.

3. George B. Bush to Lawrence Richey, November 27, 1928. RAP; Myra Nye, *Los Angeles Times*, November 25, 1928.

4. Ralph Arnold to Herbert Hoover, November 14, 1928. RAP; Ida Koverman to George Akerson/Herbert Hoover, November 16, 1928; George Akerson to Ida Koverman, November 16, 1928. HHPL.

5. *San Bernardino County Sun*, December 15, 1928, p. 13; *Los Angeles Times*, February 23, 1929, p. 25. Ida Koverman to Lawrence Richey, January 28, 1929. HHPL.

6. Ida Koverman to Lawrence Richey, January 28, 1929. HHPL. Glen Jeansonne, *The Life of Herbert Hoover: Fighting Quaker 1928–1933*, p. 56.

7. Ida Koverman to Lawrence Richey, January 28, 1929; L. M. Eginton, secretary to Ida R. Koverman to Lawrence Richey, February 2, 1929. HHPL. Eginton sent clippings at

Koverman's request to Richey regarding Louis B. Mayer's disclaimer that he was offered a diplomatic post in Turkey along with details of Hoover's Inaugural Special trains. The Los Angeles County Central Committee apparently would finance the Union Pacific and the Palo Alto Chamber of Commerce would pay for the Southern Pacific; *Los Angeles Times*, February 25, 1929, p. 17.

8. *Los Angeles Times*, February 25, 1929, p. 17. All calendar dates for Hoover from *Public Papers of the Presidents of the United States, Herbert Hoover 1930 (Jan–Dec)*, US Government Office, Appendix E, June 1, 1999; Steven J. Ross, *Hollywood Left and Right: How Movie Stars Shaped American Politics*, p. 64. Arthur Hachten, "Mayer Family Entertained by Hoovers," *Syracuse Journal*, March 14, 1929, p. 14.

9. Scott Eyman, *Lion of Hollywood*, p. 141.

10. Samuel Marx and Joyce Vanderveen, *Deadly Illusions: Jean Harlow and the Murder of Paul Bern*, pp. 199–200.

11. The name of Ernest Walker Sawyer; Ida Koverman to Lawrence Richey, February 6, 1929. HHPL; Steven Ross, *Hollywood Left and Right*, p. 64; Ida Koverman to M. L. Requa, noted in California state file, April 10, 1929; Willebrandt added another bit of advice, "Mayer also suggests that the President contact with W. R. Hearst who is coming east next week." Ida R. Koverman to Lawrence Richey, January 12, 1929, HHPL. Steven Ross and Scott Eyman, for example, suggest the lobbying for the Los Angeles IRS post was successful. Marius Moynier versus John P. Carter and Galen H. Welch, no. 6851-H; US District Court, Southern District of California, Central District, p. 3: Galen served as collector of internal revenue from April 1926 to June 30, 1933, and "left said office by expiration of his said term as Collector." Accompanying the trial was the Hearst press's dehumanization of Pantages's Greek origins, but when Jerry Giesler handled the victorious appeal to the California Supreme Court, Giesler disparaged the girl's character. Regardless, Pantages was a ruined man. Mrs. Pantages had troubles of her own, including an arrest and conviction for drunk driving and manslaughter.

12. Alma Whitaker, *Los Angeles Times*, December 2, 1928, p. C27. Maxine Davis, "Ladies Cause G.O.P. Worries: What to Do for Them Puzzles Politicians," *Pittsburgh Press*, January 20, 1929.

13. Willebrandt's resignation letter to Herbert Hoover dated May 26, 1929, effective June 15. Hoover responded May 28, 1929. Herbert Hoover: "Letter Accepting the Resignation of Mabel Walker Willebrandt as Assistant Attorney General," online by Gerhard Peters and John T. Woolley, *The American Presidency Project*. http://www.presidency.ucsb.edu/ws/?pid=22126. *Los Angeles Times*, June 12, 1929, p. A6. "Aid to Hoover Urged on Clubs: Republican Women Hear Pleas by Mrs. Koverman; Glad Mrs. Willebrandt has Quit Arduous Job," *Los Angeles Times*, June 12, 1929, p. A6.

14. Dorothy M. Brown, *Mabel Walker Willebrandt*, p. 229. She worked both in Los Angeles and in Washington, DC, on behalf Louis B. Mayer's interests with Congress and the Justice Department. Federal Bureau of Investigation FOIA subject file: Marlene Dietrich, 1942.

15. *Los Angeles Times*, June 12, 1929, and October 6, 1929; RNC's Mrs. Alvin T. Hart's lists of names to act as president of the corporation is in an undated note with a letter dated April 23, 1929. A penciled note carried the name of Miss Terhune; Ida Koverman to Lawrence Richey, August 26, 1929. HHPL.

16. Bosley Crowther, *Hollywood Raja*, p. 128; Handwritten chart, 1924, RAP. Charles Higham, *Merchant of Dreams*, p. 153.

17. Harriet B. Blackburn, *Christian Science Monitor*, October 16, 1950, p. 12.

18. Alma Whitaker, "Cards Show How Wind Blows," *Los Angeles Times*, December 26, 1929 p. A2, B10.

19. Unknown Author, possibly Edward Baber, to Ida Koverman, November 24, 1931. RAP. "There is no group more interested in the increased representation than the motion picture industry." Benton has been "unfairly and unjustly treated," while the community benefited. The men who could help him are "extremely busy and no opportunity is presented to inform them of the facts." He said, "I am writing you because I know how thoroughly informed you are in all these matters. I also know that if the matter was brought to the attention of <u>Mr. Mayer</u> with your favorable endorsement and rewards the deficit of behalf of the industry, therefore I hope that you will be good enough to render this service to your mutual friends which will be most gratefully appreciated." "In Hollywood with Patricia Dillon," *Brooklyn New York Standard Union*, July 5, 1930, p. 7.

20. Statement of Salary Paid to and Due Mrs. Ida R. Koverman, November 20, 1929. Typed note, likely from Ralph Arnold, and a list of payees attached.

21. Nellie Kelley to Ralph Arnold, May 17, 1929. Ralph Arnold to Nellie Kelley, August 10, 1929. List to whom letter regarding Miss Kelley sent, August 26, 1929: Clara M. Burdette, *Los Angeles Times* publisher Harry Chandler, Mrs. Oliver P. Clark, Judge Joe Crail, director Cecil B. DeMille, MGM's Louis B. Mayer, the attorneys Joseph Scott and Mendel B. Silberberg, and Charles C. Teague. Ralph Arnold to Col. Wm. Eric Fowler August 19, 1929; William Eric Fowler to Ralph Arnold, August 22, 1929. RAP.

22. *San Bernardino County Sun*, April 6, 1930, p. 15; Ralph Arnold to Ida Koverman, July 14, 1949. RAP.

23. A. W. McPherson to Ralph Arnold, December 8, 1929, RAP. Quote from a February 14, 1930, article by Arthur P. Jones in both the *Fresno Bee* and the *Modesto News-Herald*, and found in article by Roger M. Grace, "Thin-Skinned Buron Fitts Resigns as Lieutenant Governor to Become DA" in his column "Reminiscing," December 3, 2007, p. 7. *Metropolitan News-Enterprise*; metnews.com. Koverman telegraphed Lawrence Richey that Mr. Requa would follow up with a call to the president. January 27, 1930; typed summary of communications including attached telegram from Ida Koverman advising that Mr. Requa would call. HHPL.

24. Mabel Walker Willebrandt to Lawrence Richey, May 17, 1930. HHPL.

25. While Myra Nye's obituary attributes her and Louella Parsons as founding the Hollywood Women's Press Club in 1928, it's possible that the Women's Screen Press Club was, in fact, this same organization. Like Koverman, Myra Nye hailed from Ohio, but she had her own connection to the motion picture business. *Inside Facts of Stage and Screen*, October 4, 1930, p. 2. Other officers included Franc Dillon, re-elected president; Rosalind Shaffer as vice president; Daphne Marquette, treasurer; Ivy Wilson, secretary; and Shirley Moorman as auditor. Rosalind Shaffer was a syndicated columnist, novelist, and feature writer, publicist, and a scenarist described as a "seminal figure on the Hollywood scene." Complicating the identity further is that Jane McDonough elected president of the Women's Association of Screen Publicists as reported in the *Los Angeles Times*, January 6, 1929, p. 59, Steven J. Ross, *Hollywood Left and Right*, pg. 61.

26. "Rolph All Set for Drive," *Los Angeles Times*, October 17, 1930, p. 10 and October 26, 1930. Mrs. Van de Water was elected president; Mrs. Rolph Honored at Luncheon: Luncheon put on by Mrs. Louis B. Mayer. *Los Angeles Times*, December 9, 1930. Among the women power brokers there were Judge Georgia Bullock, Mrs. Oliver P. Clark, Mrs.

Charles Van de Water, Mrs. John C. Porter, Mrs. Thomas G. Winter, Mrs. Thornton (Mabel) Kinney, and film stars Marie Dressler and Mary Pickford. Among the men who brought their wives were Buron Fitts, Harry Chandler, Frank Merriam, L. J. Selznick, Jerry Mayer, Harry Rapf, Joe Crail, Charles Crail, Joseph Loeb, Edwin Loeb, Harry Culver, Fred Niblo, Eddie Mannix, Cecil de Mille, and Rabbi Edgar Magnin. *Los Angeles Times*, December 9, 1930, p. A3. Also present was Miss Grace Stoermer described by Alma Whitaker as, "the titan-headed chief of the Bank of Italy's woman's department at the Bank of Italy," and who was rising in capacity and esteem who "shows better leadership quality every year." Alma Whitaker, *Los Angeles Times*, date unk. CBP. *Los Angeles Times*, June 7, 1929 notes that in the interim the California Attorney General ruled that the motion picture industry is not under the eight-hour day. "Venice Woman's City Club Members to Have Charge of President's First Council," *Los Angeles Times*, September 15, 1929, pg. B8.

27. Louis B. Mayer's reference to Cecil B. DeMille came as their professional partnership was nearing its end. DeMille's three-year-three-picture contract with MGM was not renewed after the completion of *The Squaw Man*, the first sound but third version of the film. Myra Nye, "Women's Organizations Take in Louis B. Mayer—Many Promises Exacted From New Male Member," *Los Angeles Times*, March 30, 1930, p. B20. The first was Slats, from 1924 to 1928. Then, Jackie was the first whose roar was heard by an audience for MGM's first talking picture, *White Shadows on the South Seas*, directed by W.S. Van Dyke and starring Monte Blue. Slats was also the first lion to appear in Technicolor in 1932. http://www.digititles.com/content/the-story-behind-mgm-s-roaring-lion-logo

28. Lawrence Richey to Ida Koverman, January 23, 1930; Secretary of War Patrick J. Hurley to Ida Koverman, March 8, 1930. HHPL.

29. Summary of letter from Ida Koverman to Lawrence Richey, June 8, 1931. Summary of letter sent by Lawrence Richey from Ida Koverman to Secretary of State Henry Stimson, September 16, 1931. HHPL.

30. "The Watchman," *Los Angeles Times*, April 10, 1931, p. A9; Others included Judge Georgia Bullock, Mrs. Oda Faulconer, Mary Foy, and Mrs. Mary T. Workman. *Los Angeles Times*, May 17 and 27, 1931, p. A8. *Los Angeles Times*, October 13, 1933, p. A1.

CHAPTER 13: FRIENDS IN HIGH PLACES

1. Budd Schulberg, *Moving Pictures: Memories of a Hollywood Prince.*

2. November 24, 1930, Katherine Philips Edson to Hon. Hiram W. Johnson, HJPBL.

3. November 24, 1930, Katherine Philips Edson to Hon. Hiram W. Johnson, HJPBL.

4. "Rolph to Quit Old Post Today, Venice Woman Appointed to State Welfare Board," *Los Angeles Times*, January 3, 1931, p. 3.

5. After high school, she attended the Detroit Conservatory of Music and performed solos during a nine-month tour with the Thomas Normal Training School. The daughter of an Ovid, Michigan clothier, Elmer E. Cowan, and his wife Juliana (Levy), *Michigan State Gazetteer and Business Directory*, Ovid, Michigan, 1897, p. 1340. *California and Californians*, vol. 4, 1932, p. 324–25. *Ernest Holmes and the History of Religious Science* by Marilyn Leo on website Science of Mind Spiritual Heritage. Fenwicke L. Holmes, website. *California and Californians*, vol. 4, 1932, pp. 324–25.

6. "Film Clinic Plan Given," *Los Angeles Times*, November 9, 1928; "Women to Hear Film Officials," *Los Angeles Times*, February 21, 1930, p. A6.

7. Program announced on February 18, 1930 and then reported by Myra Nye in "Women to Hear Film Officials," in *Los Angeles Times*, February 21, 1930, p. A6. Mabel was often referred to as Mrs. Thornton Kinney and later as Dr. Mabel E. Kinney.

8. *Brisbane Courier*, November 27, 1929. With the advent of talking pictures, even fewer extras were employed. Edson suggested the need for an amendment to the IWC's motion picture order no. 16 where "extra" was defined as a woman or minor receiving $15.00 a day or less, or $65.00 a week or less; IWC minutes, January 20, 1930.

9. All references from IWC minutes are from April 20 and 30, 1931, p 7; pp. 2–3; 6–8; 9–11; 17–18; 22–3; June 1, 1931, pp. 2–3. Order No. 16 adopted in January 1926 for 5 years.

10. Katherine Philips Edson to unnamed source Nov. 2, 1932. Katherine Philips Edson to Mrs. Barnum and Executive Council, undated. KPE.

11. Lloyd or Dardis had the wrong name of the state commission. Tom Dardis, *Harold Lloyd: The Man on the Clock*, p. 260.

12. John Scott, "Ranks of Film Extras Slashed by NRA Action," *Los Angeles Times*, June 24, 1934, p. A1. Kerry Segrave, *Extras of Early Hollywood*, pp. 71–75; 78. Leigh Ann Wheeler, *Against Obscenity: Reform and the Politics of Womanhood in America, 1873–1935*, p. 152.

13. AFI catalog; Turner Classic Movies website; Anthony Slide, *Hollywood Unknowns*, p. 95.

14. National Lawyer's Guild, pp. 20–21: Report on Minimum Wage Enforcement, p. 5. Oral History of Hon. Gardiner Johnson, interviewed by Gabrielle Morris, 1983. Regional Oral History Office, Bancroft Library, University of California, Berkeley.

15. This resulted from practices that included removing IWC agents when they became too efficient; the stoppage of hotel payroll audits; not holding IWC or public hearings for two years; and Governor Merriam's failure to fill vacancies on the commission. The Guild also cited as evidence how one year after Kinney took over the IWC, she issued orders to employers that minimum wage laws were to be applied to a forty-eight-hour workweek. This meant that if the minimum wage were set at $16.00 per week and the employee worked a forty-hour week, the employee would receive only five-sixths pay. This directly contradicted the rules established by California's attorney general. *Report of the San Francisco Chapter of the National Lawyers Guild* (NLG); A. F. Gruger Papers, 1937; Meiklejohn Civil Liberties Institute, Berkeley, CA. Thanks to Jo Freeman for this important document. *Los Angeles Times*, October 9, p. 6, and October 27, 1939, p.13.

CHAPTER 14: SECRET MEETING, PART II

1. From "The Women Who Run the Men: Secretaries to Hollywood's Film Chiefs Are Key links in the Industry." *Variety*, October 7, 1942.

2. *Los Angeles Times*, January 29, 1932, p. A1; *San Bernardino County Sun*, April 22, 1932, p. 13; 24.

3. *Santa Cruz Sentinel*, June 16, 1932, p. 3; *Santa Rosa Press Democrat*, June 16, 1932, p. 7; *Los Angeles Times*, June 14, 1932, p. 2. Once again, she and the California delegation's reputation preceded them. Upon their arrival, the Associated Press distributed a cheery photograph of Koverman and the delegation. Nearly hidden behind her colleagues, she is identifiable by her characteristic cloche hat, round spectacles, and broad grin, standing next to Mabel Walker Willebrandt, Governor James Rolph, and Mark Requa. Another photograph prominently featured Koverman sitting with Requa.

4. *Los Angeles Times*, June 14, 1932, p. 2; *Modesto News-Herald*, June 17, 1932, p.2; cgi. cnn.com/ALLPOLITICS: Back in TIME for June 27, 1932.

5. *Los Angeles Times*, June 17, 1932, p. 4.

6. *Los Angeles Times*, July 13, 1932, p. 23. So was liberal Democrat, newspaper publisher of *The Sentinel*, Charlotte Bass. George Eells, *Hedda and Louella*, p. 130.

7. George Eells, *Hedda and Louella*. Ida Koverman shared her recollection of what happened in the wake of Paul Bern's death with MGM writer Sam Marx, and, according to Marx, her version is supported by Whitey Hendry. Virginia MacPherson, "Movie Lot Officer Has His Troubles," *Tucson Daily Citizen*, August 20, 1948.

8. Brown and Brown, *The MGM Girls*, p. 193.

9. His conversation with Ida Koverman in 1943 took place during their drive to Fort Ord for an MGM show. Subsequent accounts with a variety of details about the immediate aftermath, inquest, grand jury, and activities by law enforcement and MGM executives differ in their support or refutation of Marx's conclusions. Marx and Vanderveen, *Deadly Illusions: Jean Harlow and the Murder of Paul Bern*; Anthony Slide, *Hollywood Unknowns*, p 48.

10. Marx and Vanderveen, *Deadly Illusions*, pp. 255–56.

11. Brown and Brown, *The MGM Girls*, pp. 193–94.

12. Ida Koverman's grandniece Mary Louise Hawkins (Troffer), born January 12, 1924, had an appointment with Dr. Edward B. Jones during her extended visit in Culver City with her Aunt Ida in the 1930s. Author's interview with Mary Troffer, August 7, 2007, Palmdale, CA.

13. Brown and Brown, *The MGM Girls*, p. 193.

14. Marx and Vanderveen, *Deadly Illusions*, p. 200–201. If evidence about the accuracy of this conversation as Koverman described is lacking, perhaps its actual meaning is equivocal. Another view by Brown and Brown is that when the group agreed that Harlow was "obviously not guilty," the decision was made that Mayer would make himself and Harlow available to the DA, thus ensuring that "he'll drop the charges immediately." And, so, "it was done." Brown and Brown, *The MGM Girls*, p. 192. Scott Eyman, *Lion of Hollywood* spells it Blainie, p. 286. Described as the "notorious" and "principal villain" when the Burbank police had smashed up the Conference picket line and beat up the strikers. "Conference" is short for the Conference of Studio Unions (CSU) a progressive (and militant) group made up of painters, screen office employees, laboratory technicians, and service employees. Bernard Gordon, *Hollywood Exile: or How I Learned to Love the Blacklist*, University of Texas Press, 2013, p. 43.

15. *Oakland Tribune*, September 7, 1932, p. 2.

16. Marx and Vanderveen, *Deadly Illusions*, pp. 152–53.

17. *Monongahala Daily Republican* (PA) September 8, 1932, p. 6. One source says Silberberg was never formally Harlow's representative, but was noted as such for publicity purposes. One newspaper reported that Harlow was interviewed by police in the presence of Louis B. Mayer, Meyer [sic] Silberberg, Meyer's attorney, Bello, and Dr. Harold B. Barnard, one of her physicians. *Bakersfield Californian*, September 7, 1932, p.2.

18. *Oakland Tribune*, September 7, 1932, p. 2. *Star Press* (Muncie, Indiana) September 11, 1932, p. 1. *Monongahala Daily Republican* (PA) September 8, 1932, p. 6. *Los Angeles Times*, September 8, 1932, p. 2. *Bakersfield Californian*, September 8, 1932, p. 17. *Bradford Evening Star and Daily Record*, September 8, 1932, p. 1, 12.

19. *New York Times*, September 10, 1932, p. 18.

20. Marx and Vanderveen, *Deadly Illusions*, pp. 199–200; 202; 204–6.

21. *Los Angeles Times*, September 16, 1932, p. 18. At first, the coroner believed Millette to be thirty-eight years old. Marx and Vanderveen, *Deadly Illusions*, p. 252. *Marshfield News-Herald* (WI), September 17, 1932, p. 1; *San Bernardino County Sun*, September 17, 1932, p. 3.

22. *Pittsburgh Post-Gazette*, June 17, 1933, p. 9.

23. Irving Schulman, *Harlow*, p. 283. Virginia MacPherson, "Movie Lot Officer Has His Troubles . . . "

CHAPTER 15: WATER AND POLITICS

1. Helen Rose, *Just Make Them Beautiful: The Many Worlds of a Designing Women*, 1978.

2. Trip File, from E. H. Rathburn, December 18, 1931. HHPL. *Time* magazine, July 24, 2012, Time.com; Olivia B. Waxman, *A Brief History of U.S. Presidents and the Olympics*.

3. *Los Angeles Times*, August 6, 1932, p. 12 and August 7, 1932, p. E5.

4. *Hollywood Reporter*, January 10, 1933, p. 2. Filmsofthegoldenage.com-Jean Parker, "Cinderella Girl." James Robert Parish and Ronald L. Bowers, *The MGM Stock Company: The Golden Era*, p. 551; *Movie Classic*, January–July 1934, p. 67; 151.

5. *Los Angeles Times*, August 26, 1933, p. 6; *Los Angeles Examiner*, August 26, 1933. Thanks to Ned Comstock. Judge Georgia Bullock, Judge Oda Faulconer, Helen Laughlin, Mabel Cooper-Bigelow, Mab Copeland Lineman, Mrs. Edith Swarts, and Mrs. Samuel Blake, *San Bernardino County Sun*, August 28, 1933, p. 5. *Albuquerque Journal*, March 16, 1941.

6. *Los Angeles Times*, August 26, 1933, p. 6. Some of its champion swimmers were photographed spending time in Brooklyn.

7. *Los Angeles Examiner* and *Los Angeles Times*, August 26, 1933, p. 6.

8. Esther Williams, *Million Dollar Mermaid*, pp. 79–80.

9. Esther Williams, *Million Dollar Mermaid*, p. 82.

10. Esther Williams, *Million Dollar Mermaid*, pp. 88–90.

11. Esther Williams, *Million Dollar Mermaid*, pp. 94–95.

12. Esther Williams, *Million Dollar Mermaid*, pp. 174–75.

13. Hitchborn quoted in Royce D. Delmatier, Clarence F. McIntosh, Earl Waters, Eds. *The Rumble of California Politics*, p. 237. *San Bernardino County Sun*, October 15, 1932.

14. *Bakersfield Californian*, September 23, 1932; Steven J. Ross, *Hollywood Left and Right*, p. 69.

15. Royce D. Delmatier et al., *Rumble of California Politics*, p. 258. *Oakland Tribune*, September 9, 1932, p. 19 and September 25, 1932, p. 1; *Santa Rosa Press Democrat*, September 22, 1932, p. 1; *Los Angeles Times*, September 14, 1932, p. 17, and September 23, 1932, p. 19 and September 25, 1932, p. 6.

16. *Fresno Bee/ Republican*, September 30, 1932, p. 1.

17. Alma Whitaker, *Los Angeles Times*, September 11, 1932, p. 47; *Detroit Free Press*, August 31, 1932, p. 15; *Chicago Tribune*, August 31, 1932, p. 12; *Hartford Courant*, August 26, 1932, p. 8.

18. *Los Angeles Times*, August 29, 1932, p. 16 and September 1, 1932, p. 32 and October 12, 1932, p. 23; Alma Whitaker, *Los Angeles Times*, September 11, 1932, p. 47. *Harrisburg Telegraph*, October 11, 1932, p. 7.

19. *Los Angeles Times*, September 14, 1932, p. 17; Myra Nye, *Los Angeles Times*, October 16, 1932; CBP. Furthermore, she added, "None of the Democratic leaders has been able to give an answer to Calvin Coolidge's address. They have no program or system." One could argue that if anyone was listening at the time, Hopper's inability to interpret the reality of events around her or to call an election, she might not have been able to wreak

so much damage later on. *Los Angeles Times*, October 5, 1932, p. 17; *New York Times*, 13 October 1932; *Meridian Record*, November 4, 1932.

20. Ida Koverman to Lawrence Richey, October 5, 1932; Lawrence Richey to Ida Koverman, October 11 1932. Ida Koverman to Del Reynolds, October 16, 1935. HHPL.

21. Ida Koverman to Lawrence Richey, October 17, 1932; Lawrence Richey to Ida R. Koverman, October 18, 1932. HHPL. Myra Nye. *Los Angeles Times*, October 16, 1932; CBP. Mrs. Conrad Nagel, Darryl Zanuck, Sol Lesser, Edgar Magnin, Joe Crail, Harry Bolzer, Sam Bern, Robert Pacht, and many more. Listed by surname only: Enid Bennett, Doris Lloyd, Anita Page, Theda Bara, Julia Faye, Ida Cummings, among others.

22. The Grove was a 2,700-acre campground owned by the famed San Francisco Bohemian Club. Lawrence Richey to Ida Koverman, July 18, 1933. HHPL.

23. "Women's Club Faction Asks Writ of Control," *Los Angeles Times*, September 16, 1933 p. A2. This contest happened just five days after Mrs. Sunday's husband had jumped (or fallen) to his death from a San Francisco hotel. A year later one of her sons was killed in an automobile accident. "Breakfast Club Trial to Be Set," *Los Angeles Times*, October 3; 19, 1933, p. 7; *Los Angeles Times*, February 23, 1934, p. 25. *San Bernardino County Sun*, December 12, 1932, p. 3. Mrs. Fitts also ran unopposed and won the presidency of the Republican Study Club, while Nellie Kelley, was again elected as corresponding secretary.

CHAPTER 16: THE OTHER WIDOW

1. Matthew Kennedy, *Marie Dressler: A Biography*, p. 182.

2. *Los Angeles Times*, June 7, 1933, p. 11.

3. *Los Angeles Times*, January 22, 1933, p. 16; February 12, 1933, p. 35. Howard Charles Koverman was a student at the University of California, earning a BA in geography in 1941 and a master's degree in 1945; Email to author from Howard C. Koverman, 2003.

4. *Los Angeles Times*, July 23, 1933, p. 10.

5. *Los Angeles Examiner*, October 26, 1953. *Los Angeles Times*, August 5, 1934, p.33.

6. *Reading Times* (PA), August 29, 1934, p. 16. *Los Angeles Times*, July 30, 1934, p. 4. Aljean Harmetz, *The Making of the Wizard of Oz*, pp. 46–47.

7. In 1948, she was living at 6691 Whitley Terrace while Vignola was at 6697 Whitley Terrace. The records are ambiguous. According to a file for the Committee for the South in Los Angeles Supervisor John Anson Ford's papers, Ida Koverman's address on January 15, 1949 was 6697 Whitley Terrace, but one website has Vignola living there when he died in the 1953. Loretta Parsons, *San Antonio Light*, December 2, 1933.

8. *Who's Who In California*, 1943–1944. There are several explanations about where the name for the Academy's statue "Oscar" came from, but the most accepted is Margaret Herrick. However, it is plausible, given Ida R. Koverman's proximity to Louis B. Mayer, that she suggested the name of her by then ex-husband. US Census, 1920; District 0040. Cryptically identified as "R. Ranous," *Los Angeles Times*, July 6, 1923, p. 14. *Variety*, July 3, 1934, p. 2. *Honolulu-Star-Advertiser*, July 8, 1934, p. 9. Herbert Hoover to Ida Koverman, September 3, 1934; Miss Spooner Secy. to Hoover, September 3, 1934. HHPL.

9. *Cincinnati Enquirer*, May 25, 1924, p. 11. That newspaper reported on July 24, 1934, p. 14 that he was six feet tall and fifty-four years old. Harry N. Koverman, sister Mrs. Rudolph Ruzicka, Mrs. Bush Parker, sister Mrs. Genevieve Van Ausdale of Cincinnati, and Mrs. C. R. Chamberlain of Toledo. A Jessie Koverman married a George C. Child, but divorced him in 1937, and resumed using of her maiden name. *Cincinnati Enquirer*, November 11, 1926, p. 21.

10. *Chronicle-Telegram*, Elyria, Ohio, July 20, 1934, p. 5.

11. *Los Angeles Times*, September 15, 1934, p. 15. Gregg Mitchell, *Campaign of the Century*, p. 238; *Petaluma Argus-Courier*, September 29, 1934, p. 2.

12. *Pittsburgh Post-Gazette*, October 2, 1934, p. 1. *Indian Valley Record*, October 25, 1934, p. 1.

13. *Los Angeles Times*, October 31, 1934, p. 7.

14. *Fresno Bee/Republican*, November 1, 1934, p. 4. *St. Louis Star and Times*, October 22, 1934, p. 4. *Albany Democrat-Herald*, November 1, 1934, p. 1.

15. Michael Zmuda, *The Five Sedgwicks*, p. 223. *Los Angeles Times*, June 3, 1934, p. 48. *Movie Classic*, Jan-Jul 1934, p. 154. Biscailuz was responsible for the 1929 reorganization of the State Motor Patrol and the later Highway Patrol system, and he pioneered a program of rehabilitation to put well-behaved prisoners to work on honor farms.

16. Alma Whitaker, *Los Angeles Times*, July 14, 1935, p. A1.

17. Mary Troffer interview with author, August 7, 2007.

18. "Film Youngsters Enroll in Studio," *Los Angeles Times*, March 17, 1935, p. A7.

19. Louella Parsons, *Fresno Bee/Republican*, November 28, 1933, p. 22.

CHAPTER 17: "TIFFANY TRADEMARK"

1. *Buffalo Courier Express*, January 12, 1937, p. 13.

2. Preservation.lacity.org.

3. Harriet B. Blackburn, "Ida Koverman Makes Name in Hollywood's Movies, Thought Not on Screen," *Christian Science Monitor*, October 16, 1950, p. 12.

4. Hedda Hopper, *The Whole Truth*, p. 267.

5. Hedda Hopper, *The Whole Truth*, p. 267.

6. Vivaudou, Inc. was a formerly renowned name associated with European scents, but after legal troubles, the company was picked up by an American manufacturer that coordinated rollouts of products with movie releases. "Possibly a fictitious name; established by V. Vivaudou, Louis B. Mayer, and E. B. Hatrick in Paris in 1935 and later in Beverly Hills, CA." Hatrick was the International Secretary of International Film Service, a reporter, telegraph editor, UP bureau manager, and an editor of Hearst syndicate. Perfume Intelligence-The Encyclopedia of Perfume; *American Women, 1935–36*; *Motography*, September 1, 1917, p. 463. *Motion Picture News*, March 1, 1924, p. 972. H. C. Koverman incorporated General Bottle Jobbers, Inc., in 1934.

7. *Lansing State Journal*, November 17, 1954, p. 25

8. *Los Angeles Herald Examiner*, November 8, 1933.

9. Robert M. W. Vogel oral history, p. 101.

10. Charles Higham, *Merchant of Dreams*, p. 1; Ida Koverman didn't get a vote in the Academy Awards, but Vogel said she encouraged members to attend showings of short subjects and to attend viewings of nominated films. Vogel oral history, pp. 147, 313.

11. Adrian Kragen, *A Law Professor's Career: Teaching, Private Practice and Legislative Representative, 1934–1989*, interview by Carole Hicke, 1989. Oral History Center, the Bancroft Library, University of California, Berkeley, 1991, p. 324. *Standard-Examiner*, July 11, 1938, p. 8. *Bakersfield Californian*, August 4, 1938, p. 18. Britton's Hollywood career suffered little for his part in the scheme, and he became known as Layne "Shotgun" Britton as a Hollywood makeup artist.

12. *Los Angeles Times*, October 19, 1935, p. 29; *Waterloo Daily Courier* (Iowa) April 16, 1937; *Desert Sun*, March 15, 1983, p. 2. *Philadelphia Inquirer*, May 6, 1936, p. 6. "The Unsung Joe: Where bit-part actors go when they die," *Los Angeles Times*, December 11, 1937, p. 36 and December 21, 1937, p. 11.

13. *Modesto Bee*, Nov. 5, 1937. *Los Angeles Times*, December 13, 1940.

14. *Oakland Tribune*, Sep 27, 1939, p. 29; *Santa Ana Register*, December 8, 1939, p. 11. *Oakland Tribune*, April 11, 1943, p. 61.

15. *Los Angeles Times*, December 27, 1933, p. 21. *Oakland Tribune*, December 27, 1933, p. 6.; *Big Spring Daily Herald* (TX), July 27, 1934, p. 4. Louella Parsons, *Fresno Bee/Republican*, November 28, 1933, p. 22.

16. *Los Angeles Times*, March 14, 1934, p. 22; *Motion Picture Herald*, December 1933–March 1934. Even if Ida Koverman's mentoring didn't guarantee stardom, her efforts didn't go unnoticed. Dan Dietz, *The Complete Book of 1940s Broadway Musicals*.

17. *Los Angeles Times*, November 28, 1938, p. 10; November 29, 1938, p. 19; "Pianist Dalies Frantz Wins 'Flight Command' Role," *Los Angeles Times*, March 29, 1939, p. 13; August 20, 1939, p. 53.

18. *Hartford Courant*, July 5, 1939, p. 16.

19. *Los Angeles Times*, August 9 and 11, 1939, p. 9. *Pittsburgh Press*, October 9, 1939, p. 13 and May 13, 1940, p. 18; *Akron Beacon*, September 27, 1939, p. 10. The following year, a humorous article featured Frantz alongside stars Jeanette MacDonald and Eleanor Powell describing their troublesome idiosyncrasies. MacDonald swayed while she sang, and Powell couldn't keep her feet still when she sang. Frantz unconsciously hummed while he played the piano, which caused havoc with the studio's sound system. *Oakland Tribune*, October 3, 1941, p. 35.

20. *Los Angeles Times*, September 7, 1949, p. 46.

21. *Honolulu Star-Advertiser*, March 8, 1934, p. 6. *Los Angeles Times*, April 17, 1934, p. 13 and September 8, 1934, p. 9; *Oakland Tribune*, October 14, 1934, p. 65. Originally entitled "Ambulance Call." Producer Lucien Hubbard, *Los Angeles Times*, November 28, 1934, p. 17; *Oakland Tribune*, November 30, 1934, p. 22.

22. MGM Weekly Stock Talent Report, February 11, 1935, All Executives, Casting Department. HHPAMPAS. Either as William or Bill Henry. His brother Thomas Browne Henry also found steady work as a character actor. *Santa Rosa Press Democrat*, May 12, 1943, p. 12.

23. Kay Mulvey, of MGM's publicity department suggested Ramsey Taylor, but Koverman's choice stuck. Linda J. Alexander, *Reluctant Witness: Robert Taylor, Hollywood, and Communism*, pp. 87–8. *Daily Illinois*, November 1, 1940; *Lansing State Journal*, November 17, 1954, p. 25.

24. Linda J. Alexander, *Reluctant Witness*, p. 88.

25. "Hitting Hollywood On High with Hamm Beall," Harry Hammond (Hamm) Beall, *Hollywood*, January–December 1937, pp. 144–45.

26. Linda J. Alexander, *Reluctant Witness*, pp. 142–43. *Lodi-News Sentinel*, May 15, 1939, p. 1.

27. *Los Angeles Times*, April 28, 1933, p. A2. *Pittsburgh Post-Gazette*, February 8, 1934, p. 18; *Los Angeles Times*, January 5, 1934, p. 11 and January 26, 1934, p. 12 and February 16, 1934, p. 11.

28. Lyn Tornabene, *Long Live the King, A Biography of Clark Gable*, p. 122.

29. Lyn Tornabene, *Long Live the King*, p. 124.

30. Brown and Brown, *The MGM Girls*, pp. 65–66.

31. Brown and Brown, *The MGM Girls,* pp. 217–18.

32. Stephen Michael Shearer, *Beautiful: The Life of Hedy Lamarr.* Q & A with Patrick Agan, February 13, 2007; Andre Soares, Alternative Film Guide.

33. *Los Angeles Times,* April 21, 1940, p. 72.

CHAPTER 18: TROUBLED TENORS AND SUPERSTAR SOPRANOS

1. Gail Lulay, *Nelson Eddy: America's Favorite Baritone,* p. 39.

2. Harriet B. Blackburn, "Ida Koverman Makes Name in Hollywood's Movies, Thought Not on Screen," *Christian Science Monitor,* October 16, 1950, p. 12. Hertzel Weinstat and Bert Wechsler, *Dear Rogue: A Biography of the American Baritone, Lawrence Tibbett,* p. 96.

3. Hedda Hopper, *The Whole Truth,* p. 117–8. Robert M. W. Vogel oral history. David Shipman, *Judy Garland,* p. 45

4. Ross Hawkins, "Reel Life in Culver City, Marion Bell Remembered in Culver Historical Highlights," *Culver City Historical Society,* vol. 19, no. 1; Winter 1998.

5. Weinstat and Wechsler, *Dear Rogue,* pp. 183–201. Lawrence Tibbett Jr. interview with Sharon Rich.

6. Based on the Franz Lehar operetta *Gypsy Love* with music by Herbert Stothart, MGM's musical director. Weinstat and Wechsler, *Dear Rogue,* pp. 183–201.

7. Tip Poff, "That Certain Party," date and paper unk. *Los Angeles Times,* April 22, 1935, p. 13.

8. Anne Carre, widow of Art Director Ben Carre told Ross Hawkins. *The Fifth-Place Finisher,* May 25, 2006 by Ross Hawkins; from thefrontpageonline.com. *Los Angeles Times,* November 28, 1937, p. 71.

9. Edward Baron Turk, *Hollywood Diva: A Biography of Jeanette MacDonald,* pp. 77, 132, 135–6; 175–77; 189.

10. Edward Baron Turk, *Hollywood Diva,* pp. 177, 181, 187.

11. *Lansing State Journal,* November 17, 1954, p. 25.

12. Jane Ellen Wayne, *The Golden Girls of MGM, Glamour and Grief,* p. 12. Gail Lulay, *Nelson Eddy,* p. 50.

13. Maceddy.com. January 28, 2016.

14. *Perth Sunday Times* (WA), December 13, 1936, p. 13.

15. "Million Dollar Voice," *Time Magazine,* August 6, 1951.

16. Tom Johnson and David Fantle, "Reel to Real," *Senior Times,* August 1, 1998. Howard Thompson, "Lanza, the Bonanza, New Singer a Gold Mine for Himself and Metro," *New York Times,* May 6, 1951, p. X4.

17. *Mario Lanza: The Best of Everything,* March 2017, written, produced, directed by Alan Byron of Screenbound Entertainment. It's also not clear if she told him, "Learn opera and stick to it. If you make the Met, the world is yours—including Hollywood," or if she disagreed and instead thought, "He should get into pictures at once," and thus, "through her he was signed to a long-term film contract." Lanza told Hopper, "As an opera singer I'm still a baby at 27. Give me eight more years. But I want you to know that whatever success I may attain will be due to many people who helped me. Without Papa Innarelli, my parents, Sam Koussevitzky, Huff, Irene, Polly, Ida, Art Rush, yourself, I'd probably still be hauling pianos rather than accompanying them." "Lanza Tells of Struggle for Success," Hedda Hopper, *Los Angeles Times,* November 29, 1949, p. D8.

18. *Honolulu Star-Bulletin*, May 20, 1953, p. 23; Diana Altman, *Hollywood East: Louis B. Mayer and the Origins of the Studio System*, p. 240–41.

19. Harriet B. Blackburn, "Ida Koverman Makes Name," p. 12.

20. *Billboard,* January 10, 1948. *Shreveport Times*, February 4, 1954, p. 18; *Philadelphia Inquirer*, February 10, 1954, p. 34. *Sheboygan Press* (WI), November 25, 1952, p. 11; *Chicago Tribune*, November 4, 1965, p. 138.

21. *Los Angeles Times*, August 9, 1948, p. 31; Brandy Brent, "Carrousel," *Los Angeles Times*, November 2, 1948, p. 30. Brent misidentified Horty as Bessie.

22. Harriet B. Blackburn, "Ida Koverman Makes Name," p. 12.

CHAPTER 19: SWING VERSUS OPERA

1. Christopher Finch, *Rainbow*, 1975, p. 66.

2. Ted Gioia, *The History of Jazz*, p. 89.

3. Deanna Durbin, "Famous at Thirteen," *Spokesman Review*, Dec. 3, 1939.

4. *Winnipeg Tribune*, December 9, 1939, p. 35; David Shipman says that it was Sam Katz who had Durbin sing for Mayer over the telephone. David Shipman, *Judy Garland: The Secret Life of an American Legend*, p. 57. The Gumm Sisters were Mary Jane aka Susy, Dorothy Virginia "Jimmy" and Frances "Baby" Gumm aka Judy Garland.

5. Hedda Hopper, *The Whole Truth*, pp. 116–7.

6. *Los Angeles Times*, June 3, 1939, p. 33.

7. *Los Angeles Times*, June 17, 1938, p. 1; *Oakland Chronicle*, June 16, 1938, p. 17.

8. Hugh Fordin, *MGM's Greatest Musicals*, p. 6.

9. Christopher Finch, *Rainbow*, p. 55; David Shipman, *Judy Garland: The Secret Life of an American Legend*, p. 45.

10. Michael Balcon, *Michael Balcon Presents . . . A Lifetime of Films*, p. 104; Charles Higham, *Merchant of Dreams*, p. xi.

11. Sheilah Graham, "Take a Look Behind the Scenes at Women Who Make Film Wheels Spin," *Lincoln Sunday Journal and Star*, March 14, 1937.

12. Christopher Finch, *Rainbow*, p. 54; Brown and Brown, *The MGM Girls*, p. 177. David Shipman, *Judy Garland: The Secret Life*, p. 45.

13. David Shipman, *Judy Garland: The Secret Life*, p. 51. John Fricke in his *Judy Garland: A Portrait in Art & Anecdote* says that the first two of the auditions were before Al Rosen represented Garland. It's not clear when Al Rosen began to officially represent Judy Garland, but he was stewarding her around the complex of movie studios in Los Angeles. In August of 1935, his formal alliance with her was rejected in an unsuccessful petition to the Superior Court to enter into a contract with the twelve-year-old to serve as her manager for motion-picture and stage work. The court ruled that it didn't have jurisdiction to approve a contract involving a minor and a manager who would receive a commission for work he obtained on her behalf. *Los Angeles Times*, August 9, 1935, p. 20. *Bluefield Telegraph*, November 4, 1935, p. 6. Hedda Hopper supports Judy Garland's version. She says that it was Lew Brown who spotted the Gumm Sisters performing at the Cal-Neva Lodge in Lake Tahoe, and he then called agent Al Rosen, who knew Jack Robbins. Rosen set up a meeting with Robbins, who called Ida Koverman, who "flipped" at hearing Garland sing, after which she called Mayer, who grudgingly came in to see what all the fuss was about. Hedda Hopper, *The Whole Truth*, p. 117–8. Randy L. Schmidt, *Judy Garland on Judy Garland: Interviews and Encounters*, pp. 23, 238, 295.

14. Christopher Finch, *Rainbow*, p. 55; Gerold Frank, *Judy*.

15. David Shipman, *Judy Garland: The Secret Life*, p. 52. Gerald Clarke, *Get Happy: The Life of Judy Garland*, pp. 53–54. Richard Zelade, *Austin in the Jazz Age*, p. 201. John Fricke, *Judy Garland: A Portrait in Art & Anecdote*, p. 24.

16. John Fricke, *Judy Garland: A Portrait in Art & Anecdote*, p. 24.

17. Gerold Frank, *Judy*, pp. 62–3.

18. Gerald Clarke, *Get Happy*, p. 54. Hedda Hopper, *The Whole Truth*, p. 119. Brown and Brown, *The MGM Girls*, p. 16.

19. David Shipman, *Judy Garland: The Secret Life*, p. 46. Alternatively, Frank writes that on September 16, after Mayer heard Garland sing, he sent a memo to the legal department to prepare a contract. Hedda Hopper, *The Whole Truth*, p. 119; Clarke, *Get Happy*, p. 53–4.

20. David Shipman, *Judy Garland: The Secret Life*, p. 112.

21. *Winnipeg Tribune*, December 9, 1939, p. 35.

22. *Life Magazine*, December 28, 1936, p. 8. *Every Sunday* ad from deannadurbindevotees.com; various sources cite budget versus box office receipts.

23. Harriet B. Blackburn, "Ida Koverman Makes Name in Hollywood's Movies, Thought Not on Screen," *Christian Science Monitor*, October 16, 1950, p. 12. Gerald Clarke, *Get Happy*, p. 76

24. Gerald Clarke, *Get Happy*, p. 71. Christopher Finch, *Rainbow*, p. 70.

25. Gerald Clarke, *Get Happy*, pp. 77–78. Robert M. W. Vogel oral history. Hedda Hopper, *Off With Their Heads*, p. 260.

26. *Fresno Bee Republican*, June 14, 1944, p. 7. Tornabene, *Long Live the King*, p. 214.

27. Charles W. Tripplet on judygarlandcostumes.com.

28. Brown and Brown, *The MGM Girls*, p. 167, 173.

29. Brown and Brown, *The MGM Girls*, pp. 73, 167.

30. Hedda Hopper, *The Whole Truth*, pp. 123–4.

31. Hedda Hopper, *The Whole Truth*, p. 153; Frank, p. 153; Redlegagenda, November 20, 2015. Tip Poff, "That Certain Party," *Los Angeles Times*, January 17, 1937, p. D1.

32. Brown and Brown, *The MGM Girls*, p. 173.

33. Hedda Hopper, *Cincinnati Enquirer*, October 24, 1939, p. 15; Hedda Hopper, *Sioux Falls Argus Leader* (SD), December 10, 1944, p. 4; Gerald Clarke, *Get Happy*, p. 109.

34. Hopper incorrectly said the movie was Durbin's 1937 *100 Men and a Girl*, but the *Wizard of Oz* didn't premiere until August 1939. *First Love* premiered in November 1939. Hedda Hopper *Buffalo Courier-Express*, July 26, 1958, p. 7.

35. David Shipman, *Judy Garland*, p. 57. *Miami News*, March 19, 1939, p. 28.

CHAPTER 20: PARTY GIRLS

1. Betty Garrett, *Betty Garrett and Other Songs*, p. 94.

2. *Los Angeles Times*, May 31, 1931, p. 26.

3. "Younger Set Member Help Plan President's Ball," *Los Angeles Times* January 30, 1935, p. A7. Ida Koverman attended a tea held in his honor along with her long-time colleagues, Grace Stoermer, Mrs. Leiland Atherton Irish, Edith Van de Water, and Mrs. O. P. Clark. *Los Angeles Times*, August 18, 1935, p. 52.

4. "The Little Green Room, Ida Koverman," MGM *Studio Club News*, December 1941, and in Erin Hill, *Never Done: A History of Women's Work in Media Production*.

5. Sheilah Graham, "Take a Look Behind the Scenes at Women Who Make Film Wheels Spin," *Lincoln Sunday Journal and Star*, March 14, 1937. Charles Higham, *Merchant of Dream*, p. 41, 52; *Los Angeles Times*, January 10, 1937, p. D11. Among them, described as "Celebrities of Hollywood Greeted at Reception," were Jack Cummings (L. B. Mayer's nephew), Nelson Eddy, Cedric Gibbons (designer), Edwin Knopf (soon to be MGM producer in 1940 and brother of publisher Alfred), William Koenig, Eddie Mannix, Sam Marx, Robert Montgomery, Jerry Mayer, Ben Piazza, Harry Rapf (producer), Jack Robbins (MGM music publisher), Douglas Shearer (sound engineer and Norma Shearer's brother), Woody S. Van Dyke (versatile MGM director, Christian Scientist, and "the most ardent Roosevelt supporter in the film colony"), Eadie Adams (singer), Billie Burke (soon to be the Good Witch in *The Wizard of Oz*), Margaret Booth (film editor), Mary Carlisle (actress), Judy Garland, Hedda Hopper, Jean Harlow, Joan Marsh, Jean Parker, Eleanor Powell, Rosalind Russell, Barbara Stanwyck, Roger Edens, Clark Gable, William Powell, Jeannette MacDonald and husband Gene Raymond, Mendel Silberberg, Ben Thau, Robert Taylor, designer Adolph "Adrian" Greenburg, Gorin Igor, Norman Taurog, Frances Marion, and many others. Others included Clarence Brown, Leo Carrillo, Jack Chutck, Edward Childs Carpenter, George Converse, Harry Eddington, John Emerson, William Grady, Bernie Hyman, Lucien Hubbard, Oliver Hinsdell, Arthur Hornblow, Myrna Loy, Frank Orsatti, John Considine, Hunt Stromberg, William Thalberg, Ed Willis, Mitzi Cummings, Ruth Collier, Jane Draper, Mercedes DeAcosta, Bess Meredith, May Robson, Bea Roberts, Shirley Ross, Blanche Sewell, Gladys Unger, Florence Ryerson, Mary Garden, Edith Farrell, Charlotte Woods, Pat Casey, Gorin Igor, Leon Gordon, Denny Gray, Edmund Goulding, Leland Hayward, W. P. Henry (probably Whitey Hendry, MGM chief of police), and Edgar Allan Woolf. Ida Koverman's events provided opportunities for talent wherever she found it. Bess Gant, for example, was an African American "cook and caterer par excellence," but it was Koverman who "gave Bess cart banc [sic] to MGM and its stable of stars to write about and cater to," and some of the recipes published in her many cookbooks came "from top flight actresses and actors" from Hollywood's Golden Era. Libby Clark, "Food for Thought," *Los Angeles Sentinel*, October 7, 1982, p. C7.

6. *Los Angeles Times*, June 4 and 7, 1938; *Los Angeles Times*, October 24, 1937, p. 71.

7. David Shipman, *Judy Garland*, p. 64. *Harrisburg Telegraph*, September 3, 1942, p. 9. Joe Pasternak, *Easy the Hard Way*, p. 283.

8. Sophie Tucker, *Some of These Days*, pp. 293–94, 297. Ida Zeitlin, *Photoplay*, Oct–Dec 1937, p. 67. Cari Beauchamp, *Without Lying Down*, p. 330, 341.

9. *Los Angeles Times*, August 13, 1939, p. 8, 62. *Los Angeles Times*, March 16, 1941, p. D11.

10. *Los Angeles Times*, June 12, 1938, p. 62; *Los Angeles Times*, March 25, 1947, p. 10. Photo with misidentifications found in Brown's biography of Willebrandt and miscellaneous online sources.

11. *Philadelphia Inquirer*, June 25, 1943, p. 19. "Four Feted After Game," *Los Angeles Times*, January 9, 1938, p. D13.

12. Among the guests were Frances Marion, Hedda Hopper, Constance Collier, Laura Hope Crews, and the Countess de Maigret. Louella Parsons, *San Antonio Light*, June 24, 1935, p. 7A; *Gaffney Ledger* (SC), November 27, 1968, p. 3. Years later, Masarykova's brother, Czech foreign minister Jan Masaryk, died mysteriously one month after the communist "Czech coup," of February 1948. After World War II, Olga and her sister, Dr. Alice Masarykova, founded the National Council of Women of Free Czechoslovakia.

13. *Los Angeles Times*, February 17 and March 3, 1935, p. 43.

14. *Los Angeles Times*, May 18, 1945, p. 12. *Hobbs Flare* (NM), August 14, 1969, p. 9.

15. *Variety*, May 4, 1937, p. 5. *Los Angeles Times*, May 21, 1938, p. 6; June 18, 1939, p. 56; Hedda Hopper, *Pittsburgh Press*, May 25, 1941.

16. *Los Angeles Times*, May 17, 1938, p.34; Phyllis Powers, "Hollywood Reporter, Personal . . . but Not Confidential," *Screen & Radio Weekly*, p. 2 (referenced in *Detroit Free Press*, June 5, 1938, p. 65). *Los Angeles Times*, May 21, 1938, p. 6. *Los Angeles Times*, January 23, 1938, p. 60.

17. Louella O. Parsons, *Modesto Bee*, May 17–18, 1938, p. 3; *Fresno Bee/Republican*, May 17, 1938, p. 6; Power, *Screen & Radio Weekly*, p. 2.

18. *Look Magazine*, October 8, 1940, JGDB website.

19. Peter Evans, *Ava Gardner: The Secret Conversations*, pp. 252–53; Brown and Brown, *The MGM Girls*, pp. 56–57.

20. *Cincinnati Enquirer*, July 25, 1938, p. 2.

21. *Los Angeles Times*, September 4, 1938, p. 53. *Los Angeles Times*, August 1, 1937, p. 51. *Philadelphia Inquirer*, September 21, 1938, p. 17.

22. *Los Angeles Times*, March 30, 1941, p. 72 and May 7, 1950, p. 1; *Salt Lake Tribune*, January 2, 1941, p. 20.

23. *Los Angeles Times*, May 31, 1931, p. 26; *Los Angeles Times*, October 24, 1937, p. 71.

24. Marion Davies, *The Times We Had: Life with William Randolph Hearst*, pp. 290–92.

25. He introduced Mayer's poem with: "In their mysterious shadowy depths of the forest it is the softly whispering voices of the trees that speak serenely to the spirit of man and seem to say":

I am the forest of fir and pine,
Shadow and silence and peace are mine.
Mine are the springs and the rills and brooks,
Which rising in quiet hidden nooks,
Join hands with the river and joyously flow,
To wide spread of the stalwart trees,
And the scarlet and golden harmonies,
Of the tender shrubs which lay away,
Their garments of green for a summer day.
Mine are the paths by the riverside,
And the high steep trails over which you ride,
And the soft sweet meadow upon whose breast,
You lie down in delight to rest.
Mine is the glint of the golden sun,
Which sifts through the trees till the day is done;
Then the cool calm darkness—all too soon,
Dispersed by the light of the silvery moon.
Mine is the warmth of the summer glow.
Mine is the chill of the winter snow.
Mine is the magic of sun and air,
Which cures every ill and dispels every care.
I am the forest of fir and pine,
Which soothes and stimulates more than wine.
You need no nepenthe of vat or vine,

For the solace of silence and peace are mine.
"In the News," *San Antonio Light,* May 28, 1940, p. 1.

26. Ida Koverman to Kathryn Leighton, May 16, 1935 (a copy of which was re-sent to Hedda Hopper by Ida Koverman February 20, 1951); HHPAMPAS. Hedda Hopper, *The Whole Truth,* p. 63–64.

27. Hedda Hopper, *Los Angeles Times,* March 19, 1938, p. A7.

28. Grace Wilcox, "Screen & Radio Weekly, Hollywood Reporter, Personal . . . but Not Confidential," *Detroit Free Press,* April 10, 1938, p. 67; *Los Angeles Times,* March 20, 1938, p. D10. Hedda Hopper, *Los Angeles Times,* March 19, 1938, p. A7.

29. Hedda Hopper, *The Whole Truth,* p. 64.

30. George Eells, *Hedda and Louella: The Dual Biography of Hedda Hopper and Louella Parsons,* pp. 130–31.

CHAPTER 21: COMRADES, CANDIDATES, AND THE CANTEEN

1. "In the News," *San Antonio Light,* May 28, 1940, p. 1.

2. US Census, 1940. MGM's 1950 movie *Three Little Words* was about Kalmar, portrayed by Fred Astaire, and his partnership with Harry Ruby, played by Red Skelton.

3. *Social Justice,* November 18, 1940, pp. 12, 19.

4. Lawrence Richey to Ida overman, May 15, 1940, June 17, 1940. HHPL. *The Moguls and the Dictators: Hollywood and the Coming of World War II,* David Welky, p. 177. *Billboard,* August 30, 1952, p. 3 and September 22, 1951, p. 2.

5. Ida Koverman to Herbert Hoover, July 10, 1942. HHPL. *Biloxi Daily Herald,* April 21, 1942, p. 4. In 1944, he was a member of the National Citizens Political Action Committee, a nonpartisan organization promoting the election of Franklin Roosevelt, along with Edward G. Robinson, Orson Welles, and Ben Hecht. *Los Angeles Times,* July 4, 1942, p. 1.

6. Red Kann, "On the March," *Motion Picture Herald,* November 6, 1943, p. 16.

7. Red Kann, "On the March," *Motion Picture Herald,* November 6, 1943, p. 16. Linda A. Rapka, "Solidarity Forever! Local 47 in the Labor Movement; This Labor History Month we celebrate our connection to the greater labor movement. Musicians Open Hollywood Canteen, 'The house that labor built,'" AFM 47 archives.

8. Only to be soon loaned out for *Up In Arms. Salt Lake Tribune,* October 3, 1943, p. 57. "Hollywood Report," William Thomas Smith in *Phylon,* vol. 6, no. 1 1945, p. 13. *Wilmington Morning News* (DE), February 1, 1945, p. 9; *Joplin Globe* (MO) April 4, 1945, p. 10. Andy Williams, *Moon River and Me,* pp. 41–42.

9. *Christian Science Monitor,* October 16, 1950, p. 6. *Harrisburg Telegraph,* January 9, 1945, p. 7.

10. *Bakersfield Californian,* January 17, 1944, p. 1. *Rochester Democrat and Chronicle* (NY), May 24, 1944, p. 6; *Los Angeles Times,* June 15, 1944, pp. 1, 8. *Los Angeles Times,* October 5, 1944, p. 6. Ronald Brownstein, *The Power and the Glitter,* p.100.

11. *Santa Rosa News* December 22, 1944, p. 12.

12. Erksine Johnson, "Hollywood Column," *Bakersfield Californian,* October 3, 1945, p. 16.

13. Peter Evans, *Ava Gardner: The Secret Conversations,* pp. 135–6.

14. Cari Beauchamp, *Without Lying Down,* p. 343.

15. Steven J. Ross, *Hollywood Left and Right*, 141. Alexander, *Reluctant Witness*, p. 199.

16. *Bakersfield Californian*, February 5, 1944, p. 1. *Los Angeles Times*, February 8, 1944, p. 13.

17. Otto Frederick, *City of Nets*, p. 168; *Los Angeles Times*, May 6, 1944, p. 5. Hedda Hopper, *The Whole Truth*, p. 279.

18. Ida R. Koverman to Herbert Hoover, April 11, 1944 and June 5, 1944. HHPL. *Los Angeles Times*, April 19, 1944, p. 2.

19. Ida Koverman to Herbert Hoover, April 19, 1944. Ida R. Koverman to Herbert Hoover, June 5, 1944. HHPL.

20. Ida R. Koverman to Herbert Hoover, April 11 and June 5, 1944. HHPL.

21. *Brooklyn Daily Eagle*, June 28, 1944, p. 13; *Harrisburg Telegraph*, July 5, 1944, p. 9. Ida R. Koverman to Herbert Hoover, April 19, 1944. HHPL. Alfred Eckes, *American Conservatism: From Hoover to Nixon*, the Forum Series, 1973, p. 8. *Louisville Courier-Journal* (KY), September 21, 1944, p. 15; *Los Angeles Times*, October 16, 1944, p. 2.

22. *Oakland Tribune*, August 6, 1944, p.6. *Chula Vista Star*, October 13, 1944, p. 12. *Oakland Tribune*, August 11, 1944, p. 3. *Los Angeles Times*, October 12, 1944, p. 14.

23. Jennifer Frost, *Hedda Hopper's Hollywood*, p. 5, 14.

24. Mrs. Leiland Atherton Irish to John Anson Ford, July 3, 1942, JAF.

25. Ida Koverman to Fletcher Bowron, April 4, 1945; Louis B. Mayer to Fletcher Bowron, April 4, 1945. Fletcher Bowron Papers, Huntington Library.

26. Mary Behrens Flowers, Chapter "The Birth and the Bomb," in *Atomic Spice: A Partial Autobiography Mary Flowers*, Mary Behrens Flowers website.

27. Edward Baron Turk, *Hollywood Diva*, pp. 176–77.

28. *Los Angeles Times*, December 26, 1945, p. 1.

29. Willie Bioff, "The old brothel keeper who had found his social level among the aristocracy of Hollywood, testified in his trial for extortion that Joe had loaned Garsson $200,00.00." *Santa Cruz Sentinel*, July 16, 1946, p.2.

30. Murray W. Garsson Inc., also known as Murray W. Garsson Productions of New York City, was listed as a production company on 522 Fifth Avenue, and was active between 1920 and 1924. Metro was listed as a distribution company for Metro Pictures Corp. Also listed was Metro Pictures's president, who rented New York City's Lexington Theatre to stage "a number of scenes" for *Success*, directed by Ralph Ince and starring, among others, Mary Astor and Brandon Tynan. Silent Era website; afi.com.

31. *Los Angeles Times*, July 27, 1947, p. 1. See Robert Zom, *Cemetery John: The Undiscovered Mastermind of the Lindbergh Kidnapping*.

32. *Detroit Free Press*, November 13, 1945, p. 10.

33. "To put it more succinctly, they're the people who 'run' the men who run Hollywood." At 20th Century Fox, Bess Bearman, who "was a modified Ida Koverman in the Zanuck cabinet," and Dorothy Hechtlinger. Marcella Bennett was David Selznick's until she married Rabwin and soon was replaced by Frances Ingalls. Universal has Rosemary Foley as "Lady-in-Ambush, No. 6 on the list." From "The Women Who Run the Men: Secretaries to Hollywood's Film Chiefs Are Key Links in the Industry." *Variety*, October 7, 1942.

CHAPTER 22: MORAL CRUSADER

1. Carey McWilliams, "MRA: the 'World-arching Ideology,'" *The Nation*, July 31, 1948, p. 129.

2. *Spokesman-Review*, August 19, 1939, p.2.

3. "Group Debates Film Problems," Myra Nye, *Los Angeles Times* April 20, 1933, p. 21. LWWP. Other honored guests included Mrs. Mattison Boyd Jones, Mrs. Louise Ward Watkins, Dean Helen Matthewson Laughlin, Miss Grace Stoermer, Miss Mary Foy, and many others. *Los Angeles Times* April 20, 1933, p. 21.

4. "Group Debates Film Problems," Myra Nye, *Los Angeles Times* April 20, 1933, p. 21. LWWP.

5. "Group Debates Film Problems," Myra Nye, *Los Angeles Times* April 20, 1933, p. 21. LWWP.

6. Dr. Frank Buchman to Louis B. Mayer, June 27, 1939; July 11, [1939], Louis B. Mayer handwritten note to Dear Dr. Buchman. MRALOC. Harry "Manny" Strauss. *Advent Review and Sabbath Herald*, May 2, 1940, pp .6–7; *Wilton Bulletin* (CT) July 13, 1939, p. 13.

7. *Los Angeles Times*, June 22, 1939.

8. Daniel Sack, *The Reinventions of an American Religious Movement*; *Wilton Bulletin* (CT) July 13, 1939, p. 13; *Santa Ana Register*, July 20, 1939, p. 5. For discussion on Merritt, see Kathryn S. Olmsted, *Right Out of California*, p. 42.

9. *Santa Ana Register*, July 20, 1939, p. 5. Welford Beaton, *Hollywood Spectator*, July 22, 1939, vol. 14, no. 8, p 3. "Hays and Mayer Give Drive to 'Moral Rearmament Plan,'" *Film Daily*, July 17, 1939, p. 8. Turner Classic Movie website lists "Cece Broadhurst" as a technical advisor to the film. Rachel Crothers wrote her 1937 play *Susan and God*, inspired by a friend who was deeply involved with the MRA. Anita Loos adapted the story as the screenplay *Susan and God*, released in 1940. Charlotte Chandler, *Not the Girl Next Door: Joan Crawford, a Personal Biography*, p. 150; Filmlinc.org.

10. Photo caption: Foreman, timber worker, truck driver, and boss get together in the Moral Rearmament of their country at the Southern States Land and Timber Co. *Los Angeles Times*, September 29, 1969, p. 33. *Sarasota Herald Tribune*, November 28, 1939, p. 4.

11. *Santa Ana Register*, July 20, 1939, p. 5. Sack, *Moral Re-Armament*, p. 113. McWilliams, "MRA," p. 129. *Film Daily*, February 15, 1940, p. 1, 8. Louis B. Mayer to Frank Buchman, June 4, 1940. MRAPLOC.

12. *Oakland Tribune*, December 1, 1939, p. 29. *Berkeley Daily Gazette*, March 8, 1940, p. 3.

13. Telegram from Frank Buchman to Louis B. Mayer, June 1940; Frank Buchman letter to Mayer, February 12, 1940. MRAPLOC. *Fresno Bee/Fresno Republican*, June 2, 1940, p. 14. Chautauqua Institution Archives, Chautauqua, NY; Oliver Archive Center: The Miller Family Papers, Edison, Theodore Miller and Ann O. Correspondence (1940–1941).

14. McWilliams, "MRA," p. 129. One of the most controversial donations was made by a member of the Vanderbilt family, Mrs. John (Emily) Henry Hammond Jr., no relation to the engineer-entrepreneur John Hays Hammond, who Ida Koverman met in New York City. Like Koverman, as a devout Christian Scientist, Mrs. Hammond was drawn to the MRA. She donated millions of dollars to the MRA. Following her husband's death in 1949, Mrs. Hammond donated the family's 277-acre Mount Kisco, New York, estate to the MRA, hoping to reside in one of the dozens of rooms, but was soon evicted for fear of threatening MRA's tax-exempt status. In 1955, a reporter spotted her at the Desert Inn, dining with a group connected with the MRA. *Desert Sun*, vol. xxvii, no. 64, March 31, 1955. Arthur Bradley, *On and Off the Bandstand: A Collection of Essays Related to the Great Bands*, p. 9.

15. Frank Buchman to Louis B. Mayer, January 1, 1941. MRAPLOC.

16. *Feature*, December 20, 2002, p. 34. *Somerset Daily American* (PA) December 3, 1949, p. 9. *Time Magazine*, June 14, 1949.

17. *Kingston Gleaner*, August 15, 1948, p. 9; McWilliams, "MRA," pp. 125; 130.

18. McWilliams, "MRA," p. 129.

19. Addenda, January 6–December 6, 1943, JAF.

20. Kenneth Marcus, *Musical Metropolis: Los Angeles and the Creation of a Music Culture, 1880–1940*, p. 85.

21. Undated, Nominations for Art Association Board made at meeting in Mr. Ford's office. JAF. *The SAMOJAC*, April 25, 1945 p.3.

22. *Los Angeles Times*, May 2, 1946, p. 6; Ida Koverman cc'd letter from John Anson Ford to C. E. Toberman; October 25, 1950; JAF.

23. Frank Buchman to "My dear Ida Koverman," July 12, 1950. MRAPLOC.

24. Frank Buchman to Ida Koverman "My dear Ida," December 28, 1950. MRAPLOC.

CHAPTER 23: MUSIC, METAPHYSICS, AND MORAL CUSTODIAN

1. E. J. Fleming, *The Fixers: Eddie Mannix, Howard Strickling, and the MGM Publicity Machine*, p. 31.

2. Ann Wardell Saunders, "Hollywood-Los Angeles," Richard Drake Saunders, ed., *Music and Dance in California and the West*, p. 29; 153. Marni Nixon, *I Could Have Sung All Night*, p. 31. John Anson Ford to Roger W. Jessup, October 6, 1944. JAF. Elsa Maxwell, *Pittsburgh Post-Gazette*, July 7, 1945, p. 12. Dorothy L. Crawford, "A Windfall of Musicians," *Los Angeles Times*, October 8, 1944, p. 29. Anthony Macias, "Bringing Music to the People: Race, Urban Culture, and Municipal Politics in Postwar Los Angeles," *American Quarterly* 56, no.3 (2004).

3. John Anson Ford to Mrs. Leiland Atherton Irish, December 26, 1944. JAF. Attached with business card in what appears to be Ida Koverman's handwriting are names and phone numbers of Victor Young, Jerome Kern, Beulah Bondi, and Al Newman. Although born in Los Angeles proper, Florence Matilde Behm moved with her family to Hollywood in 1912, and soon after Leiland Atherton Irish "came a courting." The couple lived in Hollywood for fourteen years before moving closer to the water. Throughout the next four decades, Mrs. Irish established herself as a leading force in the evolution of Los Angeles's cultural and civic institutions. *The Grizzly Bear*, January 1933–35.

4. Ida R. Koverman to John Anson Ford, January 4, 1946, JAF.

5. Ida R. Koverman to John Anson Ford, January 4, 1946, JAF. Cultural Resources Assessment Plummer Park West Hollywood, California; CWH0802\Plummer Park CRA. doc, p. 21; December 5, 2008.

6. *The Score*, July–August 1946, vol. III, no. 7 and 8, p. 2. Publication of the American Society of Music Arrangers. "Encores and Echoes" by E. B. Rea, *Afro-American*, August 24, 1946. Hugh Fordin, *MGM's Greatest Musicals: The Arthur Freed Unit, p. 183–4.*

7. "Frank Sinatra Clears Misunderstanding," *Afro-American*, August 24, 1946, p.6

8. James Gavin, *Stormy Weather: The Life of Lena Horne*, p. 182.

9. *Pittsburgh Courier*, February 21, 1948, p. 14; *Afro-American*, February 21, 1948; J. E. Smyth, *Nobody's Girl Friday*, p. 80. Apparently, Horne's acceptance speech, if not her success, angered Hattie McDaniel. See W. Burlette Carter, *Finding the Oscar*, p. 124.

10. In February, the state legislature passed a bill allowing counties of 250,000 or more citizens to make contracts "with any person, firm or corporation, for performances . . . including, but not limited to, operas, symphonies, band concerts and other instrumental concerts, historical or commemorative pageants, choral concerts, plays or other related

presentations (with or without music), ballet, dance, recitals, exhibitions, and readings." Government Code-Title 3. Government and Counties [23000–33205]; Division 2. Officers [24000–28085]; Part 2. Board of Supervisors [25000–26490]; Chapter 6. Parks and Recreation [25550–25588], all added 1947, Ch. 424; Article 1. General [25550–25562] 1959, Ch. 579. "The contract shall provide that the management and control of the performances shall be under the supervision of the board of supervisors or shall provide specifically for those matters which cannot legally be delegated by the board of supervisors. The contract may also provide for the reimbursement of the county, insofar as possible, out of any net profits derived from the performance by the person, firm, or corporation."

11. *California Legislative Record*, June 7, 1947. The previous year's budget included $20,000 to sponsor band concerts throughout the city, an amount similar to the city's funding of museums and other cultural venues. Now, it sought a $5,000 increase, *Los Angeles Herald*, June 10, 1948. JAF. *Los Angeles Times*, July 6, 1948, p. 19, and January 12, 1947. City of Los Angeles Officials, cityclerk.lacity.org.

12. November 2, 1949. JAF. Koussevitsky conducted the last two weeks of the 1949 Concert Under the Stars season, unknown paper and *Los Angeles Times*, September 7, 1948, p. 31.

13. Marni Nixon, *I Could Have Sung All Night*, pp. 32; 44–45.

14. Marni Nixon, *I Could Have Sung All Night*, pp. 44–45; 48.

15. Marni Nixon, *I Could Have Sung All Night*, pp 31–32.

16. *Bulletin of America's Town Meeting of the Air.* Transcript, July 13, 1948, vol. 14, no. 12.

17. Co-authored with Fenwicke Holmes, 1982. Holly Leaves, *Hollywood*, August 12, 1922, vol. 11, no. 25–52, p. 29.

18. Louis Sahagun, *Master of the Mysteries: The Life of Manly Palmer Hall*, pp. 113; 116–17. readhowyouwant.com. Actress Barbara Fuller played Claudia in the radio drama *Our Man's Family*. "Leaders Hear of Work to Aid European Jews," *Los Angeles Times*, February 15, 1944, p. A5. Mrs. Mabel Kinney was a member of the Emergency Committee to Save the Jewish People of Europe, a multireligious and secular group of men and women. In 1948, the Woman's Club of the Institute of Religious Science held a meeting with Mabel Kinney presiding. *Los Angeles Times*, October 6, 1948, p. C2.

19. Edward Baron Turk, *Hollywood Diva*, pp. 315–6.

20. In a 1987 article for *Science of Mind* magazine, Jeannette Quinn Bisbee wrote "Hollywood and Religious Science, the Famous Who Found Their Way through Science of Mind," Hollywood and Religious Science, October 15, 2013, scienceofmindarchives.org.

21. Hollywood and Religious Science, October 15, 2013, scienceofmindarchives.org. Williams, *Million Dollar Mermaid*, p. 321; Edward Baron Turk, *Hollywood Diva*, p. 31.

22. Dorothy M. Brown,*Willebrandt*, pp. 252–3.

23. Charlotte Chandler, *Not the Girl Next Door: Joan Crawford, a Personal Biography*, p. 150.

24. Thanks to Ned Comstock, USC.

25. Neal Gabler, *An Empire of Their Own: How the Jews Invented Hollywood*, p. 286.

26. *Cincinnati Enquirer*, November 25, 1954. Sahagun, *Master of the Mysteries*, pp. 116–17. Mary Troffer interview with author. Hedda Hopper, *The While Truth*, p. 267.

27. Richard M. Fried, *Nightmare in Red: The McCarthy Era in Perspective*.

28. Quoted from the *San Francisco Examiner*, February 16, 1945, *Assembly Journal* 1947, p. 90, 118.

29. Old Time Radio Catalog: OTRCAT.com. *Anniston Star*, July 13, 1948, p. 2.

30. *Bulletin of America's Town Meeting of the Air*, p. 49. All subsequent quotes regarding sex education are from *Town Meeting* transcript.

31. *Madera Tribune*, June 22, 1948. "On the Radio Today," *New York Times*, July 13, 1948, p. 46.

32. *Bulletin of America's Town Meeting of the Air*, p. 3.

33. J. Edgar Hoover and James Madison Wood, *Woman's Home Companion*, January 1944.

34. *Bulletin of America's Town Meeting of the Air*, pp. 18–19.

CHAPTER 24: PROPAGANDA AND PUSSY WILLOWS

1. Jimmie Fidler, *Reading Eagle*, April 11, 1938, p. 12.

2. Neal Gabler, *An Empire of Their Own*, p. 361.

3. "How M-G-M Bought Up the Entire Culver City Police Force," *Jurisdictional Disputes in the Motion Picture Industry*, Thursday March 11, 1948.

4. Dorothy M. Brown, *Willebrandt*, pp. 243–44.

5. Otto Frederick, *City of Nets*, 303; Neal Gabler, *An Empire of Their Own*, p. 362. Ida Koverman to Larry Richey, April 14, 1948; HHPL.

6. Edward G. Robinson, John Garfield, Fredric March, Joseph Cotten, and Marsha Hunt, *Los Angeles Times*, October 27, 1947, p. 2. John Cogley, *Report on Blacklisting*, pp. 3–4. Joining Garland was Myrna Loy, Danny Kaye, director John Huston, Robert Young, Humphrey Bogart, *San Bernardino County Sun*, October 27, 1947, p. 1.

7. Erksine Johnson, "Hollywood Roundup," *Bakersfield Californian*, April 23, 1948, p. 12.

8. Neal Gabler, *An Empire of Their Own*, p. 373; Steven J. Ross, *Hollywood Left and Right*, pp. 376–77. Scott Eyman, *Lion of Hollywood*, p. 395. Along with Mayer were Harry Cohn of Columbia Pictures, Spyros Skouras, 20th Century Fox; Nicholas Schenck, Loews Theaters; Barney Balaban, Paramount Pictures; Samuel Goldwyn, Samuel Goldwyn Company; Albert Warner, Warner Bros.; William Goetz, Universal-International; Eric Johnston, AMPPA and MPAA; James F. Byrnes, former Secretary of State; Dore Schary, RKO Pictures.

9. Neal Gabler, *An Empire of Their Own*, pp. 382–83.

10. Dorothy M. Brown, *Willebrandt*, p. 235; James Ulmer, "A Guild Divided," *Motion Picture Production Encyclopedia* 1949, p. 593, DGA website.

11. Elsa Maxwell's "Party Line," *Pittsburgh Post Gazette*, July 21, 1945; J. E. Smyth, *Nobody's Girl Friday*, pp. 79–80.

12. Election Campaigns page: Wisconsin Center for Film & Theater Research website. Kathryn Cramer Brownell, *Showbiz Politics: Hollywood in American Political Life*, pp. 88–89.

13. Ida R. Koverman to Mr. Larry Richey, April 14, 1948. HHPL. Edwin Knopf's September 20 letter to Governor Stassen included a list of "who's who" in Hollywood, with notations about their particular political persuasion useful for future lobbying and fundraising, as well as some personal commentary. A sampling includes Atwater Kent, a "former radio manufacturer, millionaire, very possible source large contributions"; Mervyn Le Roy, "one of the four or five top directors in Hollywood, Loud-mouthed"; Adolphe Menjou, "actor—Loud-Mouthed. Very anti-New Deal"; Robert Montgomery; George Murphy; Kyle Palmer; and David Selznick; who were all described as, "you know," while Walter Pidgeon was introduced as an "actor—intelligent—valuable," and Mendel Silberberg was a "very important attorney. Always in forefront of community drives. Great influence with Jewish community. Life long Republican." Edwin H. Knopf to Governor Stassen, September 20, 1947; Minnesota Historical Society.

14. Ida Koverman was there schmoozing with, among others, Universal's Lew Wasserman, producers, executives, writers, and spouses, such as Carey Wilson, Joseph Pasternak, Arthur Freed, Cedric Gibbons, David Selznick, Irving Berlin, Dudley Nichols, Lawrence Weingarten, Lee Bowman, Richard Breen, Gene Fowler, Alvin M. Josephy Jr., journalist Harry Crocker. Rosalind Russell, Loretta Young, George Murphy, Mervyn Le Roy, Olivia Haviland, Dorothy McGuire, Dick Powell and June Allyson, Jennifer Jones, Douglas Fairbanks Jr., and all of their spouses. Writer and producer Dudley Nichols was happy to know that a "Hollywood for Stassen" committee had been formed, and he gave his five-hundred-dollar check to Knopf. Dudley Nichols was listed as a producer and writer who won an Academy Award for *The Informer*. Belva Cannan to Harold Stassen, October 3, 1947. Dudley Nichols to Harold E. Stassen, October 15, 1947. Lamar Trotti told Stassen that it was his great hope that Stassen would win the nomination. He went on to tell the former governor that what impressed him about Woodrow Wilson while working on his motion picture was Wilson's "political boldness." Then, he compared Stassen favorably to the former candidate Wendell Wilkie, whom he got to know during his work on the screenplay of Wilkie's book *One World*. The movie was never made because Wilkie withdrew from the race. Belva Cannan to Harold Stassen, October 3, 1947; Lamar Trotti to Harold E. Stassen, October 20, 1947. Cocktail party, Tuesday October 28 (1947) held at 2108 La Mesa Drive, Santa Monica. Minnesota Historical Society.

15. *Los Angeles Times*, June 24, 1948, p. 1, 5. Before modern video technology, the term "video" derived from the Latin "to see," and referred to television. *Variety*, June 23, 1948, p. 2; *Billboard*, July 3, 1948, p. 5.

16. *Los Angeles Times*, September 12, 1948, p. 4, and September 30, 1948. *Evening News*, 1948, p. 23.

17. Steven J. Ross, *Hollywood Left and Right*, p. 157. SAG-AFTRA website.

18. George Murphy, *"Say . . . Didn't You Used to Be George Murphy?" Star Tribune* (MN) on August 13, 1947, p. 2; *Los Angeles Times*, December 5, 1956, p. A1 and February 1, 1947, p. A8.

19. Other officers of the committee include Robert Montgomery, first vice president; Walt Disney, second vice president, and serving as directors Herbert Freston, Ida R. Koverman, Leo McCarey, Adolphe Menjou, Ginger Rogers, Morrie Ryskind, and Lewis Weiss. *San Bernardino Sun*, October 20, 1947, p. 1. "Film Notables Enter Politics: Murphy to Direct Republican Drive," *San Bernardino Sun*, October 20, 1947, p. 1. George Murphy, *"Say . . . ,"* p. 297.

20. Steven J. Ross, *Hollywood Left and Right*, p. 138. *Los Angeles Times*, October 1, 1939, p. 53.

21. George Murphy, *"Say . . . ,"* p. 302.

22. *Betty Garrett and Other Songs: A Life on Stage and Screen*, pp. 94–95.

23. *Betty Garrett and Other Songs: A Life on Stage and Screen*, pp. 127–28.

24. Keenan Wynn, Van Johnson, Red Skelton, Jimmy Durante, Danny Thomas, and Peter Lawford were also among the entertainers. *Variety*, June 2, 1948; *Billboard*, June 5, 1948.

25. *Betty Garrett and Other Songs: A Life on Stage and Screen*, p. 94.

26. *Chicago Tribune*, June 29, 1944. Hedda Hopper, *Pittsburgh Press*, March 8 and 23, 1946, p. 31, and April 11, 1946. *The Tennessean* (Nashville, TN) April 26, 1946, p. 37.

27. Fred Beck, "Farmers Market," *Los Angeles Times*, June 10, 1947, p. 4.

CHAPTER 25: WOUNDED WOMEN, WOMEN WARRIORS

1. Herbert Hoover to Ida Koverman, January 3, 1949. HHPL. Ida Koverman to Mayor Fletch Bowron, January 17, 1949; Fletcher Bowron to Ida Koverman, January 24, 1949. RAP.

2. January 31, 1949, date reported by Louella Parsons in *Salt Lake Tribune*, February 24, 1949. *Salt Lake Tribune*, March 19, 1949. Starting on January 10, 1949, the snowstorm blanketed the region for three days.

3. US City Directories, 1936 Los Angeles; *The Movieland Directory*, E. J. Fleming, p. 432. The 6691 address has been associated with actor Eugene O'Brien and Richard Barthelmess. Southland Centennial Committee, chaired by Ford and Koverman with a bipartisan membership, including her friend Miss Grace Stoermer. JAF. National Registry of Historic Places Inventory Nomination form #105. *Portland Press Herald*, April 26, 1949, p. 5; *Feature*, December 20, 2002, p. 34; McWilliams, "MRA," p. 129. Richard S. Weil's series on Moral Rearmament in *Daily Review-Star*, December 2, 1949, p. 7.

4. Charles Higham, *Merchant of Dreams*, p. 385.

5. After elective office, Redwine became a lobbyist for the Motion Picture Producers Distributors Association (MPPDA). Chester G. Hanson, "Sacramento Mailsack," *Los Angeles Times*, May 30, 1949, p. 5. Erwin Act, 1950.

6. Stenography, bookkeeping, accounting, and secretarial skills were among the classes adapted for employment in the 135, and growing, local movie studios and their industries. Day and evening courses were offered in a curriculum guided by studio officials such as Jesse L. Lasky, an early advisory board member. *Journal of Business Education*, 1933, vol. 9, no. 4, p.26. Taylor & Francis Online. *Los Angeles Times*, August 13, 1949, p. 6. *Los Angeles Times*, November 8, 1948, p. 31.

7. *Journal of Business Education*, 1934, vol. 9, no. 6, p. 27. Taylor & Francis Online. *Motion Picture Almanac*, 1932; Catalog of Copyright Entries, Part I, n. s, v. 6, 3482, p. 160.

8. *Los Angeles Times*, September 19, 1950, p.12.

9. *Los Angeles Times*, May 21, 1950, p. 47. Hedda Hopper, *Chicago Tribune*, September 13, 1950, p. 3. *Los Angeles Times*, September 13, 1950, p. B10. Hattie McDaniel apparently wrote to Hopper on the same day to say she would not be endorsing any candidate. McDaniel to Hopper, September 13, 1950, HHPAMPAS. Louise Beavers appeared on the KTTV telecast, *Los Angeles Times*, September 21, 1950, p. 9.

10. *Los Angeles Times*, September 20 and 21, 1950.

11. J. E. Smyth, *Nobody's Girl Friday: The Women Who Ran Hollywood*, p. 81.

12. J. E. Smyth, *Nobody's Girl Friday*, pp. 73–82.

13. Undated Hedda Hopper to Vivien Kellems. University of Connecticut Archives & Digital Collections. Hereafter UCADC.

14. "Film Stars Took Sides in a 'Tug-of-Votes,'" *Social Justice*, November 18, 1940, p. 12.

15. Jonann Sherman, "'Senator-at-Large for America's Women': Margaret Chase Smith and the Paradox of Gender Affinity," in Susan J. Carroll, ed., *The Impact of Women in Public Office*, p. 108; *San Francisco Chronicle*, January 9, 1950, pp. 89–116.

16. Darcy Richardson, uncoveredpolitics.com; Time Capsules, September 3, 2012.

17. Entitled "Hollywood Holiday," painted for the Motion Picture Relief Fund by Albert J. Kramer. Signed Ida Koverman, MGM Studio, Culver City, California 1949. UCADC.

18. Undated typed letter from Hedda Hopper to Vivien Kellems, responding to Kellems's March 31 letter. UCADC.

19. Telegram copy April 6, 1950; March 21, 1950, on MGM stationery. UCADC.

20. Ida Koverman to Kellems, March 21, 1950, on MGM stationery. Kellems to Koverman, April 7, 1950. UCADC.

21. Michelle Nickerson, *Mothers of Conservatism*, p. 44. Kellems addressed the crowd, proclaiming that "men ought to move over and make room for women in politics," because Republican men failed to lead. They "were bereft of hope, helplessness and utterly devoid of inspiration or plan," and so, "if the men are bankrupt of ideas, we're not. . . . We're teeming with them and with hope and energy." Like Koverman's able ally Joseph Scott concluded years earlier, Kellems decreed that "if the Republican party wins in 1950 it will be the achievement of the resourceful, loyal, patriotic American women, Republican, real democratic, and independent, who can no longer stomach the mad extravagance of High Tax Harry, or the futile, puerile, wishy-washy stupidity of the Republican men leaders." *New London* (CT), April 12, 1950, p. 4.; telegram from Koverman to Kellems, April 14, 1950; Kellems to Koverman, April 22, 1950. Clare D. Tuchtman, secretary to Miss Kellems to Hedda Hopper, May 9, 1950. UCADC.

22. *Los Angeles Times*, March 24, 1988. Don E. Carleton, *Red Scare: Right-Wing Hysteria, Fifties Fanaticism, and Their Legacy in Texas*, p. 116. She reached out to a local, vocal anti-communist columnist who sent her letter to J. B. Matthews, the former HUAC investigator, although she later claimed it was published without her consent or intention, first in the *New York Journal-American* on December 19, 1948, and then in the *Greenwich Times*. Adler and Draper's bookings and reputations suffered, so they sued Mrs. McCullough for libel in the fall of 1949. Carol A. Stabile, *The Broadcast 41: Women and the Anti-Communist Blacklist*, p. 108. *Cincinnati Enquirer*, May 23, 1950, p. 14. Stabile connected the McCulloughs to an anti-communist women's group that was interested in politics organized by conservative Clare Boothe Luce, wife of *Time* magazine editor Henry Luce, along with other associations linked to the American Business Consultants group tied to Matthews. Stabile, *The Broadcast 41*, p. 110. Recent scholarship on Luce argues she has been largely marginalized in revisions about modern American conservatism. Brian Thorn, *CBL and the Evolution of American Conservatism*, February 13, 2017, in online essays.

23. Mr. and Mrs. Vincent Price, Edward G. Robinson, the William Goetzs, Charles Laughton, and Fannie Brice. *Los Angeles Times*, June 5, 1950, part II, p. 9.

CHAPTER 26: THE MOGUL AND THE MATRON

1. Christopher Finch, *Rainbow*, 1975, p. 66.

2. Gerold Frank, *Judy*, pp. 213–14; *Los Angeles Examiner*, June 19, 1949.

3. Hedda Hopper and Mr. and Mrs. Ezio Pinza were among her guests. *Los Angeles Times*, July 6, 1950, p. 39; *Newark Advocate*, July 30, 1949.

4. Email to author from Pam Koverman. Charles Higham, *Merchant of Dreams*, pp. 390–91.

5. Brown and Brown, *The MGM Girls*, pp. 64–5.

6. Brown and Brown, *The MGM Girls*, pp. 64–5.

7. David Shipman, *Judy Garland*, p. 201.

8. Gerald Clarke, *Get Happy: The Life of Judy Garland*, p. 231.

9. *Detroit Free Press*, June 21, 1950, p. 1; 8.

10. *Los Angeles Times*, June 21, 1950, p. 1, 4. Brown and Brown, *The MGM Girls*, p. 166. *Daily Independent Journal*, June 29, 1950, p. 4. It is possible, as one columnist contended,

that underlying the negotiations was an implicit acknowledgement of what was troubling the entire movie industry, that is, that the new technology of television would threaten their bottom line. Therefore, "Television played a bigger role than Judy Garland was willing to publicly admit," even though in the offing, there were "several television appearances, which had been barred in her MGM contract." Erskine Johnson, *San Bernardino County Sun*, October 25, 1960, p. 4. Actually, Judy Garland didn't make her television debut until September 1955, when her CBS Saturday night live performance was a triumph, in spite of her suffering from laryngitis. *Santa Cruz Sentinel News*, September 26, 1955, p. 2.

11. Harriet B. Blackburn, "Ida Koverman Makes Name in Hollywood's Movies, Though Not on Screen," *Christian Science Monitor*, October 16, 1950, p. 12.

12. Harriet B. Blackburn, "Ida Koverman Makes Name," *CSM*.

13. Harriet B. Blackburn, "Ida Koverman Makes Name," *CSM*.

14. Herbert Hoover to "My dear Ida," October 16, 1950. HHPL.

15. Evelyn Jaeger to Herbert Hoover, October 23, 1950. HHPL.

16. Ida Koverman to Herbert Hoover, December 22, 1950; Herbert Hoover to Ida Koverman, December 30, 1950. HHPL.

17. *Altoona Mirror*, December 16, 1950, p. 18. *Los Angeles Times*, December 7, 1950, p. B6. *Pacific Stars and Stripes*, November 6, 1950, p. 1. Municipal Arts Commission to Fletcher Bowron, November 8, 1950. JAF.

18. Hedda Hopper, *The Whole Truth*, p. 271. Redcarproperty.blogspot.com.

19. Brown and Brown, *The MGM Girls*, p. 19.

20. Dorothy M. Brown, *Willebrandt*, p. 231; Hedda Hopper, *The Whole Truth*, p. 270–71.

21. Hedda Hopper, *From Under My Hat*, p. 187; Brown and Brown, *The MGM Girls*, pp. 19; 22. *Salt Lake Tribune*, May 14, 1951.

22. *Hartford Courant*, September 20, 1962, p. 12.

23. Frank Buchman to "My dear Louis B. Mayer, October 17, 1950. MRALOC.

24. Frank Buchman to Ida Koverman "My dear Ida" December 28, 1950; Frank Buchman to Ida Koverman, January 30, 1951. MRALOC. Peter Howland, *The World Rebuilt: The True Story of Frank Buchman and the Achievements of Moral Re-Armament*, p. 169.

25. Evelyn Jaeger, Secretary [to Ida Koverman] to Dr. Frank N. D. Buchman at address of Moral Re-Armament, 2419 Massachusetts Avenue, Washington, DC, February 8, 1951. Frank Buchman to "My dear Ida" February 21, 1951. MRALOC.

26. Frank Buchman to Ida Koverman, July 20, 1951. MRALOC.

27. Frank Buchman to Ida Koverman, August 22 and 23, 1951. MRALOC.

28. Jack Currie and Bennet Hall to Miss Ida May [sic] Koverman, June 23, 1952. Jack Currie and Bennet Hall from Ida Koverman, June 25, 1952. MRALOC.

29. The *Times* likely relied upon Hedda Hopper's testimony for the short biography. *Los Angeles Times*, December 31, 1950, p. C1.

30. Evelyn Jaeger to Bernice Miller, January 11, 1951; Bernice Miller to Evelyn Jaeger, January 19, 1951, HHPL. He also said that Koverman's best wishes were extended by Milton Silverberg [sic], a Long Beach [sic] attorney, who had recently called him, and to thank her for the nice thought. It is likely he meant Mendel Silberberg, Koverman's longtime ally and MGM attorney. Resolution authored by Lester A. McMillan of Cheviot Hills and Charles W. Lyon of Beverly Hills, No. 16, resolution chapter 29 in Appendix to Assembly Journal—1951 Regular Session and Recapitulation of Assembly Measures, p. 6907. ACR. 16, 4257. Assembly Concurrent Resolution No. 16-filed with Secretary of State, January 24, 1951, Chapter 29.

31. *Los Angeles Times*, April 4, 1951, p. 31. Patricia Mahon, *Mrs. Spencer Tracy and the John Tracy Clinic: A Tireless Drive to Educate Deaf Children*, p. 122. *Los Angeles Times*, April 6, 1951, p. 54.

32. *Los Angeles Times*, April 7, 1951; Hedda Hopper, *The Whole Truth*, p. 278.

33. *Variety*, May 30, 1951, p. 3, 8; Scott Eyman, *Lion of Hollywood*, p. 442–3.

34. Charles Higham, *Merchant of Dreams*, p. 387.

35. Bosley Crowther, *Hollywood Rajah*, p. 290.

36. Hedda Hopper, *The Whole Truth*, p. 278.

37. Hedda Hopper, *The Whole Truth*, p. 269.

38. Charles Higham, *Merchant of Dreams*, p. 419.

39. Hedda Hopper, *The Whole Truth*, p. 276.

40. Hedda Hopper, *The Whole Truth*, p. 271.

41. *Evening Telegram*, August 27, 1952, p. 8; Scott Eyman, *Lion of Hollywood*, p. 468.

CHAPTER 27: OUTSTANDING WOMAN OF THE STATE

1. Cari Beauchamp, *Without Lying Down: Frances Marion and the Powerful Women of Early Hollywood*, p. 248.

2. *Billboard*, May 19, 1951, p. 16. *Los Angeles Times*, January 6, 1954, p. B3. *Los Angeles Times*, May 5, 1954, p. B3.

3. Ida Koverman to Herbert Hoover, May 1, 1952; October 1, 1952. HHPL.

4. Frank Buchman to Ida Koverman, June 26, 1952. Frank Buchman to Ida Koverman, June 30, 1952; Ida Koverman to Frank Buchman, June 30, 1952; MRALOC. T. Christopher Jespersen, *American Images of China, 1931–1949*, p. 166. Sack, *Moral Re-Armament*, p. 145.

5. "Working Women Open Drive for Mrs. Younger," March 28, 1954, *Los Angeles Times*, p. 1.

6. Ruth N. Harmer, "Hedda Hopper: Ike's Hollywood Helper," *Frontier*, November 1956, pp. 24–5. *Los Angeles Times*, September 29, 1952, p. 6; October 1, 1952, p. 31. Ida Koverman to Herbert Hoover, May 1, 1952; October 1, 1952. HHPL.

7. Ida Koverman to "Dear Chief," Herbert Hoover, October 1, 1952. Ida Koverman to "Dear Chief" Herbert Hoover, May 1, 1952. HHPL.

8. *Los Angeles Times*, November 23, 1948, p. 37; *Hollywood Citizen-News*, December 31, 1952.

9. *Shreveport Times* (LA), September 23, 1952, p. 8.

10. Cheryl Krasnick Warsh and Dan Mallek, eds, *Consuming Modernity: Gendered Behavior and Consumerism before the Baby Boom*. Esther Williams, *The Million Dollar Mermaid*, p. 277.

11. *Los Angeles Times*, July 27, 1951, p. 24. Lloyd Shearer, "Judy Garland's Sister: The Happy One in the Family," *Parade*, October 4, 1964, pp. 6–7.

12. *San Bernardino Sun*, January 6, 1953, p. 4.

13. *Los Angeles Times*, February 10, 1953, p.15. Bernice Miller to Mrs. Ida Koverman, March 27, 1953; Ida Koverman to Bernice Miller, April 2, 1953, HHPL. *Los Angeles Times*, May 15, 1953, p. 14.

14. Peter Meremblum to John Anson Ford, February 6, 1953. JAF. Vladimir Rosing was a tenor who advanced innovative ideas about opera production, such as English-speaking performances, and innovative staging for the BBC's televised operas, and later in Southern California. He directed the 1950 *Grounds for Marriage* with Kathryn Grayson,

Strictly Dishonorable (1951) with Ezio Pinza, and *Interrupted Melody* with Eleanor Parker in 1955. Attorney Harry Rabwin was Dr. Marus Rabwin's brother. "Leaders Get Invitations to Anti-Red Play," *Los Angeles Times*, February 18, 1953, p. 21.

15. Governor Warren said, "This is a bizarre case, perhaps more fantastic than any moving picture in which the defendant acted—but certainly having many of the attributes of a scenario." Madge Meredith Becomes Bride, *Los Angeles Times*, September 30, 1953, p. A1. Eventually, two amateur sleuths inspired the California legislature to declare the case was "from the beginning to end . . . a mockery of investigation, of defense counseling, of trial procedure, and justice itself," after finding "shocking evidence of perjury, suppression of evidence, prejudice, and an almost unbelievable reluctance on the part of defense counsel to investigate the cause of defendant." Prosecutors had intimidated witnesses, and "one of the most disturbing factors . . . was the failure of defense counsel to call three key witnesses." Unknown newspaper, March 27, 1951; Joan Renner "A Story Fit for Film," *Los Angeles Magazine* website, June 20, 2013.

16. James Copp, "Sklylarking," *Los Angeles Times*, October 10, 1953, p. 8. Hulda McGinn to Hon. Herbert Hoover, October 22, 1953. HHPL.

17. Herbert Hoover to Hulda McGinn, October 27, 1953; Hulda McGinn to Hon. Herbert Hoover, November 2, 1953. Herbert Hoover to Miss. Hulda McGinn November 5, 1953. HHPL.

18. *Journal of the Senate, Legislature of the State of California, statement of expenses for March*, Hulda McGinn, April 1950; *Daily Independent Journal*, San Rafael, December 15, 1961, p. 16; *The Times*, San Mateo, May 5, 1944, p. 7.

19. JAF; *Los Angeles Times*, November 27, 1953, p. A6. "Chamber Unit Has Yule Lunch," *Los Angeles Times*, December 10, 1953, p. B5.

20. Ann Wardell Saunders, "Hollywood—Los Angeles," in *Music and Dance in California and the West*, edited by Richard Drake Saunders, p. 126, 153. Ida Koverman to Bernice Miller, January 16, 1954. HHPL.

CHAPTER 28: EXIT STAGE RIGHT

1. Virginia Kellogg, "Nobody Called, All Came for Last Rites of Ida Koverman," unknown newspaper clipping. HHPL.

2. As of July 1, presumably in 1953, Koverman sent out announcements that her residence address would be 1343 North Laurel Avenue in Hollywood. Announcement card in HHPL. Hedda Hopper, *The Whole Truth*, p. 268. James Copp, "Skylarking" *Los Angeles Times*, September 2, 1954, p. B1.

3. *Los Angeles Times*, September 9, 1954, p. B4. Kurt Schuparra, *Triumph of the Right*, pp. 22–3.

4. Don Iddon's "American Diary," *The Advertiser* (Adelaide, SA), October 21, 1954. *Los Angeles Times*, August 2, 1998, p. 53.

5. "Knowland Stresses Election Significance," *Los Angeles Times*, October 22, 1954, p. B1.

6. Hedda Hopper "Guiding Light Lost, Says Hedda," unknown newspaper. HHPL. Misc. and Masterworks Broadway websites. Ray Zeman, "Hollywood Pays Tribute to Lionel Barrymore," *Los Angeles Times*, November 19, 1954, p. 2.

7. Virginia Kellogg, "Nobody Called, All Came for Last Rites of Ida Koverman," unknown newspaper clipping. HHPL.

8. Evelyn Jaeger to Bernice Miller, November 24, 1954. Virginia Kellogg, "Nobody Called." HHPL.

9. Virginia Kellogg, "Nobody Called."

10. The rose was from Patrick Gleason, "the favorite Godchild she had found for friends to complete their childless home." Virginia Kellogg, "Nobody Called."

11. Virginia Kellogg, "Nobody Called."

12. Obituaries include Kellogg's tribute, Charles Higham's 1993 *Merchant of Dreams, Louis B. Mayer, MGM, and the Secret Hollywood*, pp. 124, 448, 457; from original sources in HHPL and Los Angeles probate files.

13. Virginia Kellogg, "Nobody Called." HHPL.

14. *Los Angeles Examiner* and *Los Angeles Times*, November 25, 1954.

15. Virginia Kellogg, "Nobody Called." HHPL.

16. Virginia Kellogg, "Nobody Called." HHPL.

17. *Los Angeles Examiner*, November 27, 1954.

18. *Los Angeles Examiner*, November 27, 1954. Unknown newspaper, January 20, 1957, p. 49.

19. Hedda Hopper to Herbert Hoover, November 29, 1954, and Hoover's handwritten response and typed letter of same, December 3, 1954. HHPL.

20. L. Sherman Adams to Hedda Hopper, November 26, 1954; J. W. Ehrlich to Hedda Hopper; Harry Brand to Hedda Hopper, November 26, 1954. HHPAMPAS.

21. *Pittsburgh Courier*, November 6, 1954, p. 11.

22. 1955 Regular Session, Chapter 54, Senate Concurrent Resolution No. 36, filed with Secretary of State, January 21, 1955, p. 3901–2.

23. *Los Angeles Examiner*, December 2, 1954.

24. Hedda Hopper, *The Whole Truth*, p. 268. Ida R. Koverman will, September 16, 1953; Courtesy of Mary Troffer.

25. *Los Angeles Times*, May 21, 1951, p. B8.

26. Charles Higham, *Merchant of Dreams*, p. 419. Koverman will 1953; Courtesy of Mary Troffer.

27. The story led with, "Widow says Mrs. Ida Koverman, former Cincinnatian and motion picture executive who died last week in Hollywood, was the divorced wife of the late Oscar Koverman of Cincinnati." Cincinnati, Ohio, *City Directory*, 1948. *Cincinnati Enquirer*, May 3, 1963, p. 36. She had been living at 4121 Edwards Road. The services were held at the Christ Church Chapel. *Cincinnati Enquirer*, December 2, 1954, p. 5. The unusual tragedy never made it into the family's folklore, or if it did, no one passed it on. Some had posited that Oscar died of tuberculosis, and that he was living in California at the time. *Cincinnati Enquirer*, May 3, 1963, p. 36.

28. Donald T. Critchlow, *When Hollywood Was Right*, p. 145.

CHAPTER 29: EPILOGUE: GUIDING LIGHT LEGACY

1. *Los Angeles Times*, November 25, 1954.

2. Michelle Nickerson, *Mothers of Conservatism*, p. 167. Unlike Kathryn Olmsted's argument that California conservatism grew out of a reaction to the New Deal in the 1930s, this work on Ida Koverman and her allies suggest the origins of an organized partisan conservatism go further back to the immediate post-WWI era. See Kathryn Olmsted, *Right Out of California*.

3. Lary May, "Anti-Communism in Hollywood," James G. Rawls, *New Directions in California History: A Book of Readings*, pp. 319–30. United States Congress House Committee on Un-American Activities; Washington, DC, US Goverment Printing Office, 1956: "It is hardly necessary to point out that this inadvertently compiled honor roll of Americans in Hollywood was far from complete. To it we should add the names of hundreds of Hollywood celebrities who never at any time in their careers have had any truck with communism and have been actively in opposition to it when it was stylish to flirt with treason." "At risk of unwittingly omitting some of the best anti-Communist fighters in Hollywood, let us add to the *Daily Worker's* list the following names of good Americans in filmdom: John Wayne, Charles Coburn, Roy Brewer, Ward Bond, Bob Arthur, John Ford, Clark Gable, the late lamented and irreplaceable James K. McGuinness, Fred Niblo Jr., Pat O'Brien, Lela Rogers (mother of Ginger), Robert Taylor, and the late Sam Wood." *Investigation of So-Called 'Blacklisting*, p. 5259, 5265–6. Hearings by United States Congress. House Committee on Un-American Activities, June 18, 1956, p. 5266.

4. In 1954, when the Directors Guild won a new working agreement including a pension plan, Mendel Silberberg and many of the same personnel represented the Association of Motion Picture Producers, and Mabel Walker Willebrandt represented the directors. Just over a month before Ida Koverman passed away, a photograph captures Ida Koverman's old Republican Party colleague, attorney Joseph Scott, and the MRA's Dr. Frank Buchman on the platform at the Moral Rearmament World Assembly in Mackinac Island, Michigan. Attorney Scott, "who flew to Europe to arrange the session, calls the Assembly's principles the 'one hope of humanity,' in an age threatened by the hydrogen bomb." By then, the Mackinac Singers were getting rave reviews offering music with a cause and as part of the MRA's spreading of song throughout the world. Ida Koverman's name still carried weight. That same month, she was listed among MRA devotees along with Joel McCrea, Ronald Reagan, Ward Bond, Charles Skouras, Louis B. Mayer, Mr. and Mrs. Robert Cummings, and George Murphy. *Miami News*, January 18, 1955, p. 3.

5. Kurt Schuppara, *Triumph of the Right: The Rise of the California Conservative Movement, 1945–1966*, pp. 103–4. Kathyrn Cramer Brownell, *Showbiz Politics, Hollywood in American Political Life*. pp. 195–6; *San Francisco Chronicle*, July 11, 1966, p. 5; Steven J. Ross, *Hollywood Left and Right*, p. 181.

6. Mary Troffer interview with author. Ida R. Koverman was Mary's great-aunt. Interview facilitated by Victoria McAllister, Mary's niece. August 7, 2007, Palmdale, CA.

7. Hedda Hopper, *Off With Their Heads*, p. 199. Norman J. Zierold, *The Moguls, Hollywood's Merchants of Myth*, p. 310. Frank Buchman to Louis B. Mayer, June 12, 1957; Lorena Mayer, undated, following Louis B. Mayer's death, October 29, 1957. MRALOC.

BIBLIOGRAPHY

PRIMARY SOURCES (WITH ABBREVIATIONS)

Business Women's Legislative Council, Huntington Library. BWLC

Clara Burdette Papers, Huntington Library. CBP

Edwin H. Knopf letters, Minnesota Historical Society. EHKMHS

Hedda Hopper Papers, Margaret Herrick Library, Academy of Motion Pictures Arts and Sciences. HHPAMPAS

Hiram Johnson Papers, Bancroft Library, University of California, Berkeley. HJPBL

Industrial Welfare Commission Minutes, Sacramento Office. IWC minutes

John Anson Ford Papers, Huntington Library. JAF

Katherine Philips Edson Papers, Special Collections, University of California, Los Angeles. KPE

Louis Ward Watkins Papers, Huntington Library. LWWP

Mabel Walker Willebrandt Papers, Library of Congress. MWWLOC

Moral Rearmament Papers, Library of Congress. MRALOC

National Archives and Records Administration, Library of Congress

Ralph Arnold Papers, Huntington Library. RAP

Special Collections, University of California, Santa Cruz

Women's Swimming Association Archives website, The Henning Library, International Swimming Hall of Fame, Fort Lauderdale, Florida; scrapbooks, 1915–1917.

GOVERNMENT PUBLICATIONS

Assembly Concurrent Resolution No. 16, filed with Secretary of State, January 24, 1951, Chapter 29.

California Legislative record, *Assembly Final History*, June 7, 1947.

Cultural Resources Assessment Plummer Park, West Hollywood, California; CWH0802\ Plummer Park CRA.doc, p. 21. 12/5/2008.

Government Code-Title 3. Government and Counties [23000–33205]; Division 2. Officers [24000–28085]; Part 2. Board of Supervisors [25000–26490]; Chapter 6. Parks and Recreation [25550–25588], all added 1947, Ch. 424; Article 1. General [25550–25562] 1959, Ch. 579.

Handbook, California Legislature, fortieth session, 1913, p. 21; *Journal of the Senate of the State of California*, vol. 1, April 2, 1913.

Hoover from Public Papers of the Presidents of the United States, Herbert Hoover 1930 (Jan–Dec) US Government Office, Appendix E, June 1, 1999.

Investigation of So-Called 'Blacklisting, p. 5259, 5265–66. Hearings. By United States Congress. House Committee on Un-American Activities, June 18, 1956.

Journal of the Senate, Legislature of the State of California, statement of expenses for March, Hulda McGinn, April 1950.

Jurisdictional Disputes in the Motion Picture Industry, Thursday, March 11, 1948.

National Registry of Historic Places Inventory Nomination form; #105.

No. 16, resolution chapter 29 in Appendix to Assembly Journal—1951 Regular Session and Recapitulation of Assembly Measures, p. 6907. ACR. 16, 4257.

US Census (various decades); District 0040.

United States Congress, House Committee on Un-American Activities; Washington, US Government. Printing Office, 1956.

BOOKS

Alexander, Linda J. *Reluctant Witness: Robert Taylor, Hollywood, and Communism.* North Carolina: Tease Publishing, 2008.

Alleman, Richard. *Hollywood: The Movie Lover's Guide.* New York: Broadway Books, 2005.

Altman, Diana. *Hollywood East: Louis B. Mayer and the Origins of the Studio System.* New York: A Birch Lane Press Book, 1992.

Austin, John. *More of Hollywood's Unsolved Mysteries.* New York: Shapolsky Publishers, Inc., 1991.

Baker, Lorin L. *That Imperiled Freedom.* Los Angeles: Graphic Press Publishing Co., 1934.

Bakeweal, William. *Hollywood Be Thy Name: Random Recollections of a Movie Veteran from Silents to Talkie to TV.* Scarecrow Press, 1991.

Balcon, Michael. *Michael Balcon Presents . . . A Lifetime of Films.* Hutchison of London, 1969.

Barbas, Samantha. *The First Lady of Hollywood.* Berkeley: University of California Press, 2005.

Barney, David E. "American Genesis: The Archeology of Women's Swimming at the 1920 Olympic Games," in *Pathways: Critiques and Discourse in Olympic Research,* 9th Annual Symposium for Olympic Research, Robert K. Barney et al., Beijing, PRC, August 5–7, 2008.

Batman, Richard Dale. *The Road to the Presidency: Hoover, Johnson, and the California Republican Party, 1920–1924.* PhD dissertation, University of Southern California, 1965.

Beauchamp, Cari. *Without Lying Down: Frances Marion and the Powerful Women of Early Hollywood.* Berkeley: University of California Press, 1997.

Bender's Lawyers' Diary and Directory for the State of New York, vol. 27. Matthew Bender & Company, 1918.

Best, Gary Dean. *The Politics of American Individualism: Herbert Hoover in Transition, 1918–1921.* Westport, CT: Greenwood Press, 1975.

Best, Gary Dean. *Herbert Hoover: The Postpresidential Years, 1933–1964.* Stanford: Hoover Institution Press, 1983.

Braitman, Jacqueline R. *Katherine Philips Edson: A Progressive-Feminist in California's Era of Reform.* PhD dissertation, University of California, Los Angeles, 1988.

Brennan, Mary, C. *Wives, Mothers, and the Red Menace: Conservative Women and the Crusade against Communism.* University Press of Colorado, 2009.

Brown, Dorothy M. *Mabel Walker Willebrandt.* Knoxville: University of Tennessee Press, 1984.

Brown, Peter Harry, and Pamela Ann Brown. *The MGM Girls: Behind the Velvet Curtain*. New York: St. Martin's Press, 1983.

Brownell, Kathryn Cramer, *Showbiz Politics, Hollywood in American Political Life*. Chapel Hill: University of North Carolina Press, 2014.

Brownstein, Ronald. *The Power and the Glitter: The Hollywood-Washington Connection*. New York: Pantheon Books, 1990.

Button, John. *L.A. Noir: The Struggle for the Soul of America's Most Seductive City*. New York: Three Rivers Press, 2009.

Carleton, Don E. *Red Scare! Right-Wing Hysteria, Fifties Fanaticism, and Their Legacy in Texas*. Texas Monthly Press, 1985.

Cartwright, A. P. *Gold Fields Paved the Way: The Story of the Gold Field Group of Companies*. London: MacMillian, 1967.

Clarke, Gerald. *Get Happy: The Life of Judy Garland*. New York: Random House, 2000.

Cogley, John. *Report on Blacklisting, I, 1954. The Fund for the Republic, Inc.* San Francisco: Prelinger Library, 2006.

Cooper, Jackie, with Dick Kleiner. *Please Don't Shoot My Dog: The Autobiography of Jackie Cooper*. New York: William Morrow and Company, 1981.

Critchlow, Donald T. *When Hollywood Was Right: How Movie Stars, Studio Moguls, and Big Business Remade American Politics*. Cambridge: Cambridge University Press, 2013.

Crowther, Bosley. *Hollywood Rajah: the Life and Times of Louis B. Mayer*. New York: Holt, Rinehart, and Winston, 1960.

Dallek, Matthew. *The Right Moment: Ronald Reagan's First Victory and the Decisive Turning Point in American Politics*. New York: The Free Press, 2000.

Davis, Ronald L. *The Glamour Factory: Inside Hollywood's Big Studio System*. Dallas: Southern Methodist University Press, 1993.

Delmatier, Royce D., Clarence F. McIntosh, and Earl Waters, eds. *The Rumble of California Politics*. New York: John Wiley & Sons, 1970.

Dietz, Dan. *The Complete Book of 1940s Broadway Musicals*. New York: Rowman & Littlefield Publishers, 2015.

Edwards, Anne. *Judy Garland*. New York: Simon and Schuster, 1975.

Eells, George. *Hedda and Louella: The Dual Biography of Hedda Hopper and Louella Parsons*. New York: Warner Paperback Edition, June 1973.

Evans, Peter. *Ava Gardner: The Secret Conversations*. Simon & Schuster, 2013.

Eyman, Scott. *Lion of Hollywood: The Life and Legend of Louis B. Mayer*. New York: Simon & Schuster, 2005.

Finch, Christopher. *Rainbow: The Stormy Life of Judy Garland*. New York: Grosset & Dunlap, 1975.

Fleming, E. J. *The Fixers: Eddie Mannix, Howard Strickling, and the MGM Publicity Machine*. North Carolina: McFarland & Company, 2005.

Fleming, E. J. *The Movieland Directory: Nearly 30,000 Addresses and Historical Sites in the Los Angeles Area, 1900–Present*. McFarland & Company, 2009.

Fletcher, Russell Holmes, ed. *Who's Who In California, Vol. I, 1942–1943*. Los Angeles: Who's Who Publications Company.

Fordin, Hugh. *MGM's Greatest Musicals: The Arthur Freed Unit*. Da Capo Press, 1996.

Frank, Gerold. *Judy*. Boston: Da Capo Press, 1999.

Frederick, Otto. *City of Nets: A Portrait of Hollywood in the 1940s*. New York: Perennial Library, 1987.

Fricke, John. *Judy Garland: A Portrait in Art & Anecdote*. Bulfinch, 2003.

Fried, Richard M. *Nightmare in Red: The McCarthy Era in Perspective.* Oxford University Press, 1991.

Frost, Jennifer. *Hedda Hopper's Hollywood: Celebrity Gossip and American Conservatism.* New York: New York University Press, 2011.

Gabler, Neal. *An Empire of Their Own: How the Jews Invented Hollywood.* New York: Anchor Books, 1988.

Garrett, Betty, with Ron Rapoport. *Betty Garrett and Other Songs: A Life on Stage and Screen.* Lanham, MD: Madison Books, 2000.

Gavin, James. *Stormy Weather: The Life of Lena Horne.* Atria Books, 2010.

Gioia, Ted. *The History of Jazz.* Oxford University Press, 1997.

Gleason, Lafayette B. *Official Report of the Nineteenth Republican National Convention.* The Tenny Press, 1928.

Gordon, Bernard. *Hollywood Exile: or How I Learned to Love the Blacklist.* Austin: University of Texas Press, 2013.

Gustafson, Melanie Susan. *Women and the Republican Party, 1854–1924.* Urbana and Chicago: University of Illinois Press, 2001.

Harmetz, Aljean. *The Making of the Wizard of Oz: Movie Magic and the Studio Power in the Prime of MGM and the Miracle of Production #1060.* Delta, 1977.

Harvey, Anna L. *Votes without Leverage: Women in American Electoral Politics, 1920–1970,* Cambridge University Press, 1998.

Higham, Charles. *Merchant of Dreams: Louis B. Mayer, MGM and the Secret Hollywood.* New York: Donald I. Fine, Inc., 1993.

Hill, Erin. *Never Done: A History of Women's Work in Media Production.* New Brunswick: Rutgers University Press, 2016.

Hopper, Hedda. *From Under My Hat.* New York: A Macfadden Book, 1964.

Hopper, Hedda, and James Brough. *The Whole Truth and Nothing But the Truth.* Garden City: Doubleday, 1963.

Jeansonne, Glen. *The Life of Herbert Hoover: Fighting Quaker 1928–1933.* Palgrave MacMillian, 2012.

Jensen, Joan M., and Gloria Ricci Lothrop. *California Women: A History,* Golden State Series, 1987.

Kennedy, Matthew. *Marie Dressler: A Biography, with a Listing of Major Stage Performances, a Filmography and a Discography.* McFarland & Company, 2005.

Kenny, D. J. *Illustrated Cincinnati: A Pictorial Hand-Book of the Queen City,* 1875; Over-the-Rhine blog, otrmatters.com/history.

La Salle, Mick. *Complicated Women: Sex and Power in Pre-Code Hollywood.* New York: Thomas Dunne Books, 2000.

Larch, Harold A., and Paula D. Welch. "The Women's Swimming Association: The Golden Years, 1920–1940," in *AAMPER Research Consortium Symposium Papers: Teaching Behavior and Women in Sport.* Richard H. Cox, ed., Department of Health Physical Education and Recreation, Kansas State Univeristy, 1970.

Lewis, Kevin. *The Moviola Mavens and the Moguls.* The Motion Picture Editors Guild, IATSE Local 700, 2005.

Lower, Richard Coke. *A Bloc of One: The Political Career of Hiram H. Johnson.* Stanford: Stanford University Press, 1993.

Lulay, Gail. *Nelson Eddy, America's Favorite Baritone: An Authorized Tribute.* Authors Choice Press, 2000.

Lyons, Louis S. *Who's Who Among the Women of California: An Annual Devoted to the Representative Women of California, With an Authoritative Review of Their Activities.* Los Angeles: Security Publishing Company, 1922.

Marcus, Kenneth. *Musical Metropolis: Los Angeles and the Creation of a Music Culture, 1880–1940.* New York: Palgrave MacMillian, 2004.

Marx, Samuel, and Joyce Vanderveen. *Deadly Illusions: Jean Harlow and the Murder of Paul Bern.* New York: Random House, 1990.

Marx, Samuel. *Mayer and Thalberg: The Make Believe Saints.* Hollywood: Samuel French Trade, 1988.

Mitchell, Greg. *Campaign of the Century: Upton Sinclair's Race for Governor of California and the Birth of Modern Politics.* New York: Random House, 1992.

Moley, Raymond. *The Hays Office*, Bobbs-Merrill, 1945.

Morris, Peter, et al. *Base Ball Pioneers, 1850–1870: The Clubs and Players Who Spread the Sport.* New York: McFarland & Company, 2012.

Murphy, George, with Victor Lasky. *"Say . . . Didn't You Used to Be George Murphy?"* Bartholomew House, Ltd., 1970.

Nickerson, Nickerson. *Mothers of Conservatism: Women and the Postwar Right.* Princeton: Princeton University Press, 2012.

Nixon, Marni, with Stephen Cole. *I Could Have Sung All Night: My Story.* New York: Billboard Books, 2006.

Olmsted, Kathryn S. *Right Out of California: The 1930s and the Big Business Roots of Modern Conservatism.* New York: The New Press, 2015.

Parish, James Robert, and Ronald L. Bowers. *The MGM Stock Company*: The Golden Era. New York: Bonanza Books, Crown Pub., 1972.

Rogin, Michael P., and John L. Shover. *Political Change in California: Critical Elections and Social Movements, 1890–196.* Greenwood Publishing Corp., 1970.

Ross, Steven J. *Hollywood Left and Right: How Movie Stars Shaped American Politics.* New York: Oxford University Press, 2011.

Rymph, Catherine E. *Republican Women: Feminism and Conservatism from Suffrage through the Rise of the New Right.* Chapel Hill: University of North Carolina Press, 2006.

Sack, Daniel. *Moral Re-Armament: The Reinventions of an American Religious Movement.* Palgrave Macmillan, 2008; *Wilton Bulletin* (Conn.) July 13, 1939.

Schmidt, Randy L. *Judy Garland on Judy Garland: Interviews and Encounter.* Chicago Review Press; reprint June 1, 2016.

Schuppara, Kurt. *Triumph of the Right: The Rise of the California Conservative Movement, 1945–1966.* New York: M. E. Sharpe, 1998.

Scobie, Ingrid. *Center Stage: Helen Gahagan Douglas, a Life.* Oxford Univ. Press, 1992.

Segrave, Kerry. *Extras of Early Hollywood: A History of the Crowd, 1913–1945.* Jefferson: McFarland & Co., 2013.

Selznick, Irene Mayer. *A Private View.* New York: Alfred A. Knopf, 1993.

Sennett, Robert S. *Hollywood Hoopla: Creating Stars and Selling Movies in the Golden Age of Hollywood.* New York: Billboard Books, 1998.

Shearer, Stephen Michael. *Beautiful: The Life of Hedy Lamar.* MacMillian, 2010.

Shindler, Colin. *Hollywood in Crisis: Cinema and American Society, 1929–1939.* New York, Routledge, 1996.

Shipman, David. *Judy Garland: The Secret Life of an American Legend.* New York: Hyperion, 1992.

Shulmen, Irving. *Harlow, an Intimate Biography*. New York: Bernard Gels Associates; distributed by Random House, 1964.

Sitton, Tom, and William Deverell. *Metropolis in the Making: Los Angeles in the 1920s*. Berkeley: University of California Press, 2001.

Slide, Anthony. *Hollywood Unknowns: A History of Extras, Bit Players, and Stand-Ins*. Jackson: University Press of Mississippi, 2012.

Slide, Anthony. *Inside the Hollywood Fan Magazine: A History of Star Makers, Fabricators, and Gossip Mongers*. Jackson: University Press of Mississippi, 2010.

Smyth, J. E. *Nobody's Girl Friday: The Women Who Ran Hollywood*. New York: Oxford University Press, 2018.

Stabile, Carol A. *The Broadcast 41: Women and the Anti-Communist Blacklist*. Goldsmiths Press, 2018.

Starr, Kevin. *Material Dreams: Southern California through the 1920s*. Oxford University Press, 1990.

Thomson, David. *Showman: The Life of David O. Selznick*. New York: Alfred A. Knopf, 1992.

Tornabene, Lyn. *Long Live the King: A Biography of Clark Gable*. New York: G. P. Putnam's & Sons, 1976.

Tucker, Sophie. *Some of These Days: The Autobiography of Sophie Tucker*. New York: Doubleday, Doran and Company, Inc. 1945.

Turk, Edward Baron. *Hollywood Diva: A Biography of Jeanette MacDonald*. Berkeley: University of California Press, 1998.

Tygiel, Jules. *The Great Los Angeles Swindle: Oil, Stocks, and Scandal during the Roaring Twenties*. New York: Oxford University Press, 1994.

Walcott, David B. *Cops and Kids: Policing Juvenile Delinquency in Urban America, 1890–1940*. Columbus: Ohio State University Press, 2005.

Warsh, Cheryl Krasnick, and Dan Mallek, eds. *Consuming Modernity: Gendered Behavior and Consumerism before the Baby Boom*. Vancouver: University of British Columbia Press 2013.

Wayne, Jane Ellen. *The Golden Girls of MGM: Glamour and Grief*. London: Robson Books, 2004.

Weidman, Jeffrey. *Artists in Ohio, 1787–1900: A Biographical Dictionary*. Ohio: Kent State University Press, 2000.

Weinstat, Hertzel, and Bert Wechsler. *Dear Rogue: A Biography of the American Baritone, Lawrence Tibbett*. Portland: Amadeus Press, 1996.

Welky, David. *The Moguls and the Dictators: Hollywood and the Coming of World War II*. Baltimore: Johns Hopkins University Press, 2009.

Wheeler, Leigh Ann. *Against Obscenity: Reform and the Politics of Womanhood in America, 1873–1935*. Baltimore: Johns Hopkins University Press, 2007.

Williams, Esther, with Digby Diehl. *The Million Dollar Mermaid: An Autobiography*. Simon & Schuster, 1999.

Wilson, Joan Hoff. *Herbert Hoover: Forgotten Progressive*. New York: Little, Brown and Company, 1975.

Zmuda, Michael. *The Five Sedgwicks: Pioneer Entertainers of Vaudeville, Film, and Television*. New York: McFarland, 2015.

ARTICLES

Arnold, Ralph. "Laying Foundation Stones, Chapter I: My Acquaintanceship with Herbert Hoover," *Historical Society of Southern California Quarterly* 37, no. 2 (June 1955): 99–124.

Arnold, Ralph. "Laying Foundation Stones, Part II: The 1922 Senatorial Campaign," *Historical Society of Southern California Quarterly* 37, no. 3 (September 1955): 243–60.

Arnold, Ralph. "Laying Foundation Stones, Part III: Women in Politics," *Historical Society of Southern California Quarterly* 37, no. 4 (December 1955): 297–319.

Bearings: The Cycling Authority of America, vol. 4–6: (vol. 5, no. 21; June 21, 1892).

Blackburn, Harriet B., "Ida Koverman Makes Name in Hollywood's Movies, Thought Not on Screen," *The Christian Science Monitor,* October 16, 1950.

Borish, Linda J. "Women, Sport and American Jewish Identity in the Late Nineteenth and Early Twentieth Centuries," in Timothy Chandler and Tara Magdalinski, *With God on Their Side: Sport in the Service of Religion.* New York: Routledge, 2002.

Carlson, Edna M. "The Public Library and Sex Education," *Journal of Social Hygiene* 29 (1943): 353–70.

Fisher, Marguerite J., and Betty Whitehead. "Women and National Party Organization," *American Political Science Review* 38 (October 1944).

Francke, Lizzie. "Script Girls: Women Screenwriters in Hollywood." *Historical Journal of Film, Radio, and Television.* London: British Film Institute, 1994.

Hawkins, Ross. "Reel Life in Culver City, Marion Bell Remembered in Culver Historical Highlights," *Culver City Historical Society,* vol. 19, no. 1; Winter 1998.

Hawkins, Ross. "The Fifth-Place Finisher." The Front Page Online: The Voice of Culver City and Beyond, May 25, 2006.

Leo, Marilyn. *Ernest Holmes and the History of Religious Science.* Science of Mind Spiritual Heritage website.

Macias, Anthony. "Bringing Music to the People: Race, Urban Culture, and Municipal Politics in Postwar Los Angeles," in *Los Angeles and the Future of Urban Cultures,* Special ssue of *American Quarterly* 56, no. 3 (2004).

May, Lary. "Anti-Communism in Hollywood," in James G. Rawls, *New Directions in California History: A Book of Readings.* New York: McGraw-Hill, 1988.

Mondout, Patrick. "Baseball in Cincinnati: A History," *Baseball Chronology: The Game Since 1845,* June 1, 2008.

Rapka, Linda A. "Solidarity Forever! Local 47 in the Labor Movement; This Labor History Month Our Connection to the Greater Labor Movement, Musicians Open Hollywood Canteen, 'The House That Labor Built,'" AFM 47 archives.

Sahagun, Louis. *Master of the Mysteries: The Life of Manly Palmer Hall* (Large Print 16 pt) readhowyouwant.com, 2011.

Saunders, Ann Wardell. "Hollywood—Los Angeles," in Richard Drake Saunders, ed., *Music and Dance in California and the West.* Hollywood: Bureau of Musical Research, Inc., 1948.

The Score. July–Aug. 1946, vol. III, no. 7 and 8, p. 2. Publication of the American Society of Music Arrangers.

Suber, Howard. "Politics and Popular Culture: Hollywood at Bay, 1933-1953," *American Jewish History,* vol. 68, no. 4 (June 1979), 517–533.

Thorn, Brian. "Clare Boothe Luce and the Evolution of American Conservatism," AN-AMNESIS Journal. February 13, 2017, (online edition).

CITY DIRECTORIES

Los Angeles County, California Online Historical Directories.

US City Directories, 1821–1989, Ancestry.com.

Norwood City Directory, cinncinatilibrary.org.

Williams' Covington and Newport directory; The Public Library of Cincinnati and Hamilton County.

ORAL HISTORIES/AUTHOR INTERVIEWS

An Oral History with Robert M. W. Vogel. Academy of Motion Picture Arts and Sciences, Oral History Program. Interviewed by Barbara Hall, 1991.

Cari Beauchamp, interview with author, August 7, 2008, Los Angeles, California.

Jean Wood Fuller, Organizing Women: Career in Volunteer Politics and Government Administration. Interviewed by Miriam Feingold Stein. Regional Oral History Office University of California, the Bancroft Library, Berkeley, California, Women in Politics Oral History Project, 1972.

Marni Nixon, telephone interview with author, February 5, 2015.

Mary Troffer, interview with author, August 7, 2007, Palmdale, California. Mary was the granddaughter of Ida Koverman's older sister, Phoebe May Brockway. Interview facilitated by Mary's niece, Victoria "Vikki" McAllister.

Oral History Interview with Hon. Gardiner Johnson. Regional Oral History Office, the Bancroft Library and the State Government Oral History Program, California State Archives, Office of the Secretary of State, Sacramento, 1989. Interviewed by Gabrielle Morris, 1983.

SELECTED PERIODICALS

(Newspapers.com; ProQuest; Ancestry.com, various websites, and library collections)
Billboard
Bulletin of America's Town Meeting of the Air
Chemical & Metallurgical Engineering
Compressed Air Magazine
Engineering and Mining Journal
Hollywood Filmograph
Hollywood Reporter
Life Magazine
Look Magazine
Mines Register: Successor to the Mines Handbook and the Copper Handbook
Motion Picture News
Movie Classic
Opera News
Photoplay
Silver Screen
Time
Variety

SELECTED NEWSPAPERS

(Newspapers.com; ProQuest; Ancestry.com and various websites and library collections)
Akron Beacon Journal
Bakersfield Californian
Brooklyn Daily Eagle
Buffalo Courier Express

Daily Illinois
Detroit Free Press
Harrisburg Telegraph
Hartford Courant
Honolulu Star-Advertiser
Illinois Digital Newspaper Collections
Lansing State Journal
Lodi-News Sentinel
Los Angeles Examiner
Los Angeles Times
Modesto Bee
Motion Picture Herald
Oakland Tribune
Philadelphia Inquirer
Pittsburgh Courier
Pittsburgh Post-Gazette
San Francisco Chronicle
San Jose News
Santa Ana Register
The Desert Sun
The Dispatch, Lexington, NC
The Fresno Bee Republican
The Miami News
The Nation
The Press Democrat (Santa Rosa, CA)
Waterloo Daily Courier

INTERNET SOURCES

Ancestry.com.
"Encores and Echoes" by E. B. Rea, *Afro-American*, August 24, 1946.
Denver Public Library website.
Election Campaigns page: Wisconsin Center for Film & Theater Research website.
Fenwicke L. Holmes website.
Genealogy.com.
fultonhistory.com.
Hollywood and Religious Science, October 15, 2013, scienceofmindarchives.org.
Mediahist.org.
No. Am. Newspaper Alliance: Deanna Durbin Devotees website.
Northern Kentucky Photographers' Index, Kenton County Public Library, Northern Kentucky.
Parker, Jean. "Cinderella girl." lmsofthegoldenage.com/foga/1997/summer97/jeanparker
     .shtml.
Perfume Intelligence—The Encyclopedia of Perfume.
Preservation.lacity.org.
Regarding Ben Carre; The Front Page Online.
Research Hints, Helps and Links: Photographic Artists and Studios in Cincinnati website.
The.hitchcock.zone.
The Unsung Joe: Where bit-part actors go when they die.
Science of Mind Spiritual Heritage website.

INDEX

ABOUT THE AUTHOR

Jacqueline R. Braitman is a historian of American history who specializes in California and women's politics. She is coauthor of *Justice Stanley Mosk: Life at the Center of California Politics and Justice*.